Polaroids

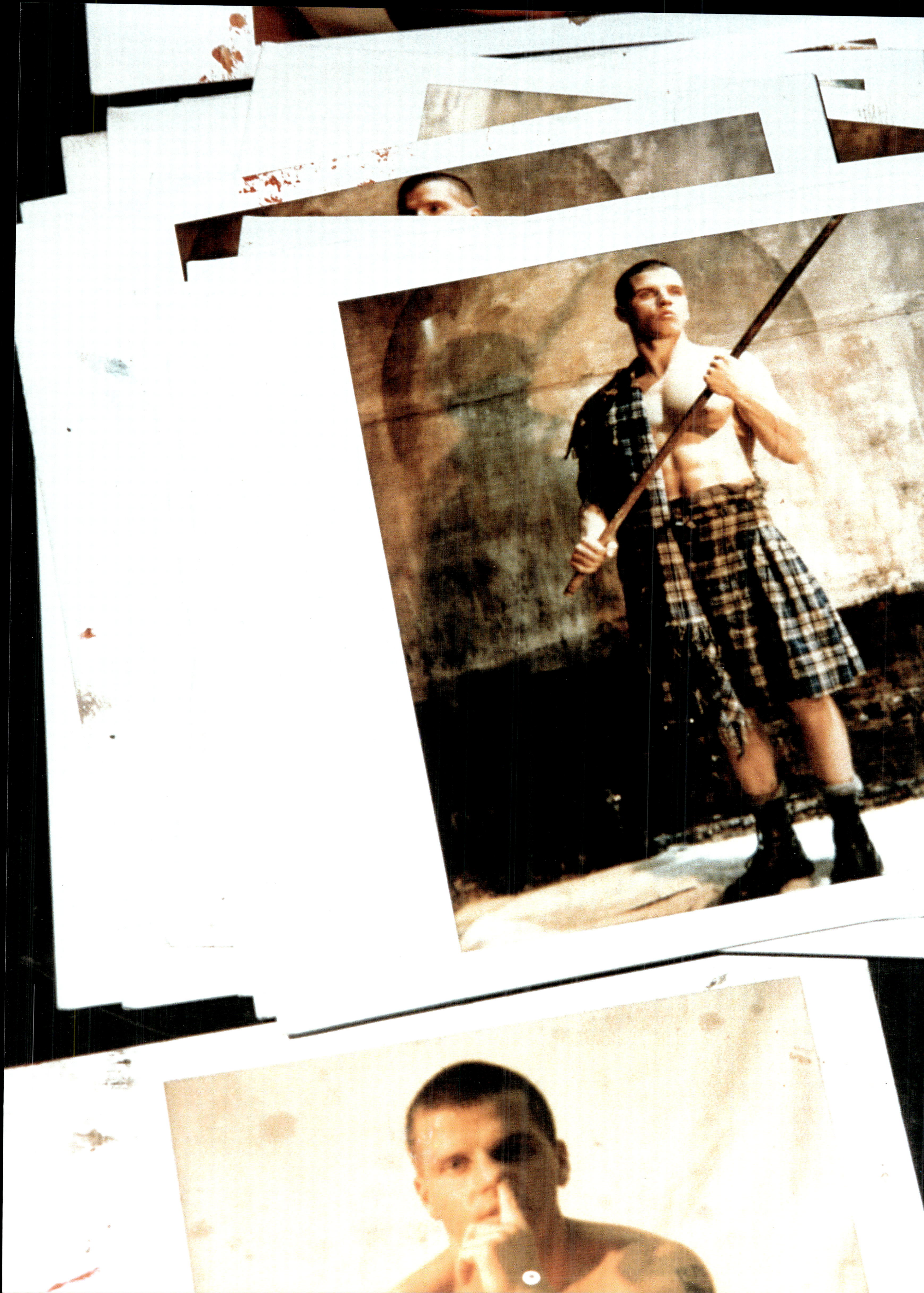

Polaroids: Attila Richard Lukacs and Michael Morris

Editing by Catherine Crowston and Reid Shier
Printed and bound in South Korea

Arsenal Pulp Press
Suite 101, 211 East Georgia Street, Vancouver, BC Canada V6A 1Z6
arsenalpulp.com

Art Gallery Of Alberta
2 Sir Winston Churchill Square, Edmonton, AB Canada T5J 2C1
youraga.ca

Illingworth Kerr Gallery
Alberta College of Art + Design, 1407-14 Avenue NW, Calgary, AB Canada T2N 4R3
acad.ab.ca/ikg.html

Presentation House Gallery
333 Chesterfield Avenue, North Vancouver, BC Canada V7M 3G9
presentationhousegall.com

Arsenal Pulp Press gratefully acknowledges the support of the Canada Council of the Arts (Support for Art Books) and the British Columbia Arts Council for its publishing program, and the Government of Canada (through the Canada Book Fund) and the Government of British Columbia (through the Book Publishing Tax Credit Program) for its publishing activities.

Attila Richard Lukacs/Polaroids/Michael Morris was presented at the Art Gallery of Alberta with the generous support of the Audain Foundation. The Art Gallery of Alberta gratefully acknowledges the ongoing support of the Canada Council for the Arts, the Alberta Foundation for the Arts and the City of Edmonton for all of its programming activitiess.

The presentation of *Attila Richard Lukacs/Polaroids/Michael Morris* at Presentation House Gallery, North Vancouver would not have been possible without the generous support of The Canada Council for the Arts, the North Vancouver Office of Cultural Affairs, the City of North Vancouver, The District of North Vancouver, The BC Gaming Commission, the BC Arts Council and Metro Vancouver.

The presentation of *Attila Richard Lukacs: Polaroids* at the IKG would not have been possible without the generous support of the ACAD, the Alberta Foundation for the Arts, The Canada Council for the Arts, and the Lukacs family. Appreciation is extended to Denise Mullen, Provost, ACAD, and Anthea Black, Exhibitions Manager, AGA.

Installation photographs: Art Gallery of Alberta. Photos by M.N. Hutchinson

Library and Archives Canada Cataloguing in Publication

Lukacs, Attila Richard, 1962–
Polaroids / Attila Richard Lukacs and Michael Morris.

Co-published by: Presentation House Gallery and the Art Gallery of Alberta and the Illingworth Kerr Gallery.
Essays by Michael Turner, Scott Watson, Vince Aletti and Stan Persky.
ISBN 978-1-55152-295-1

1. Lukacs, Attila Richard, 1962–. 2. Morris, Michael, 1942–. 3. Men in art. 4. Photography, Artistic. I. Morris, Michael, 1942– II. Turner, Michael, 1962– III. Watson, Scott, 1950– IV. Aletti, Vince V. Presentation House Gallery VI. Art Gallery of Alberta VII. Illingworth Kerr Gallery VIII. Title.

ND249.L85A4 2009 779.092 C2009-904298-3

Polaroids

Photographs by Attila Richard Lukacs

conceptualized and assembled by Michael Morris

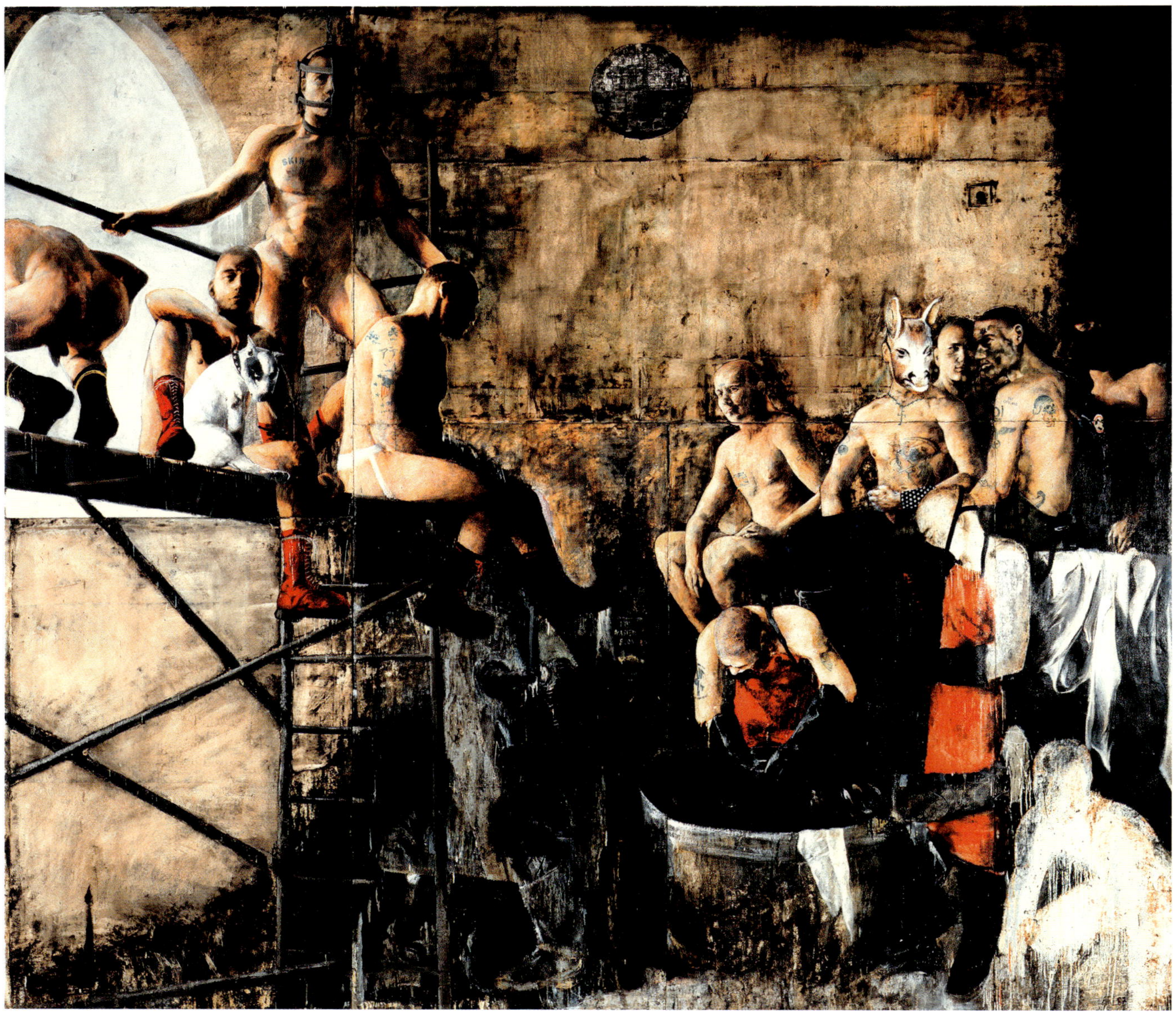

Attila Richard Lukacs, *Where the Finest Young Men*, 1987, asphalt, oil, enamel on canvas, 427 x 484 cm, Collection of the National Gallery of Canada.

Foreword

Attila Richard Lukacs had firmly established himself as a gifted and precocious artist by the mid-1980s. While still an art student in Vancouver, he had absorbed and synthesized the lessons of European neo-expressionism and was making aggressive, heroically scaled paintings of young men at play or at war with one another in refined and (at the time provocatively) classical compositions. We had not seen contemporary youth portrayed this way. Lukacs was showing us something new through the lens of the past, and was re-enacting and redeploying historical art in paintings that were charged and freshly visceral. As Michael Turner describes in his essay, his subjects were "... skinheads mostly ... in various states of inversion, transformation and decay ... on the verge of ritual, in dungeons or in ruins, surrounded by monkeys, pigs, totalitarian paraphernalia—a broken army of disenfranchised youth." Fighting under the weight of a rigid and conservative political momentum, these young men suggested for Lukacs a need for an artistic milieu much different than what Vancouver could—at the time—provide.

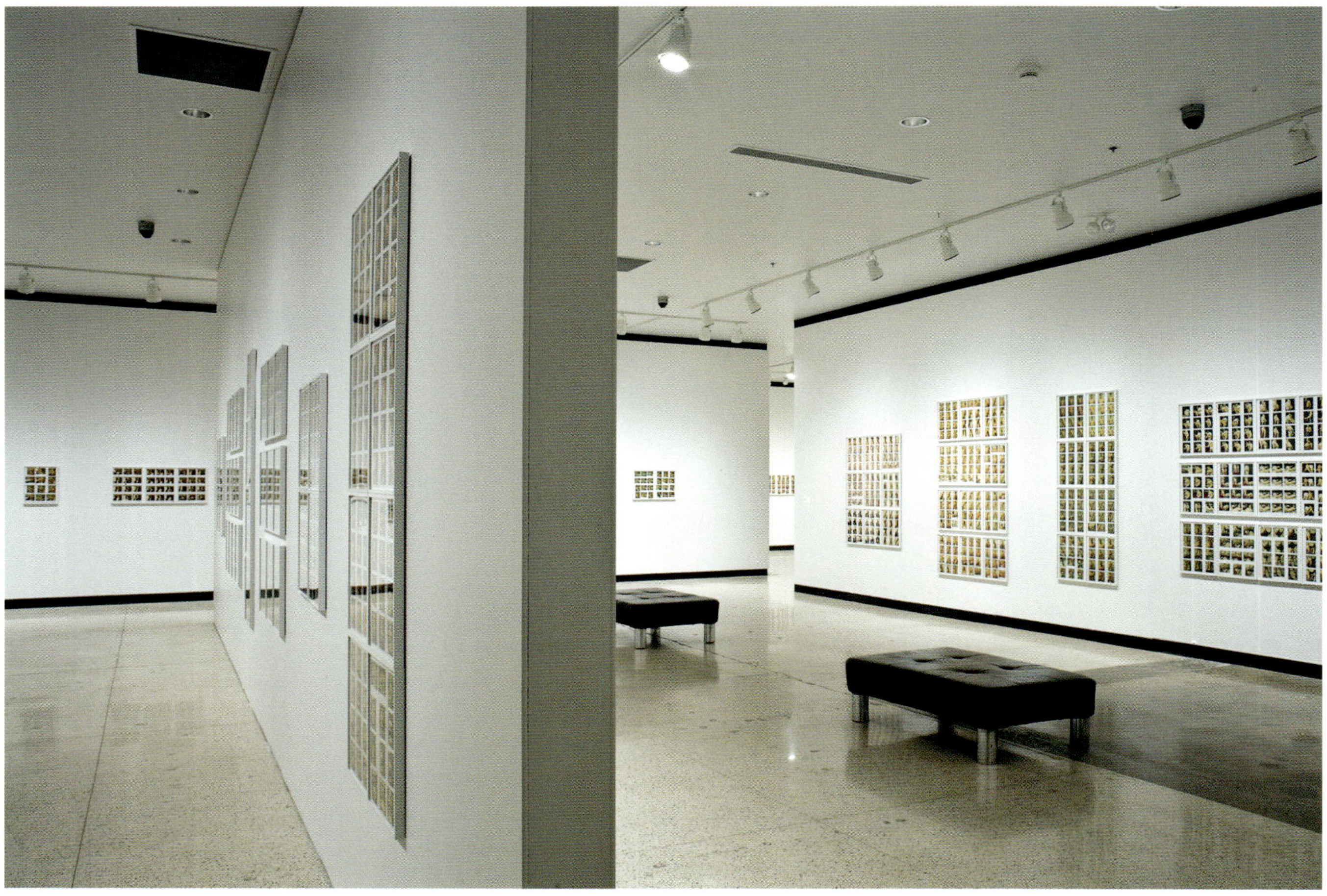

Installation of Polaroids: Attila Richard Lukacs and Michael Morris, Art Gallery of Alberta, Edmonton, 2009.

Lukacs moved to Berlin in 1986. There, he met Michael Morris, a senior artist and fellow Canadian expatriot. Morris tutored Lukacs, providing lessons in art history and, no doubt, opening important doors to Lukacs's voracious historical appetite. Pre-1989 Berlin was circumscript and surreal, an artist's playground. Yet one of the more significant offerings the city must have inspired in—and in hindsight provided for—Lukacs would have been the proximity to paintings that were becoming close objects of his study and affection, particularly by artists such as Botticelli, Goya, and Degas. It was during this first year in Berlin that Lukacs began to take Polaroid photographs as studies for his paintings. Lukacs used these images as building blocks for increasingly complex compositions and to arrange and reorganize parts against a whole. As he would also discover, Lukacs's intense chiaroscuro palette was aided by the rich, vibrant colours of the Polaroids themselves, which provided an uncannily proximate referent to the work of one of Lukacs most significant inspirations, Caravaggio.

Over the ensuing years and continuing (while stock lasts), Lukacs has taken thousands of Polaroid studies. They are almost all of nude or semi-costumed young men, and are reminescent of a nineteenth- and twentieth-century Northern European ideal—a well proportioned, masculine,

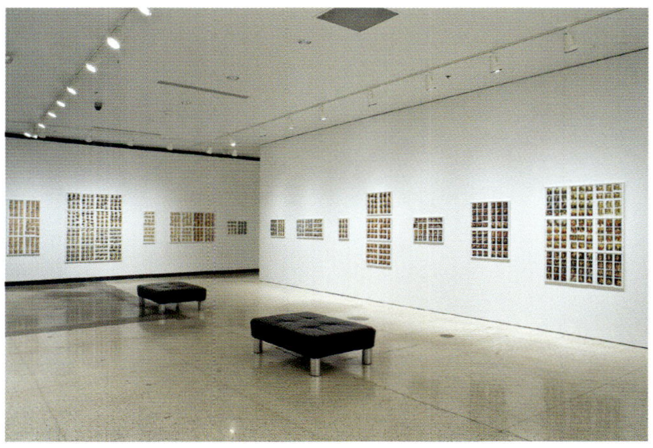

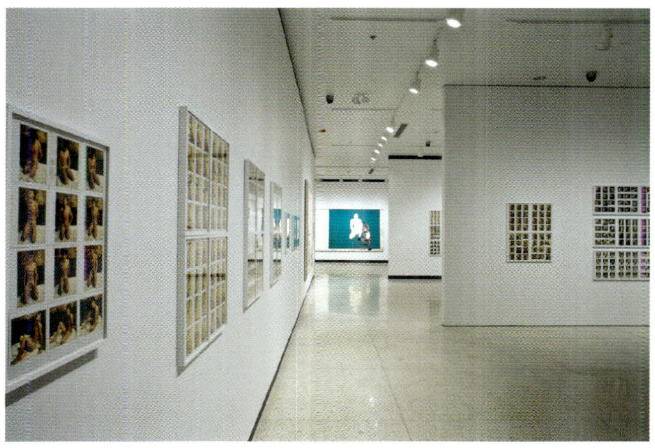

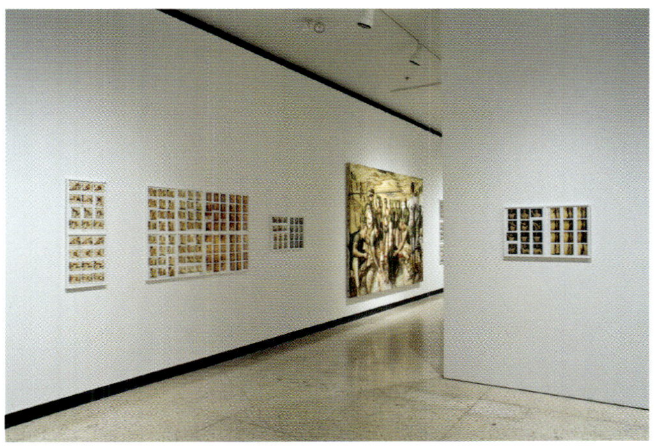

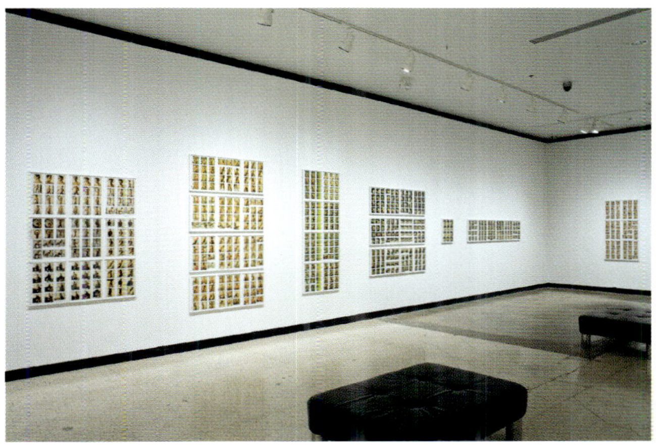

unself-consciously sensual male. One can detect the historical inspirations in the model's poses, or in the photograph's allusions to social realist heroicism, but this is disrupted as the young men pose with their pants down, bent over, vomiting and shooting up. Taken in rapid succession, Lukacs's Polaroids document these gestures as if stills for short films. They are extraordinary images, the result of a painter's keen sense of colour coupled with a photographer's expertise in light and framing. They are also a unique historical document (almost completely) realized within the confines of Lukacs's succession of studios in Berlin, New York, and Vancouver over the past twenty-three years.

Michael Morris has watched the production of this "archive" since its inception in 1986, and starting two years ago, has devoted himself to categorizing and arranging the Polaroids into their current 3 x 4 grid forms, re-constructing Lukacs photo shoots and re-presenting this history. These photographic orchestrations are the focus of the exhibition *Attila Richard Lukacs/Polaroids/Michael Morris* and of this accompanying publication. We would like to acknowledge and thank Michael Morris for his dedication to this project and for providing such integrity to its organization. Thank you to the authors for their inspired work, to Vince Aletti who conducted an extensive interview with Attila Richard Lukacs, and to Stan Persky, Michael Turner, and Scott Watson for their insightful essays. Finally, thank you to Attila Richard Lukacs for whom this publication has been an honour to produce.

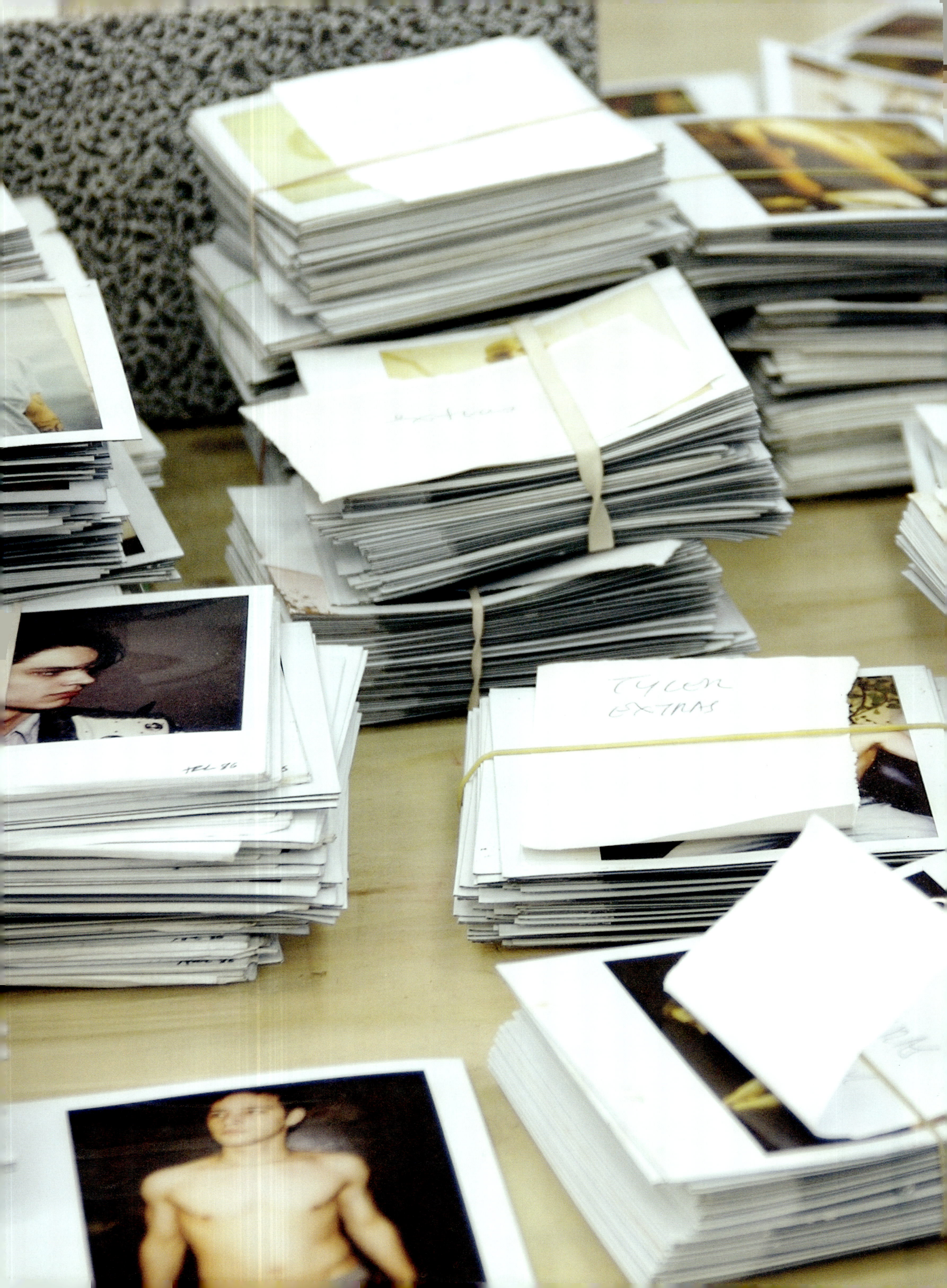
TYLER
EXTRAS

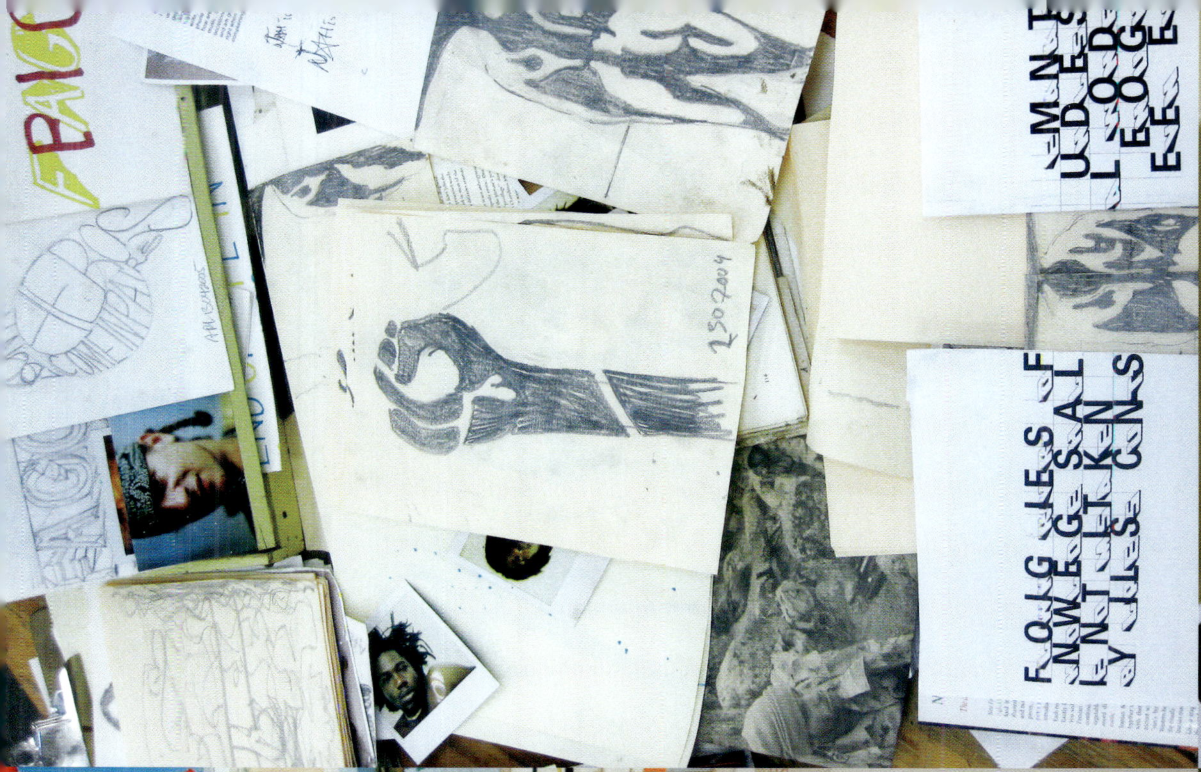

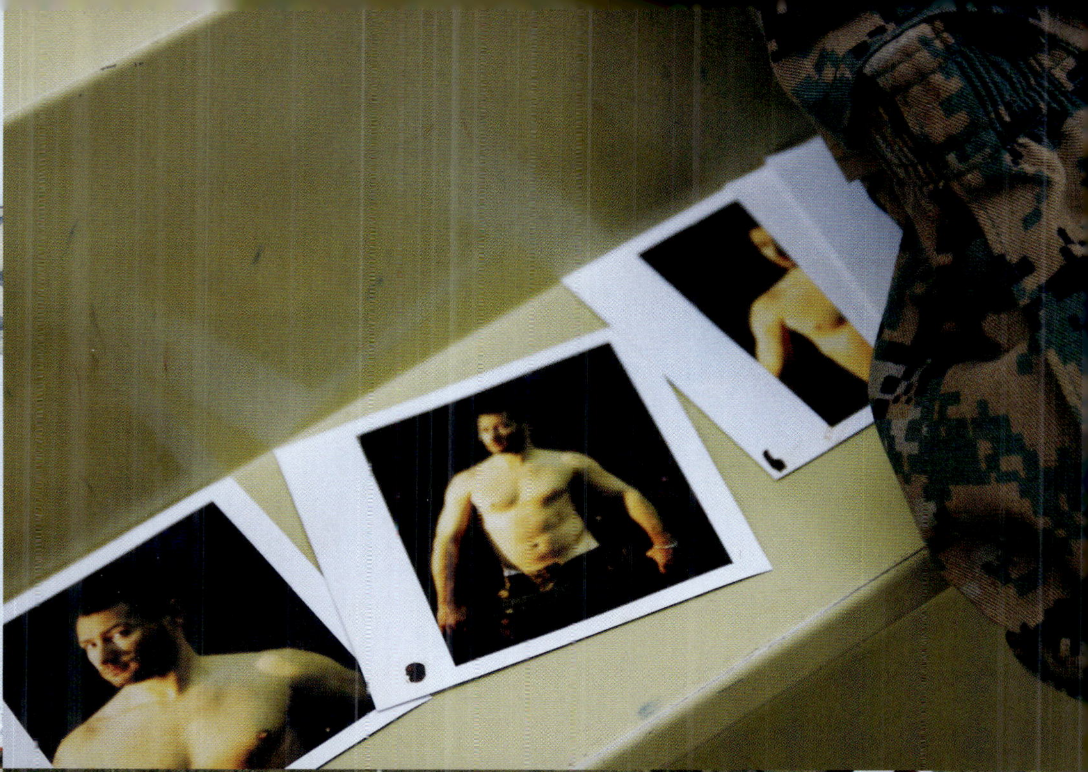

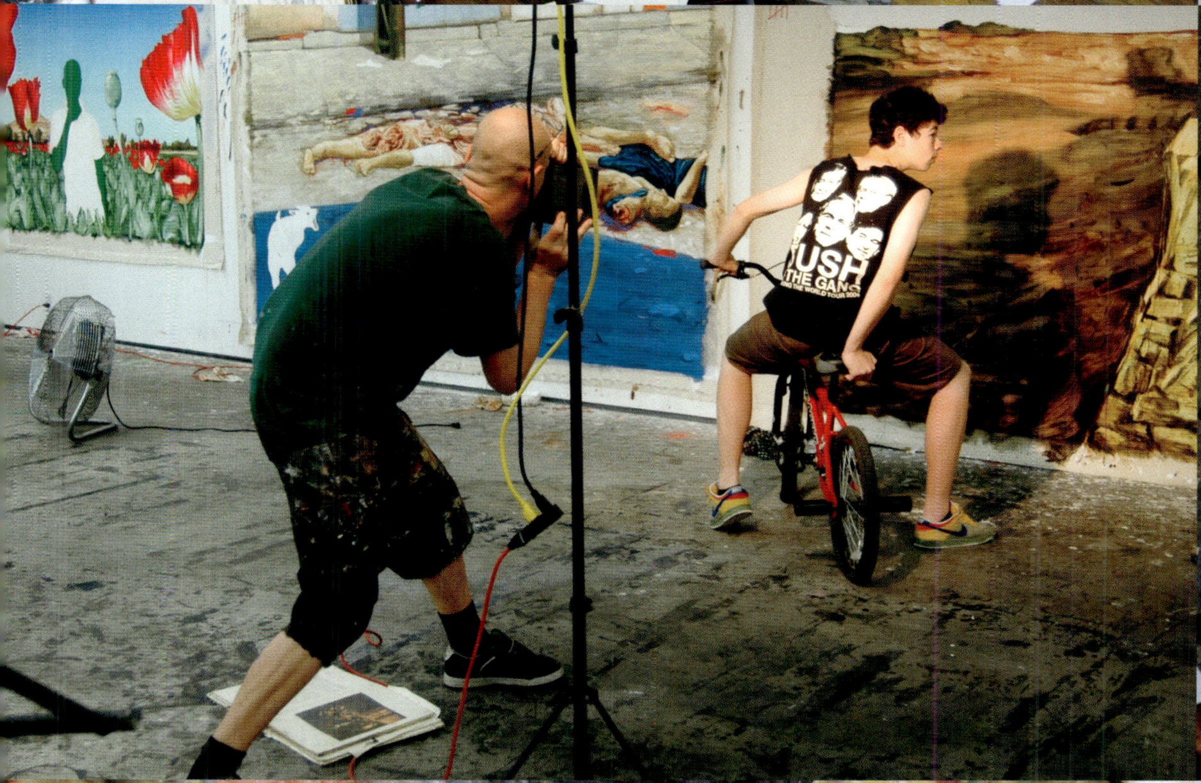

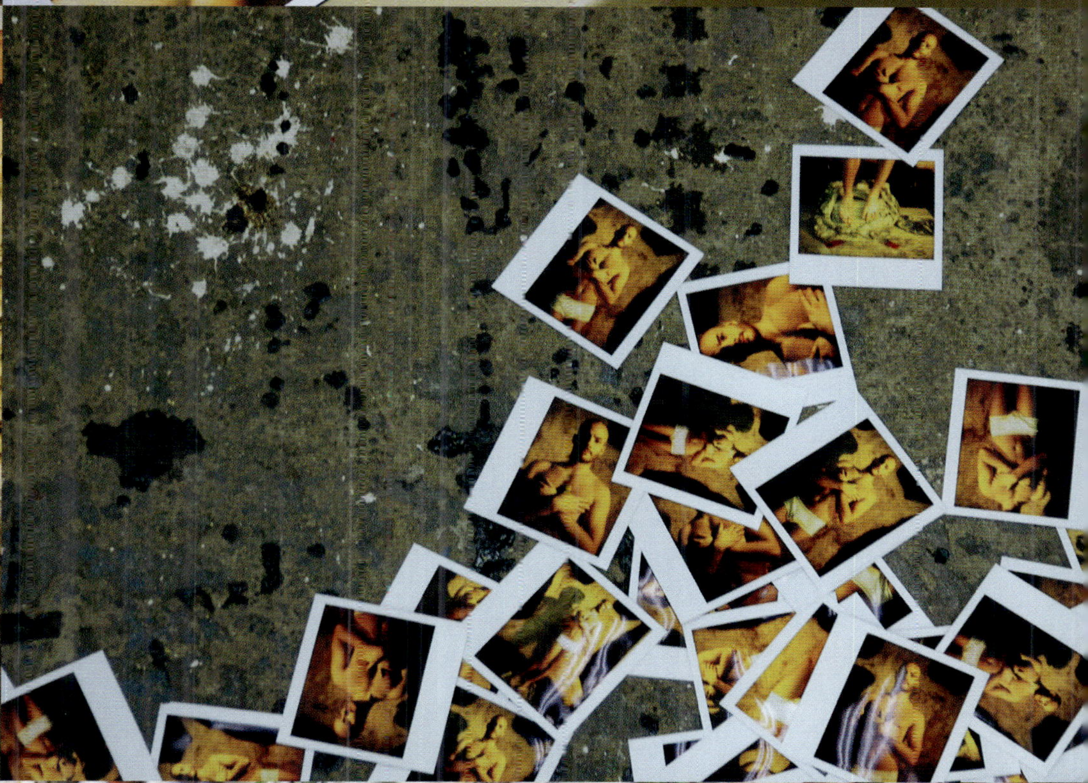

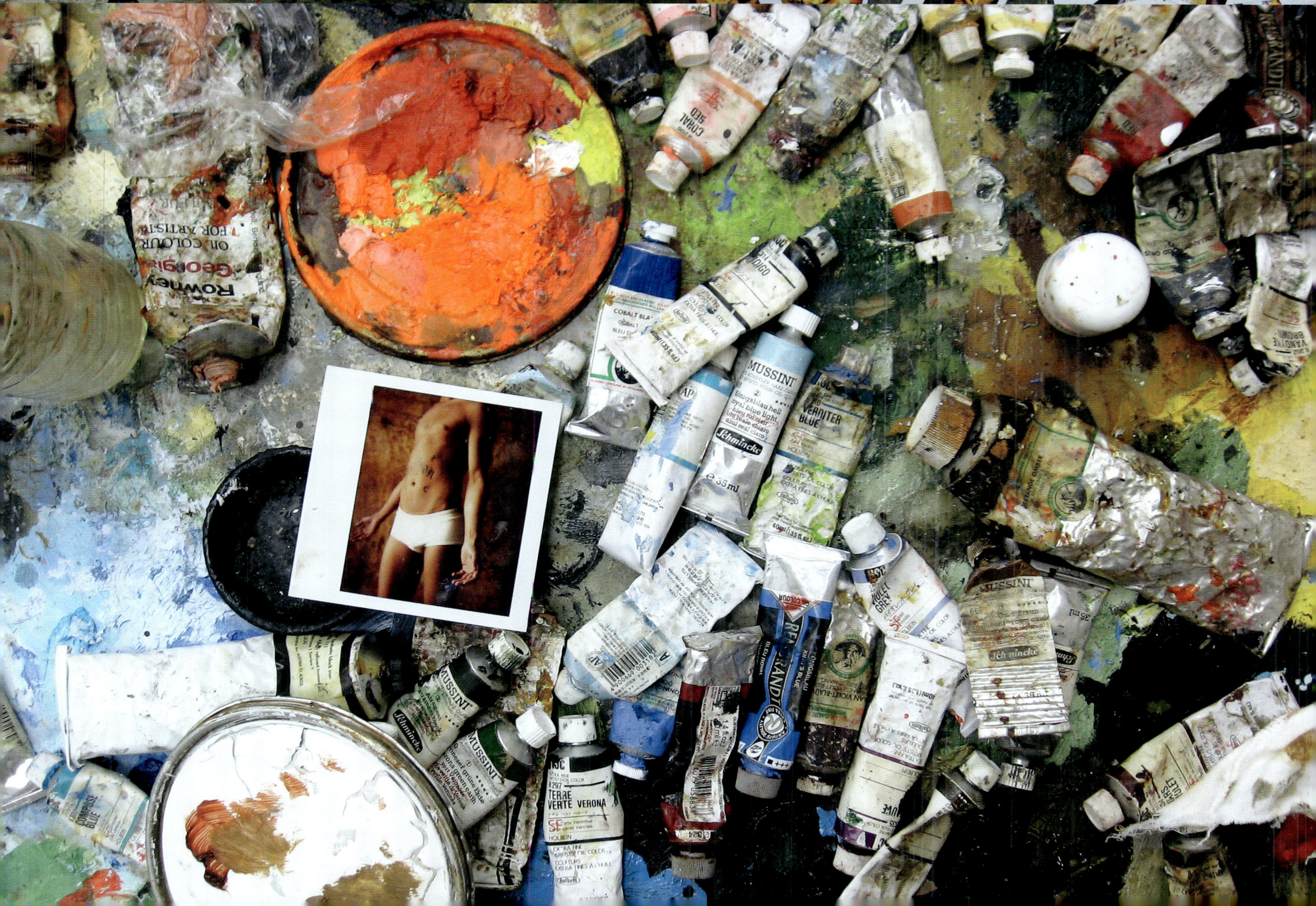
MUSSINI
Schmincke
TERRE VERTE VERONA

Pola

roids

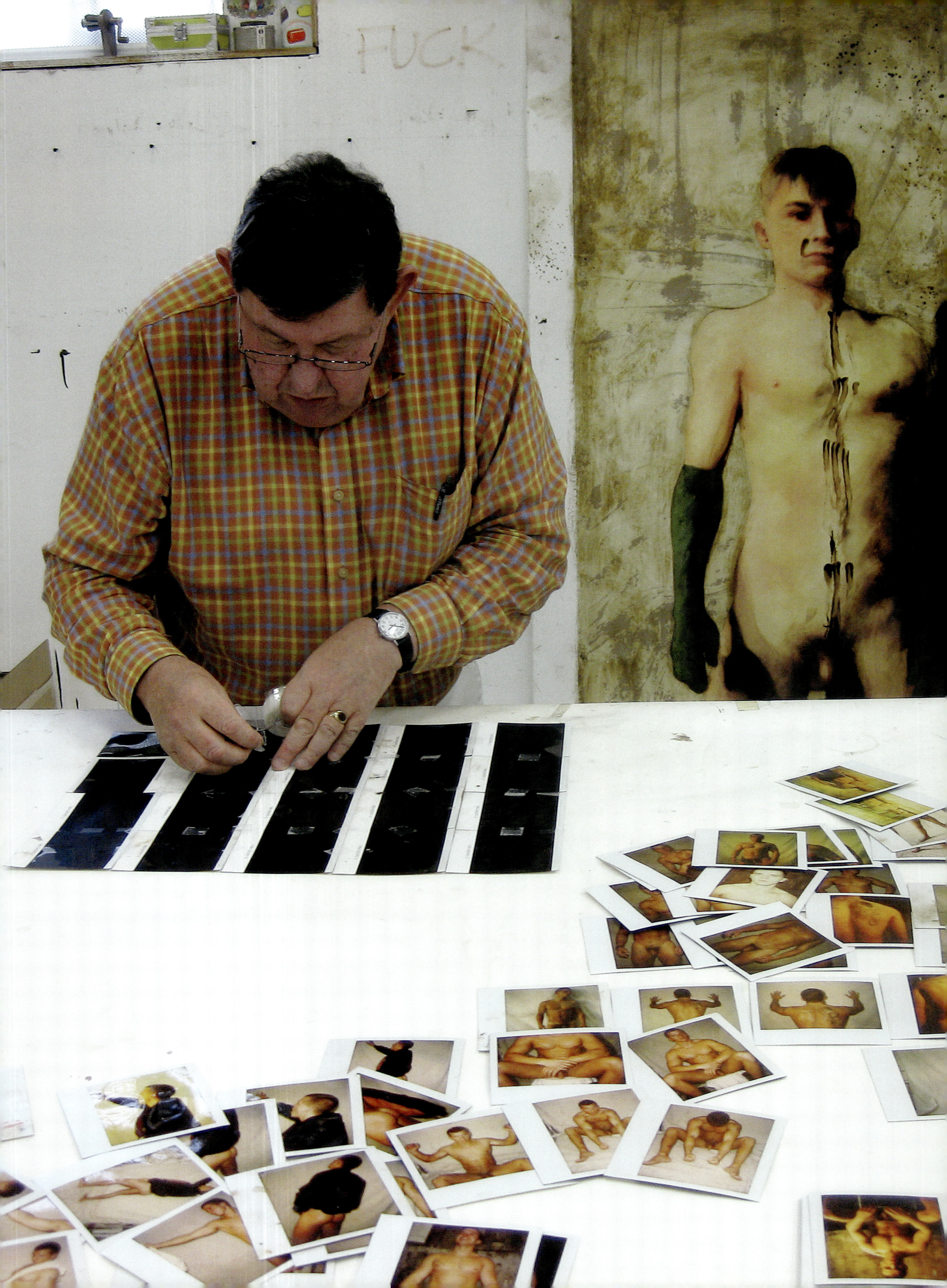
FUCK

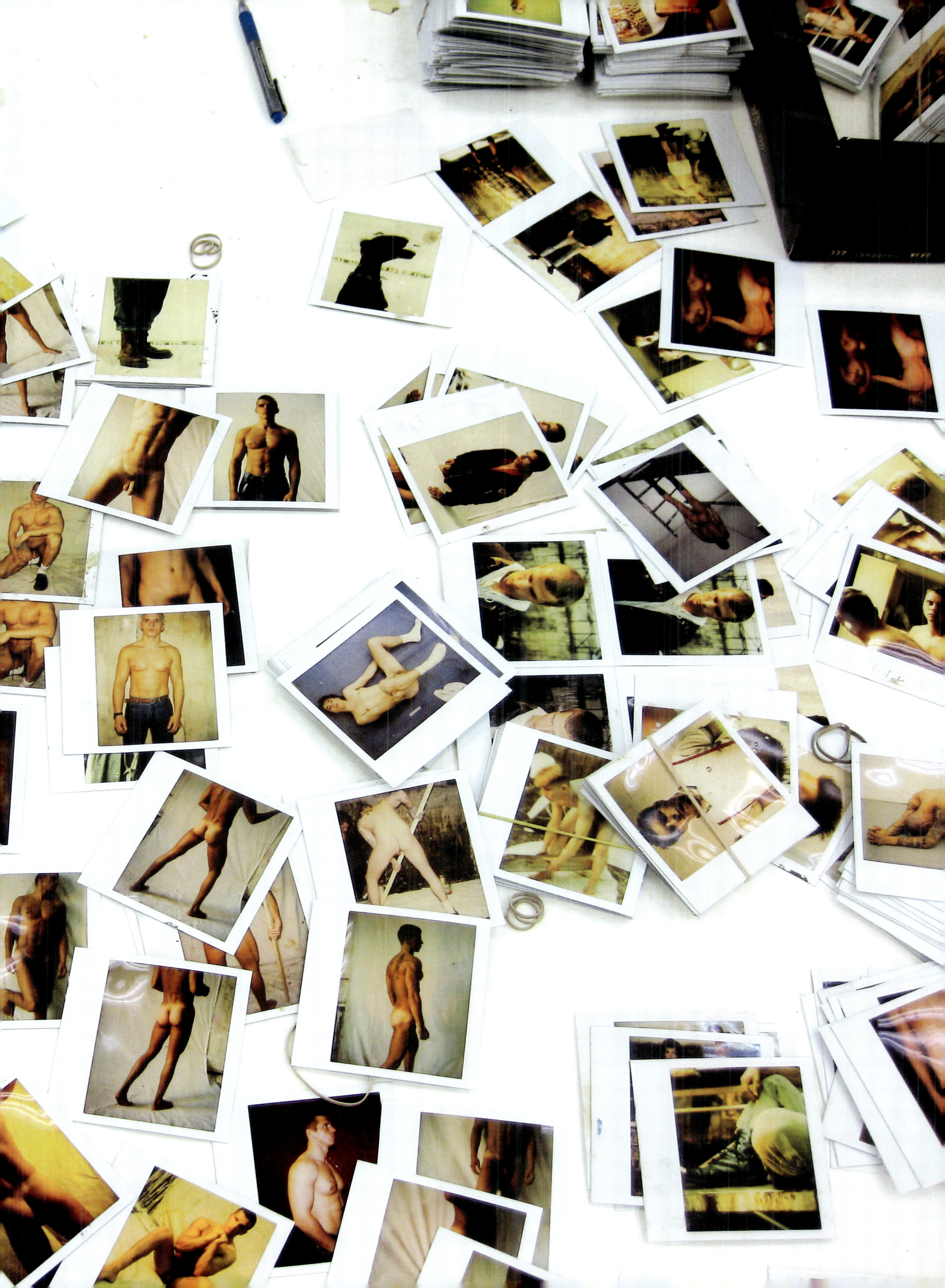

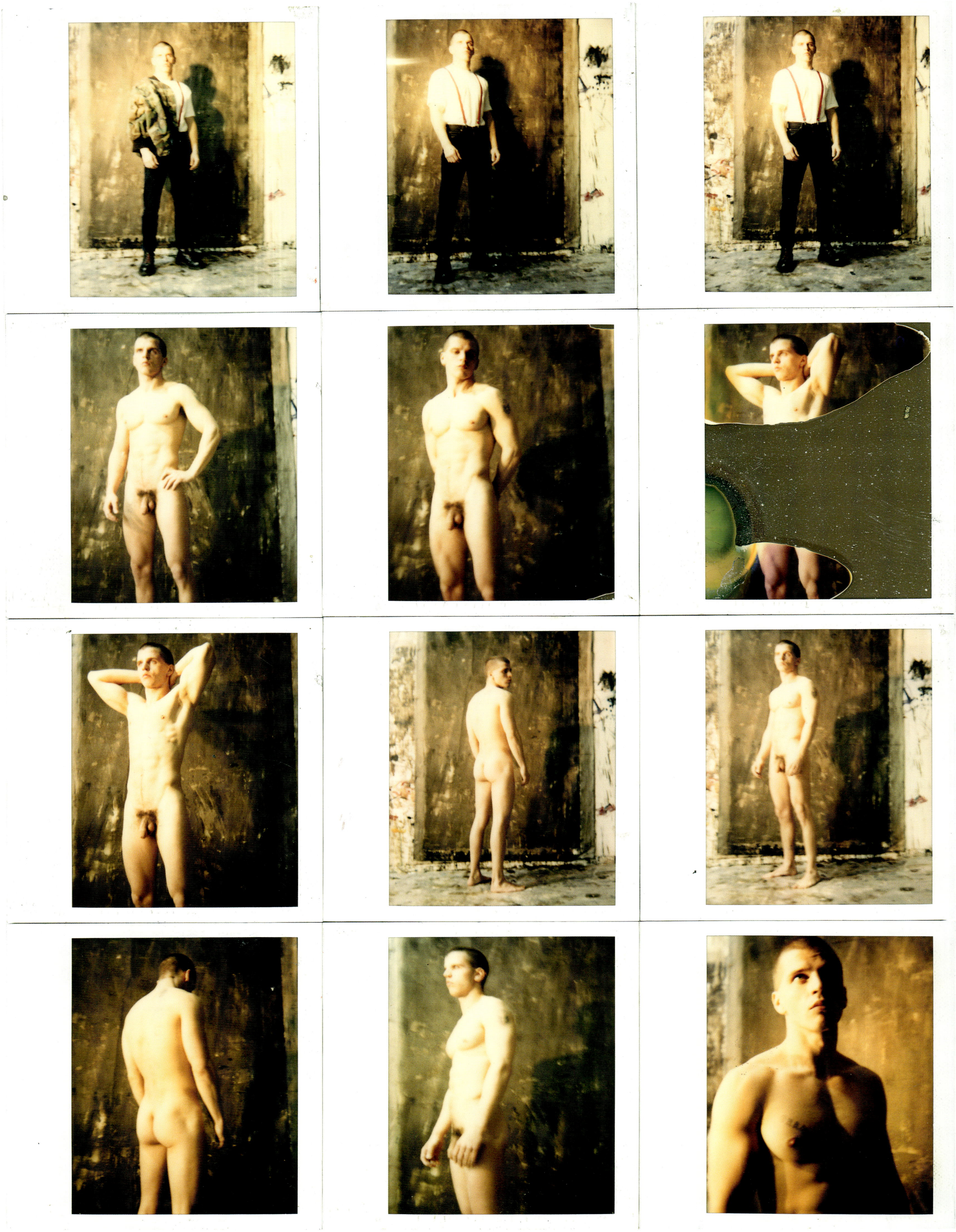

Alex, Berlin, 1987

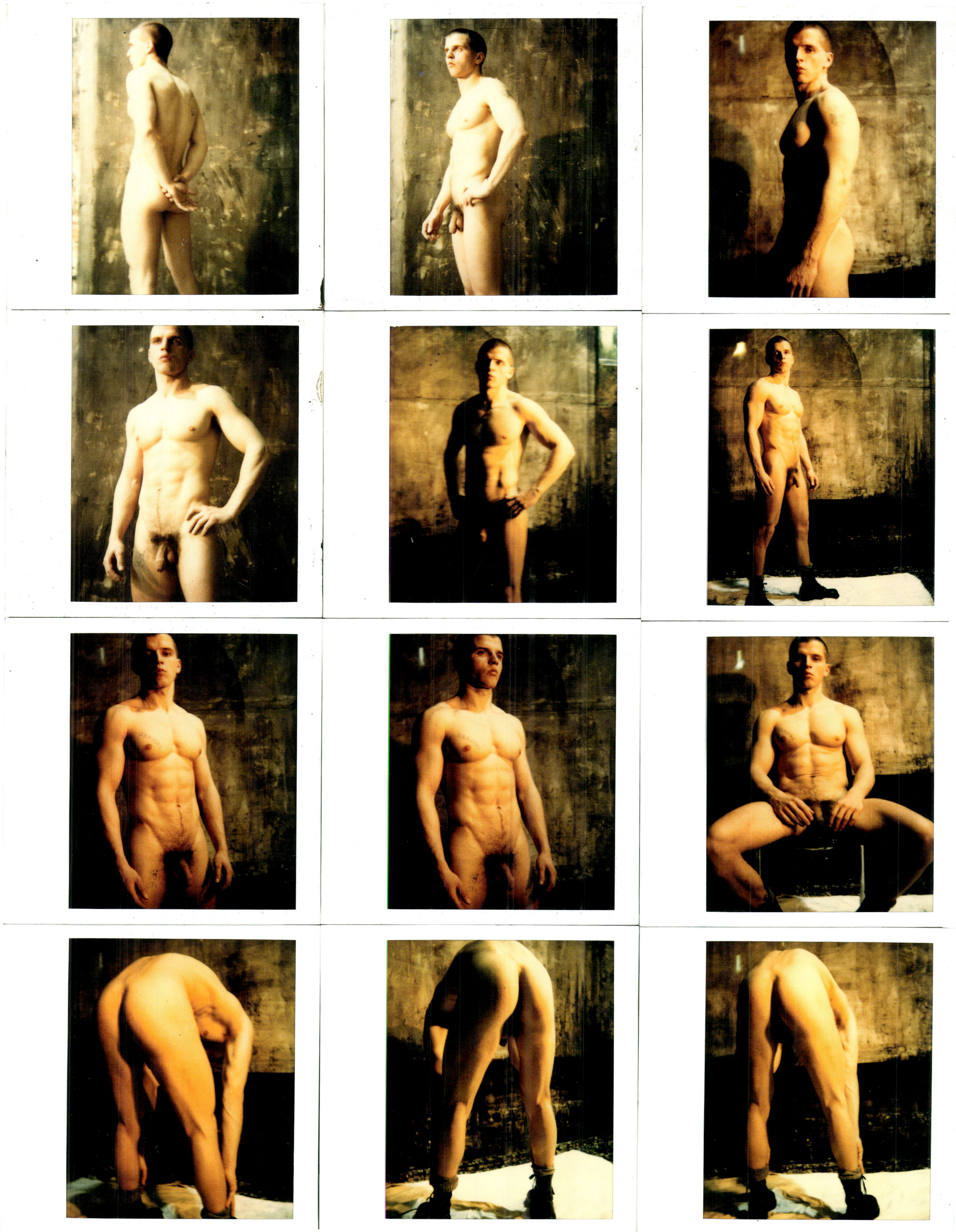

Alex, Berlin, 1987

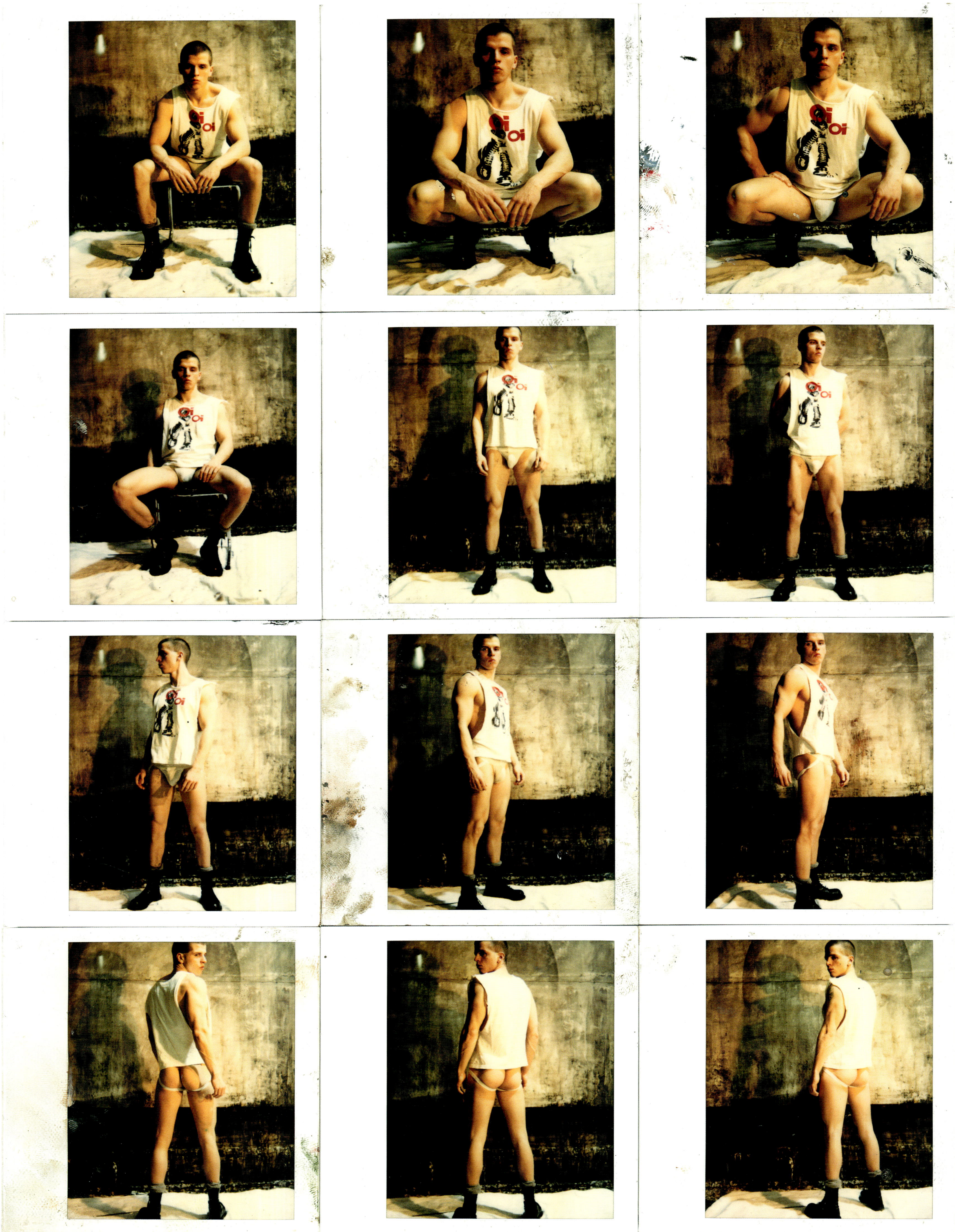

Alex, Berlin, 1987

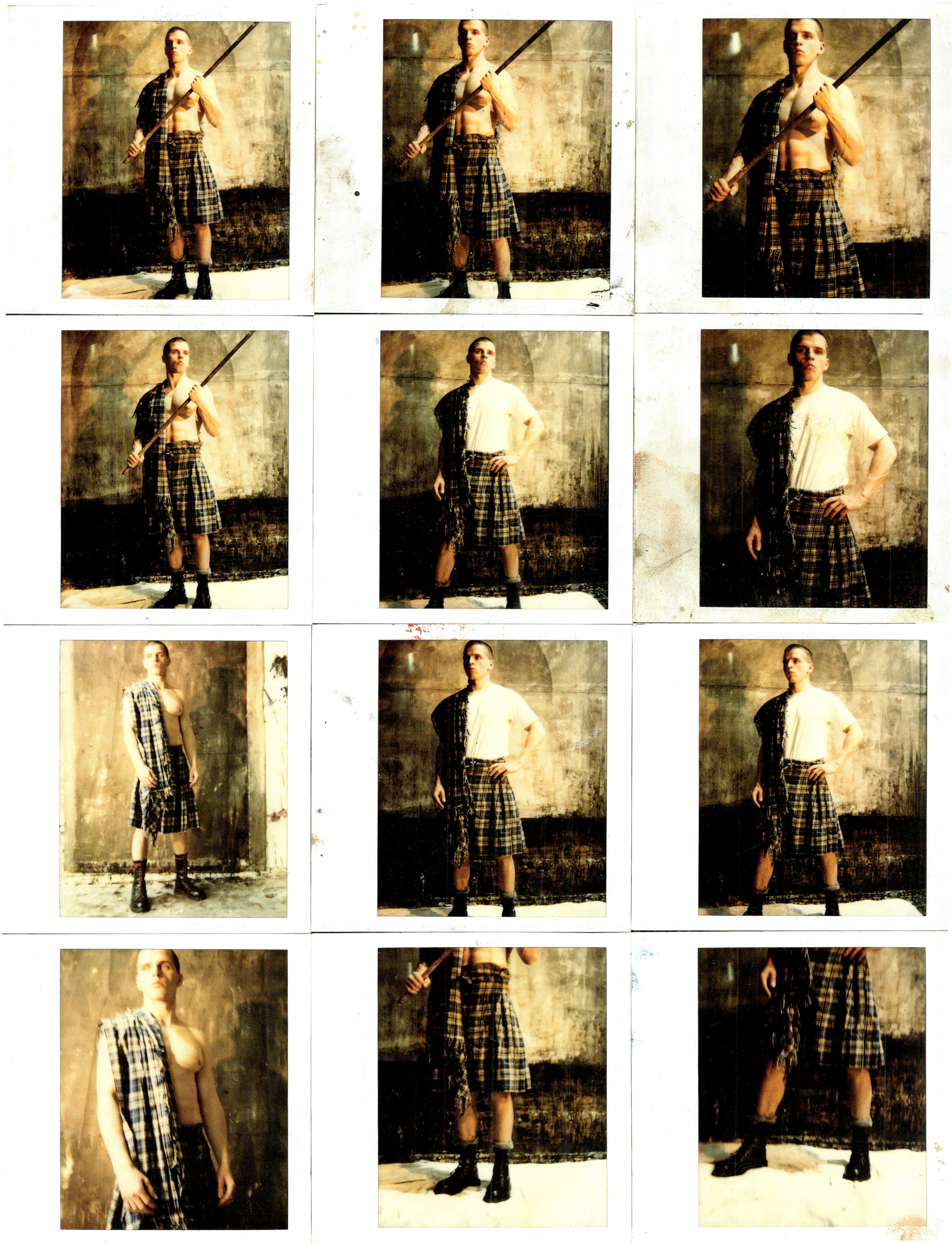

Alex with Kilt, Berlin, 1987

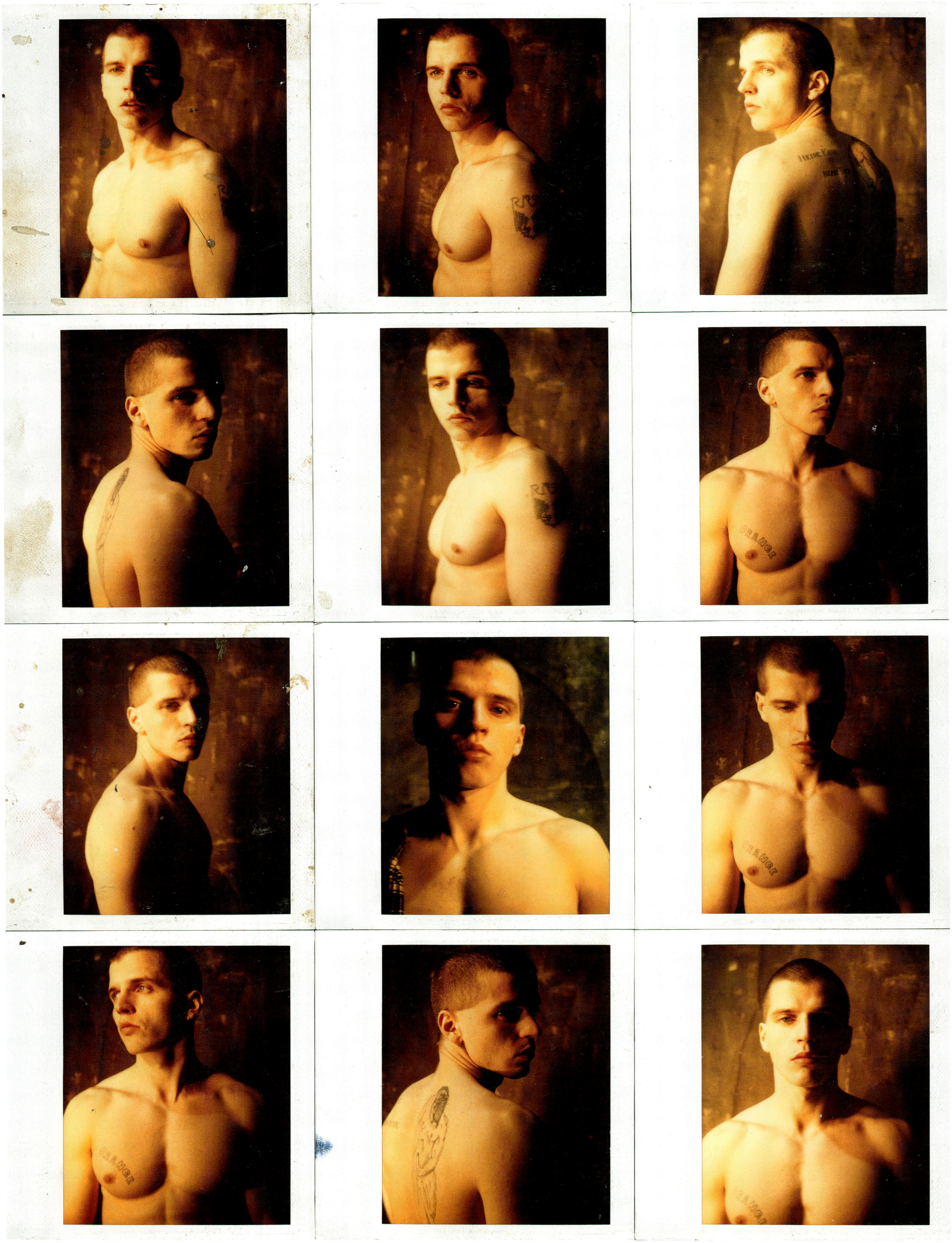

Alex, Berlin, 1987

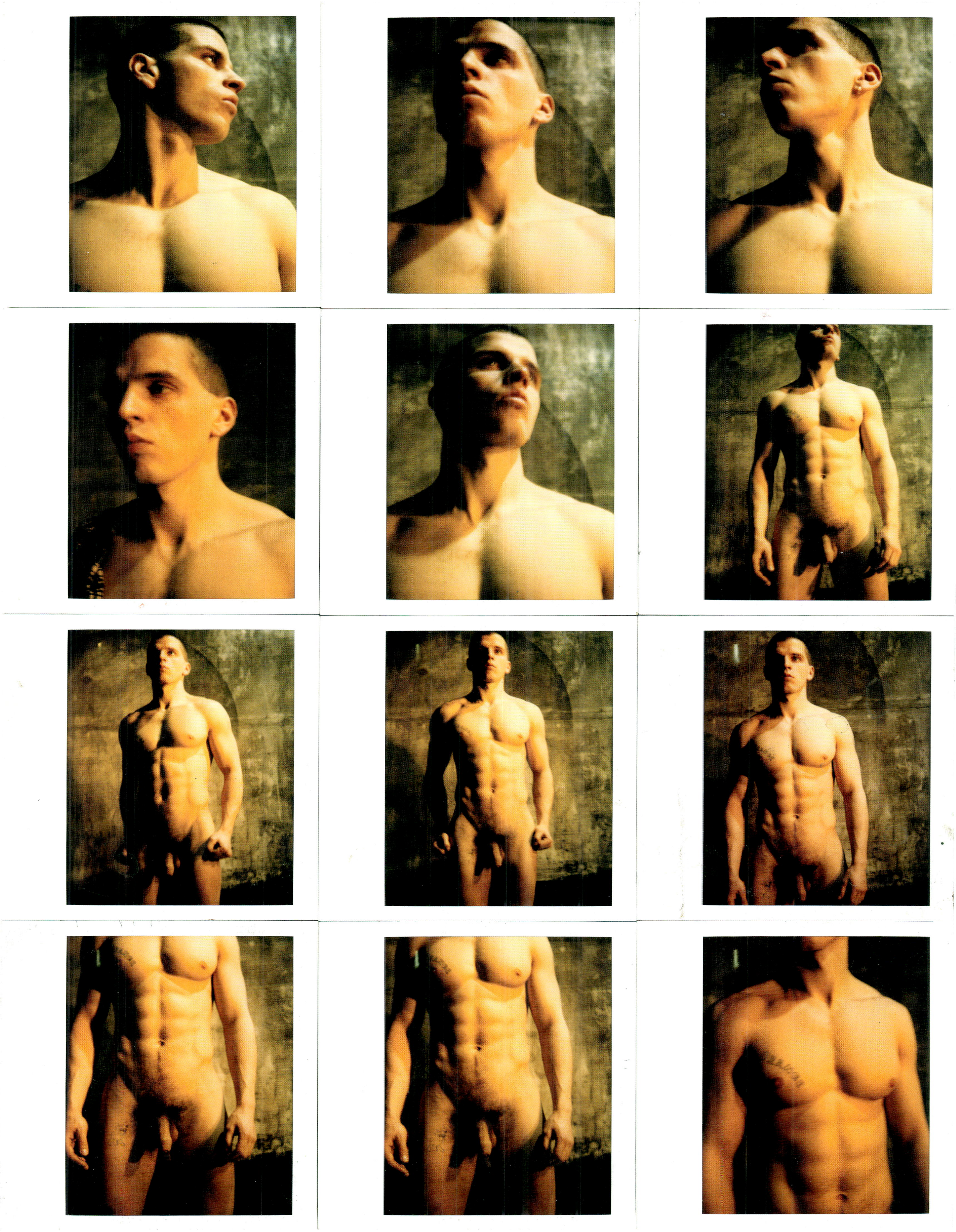

Alex, Berlin, 1987

In Advance of a Broken Army

Michael Turner

Nothing changes from generation to generation except the thing seen and that makes a composition.
—Gertrude Stein, "Composition As Explanation"[1]

After the identification of the postwar Baby Boom (1950s), Corporate America, eager to put a face on a new wave of consumers, announced the Pepsi Generation (1960s).[2] A decade later, once those cola-swilling teens became daiquiri-sipping adults: the Me Generation (1970s).[3] Then, as the last wave of Boomers entered adulthood (those born between 1958-1965), a subdivison—Generation X (1980s).[4] This last category is significant, for it recalls the gap between first-born Baby Boomers and their parents (those who grew up during the Great Depression)—only this time the generation gap is within a single reproductive cycle.

Michael Morris and Attila Richard Lukacs were born twenty years apart—Morris in 1942, Lukacs in 1962. A hundred years ago, twenty years was a generation: roughly the time it took to grow up, marry, and reproduce. Today, generations are no longer spoken of in biological terms but as markets, some as small as five years (depending on who is doing the talking).[5] Morris is not a baby boomer. Born in wartime England, he and his mother came to Victoria, BC, in 1946, where he was encouraged to pursue a life in art (his father, a Canadian soldier serving with the Carlton and York regiment, was killed in action in Sicily). Like those who made the art, film, music, and literature that characterized the baby boom generation, Morris was older, in advance of his audience, a leader. Lukacs, on the other hand, was born near the end of the boom, when live births, though not at their peak, blossomed once more before petering out. Some believe this relative surge in births accounts for an anxiety amongst last-born boomers—an anxiety over everything from career advancement (increased competition for jobs, with the "good jobs" being taken) to the survival of the planet (the threat of nuclear war).[6]

Like Morris, the Alberta-born Lukacs was also the child of immigrants; he too was encouraged to pursue a life in art. However, the art of Morris and the art of Lukacs are as different as the times they grew up in, not to imply that both are emblematic of their generations so much as ask what the basis for their collaboration might be, assuming collaborations begin with something in common.

In a 1995 interview, Morris spoke of arriving at London in 1964 to attend the Slade School of Fine Art, only to be told that the art everybody was talking about was coming from Southern California, down the coast from whence he came, epitomized by the post-medium forays of the painter Ed Ruscha.[7] Morris could be excused for having missed this, growing up as he did with the belief that an art education and a vital art community required proximity to the great museums of Britain and Europe. Although aware of the New York abstractionists—Pollock and de Kooning, Rothko and Newman—Morris would not have had media or institutional access to the Southern California scene, nor a belief that anything as generative could emerge within minutes of Disneyland.

By 1970 Morris was arguably the leading Vancouver artist of his generation, fluent in numerous media, from painting, sculpture, and collage to new practices of performance, installation, photography, and video. Through extensive research and travel, Morris had cultivated relationships with international artists such as Robert Rauschenberg, whom he introduced to Vancouver gallerist Doug Christmas, as well as "destruction" artist Ralph Ortiz, whom he arranged an exhibition for at the Vancouver Art Gallery. A letter from Ray Johnson (dated May 11, 1968), written in response

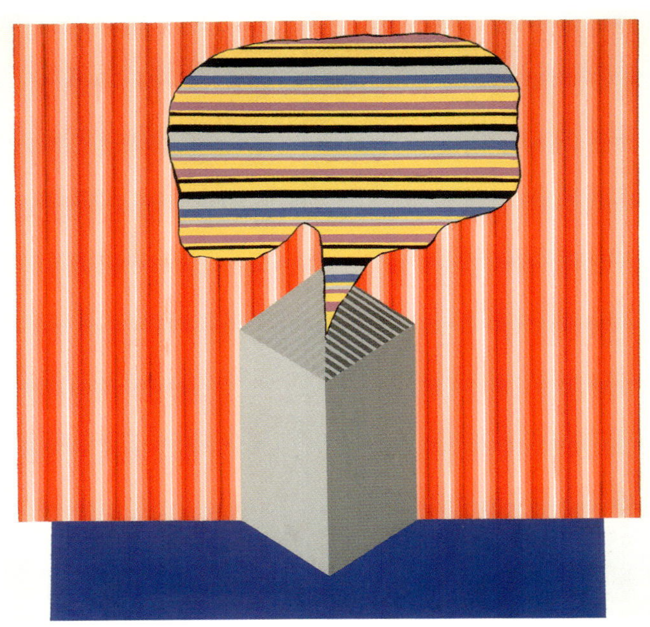

Michael Morris, *The Problem of Nothing*, 1966, acrylic on canvas, 137 x 152 cm, Collection of the Vancouver Art Gallery, Vancouver Centennial Award Purchase Prize. Photo: Robert Keziere, Vancouver Art Gallery

to a reproduction of Morris's 1967 painting *The Problem of Nothing* (as seen in *Artforum*), marked the beginning of correspondence art in Vancouver, a relationship which inspired both an instrumental Concrete Poetry exhibition at the UBC Fine Arts Gallery in 1969 and his most enduring work, the Image Bank archive (now the Morris/Trasov Archive), which he began that same year with Gary Lee-Nova and Vincent Trasov. In 1973 Morris and Trasov, et al., cofounded the Western Front, one of Canada's best-known artist-run centres.

In looking back on Morris's career, one might ask: What happened? Perhaps the question could be framed in relation to the 1946 cartoon by Ad Reinhardt, in which a man points to an abstract painting and says, "Ha Ha What does this represent?" while below, the recomposed (and suddenly figurative) painting replies, "What do you represent?" which is to say that any question of Morris's

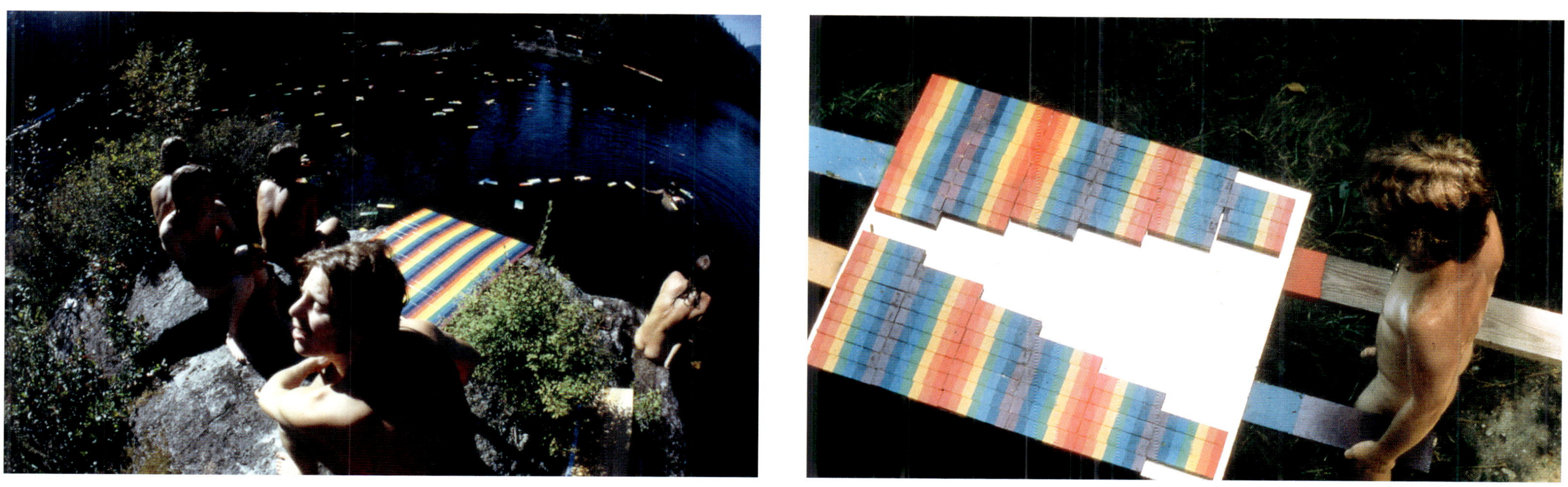

Slides from "Colour Research in Babyland, Summer of '72–'74," Collection of the Morris/Trasov Archive, The Morris and Helen Belkin Art Gallery.

activity over the past thirty years—from his arrival in West Berlin in 1981 to his return to Vancouver in 1998, and onward—is contingent on where one stands relative to the shifting interests of artists and audiences, the conversations that transpire from generation to generation. Because every time Morris opens a Morris/Trasov Archive box, whether to add to its contents or remove items for arrangement and display, he is making art. No matter that these (inter)actions are carried out informally—as gestures they are equivalent to a brush dipped in paint. True, Morris's 1980s exhibition record was nowhere as robust as it had been in the '60s and '70s, but neither was the Morris/Trasov Archive—until 1990, when it was accessioned to the Banff Centre and, in 1993, housed at the Morris and Helen Belkin Art Gallery. It was only in the 1990s that this collection of correspondences and "exhibition[s] destined for the mail"[8] began its transformation from ephemera to artist material.

Attila Richard Lukacs arrived in Vancouver in 1982 to attend the Emily Carr College of Art + Design. Like Morris, Lukacs came to paint. But where the painting of Morris's undergraduate era concerned itself with abstraction (and its rules), Lukacs was drawn to representational work, encouraged in part by a revival in figuration, as evidenced by the neo-expressionism of Jörg Immendorff and Georg Baselitz, as well as magazine superstars Jean-Michel Basquiat and Julian Schnabel—all of whom were engaged in this new and sudden world of the 1980s, where brushes dipped in the dark recesses of the past were wielded like conductors' batons at a bleak and certain future.

In Lukacs's art, young men, skinheads mostly, populated this world in various states of inversion, transformation, and decay. Rendered in deep chiaroscuro over large canvases, these men (naked and clothed, alone or in groups) stood on the verge of ritual, in dungeons or in ruins, surrounded by monkeys, pigs, totalitarian paraphernalia—a broken army of disenfranchised youth. Stylistically, the paintings were reminiscent of Caravaggio, infused with Renaissance symbolism and punk rage. And they were popular, not only with his contemporaries but with Vancouverites young and old—from the pogo-centric dancers of the Smilin' Buddha Cabaret to the crumbling middle-aged homotopians of Vancouver's West End. For them, Lukacs was a heroic figure, a chronicler of the world as they knew it, dreamed it, and feared it.

But what was this new world? And how, if at all, did it differ from Morris's?

The 1980 election of American President Ronald Reagan marked a shift in relations between the so-called democratic world and its ideological other, the Soviet Union. Like Britain's Margaret Thatcher (and British Columbia's Social Credit government), Reagan accelerated government deregulation, arguing that the unseen hand of

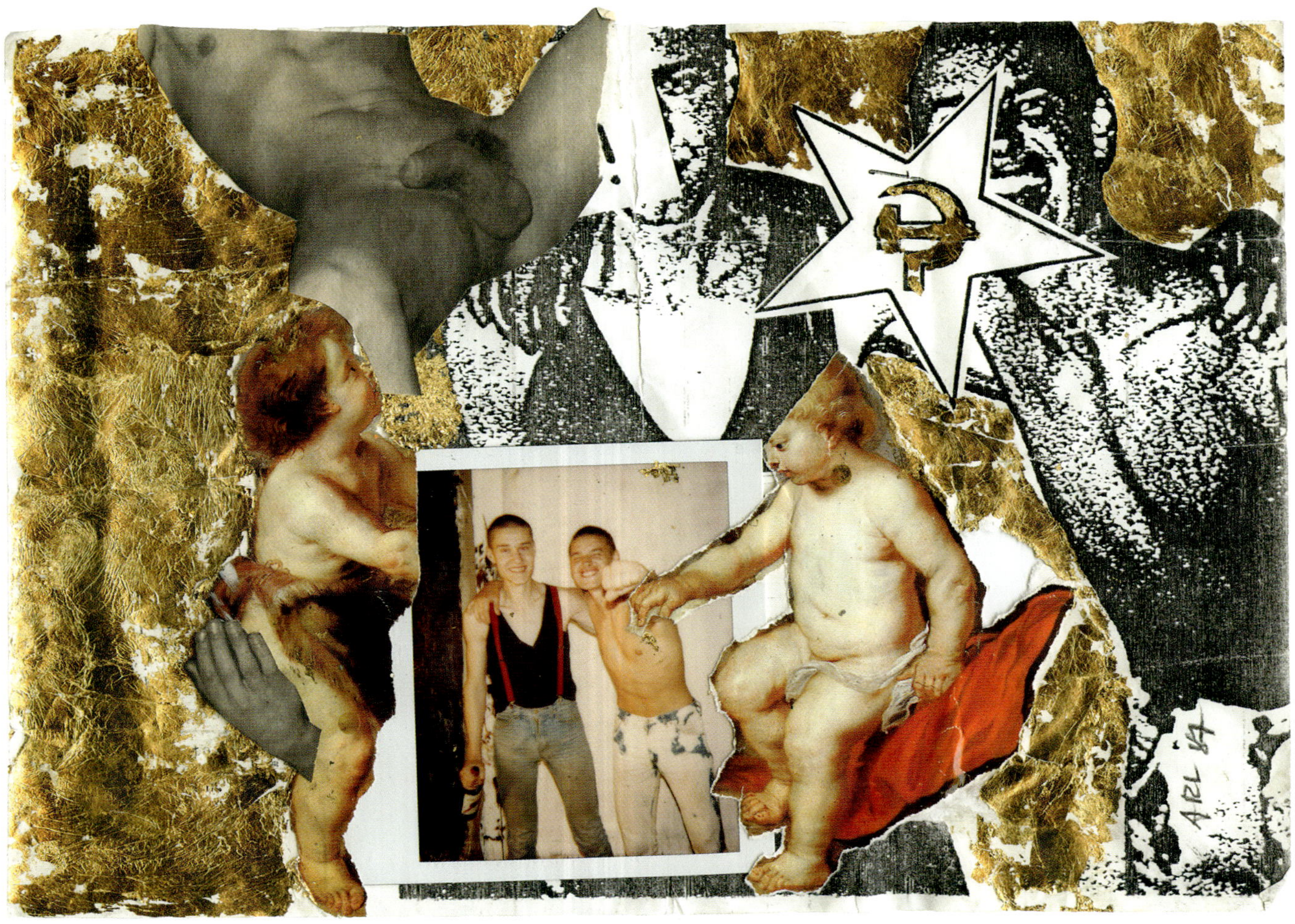

Attila Richard Lukacs, Untitled, 1987, goldleaf and collage on paper, 17 x 20 cm, Collection of Morris/Trasov Archive, The Morris and Helen Belkin Art Gallery.

capitalism, not the welfare state, would lead us to the future. Concurrently, he increased military spending, amplified anti-Soviet rhetoric, and aligned himself with the Christian Right, the same people who denied the science behind Acquired Immune Deficiency Syndrome (AIDS) in favour of the near-Biblical term "Gay Plague." The result was a cold and brittle world, particularly for those entering adulthood, and a feeling that the planet, now porcupined with warheads, could explode at a moment's notice—with the losers going to Hell. Although Morris would have experienced something similar at Lukacs's age (the Cuban Missile Crisis), the fear stoked by this toxic conflation of politics, economics, and religion was, by the mid-1980s, particularly acute, especially for those who identified as homosexual.

In 1986, with Vancouver disfigured by an international exposition, Lukacs left North America for West Berlin. It was a move consistent with the artist's subject matter—Berlin being a city steeped in artistic and homosexual tradition, where being a skinhead had more to do with politics than fashion, and where neo-expressionist figuration (an inadvertent critique of socialist realism?) remained popular. Lukacs would spend the next ten years in Berlin's Kreuzberg district, painting, hanging out with Morris, and watching as the first stream of young Eastern European men stepped over the Wall in search of work. Lukacs hired some of these men as studio models and painted them with the aid of Polaroid images. Over the next twenty years, Lukacs would take thousands of Polaroids. It was in 2008 that Morris began to work with them, in earnest.

In her 1926 essay "Composition as Explanation," Gertrude Stein, in an attempt to explain her writing, makes a case for generational change not as a change of elements but a change in the relationships between elements. This change applied to art when Morris arrived in England to learn that painting had once again exhausted itself, giving rise to designer painters like Ruscha and Andy Warhol, both of whom worked in graphic media. That this fusion of painting with the so-called lower arts (photography, silkscreening) came at a time when the governments of Canada, Great Britain, the United States, and West Germany were increasingly regulatory is notable when contrasted with the reemergence of representational painters such as Baselitz, Immendorff, Schnabel, Basquiat, and Lukacs, occurring as they did in the 1980s while their countries were undoing the regulatory policies of previous governments. The reemergence of representational painting in this milieu was supported by a number of material conditions—significantly, commercial gallerists were eager to sell work to those who had benefited from the new deregulated economy and were determined to build art collections. But these collections would not feature the dry and distant works of 1970s minimal and conceptual art but big, expressive oil paintings, ideally for homes big enough to dwarf them.

In a recent conversation, Lukacs spoke of his years in Berlin, in particular, his friendship with Morris. Morris found him his first apartment, introduced him to gallerists, curators, and collectors, secured for him a two-year residency at the Künstlerhaus Bethanien and made himself available for "lessons in art history" and late-night "emergency crits."[9] Most relevant to this discussion was Morris's collaged notes, slipped under Lukacs's door or given to him "on any occasion—Easter, Christmas, Mother's Day." It was from these collages that Lukacs came to understand the Morris/Trasov Archive not only as a record of Morris's conversations with art and artists but as a collective unconscious, an artist material, and in doing so, exchanged with Morris collages of his own, a practice he took up as a kind of palette cleanser, "something to do between paintings." However, these were not the collages Lukacs did with schoolmates Angela Grossmann and Derek Root (attempts, as he put it, "to get at something worth painting"), but correspondences related to past conversations—jokes, reminiscences, lessons—all of which can be found in the Morris/Trasov Archive, and within Lukacs's own.

When asked about his Polaroids, what they mean to him, Lukacs said he knew something would "probably come of them someday," though he was "probably not the one to do it." When asked if his uncertainty was related to his models, if it was a privacy issue, he said no, he had their consent. Morris knew the young models, and when he asked to look at the Polaroids (in disarray after Lukacs's return from five chemically altered years in New York City) he found that he could resequence them based on his memory of visits to Lukacs's Berlin studio. Thus what began as an archaeological dig

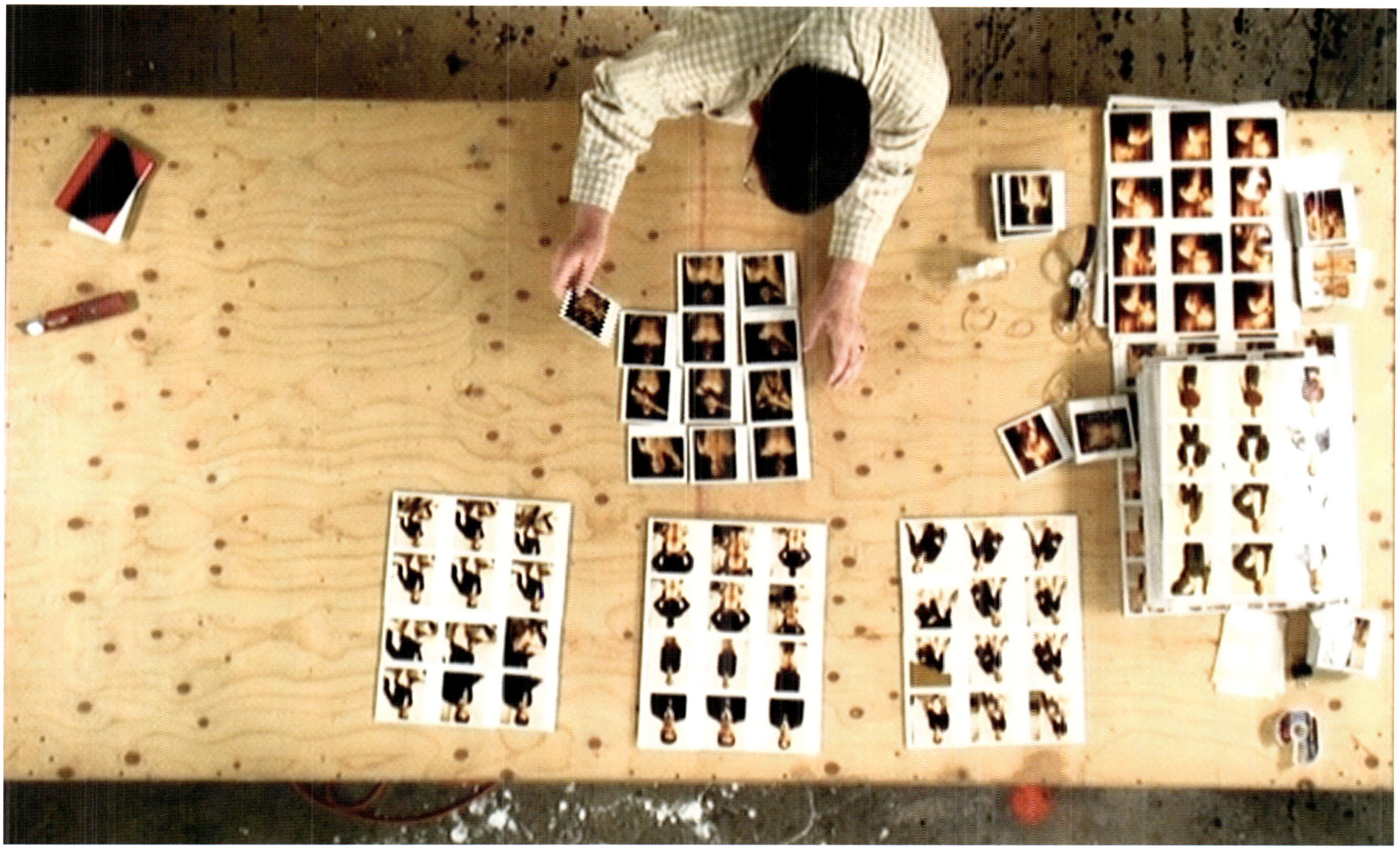

Michael Morris assembling Polaroids; still from a video by Paul Wong.

evolved into a wholesale spatial reorientation, the Polaroids undergoing numerous arrangements before settling into the systematized 3 x 4 image grids we see now. Most remarkable is the speed with which Morris composes these grids and grid sequences—in most instances quicker than the time it takes for one of these images to develop. Watching him at work, I am reminded of a night-club DJ, but also an artist who has been working with photo sequences since the late-1960s.

Indeed, it is this reminder of the younger Morris that unites him with the artist he is today: his desire (like that of Lukacs's contemporary Steven Shearer) to take what is around him and bring it to an aesthetic conclusion. Lukacs does something different. His paintings (from his model studies to his recurrent use of nonpainterly materials and his abiding interest in ideological conflicts and private rituals) appear concerned more with premise than conclusion ("on the verge of ritual," as mentioned earlier), as well as that which goes unseen—be it capitalism's hand or the Polaroid process, how the image develops, untouched, before your very eye. Having used these images to make his paintings, Lukacs would think nothing of allowing them to travel onward, transformed, not only in recognition of what Morris has done for him as both a mentor and a friend, but as someone who sees a parallel in his paintings as a site of transformation.

NOTES

1. Gertrude Stein, "Composition As Explanation," in *Look At Me Now and Here I Am: Writings and Lectures 1909–1945* (Harmondsworth: Penguin, 1990) 21.

2. The "Pepsi Generation" campaign was conceived by PepsiCo advertising executive Alan Maxwell Pottasch in 1963. Prior to Pottasch's campaign, advertisers focused on a product's attributes, not the consumer's. The emphasis on the consumer (audience) over the product (object) provides an interesting parallel to the development of late-twentieth century Western art and theory.

3. Christopher Lasch, *The Culture of Narcissism: American Life in an Age of Diminishing Expectations* (London: W.W. Norton, 1979).

4. Douglas Coupland, *Generation X: Tales for an Accelerated Culture* (New York: St. Martin's Griffin, 1991).

5. Gertrude Stein, "Portraits and Repitition," in *Look At Me Now and Here I Am: Writings and Lectures: 1909–1945* (Harmondsworth: Penguin, 1990) 99.

6. William Strauss and Neil Howe, *Generations: The History of America's Future, 1584 to 2069* (New York: Harper Perennial, 1992).

7. Sharla Sava interview with Michael Morris, unpublished, 1995.

8. Scott Watson, "Hand of the Spirit: Documents of the Seventies from the Morris/Trasov Archive," (University of British Columbia Fine Arts Gallery: Vancouver, 1992).

9. Interview with Attila Richard Lukacs, 2009.

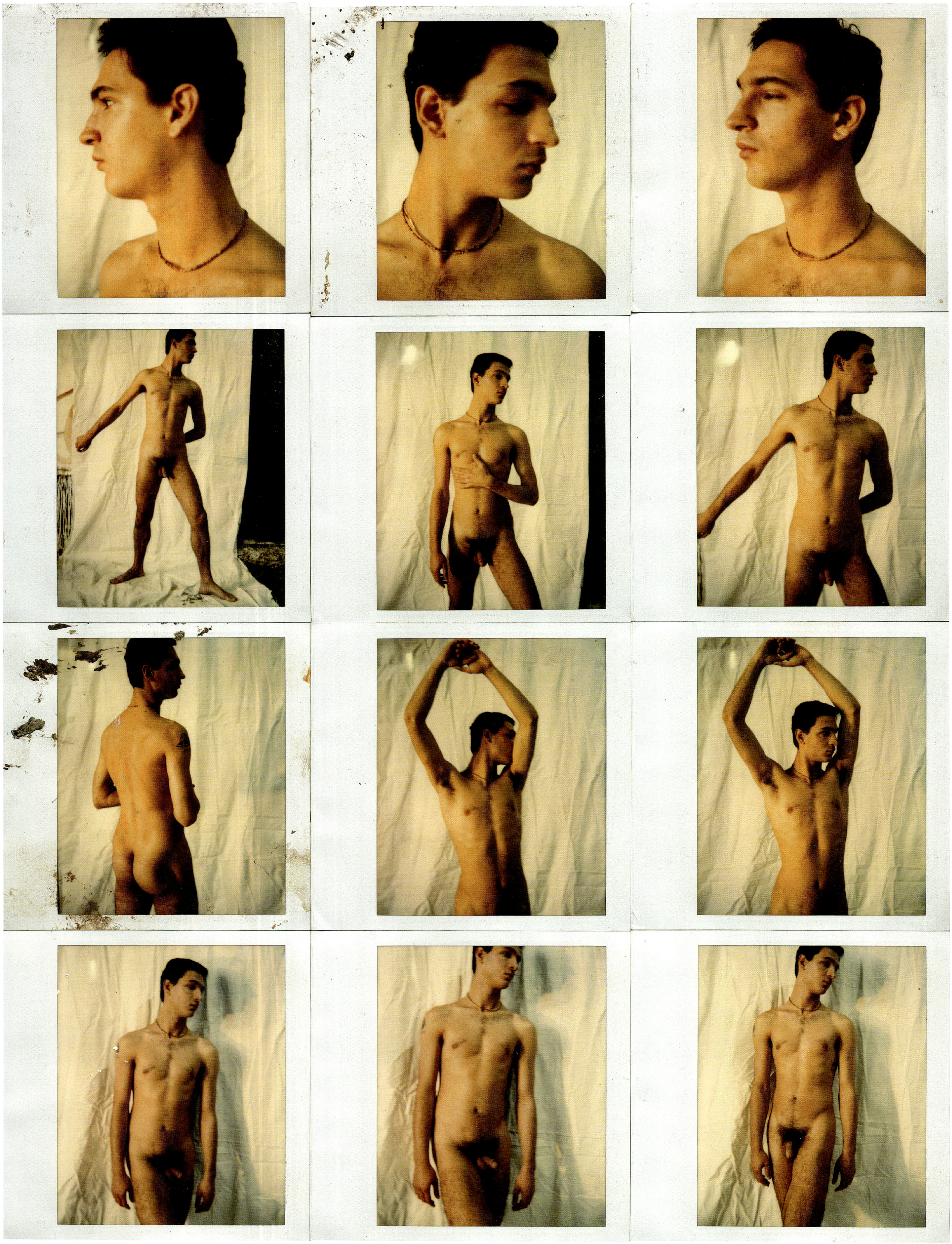

Study for *The Young Spartans...* after Degas, Berlin, 1987

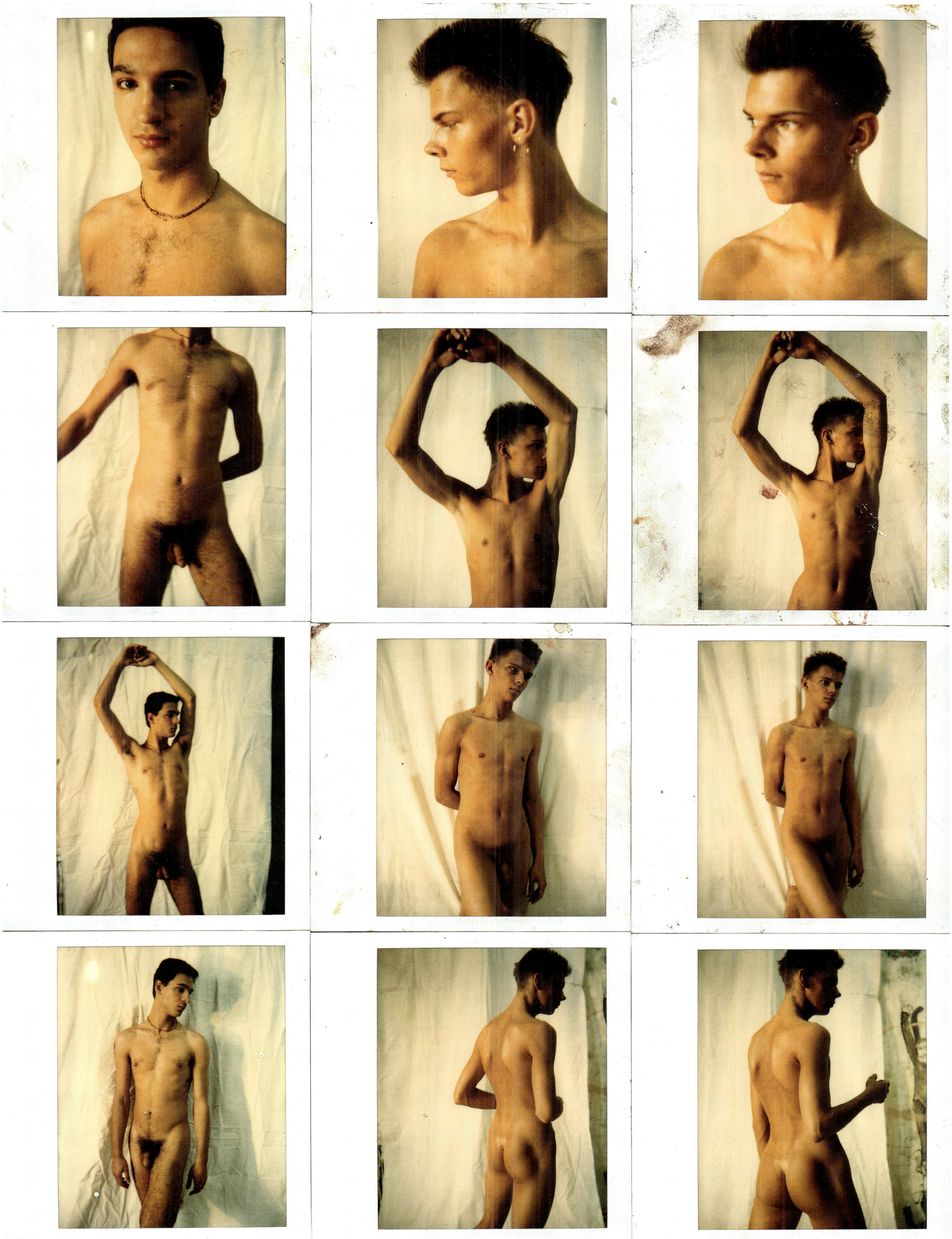

Study for *The Young Spartans...* after Degas, Berlin, 1987

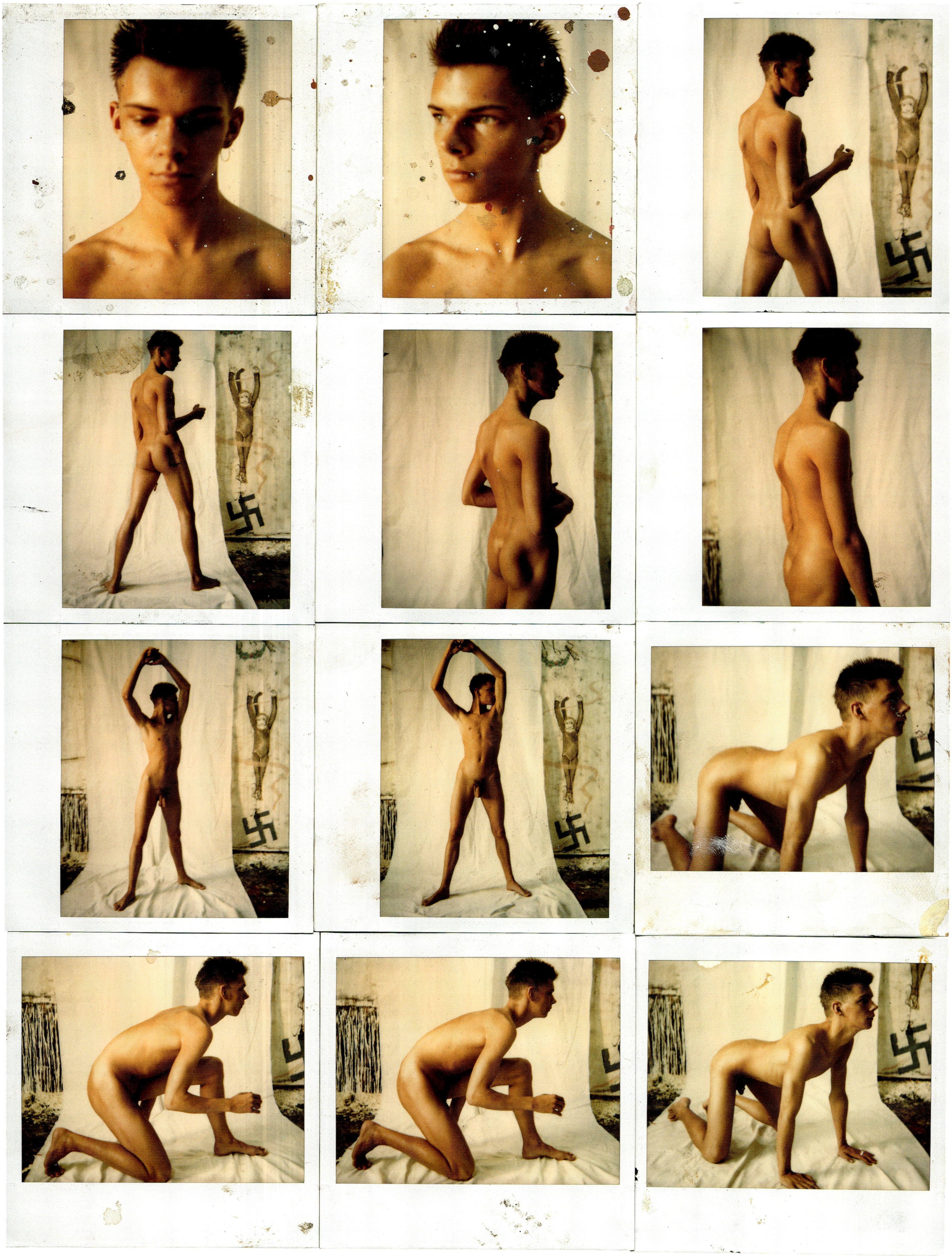

Study for *The Young Spartans*... after Degas, Berlin, 1987

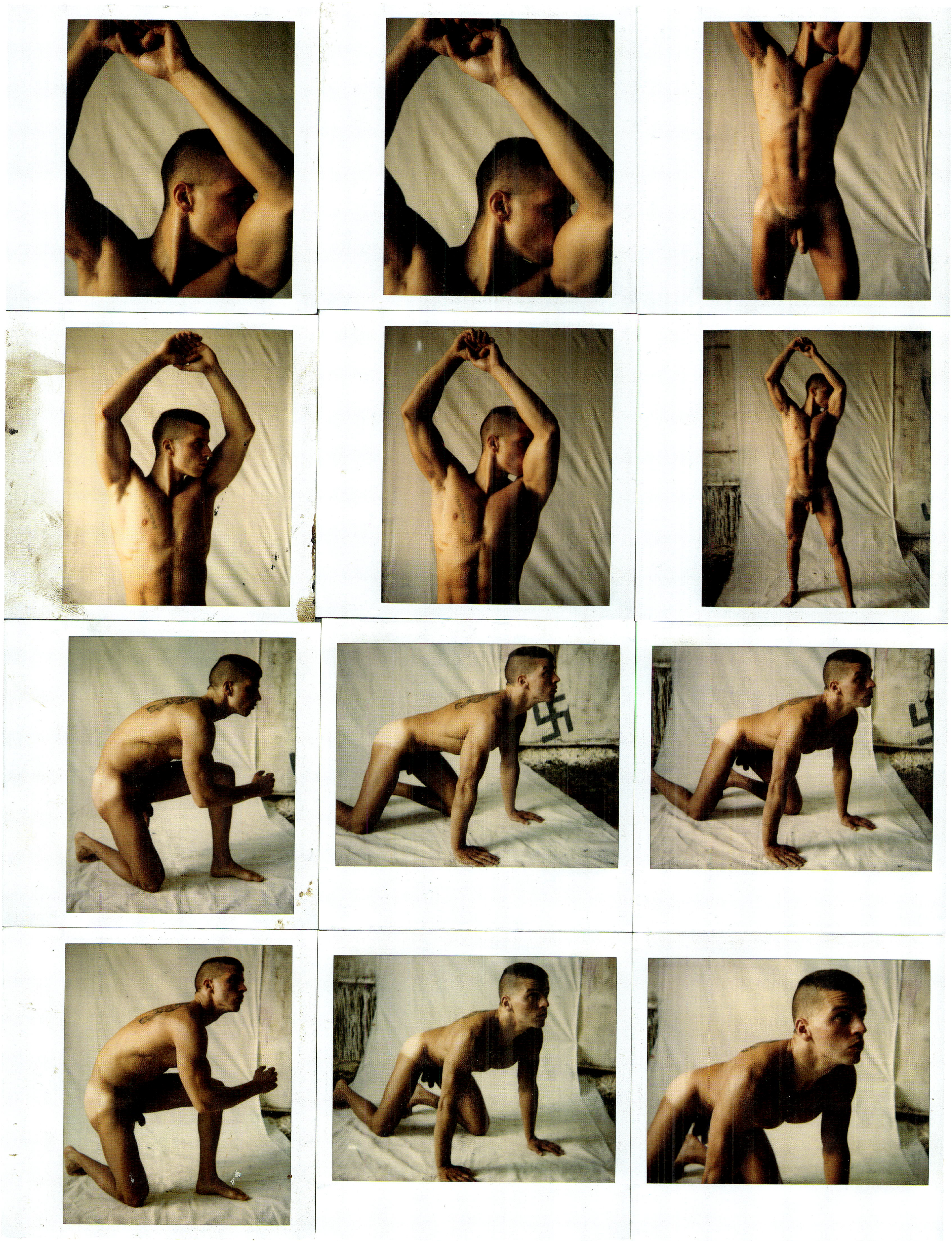

Study for *The Young Spartans*... after Degas, Berlin, 1987

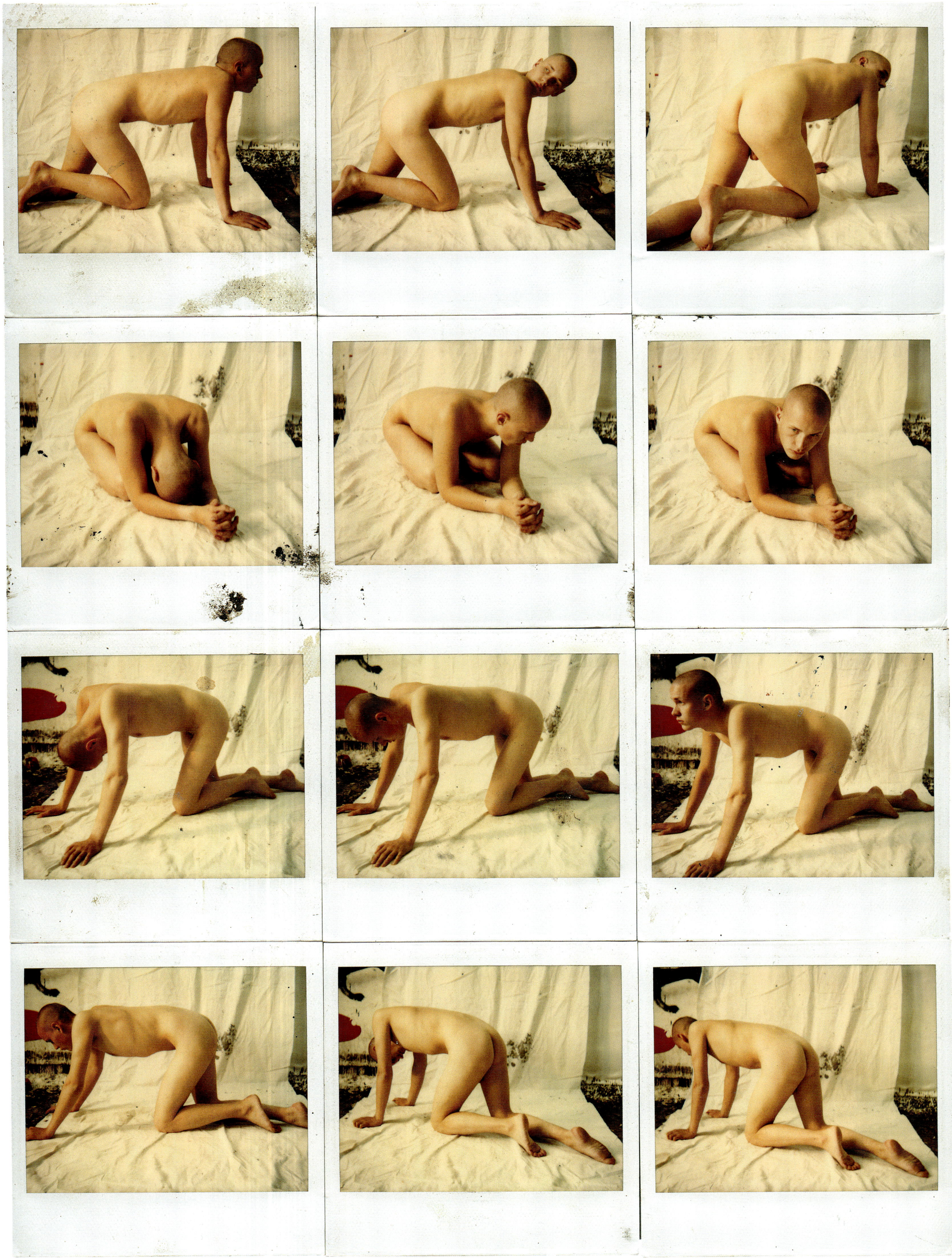

Finn Skin, Berlin, 1987

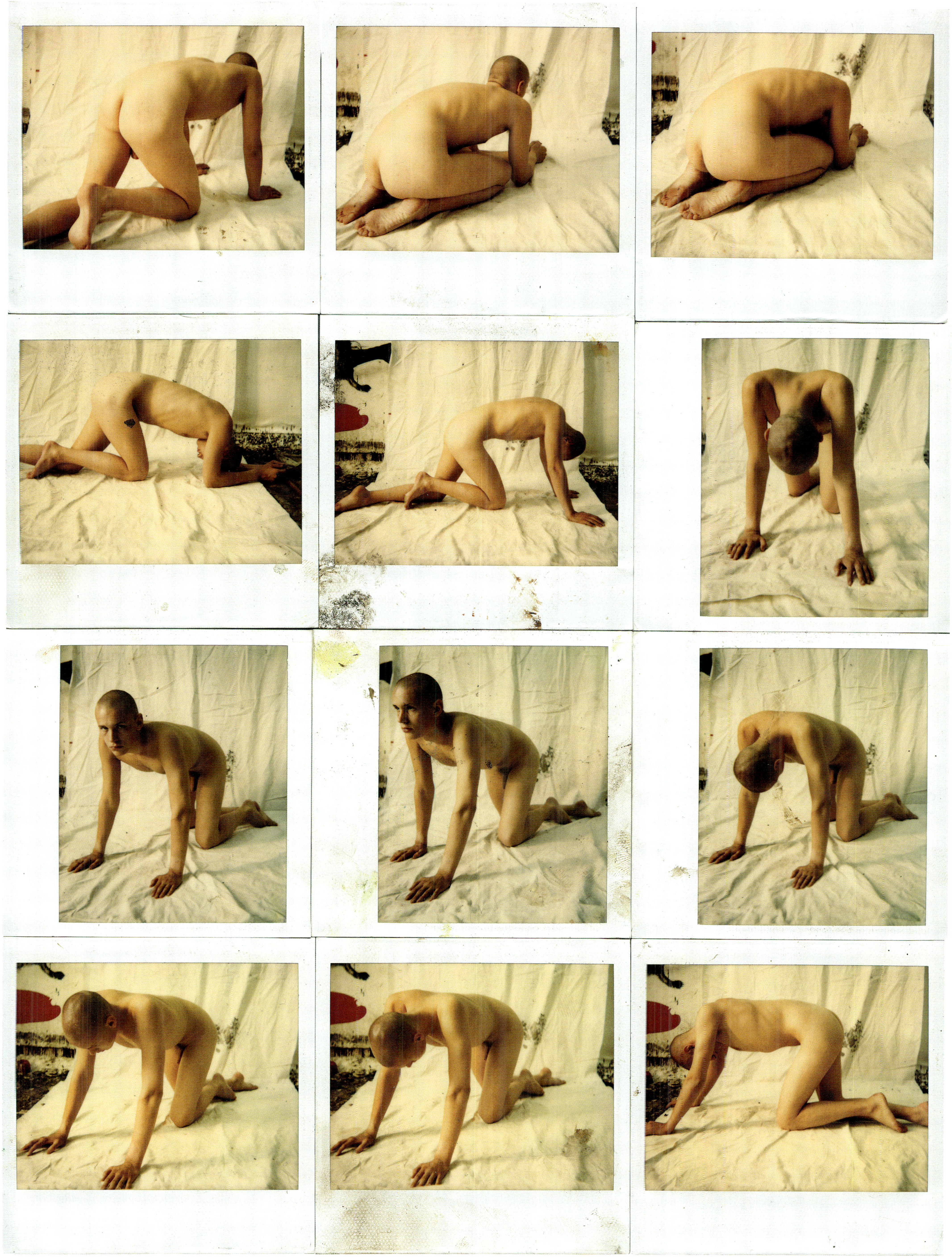

Finn Skin, Berlin, 1987

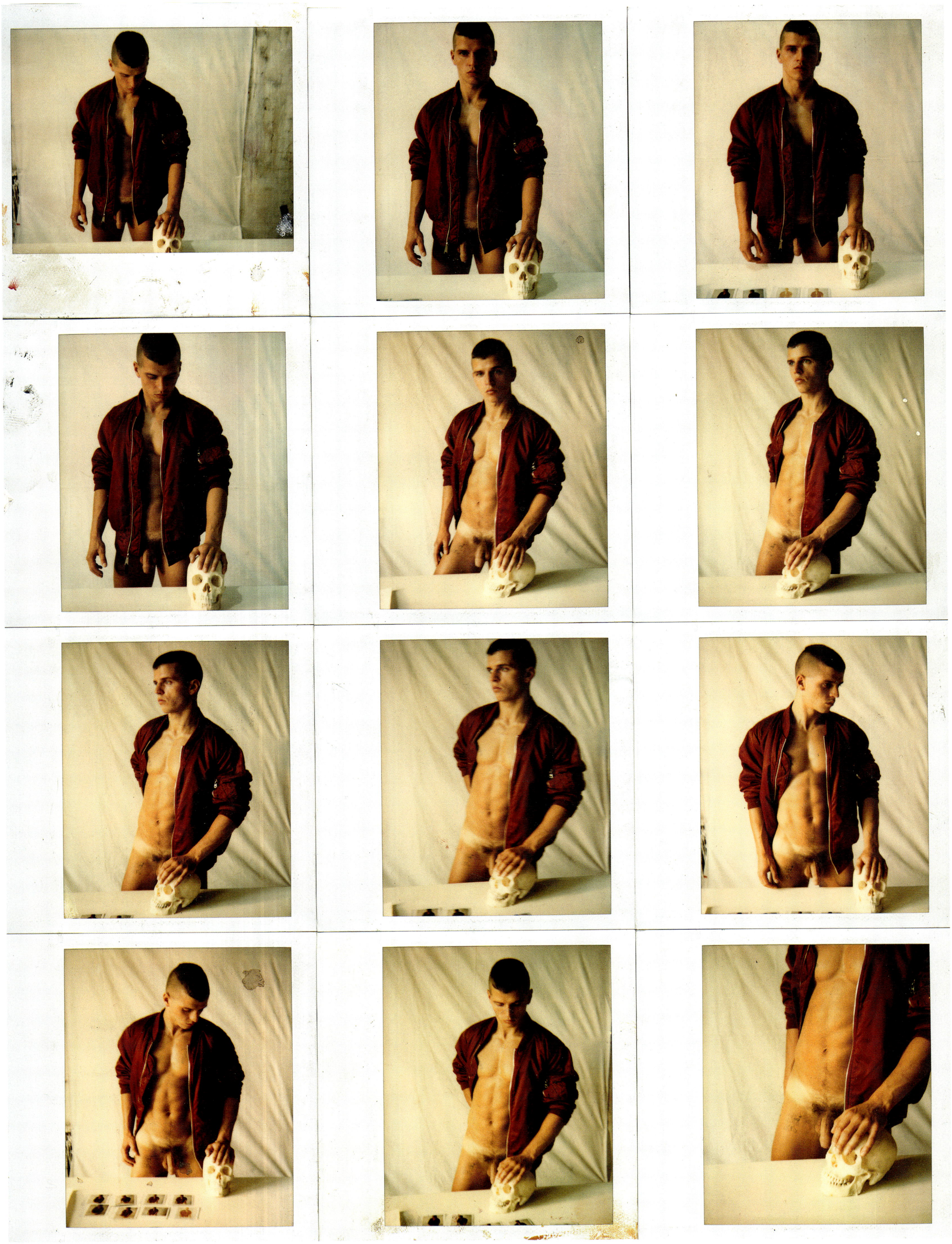

Alex, after *The Calling of Saint Matthew*, Caravaggio, Berlin, 1987

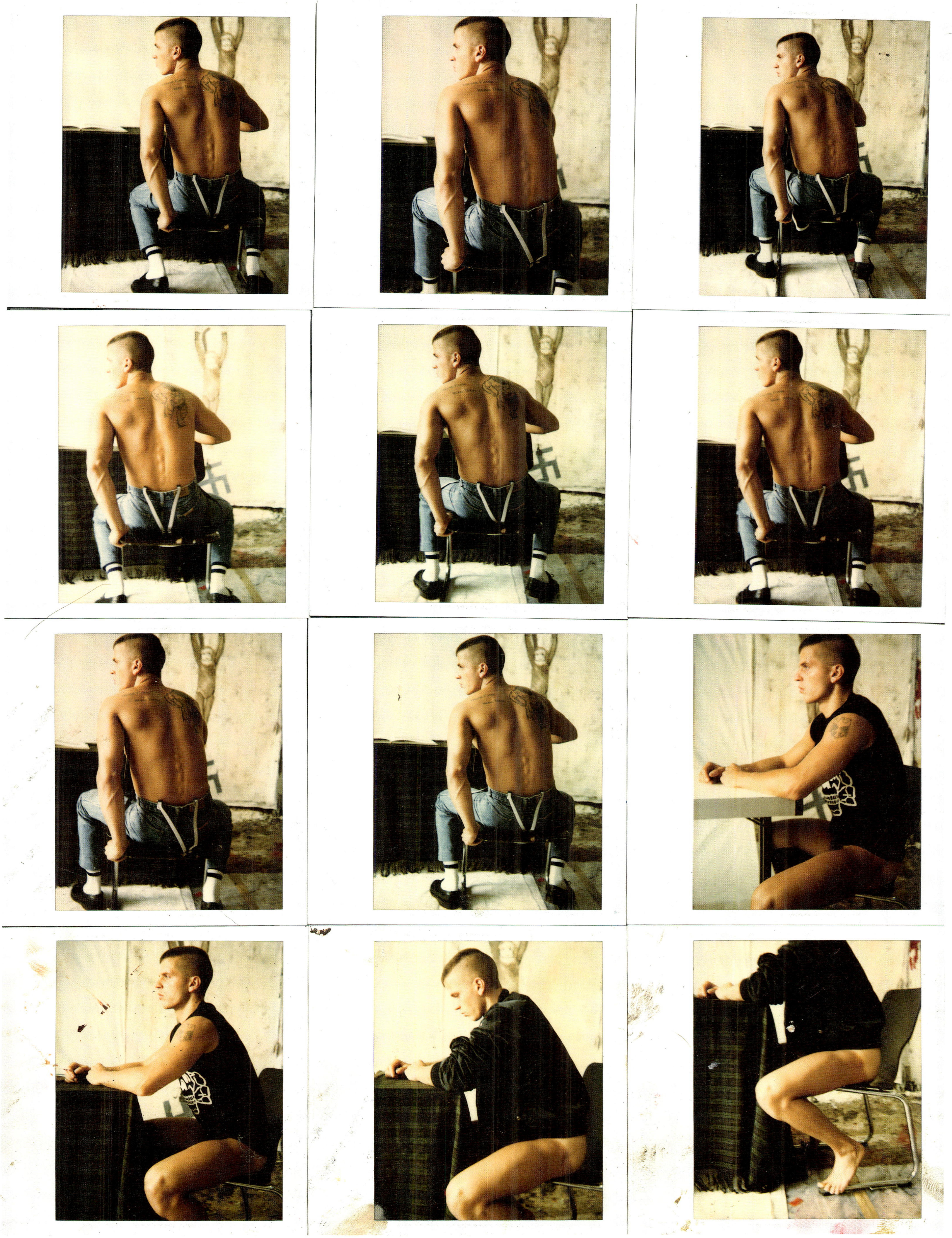

Alex, after *The Calling of Saint Matthew*, Caravaggio, Berlin, 1987

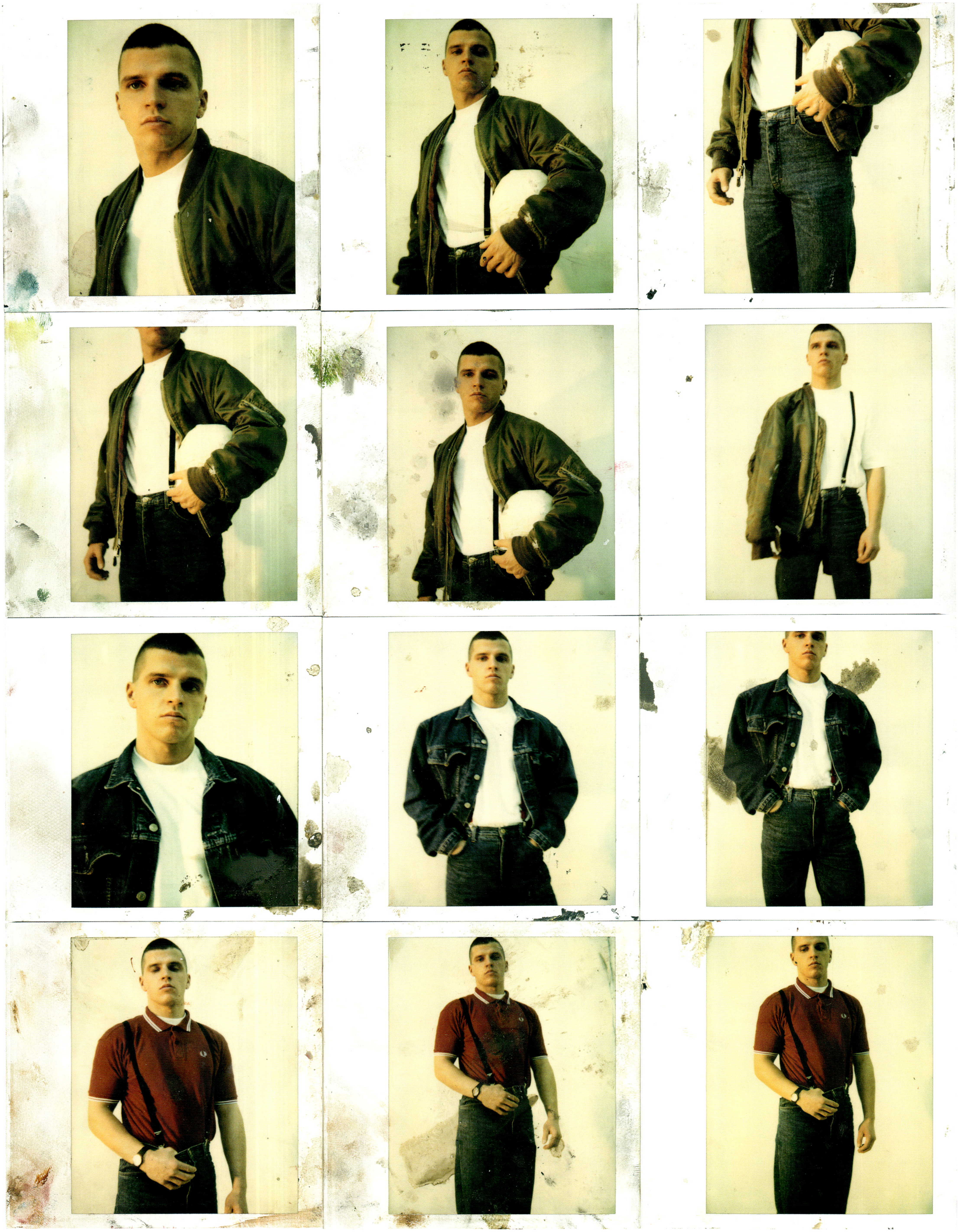

Alex for *True North*, Berlin, 1988

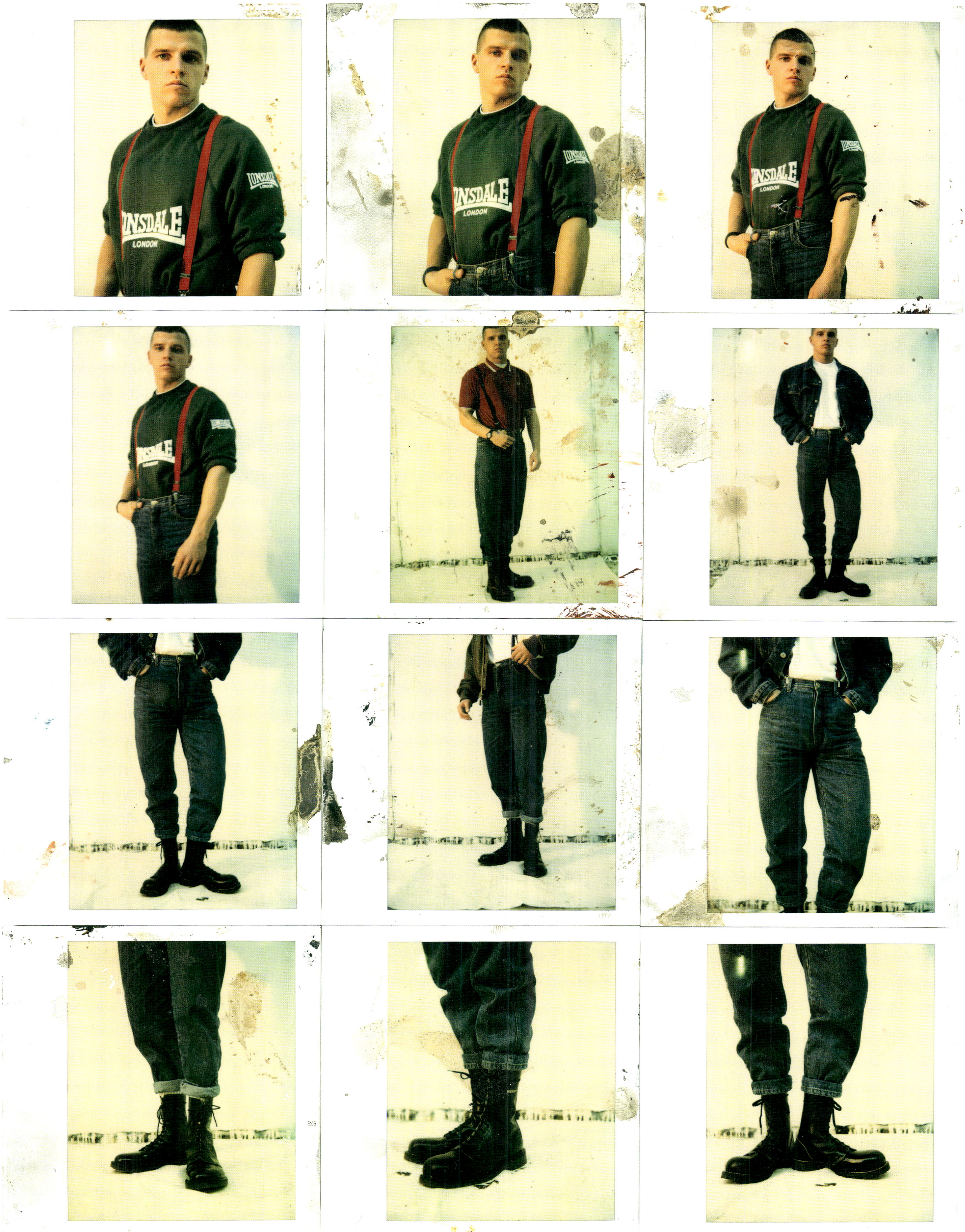

Alex for *True North*, Berlin, 1988

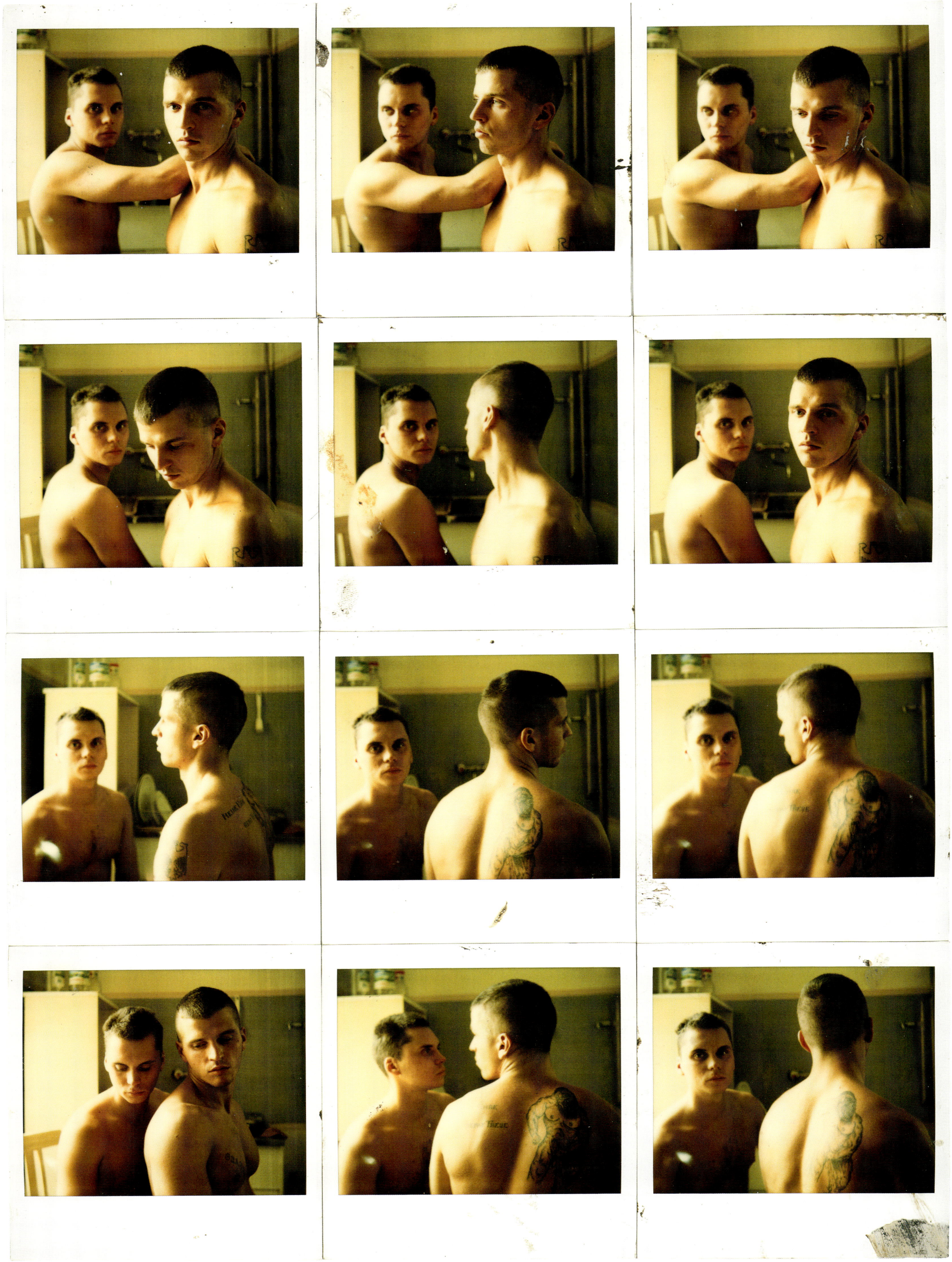

Alex & Ingo, Oranienstr. 33, Berlin, 1988

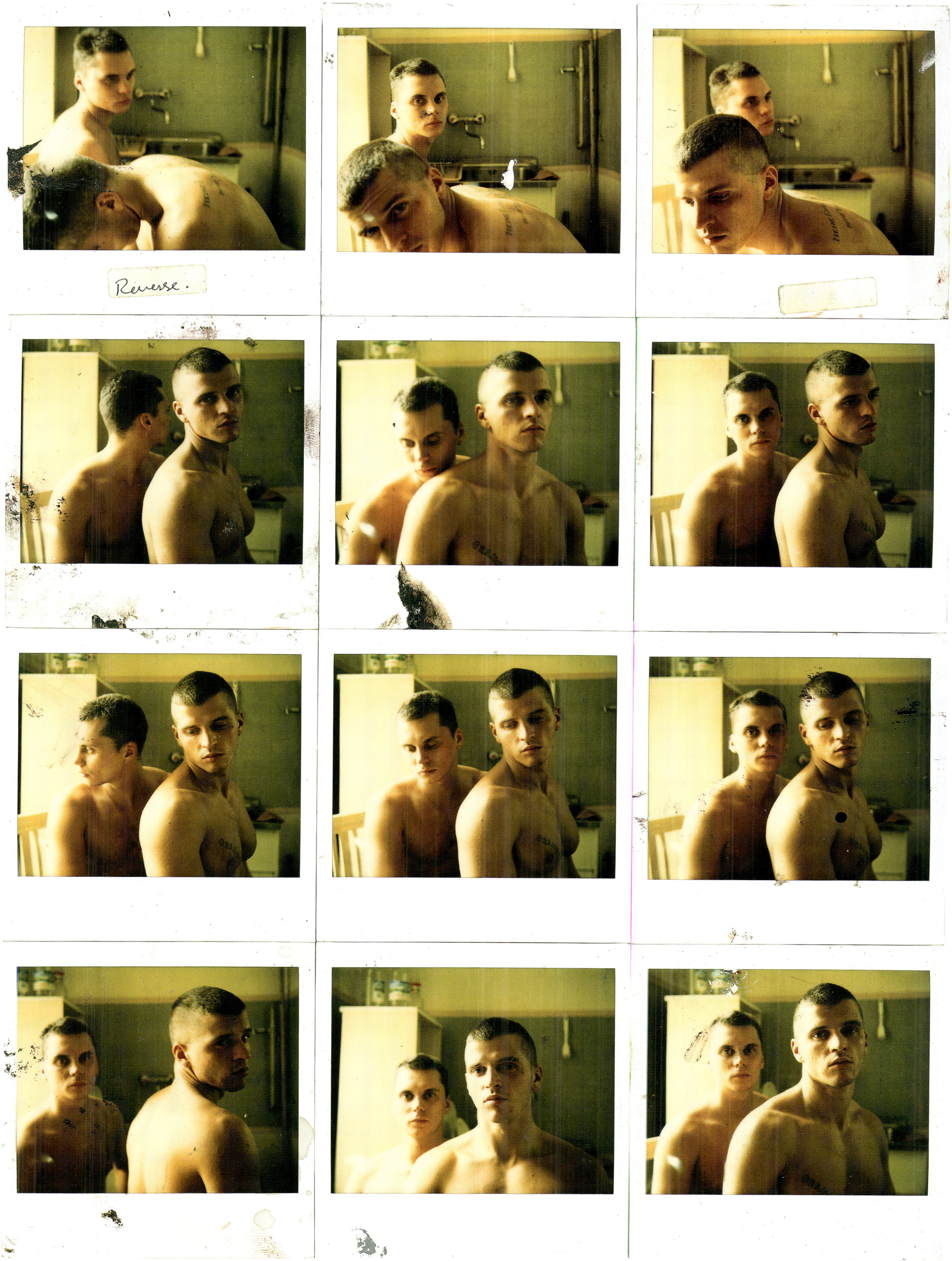

Alex & Ingo, Oranienstr. 33, Berlin, 1988

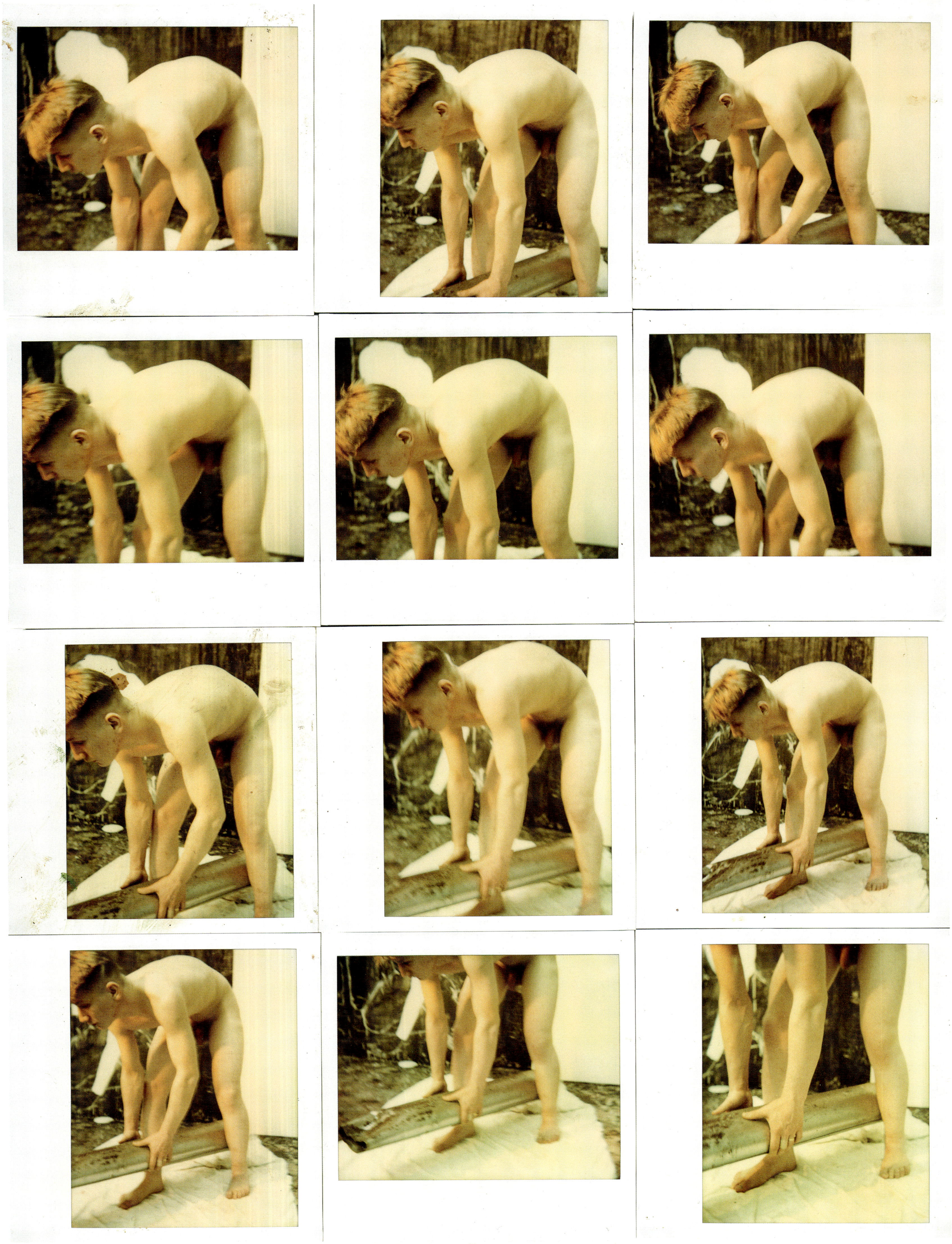

Zoo Boy, Berlin, 1988

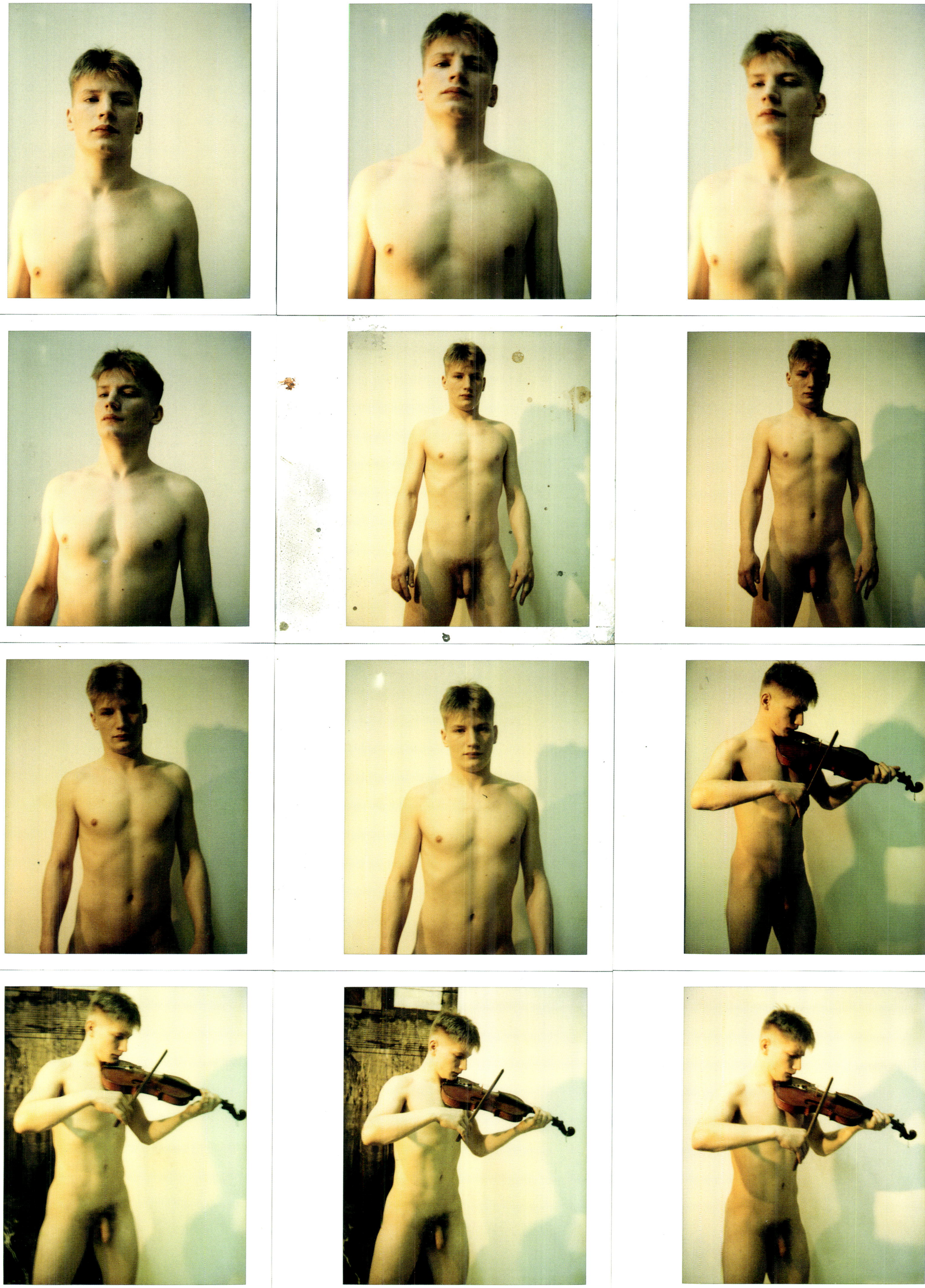

Zoe Boy with Violin, Berlin, 1988

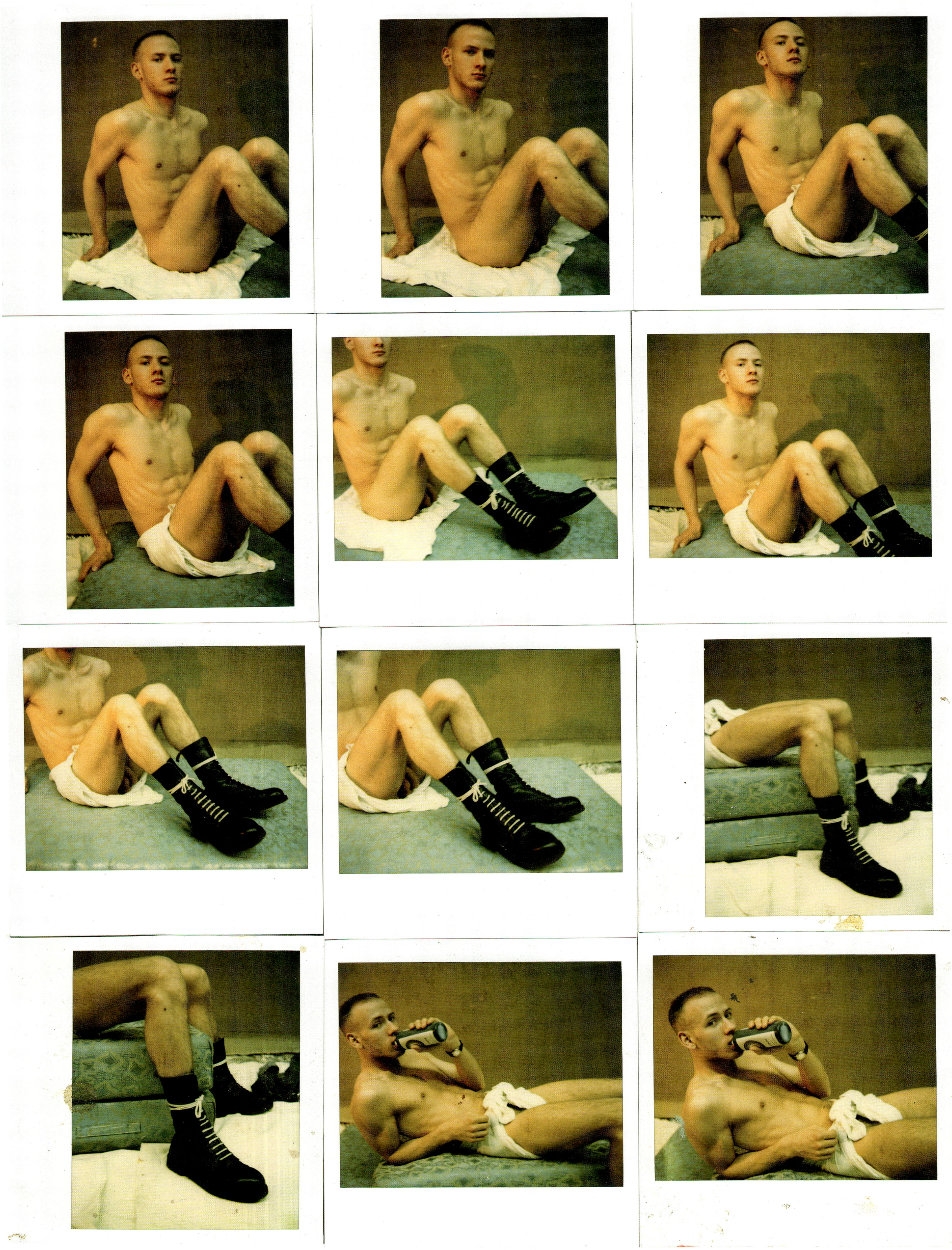

Stephan with Boots & Bottle, Berlin, 1989

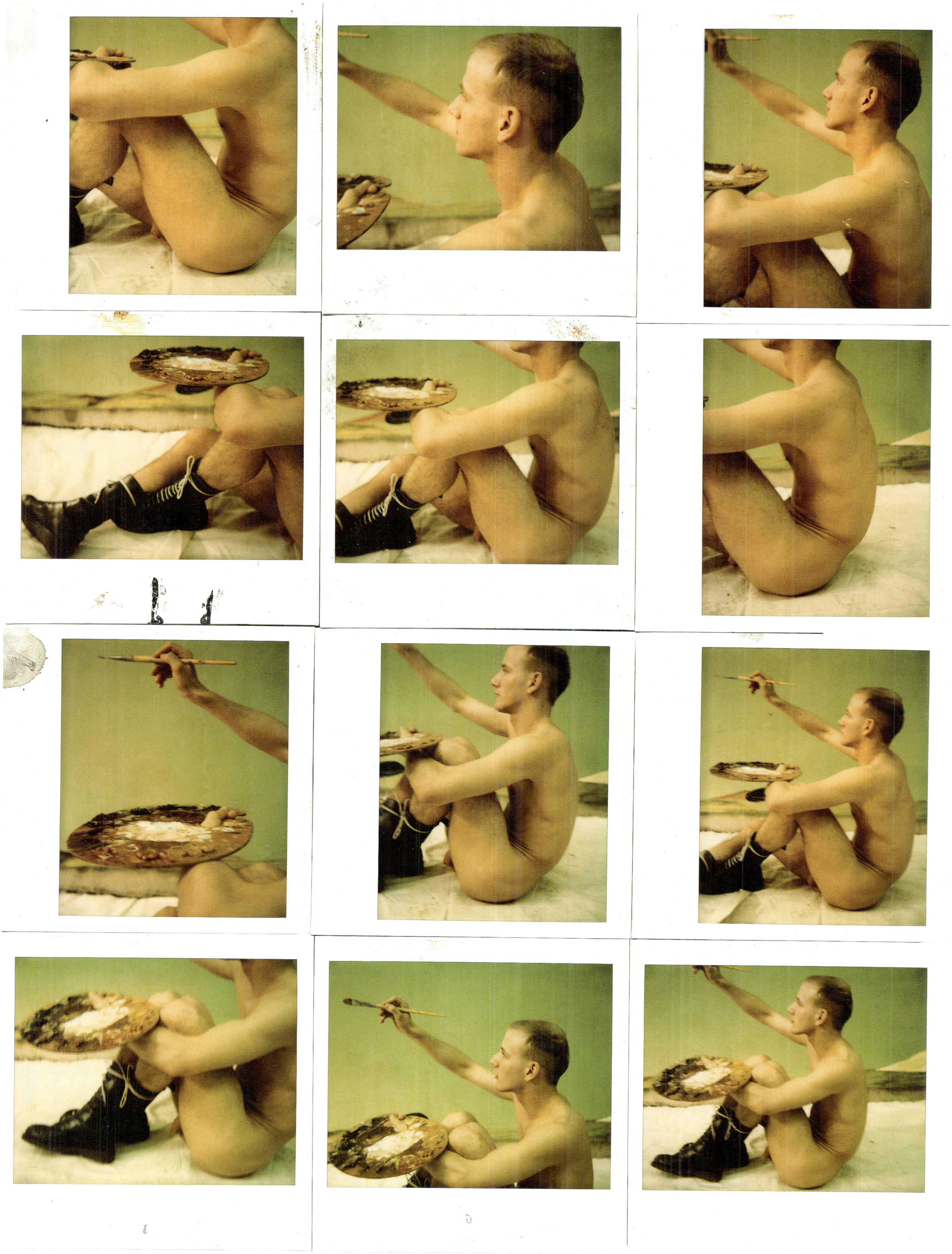

Stephan with Palette, Berlin, 1989

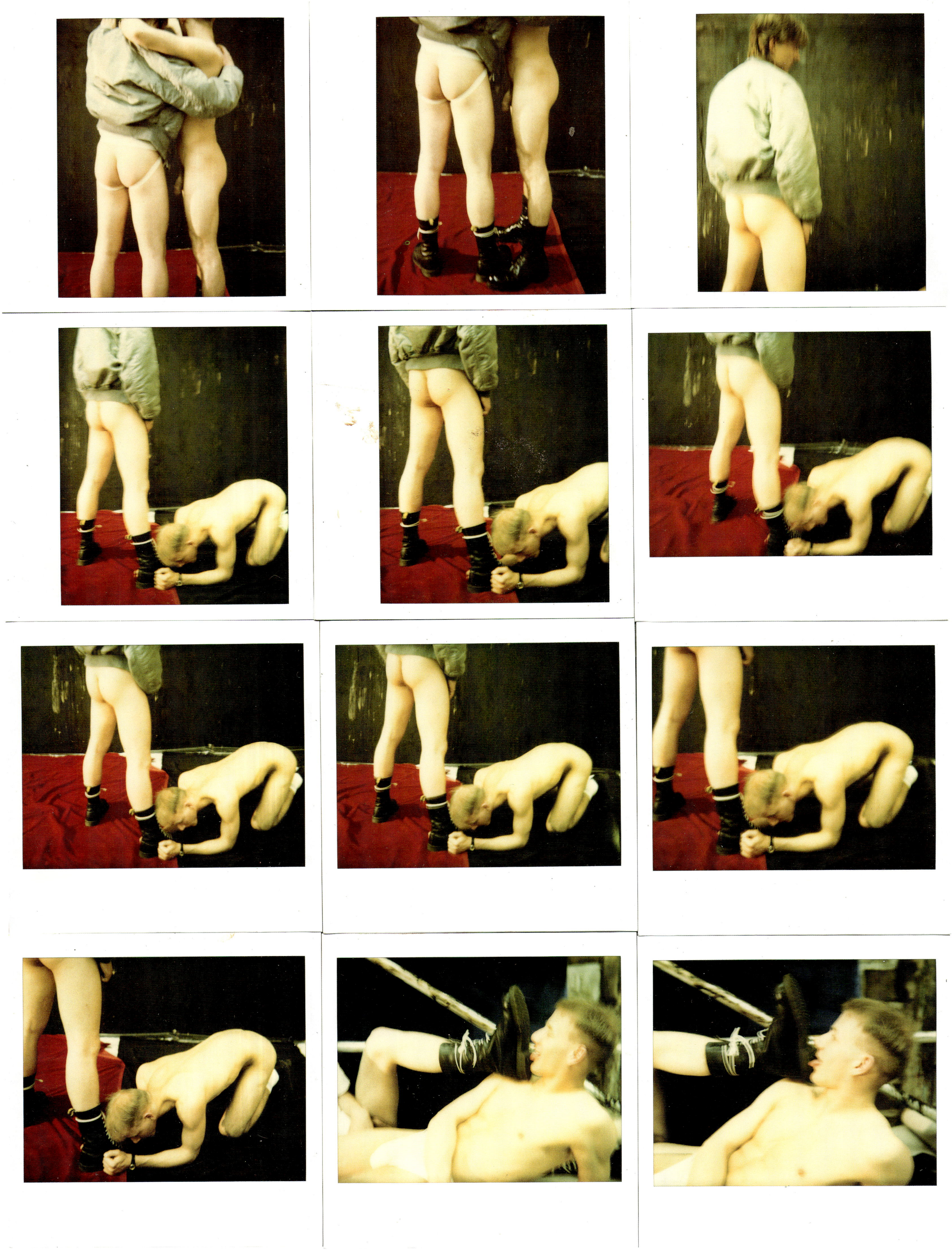

Stephan Boot Licking, Berlin, 1989

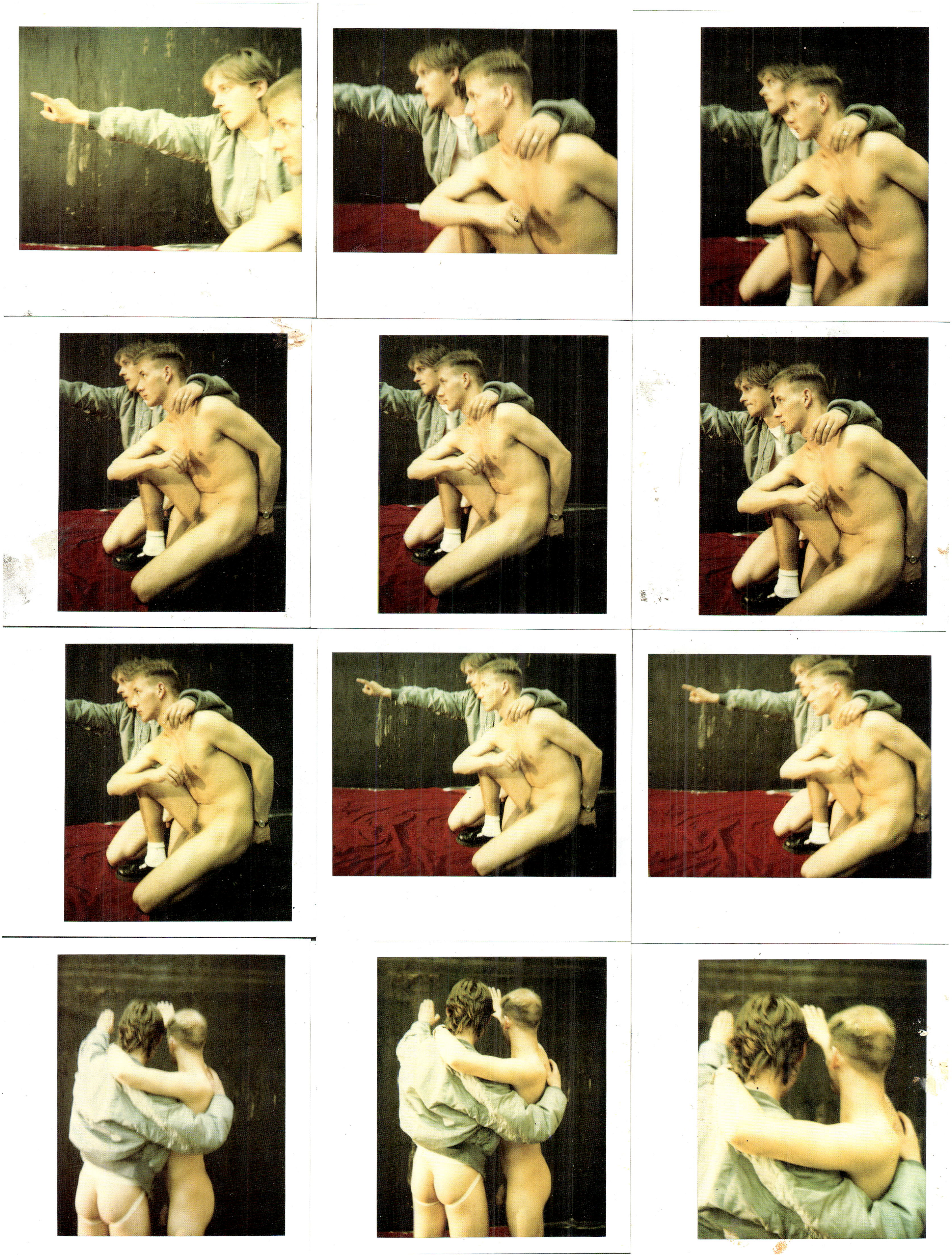

Stephan & Marek, Berlin, 1989

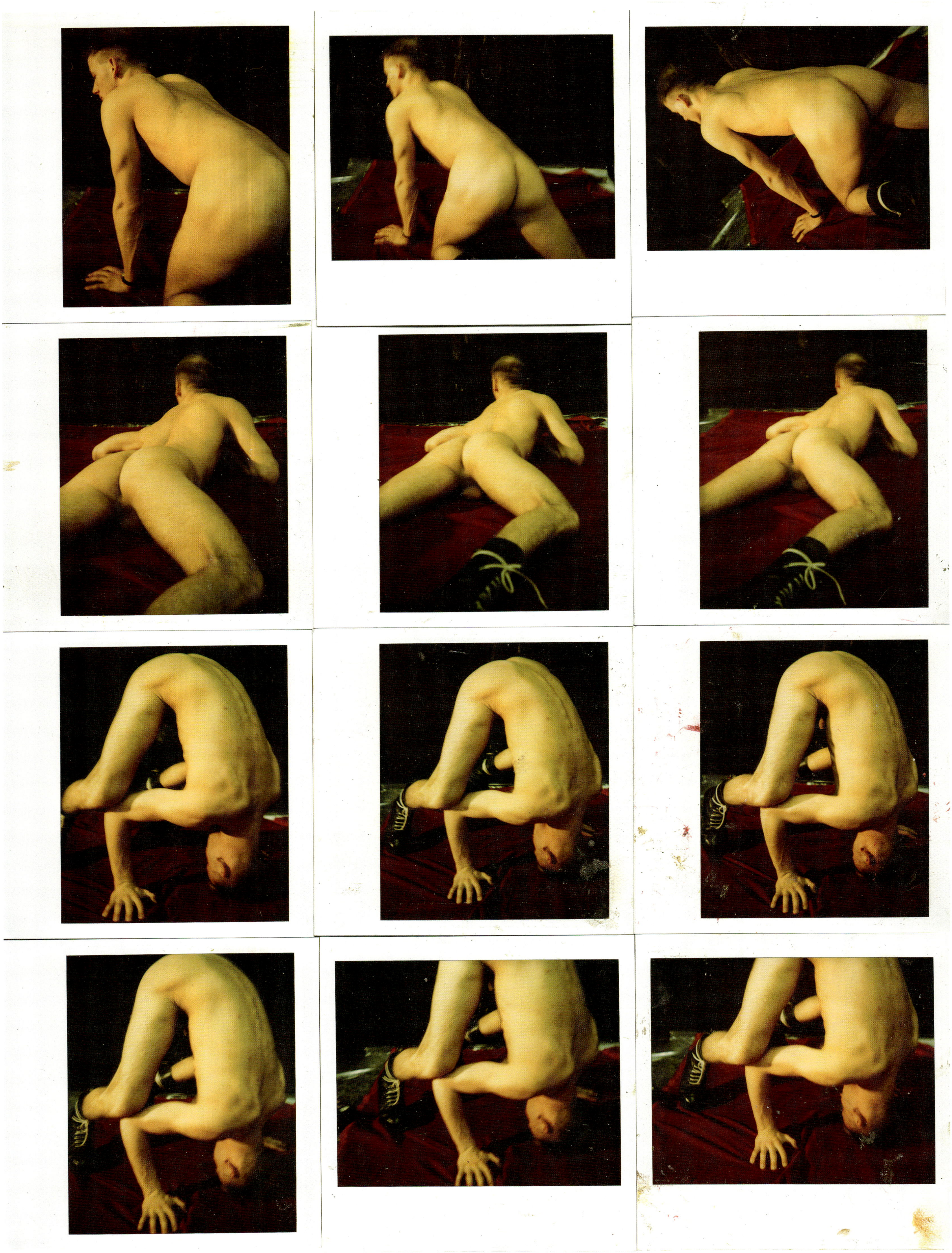

Stephan, Berlin, 1989

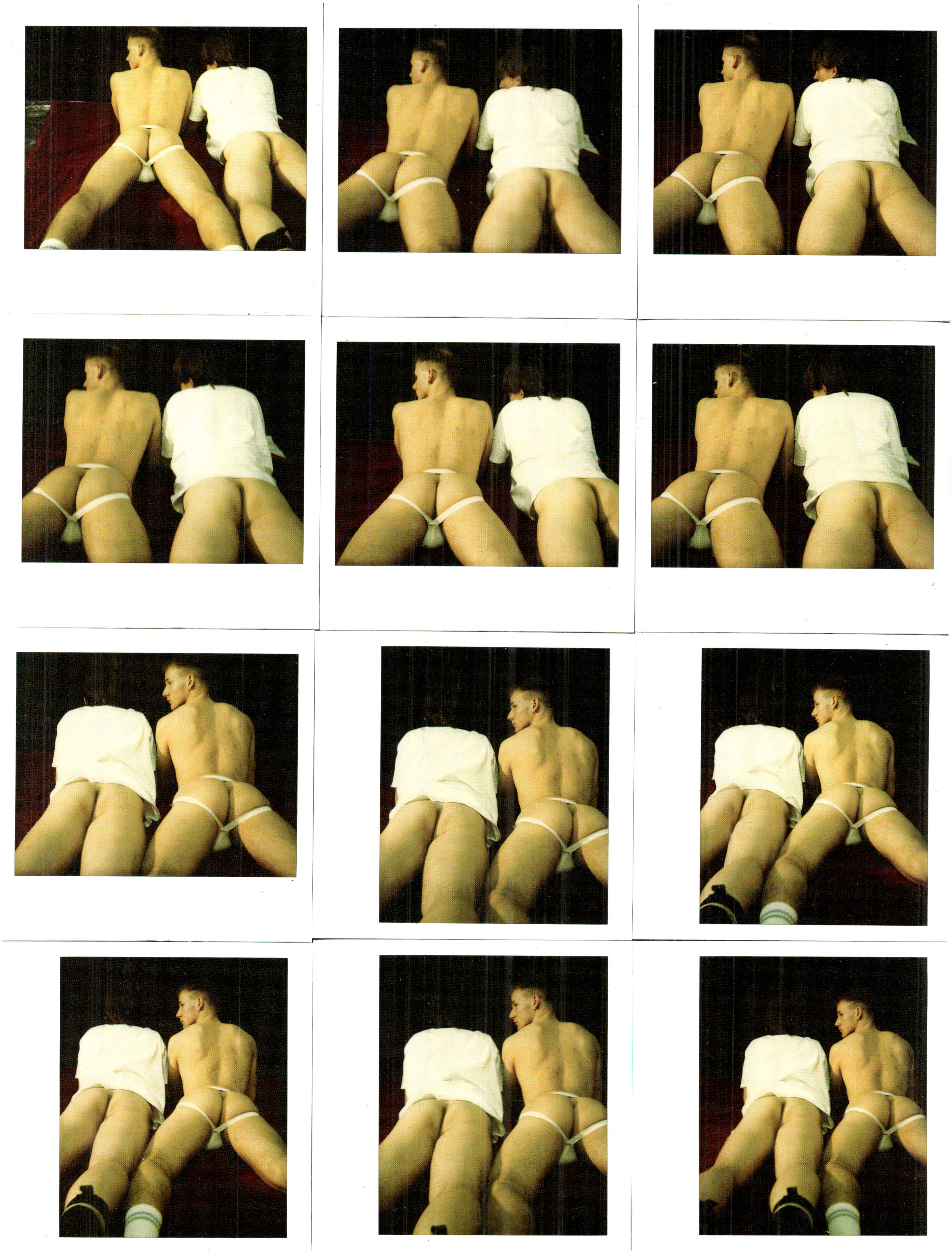

Stephan & Marek, Berlin, 1989

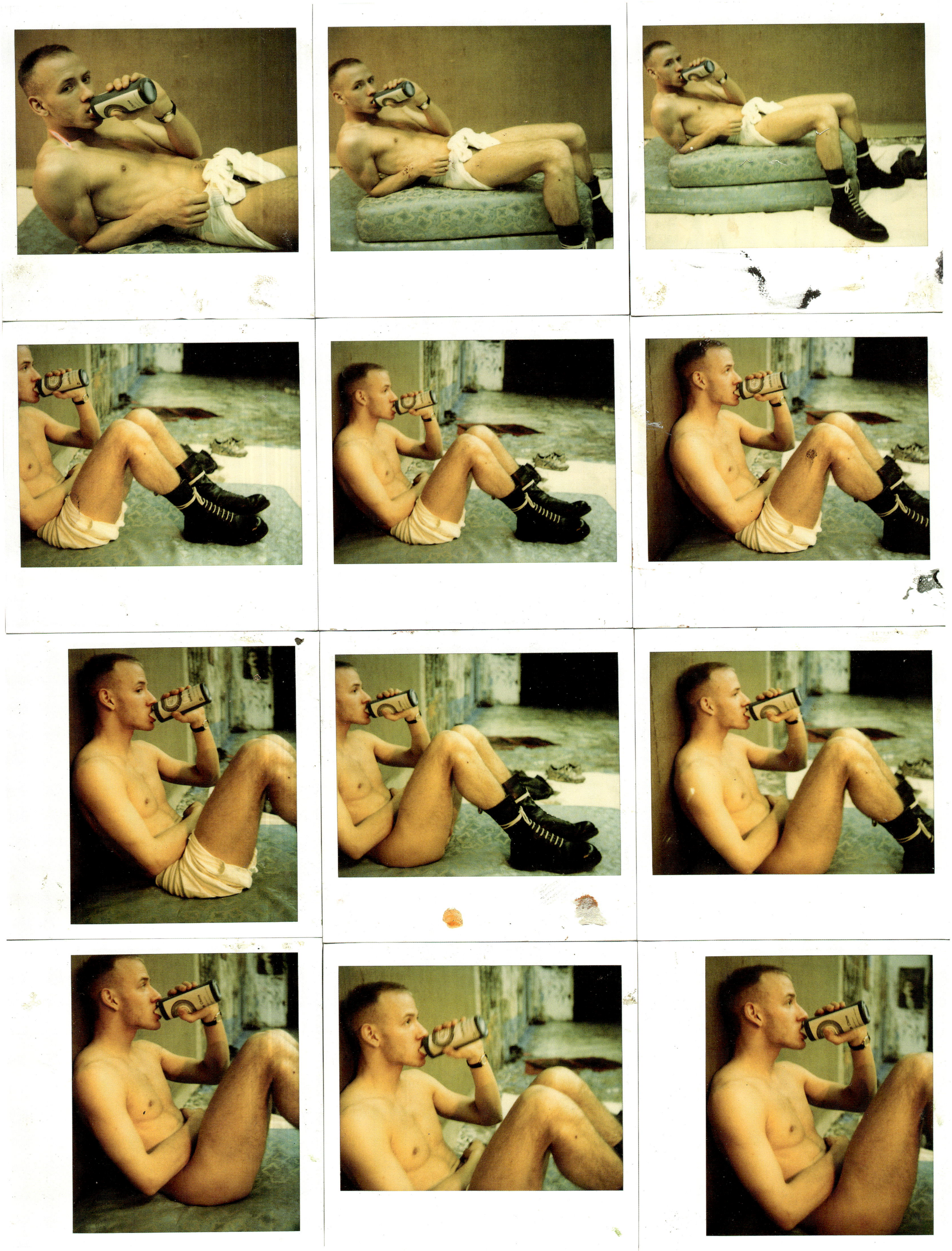

Stephan with Boots & Bottle, Berlin, 1989

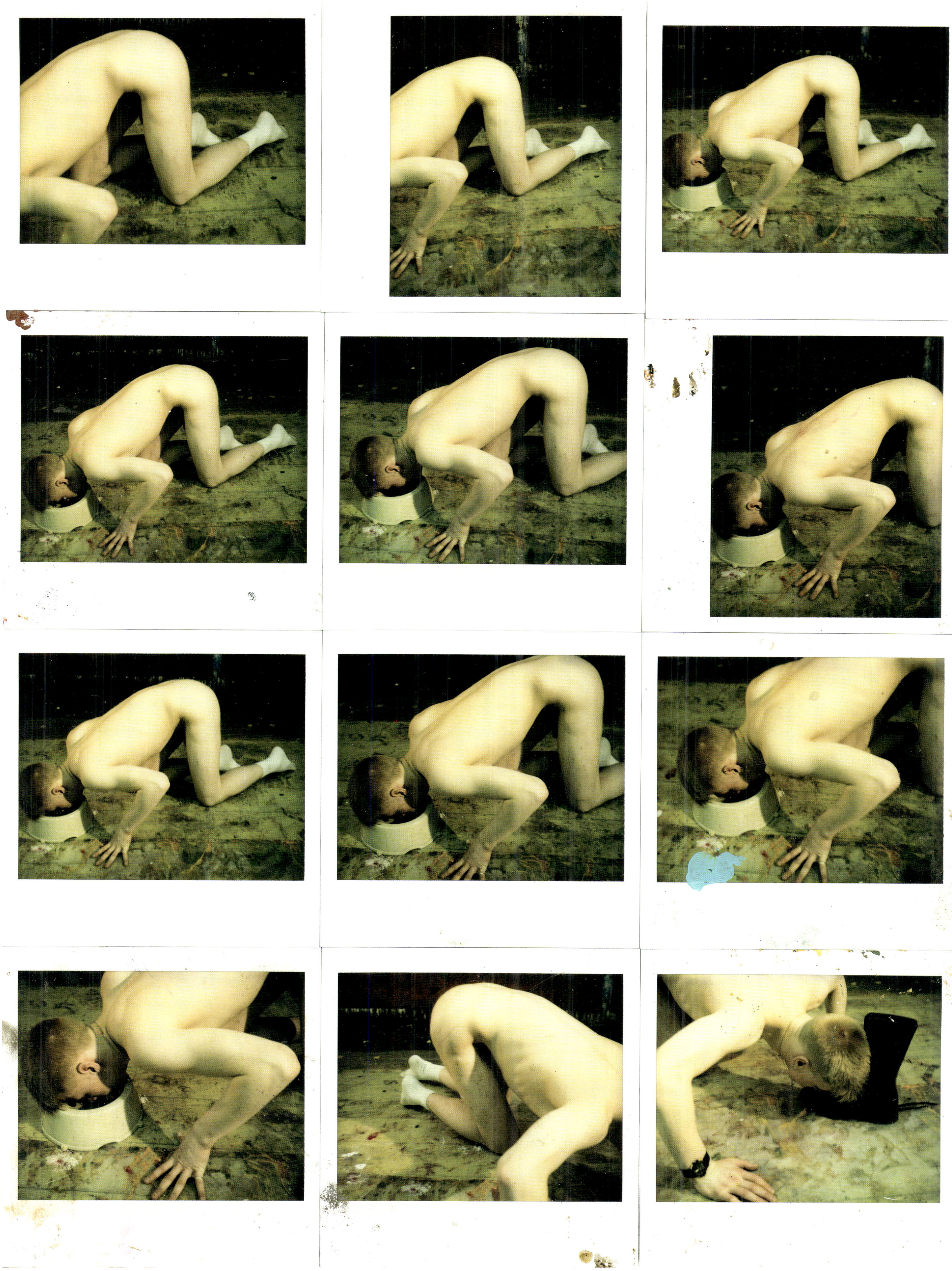

Zoo Boy, Berlin, 1989

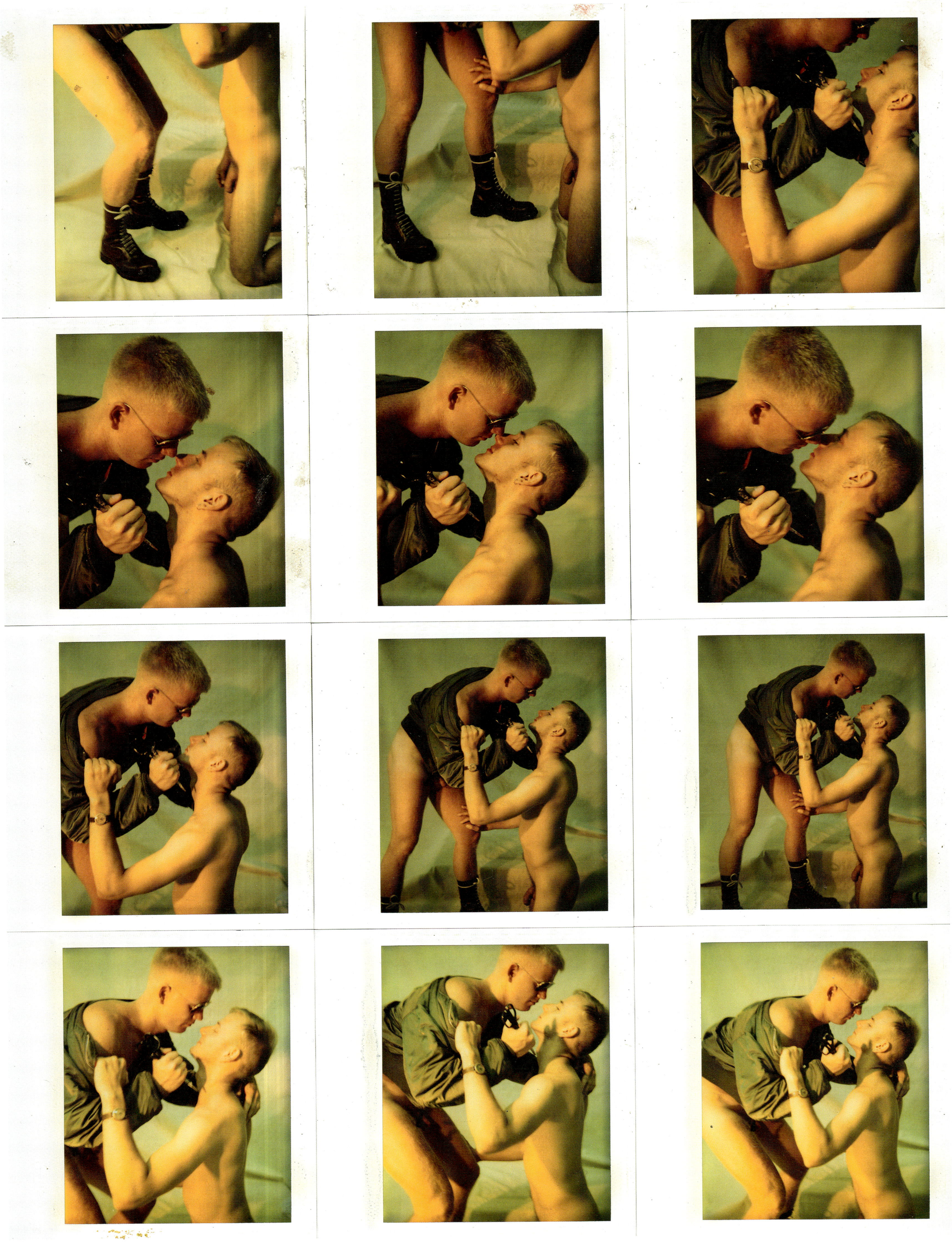

Stephan & Stefan, Berlin, 1990

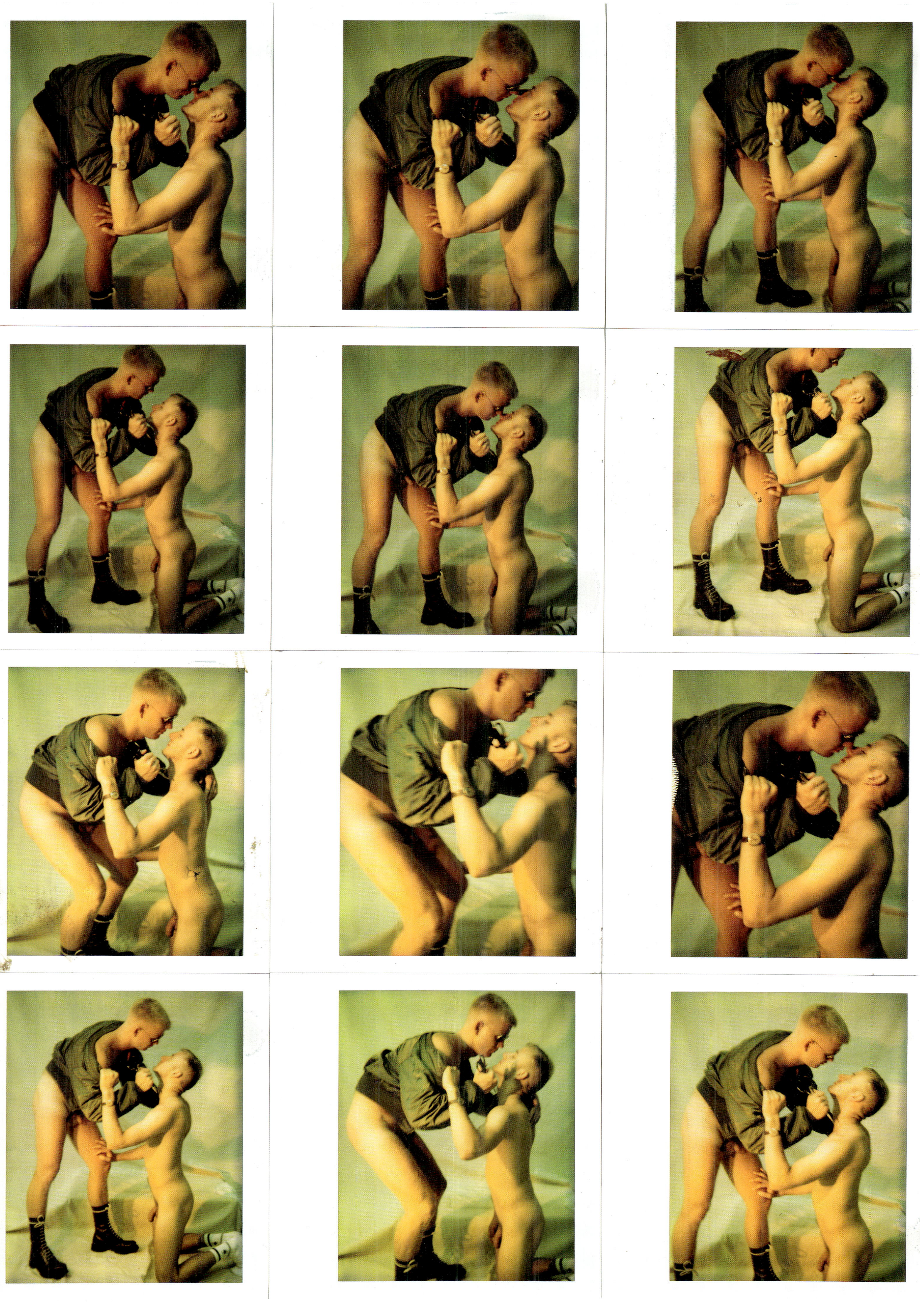

Stephan & Stefan, Berlin, 1990

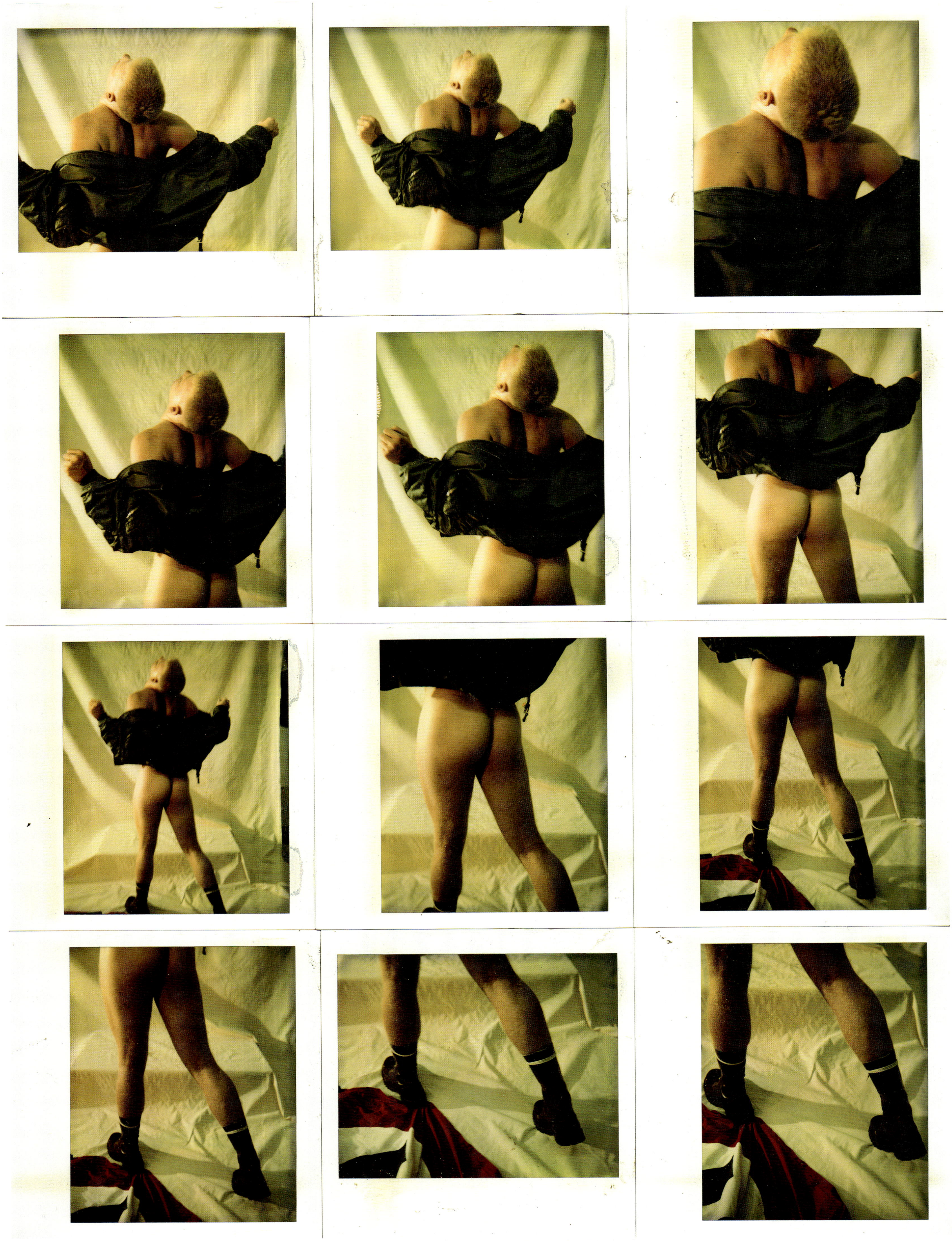

Stefan, study for *The Death of Orpheus*, Berlin, 1990

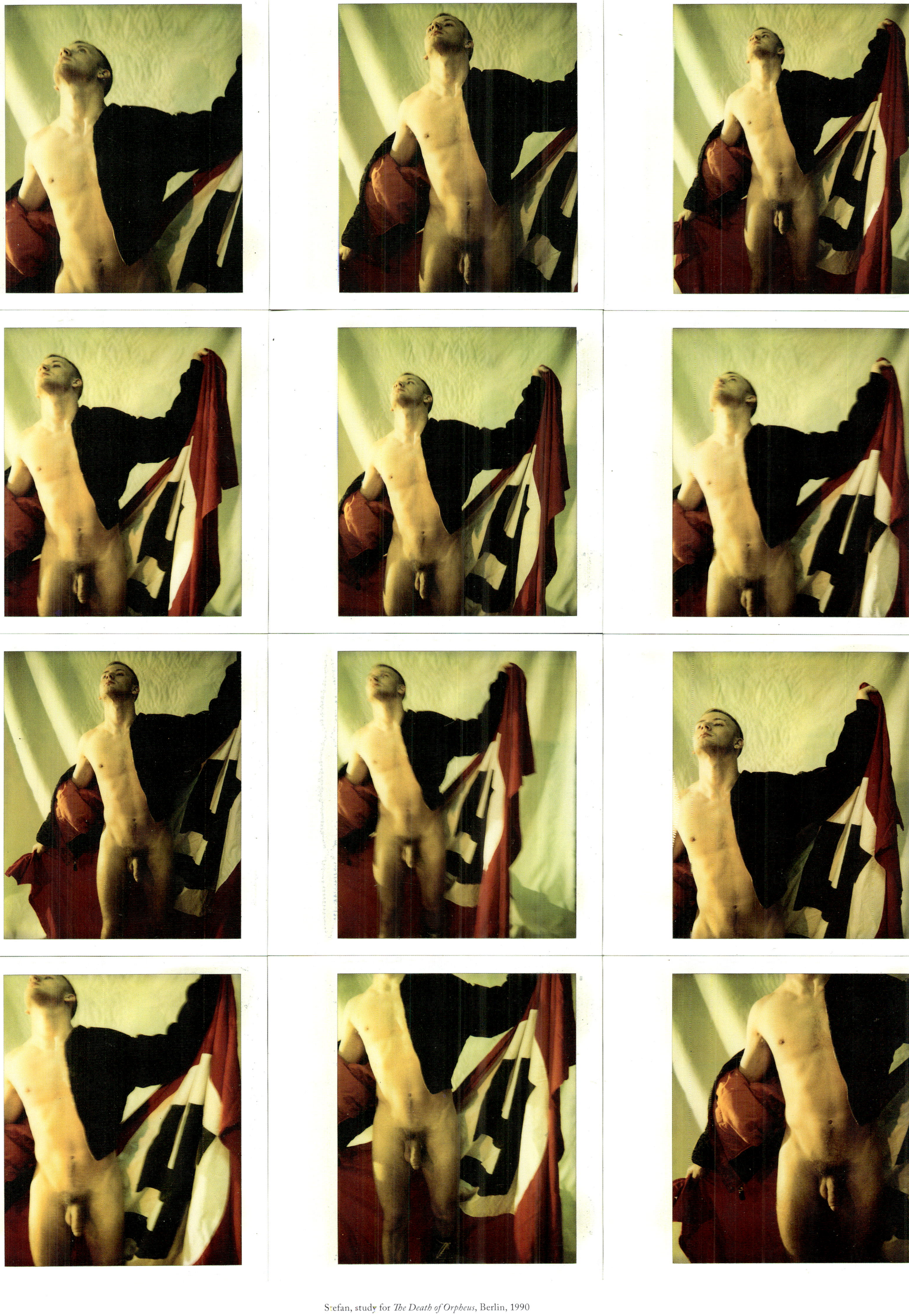

Stefan, study for *The Death of Orpheus*, Berlin, 1990

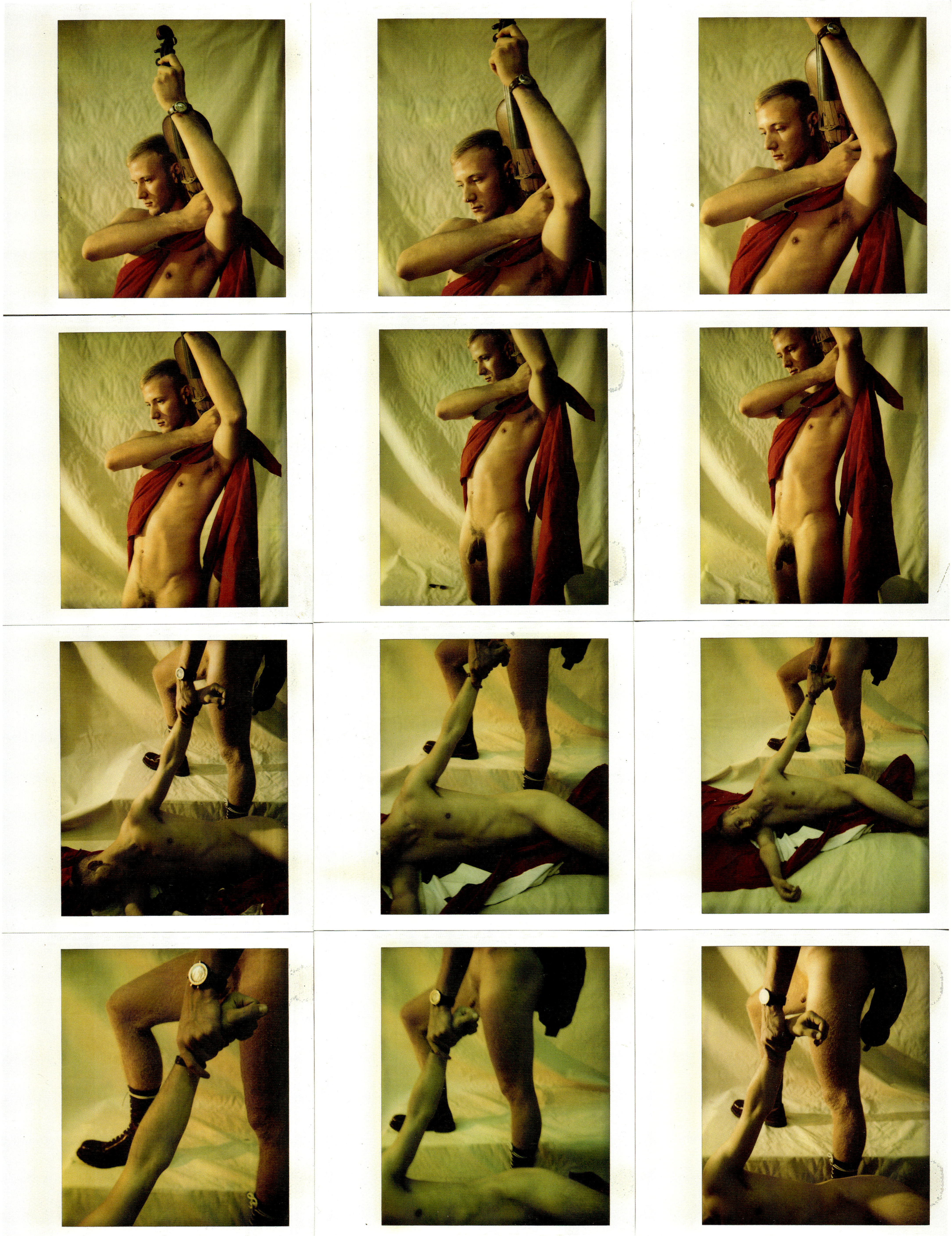

S & S, study for *The Death of Orpheus*, Berlin, 1990

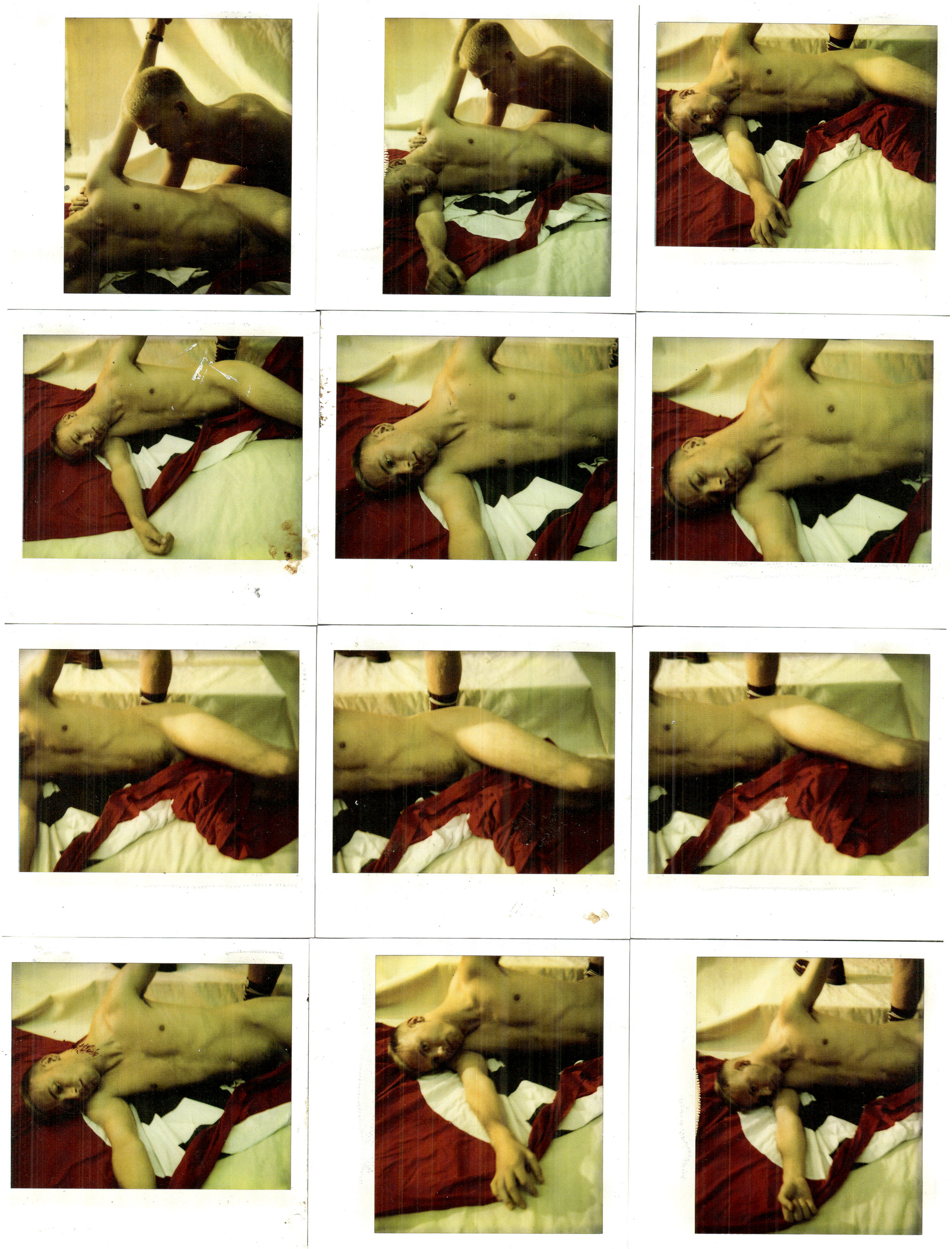

S & S, study for *The Death of Orpheus*, Berlin, 1990

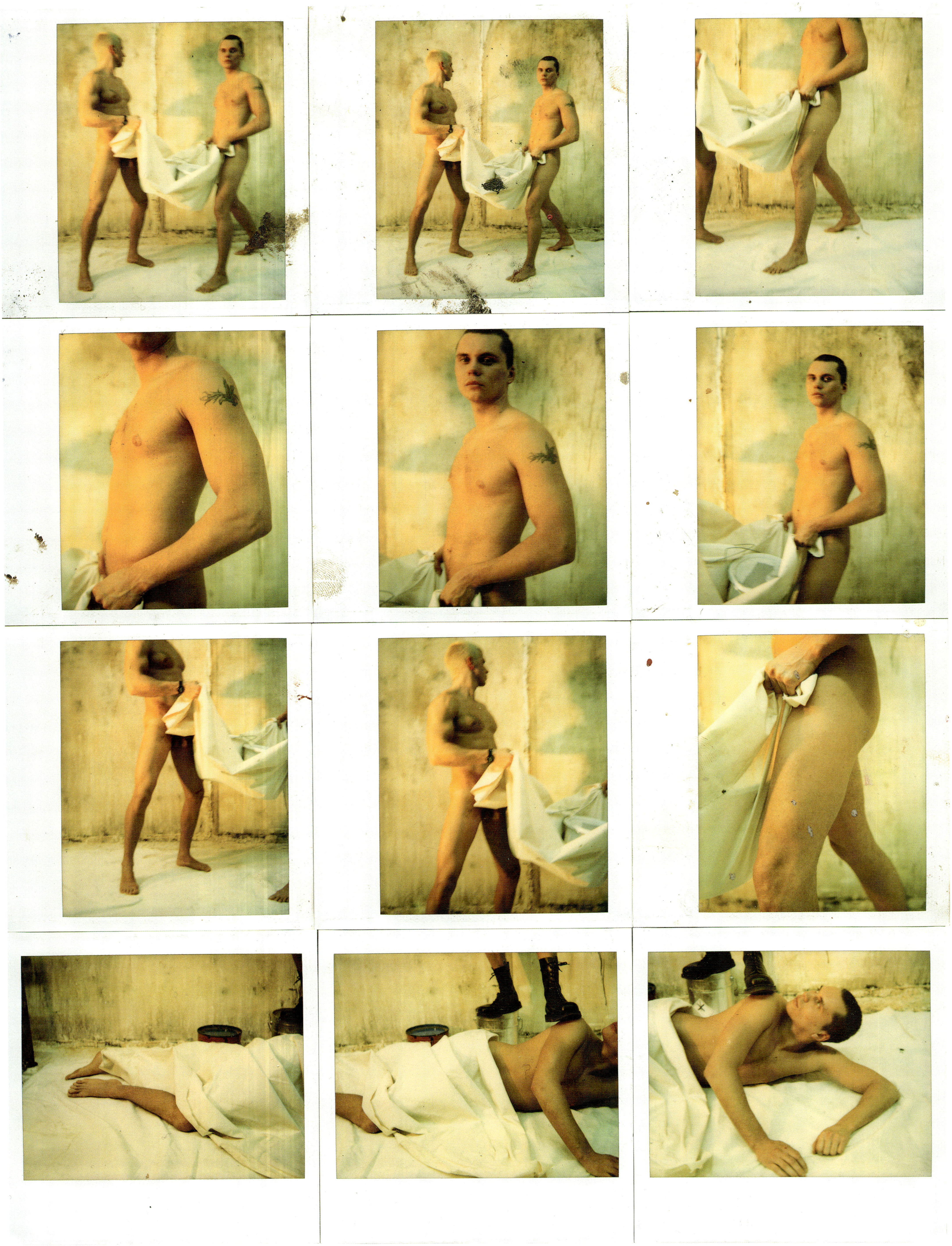

Alex & Ingo, Berlin, 1990

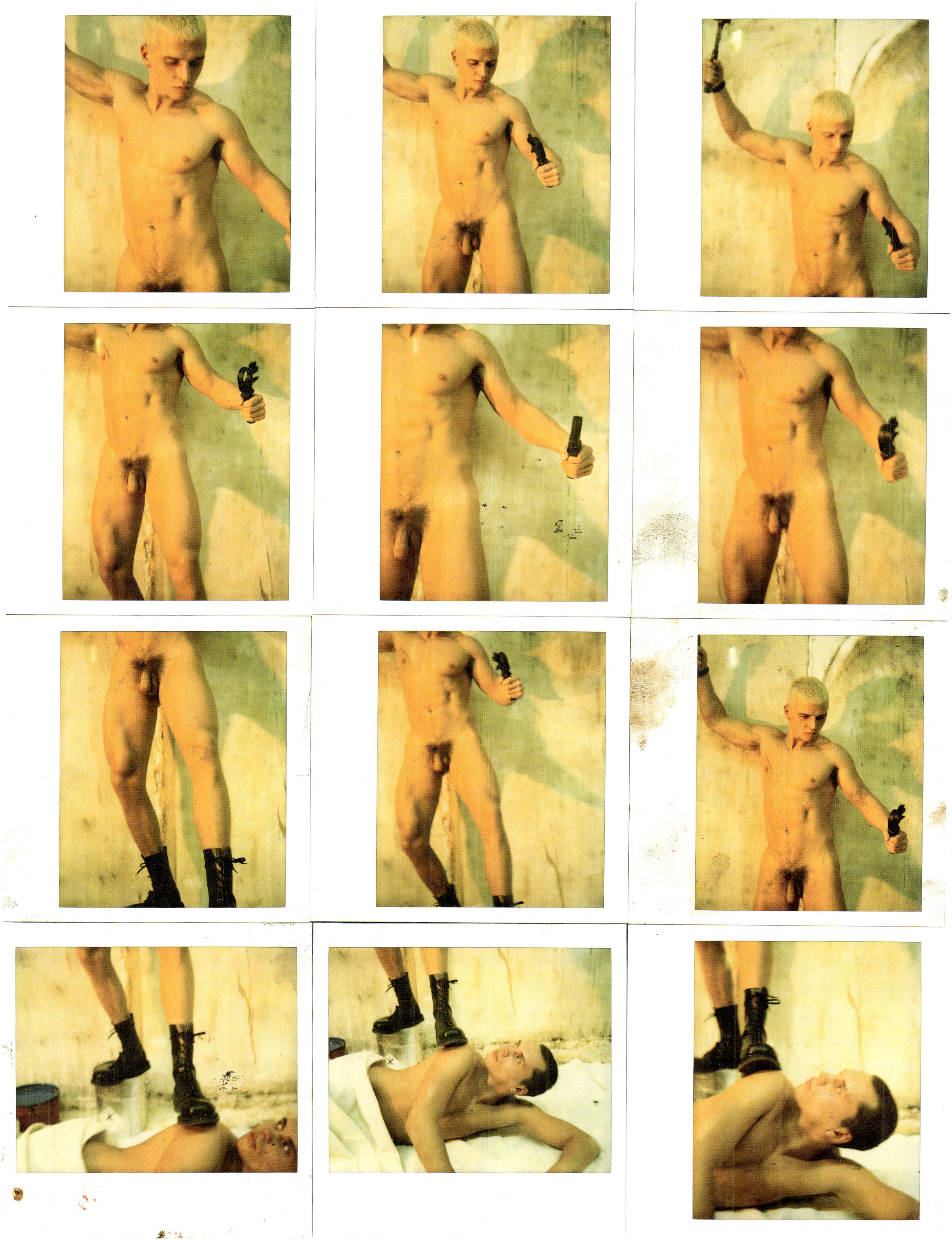

Alex as St Michael, Berlin, 1990

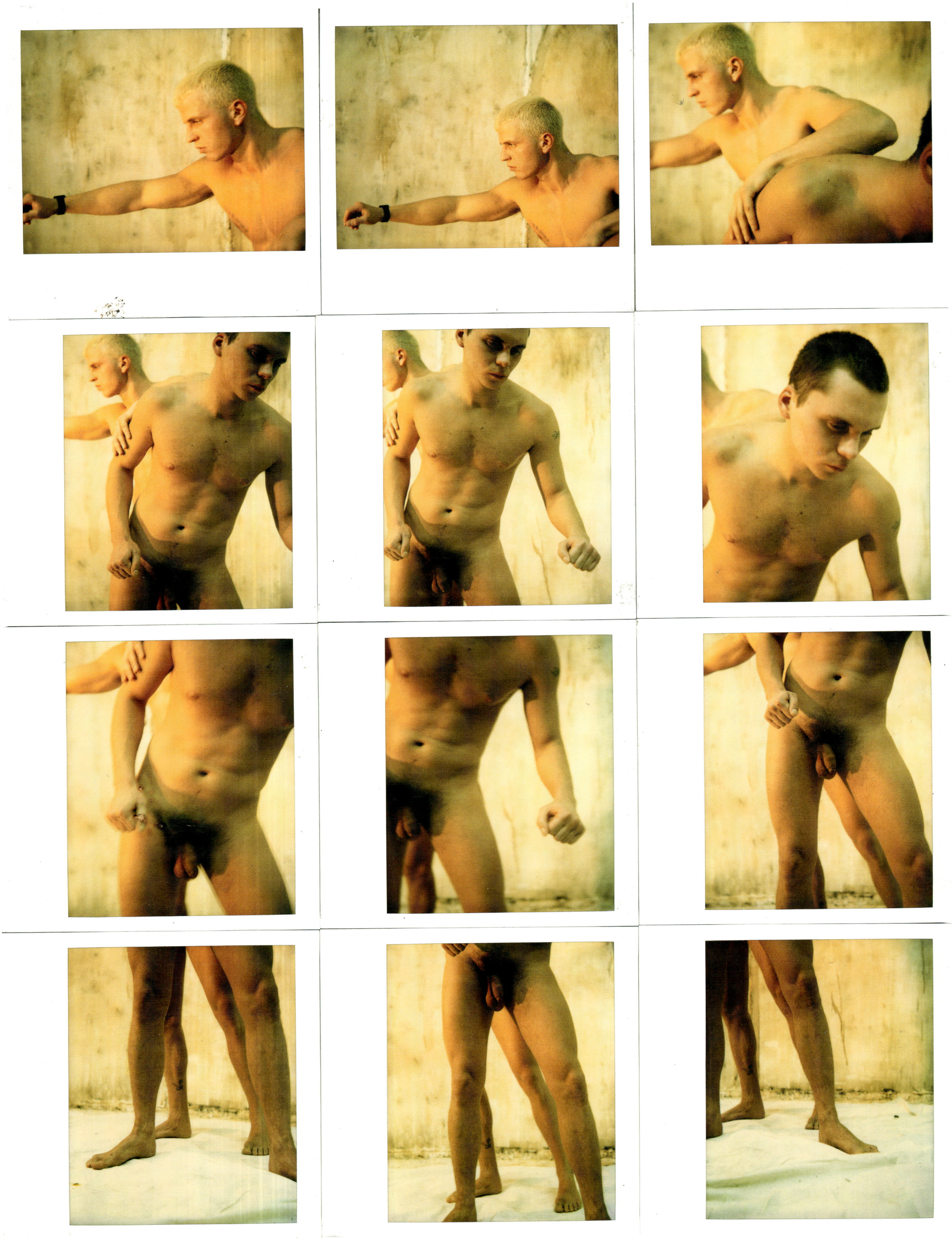

Alex & Ingo, Berlin, 1990

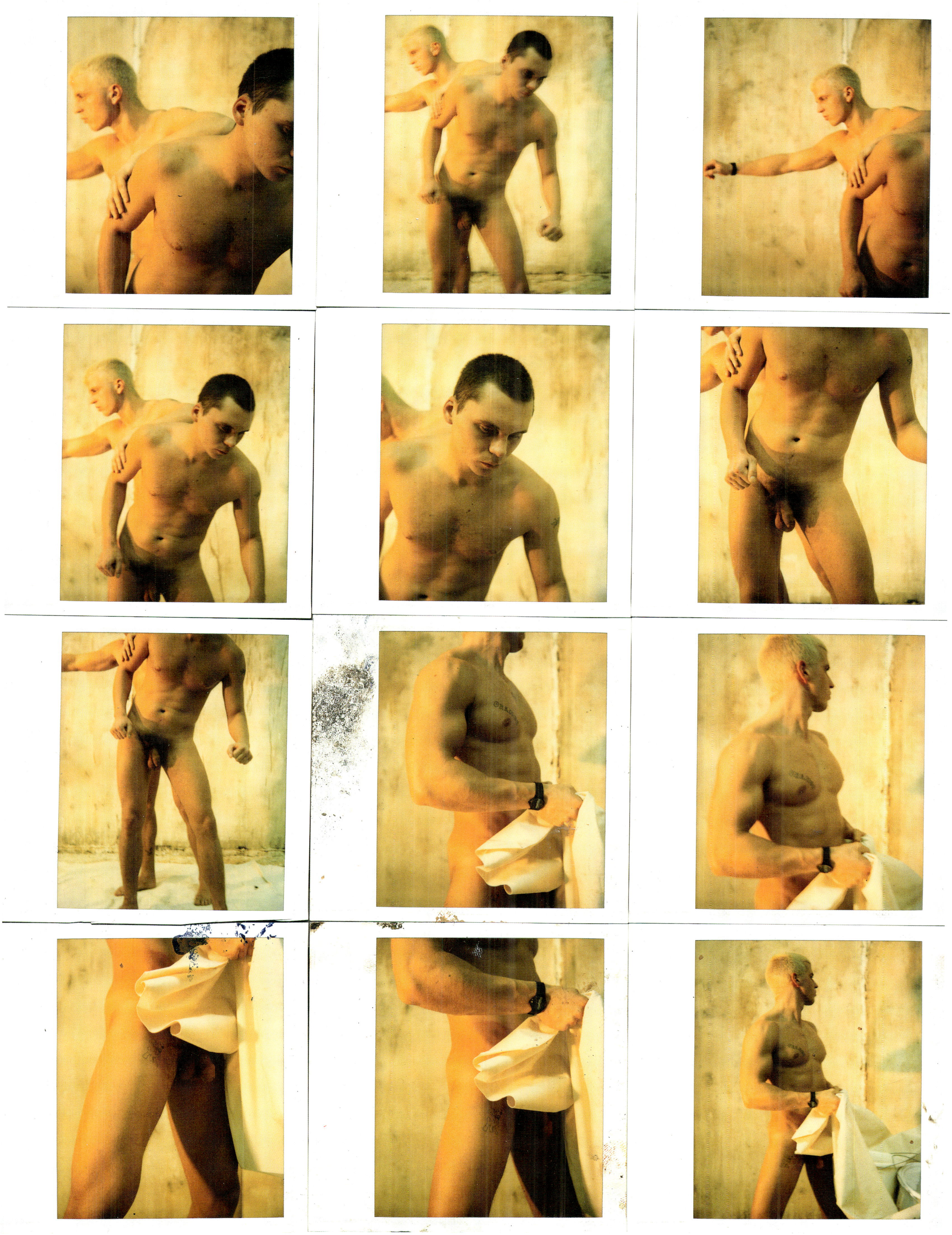

Alex & Ingo, Berlin, 1990

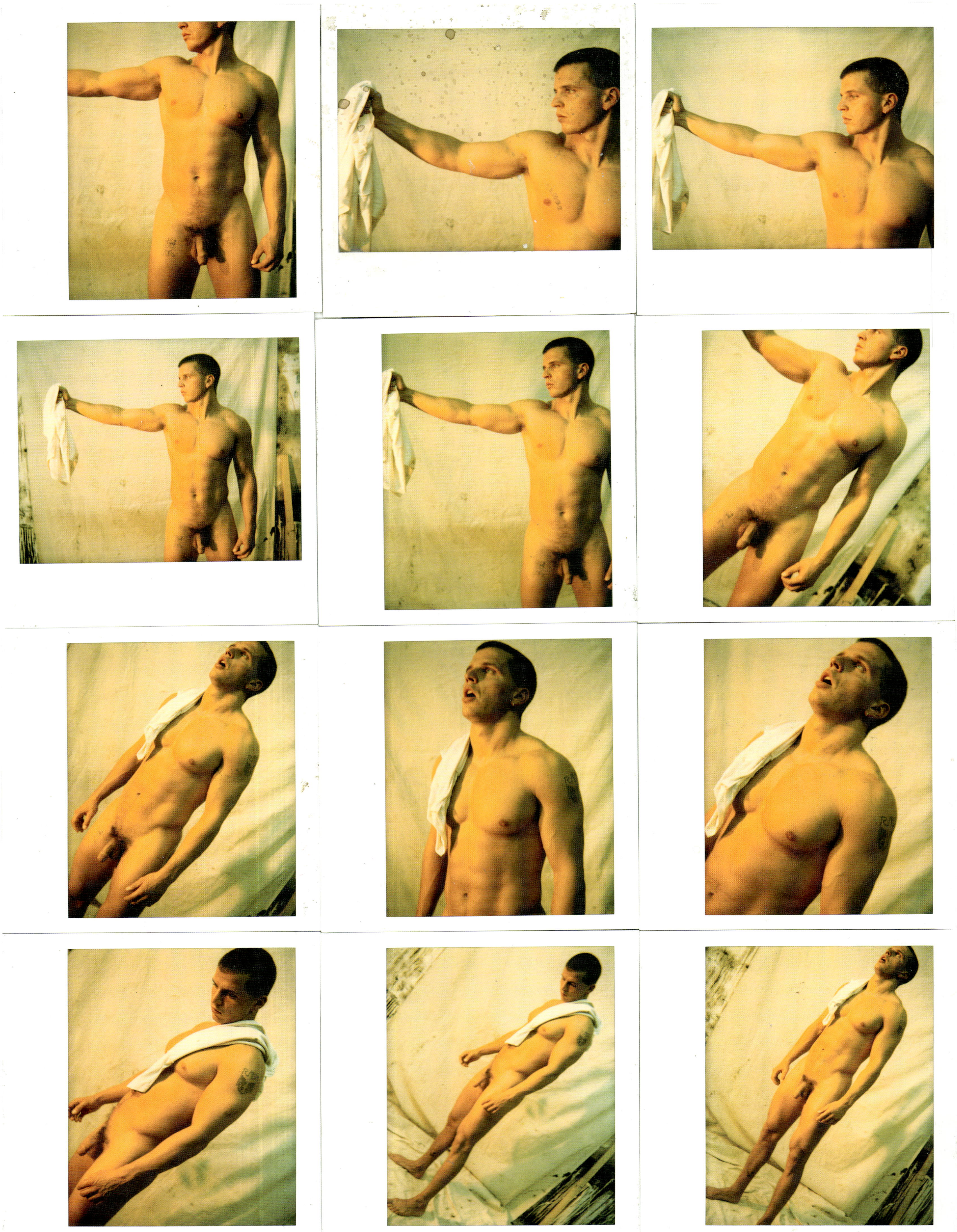

Alex, Berlin, 1990

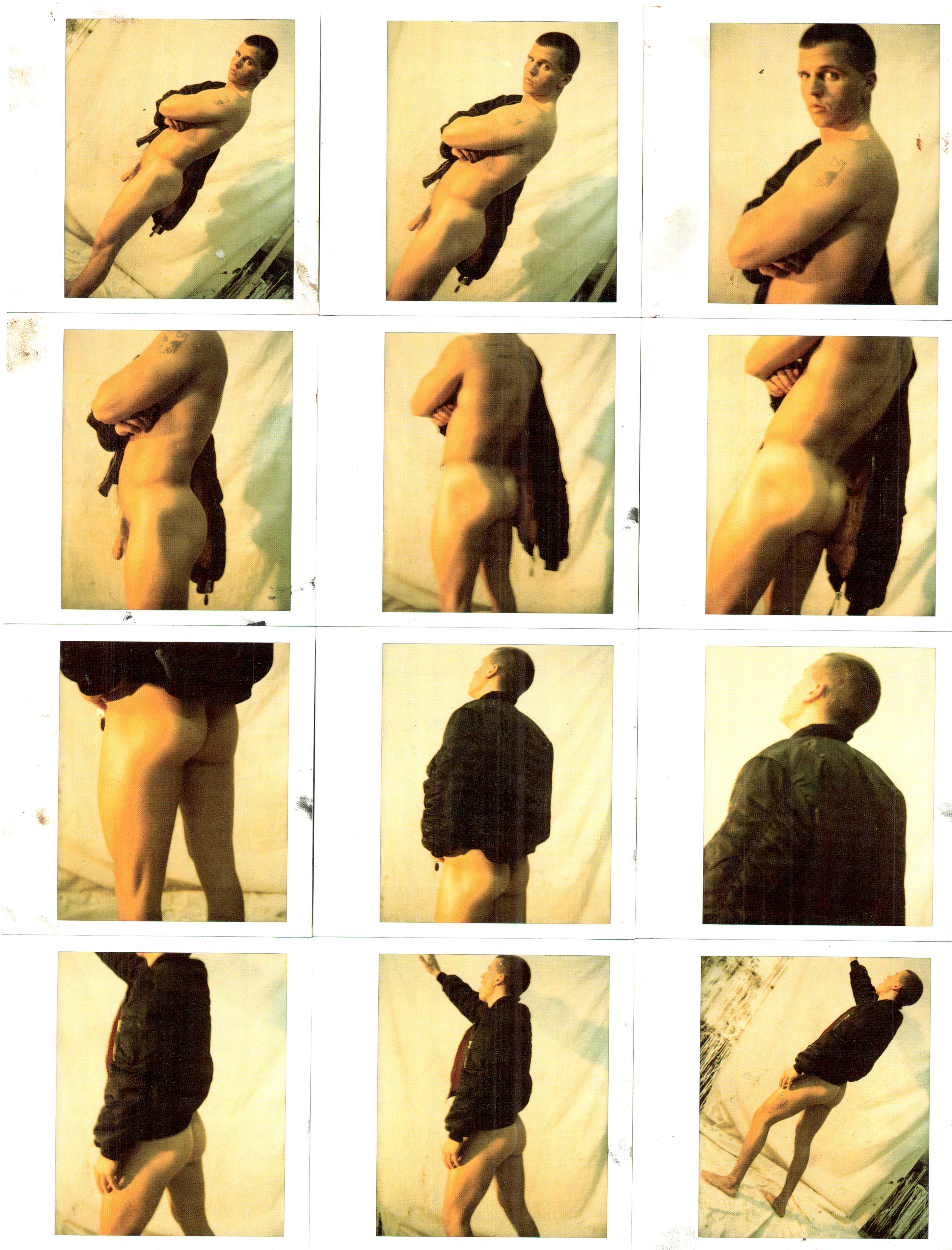

Alex, Berlin, 1990

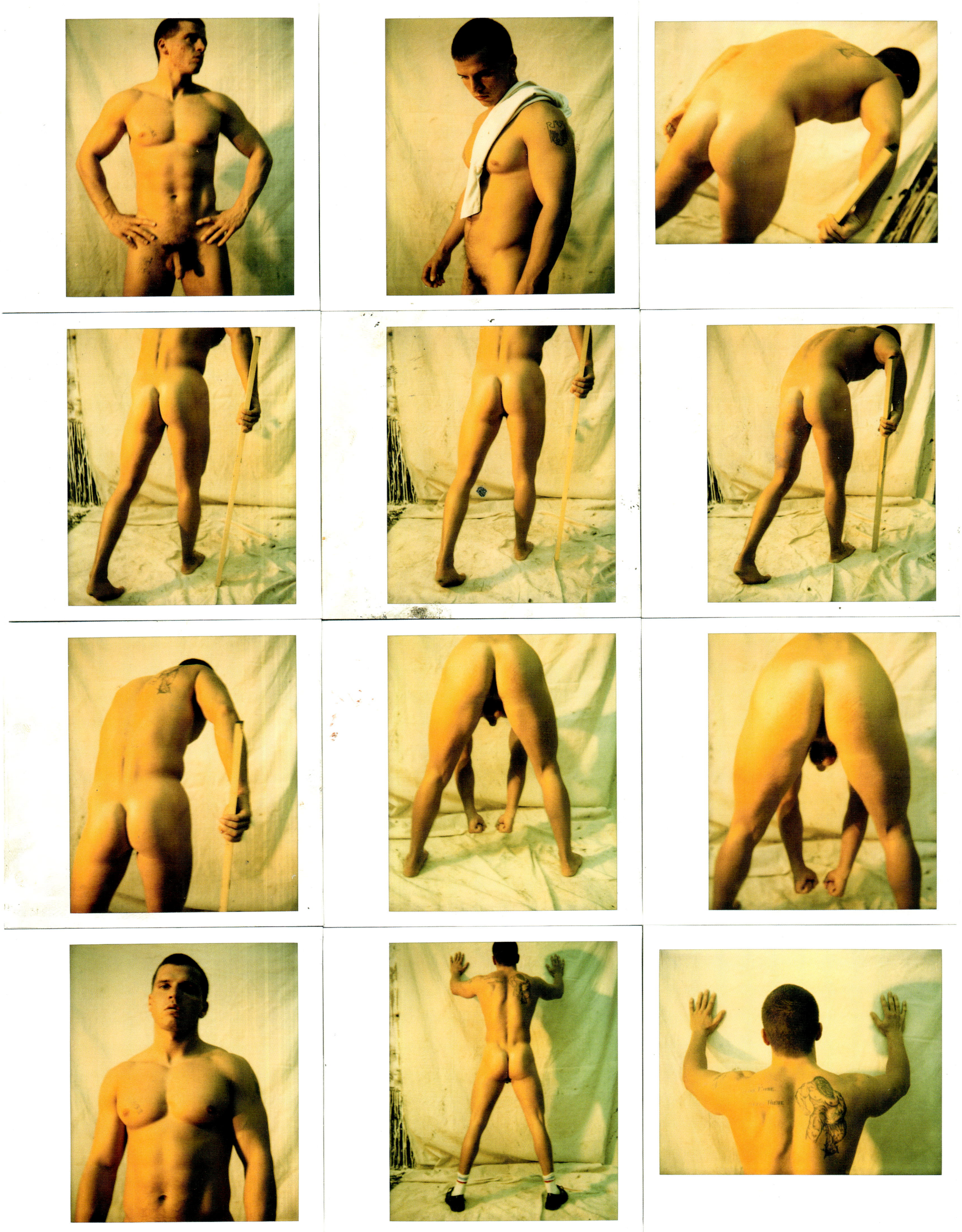

Alex, Berlin, 1990

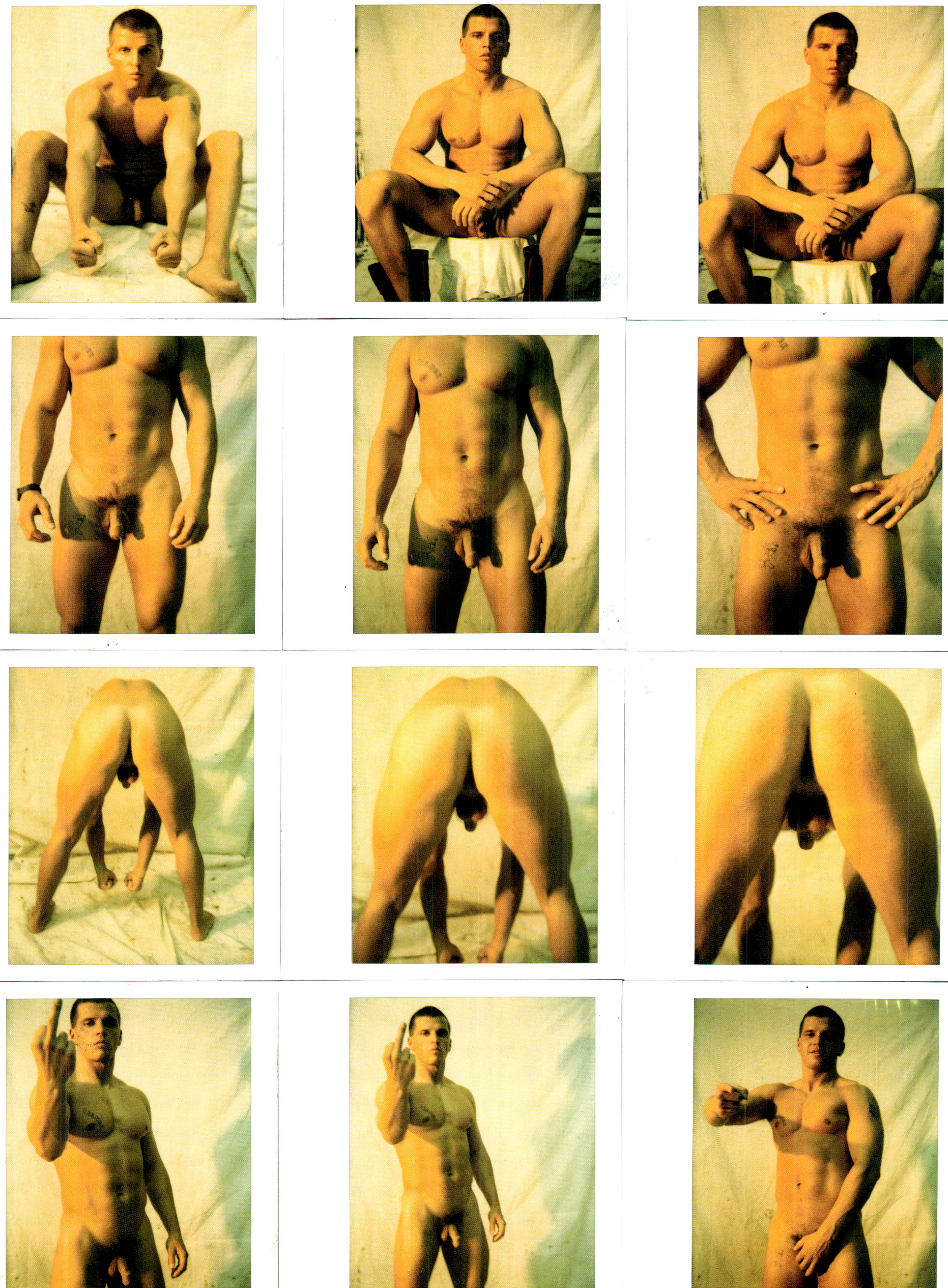

Alex, Berlin, 1990

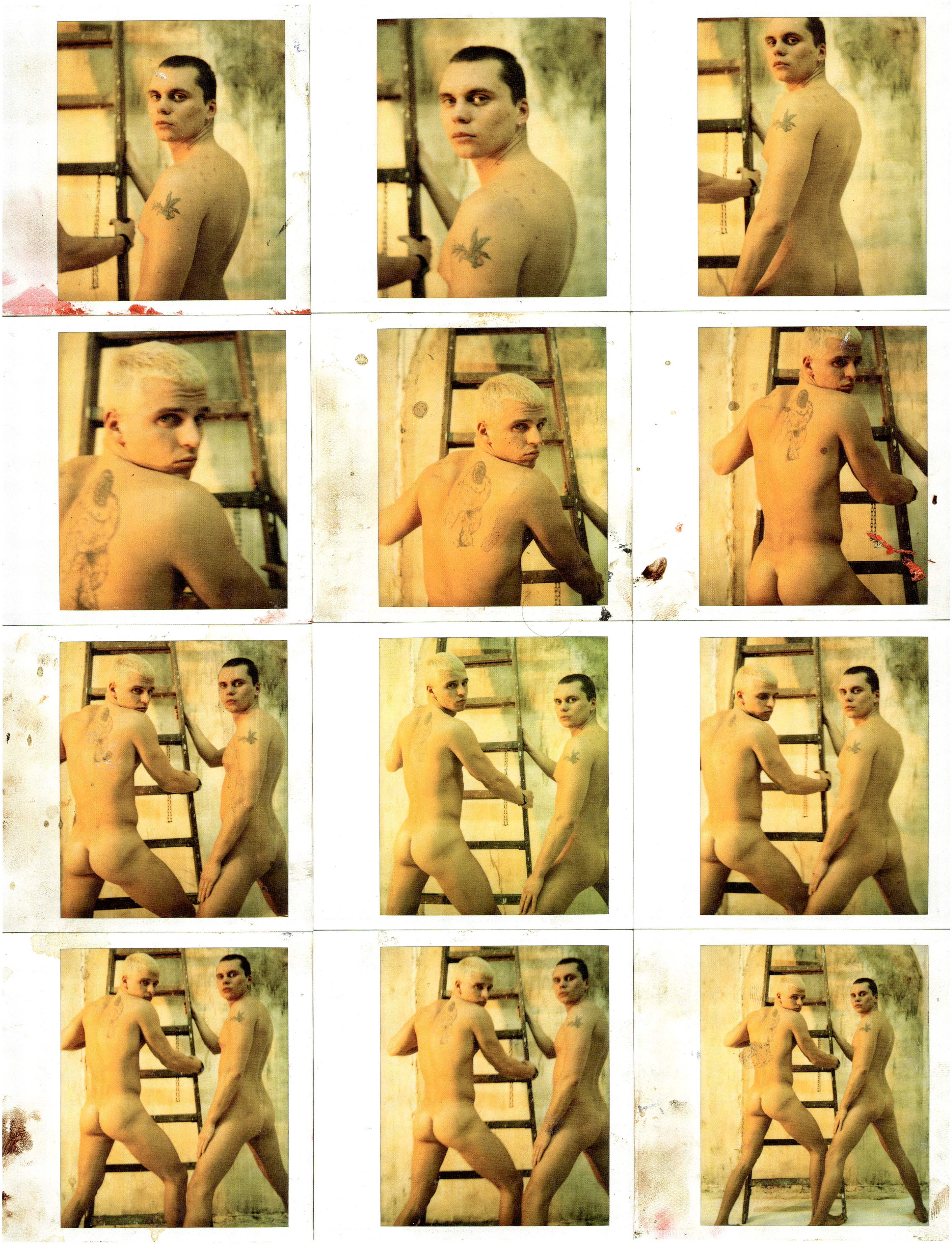

Alex & Ingo, Berlin, 1990

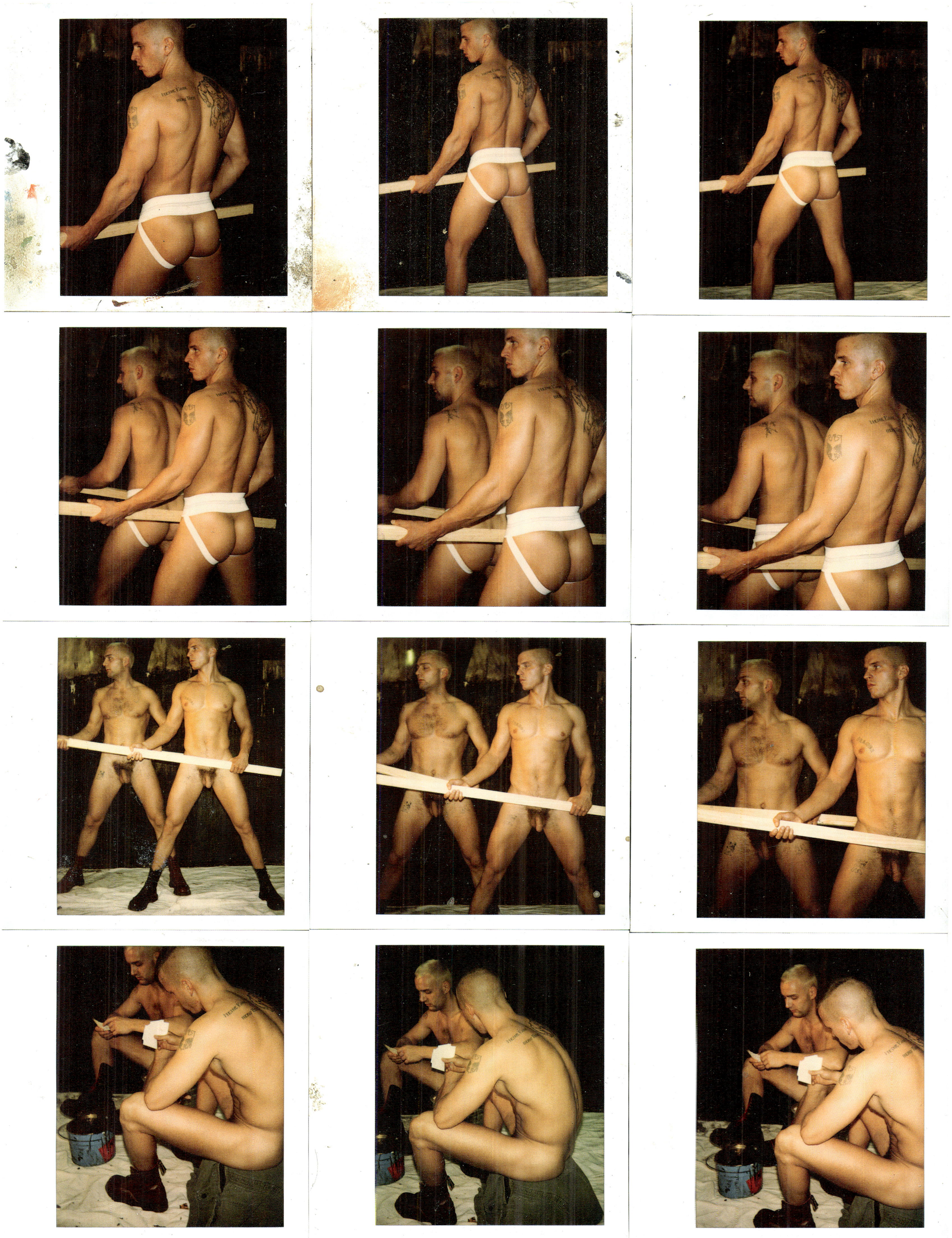

Alex & Friend, Berlin, 1990

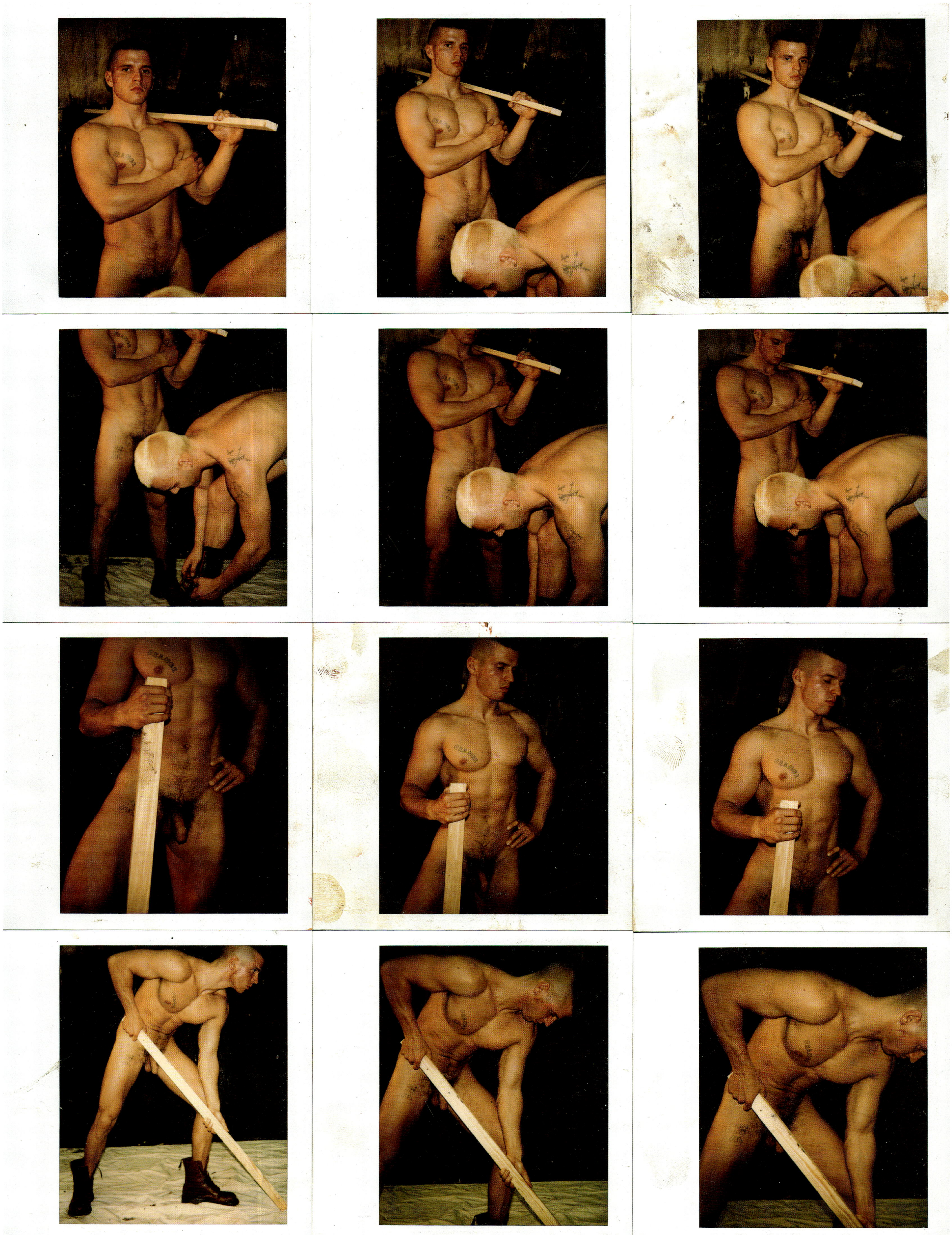

Alex & Friend, Berlin, 1990

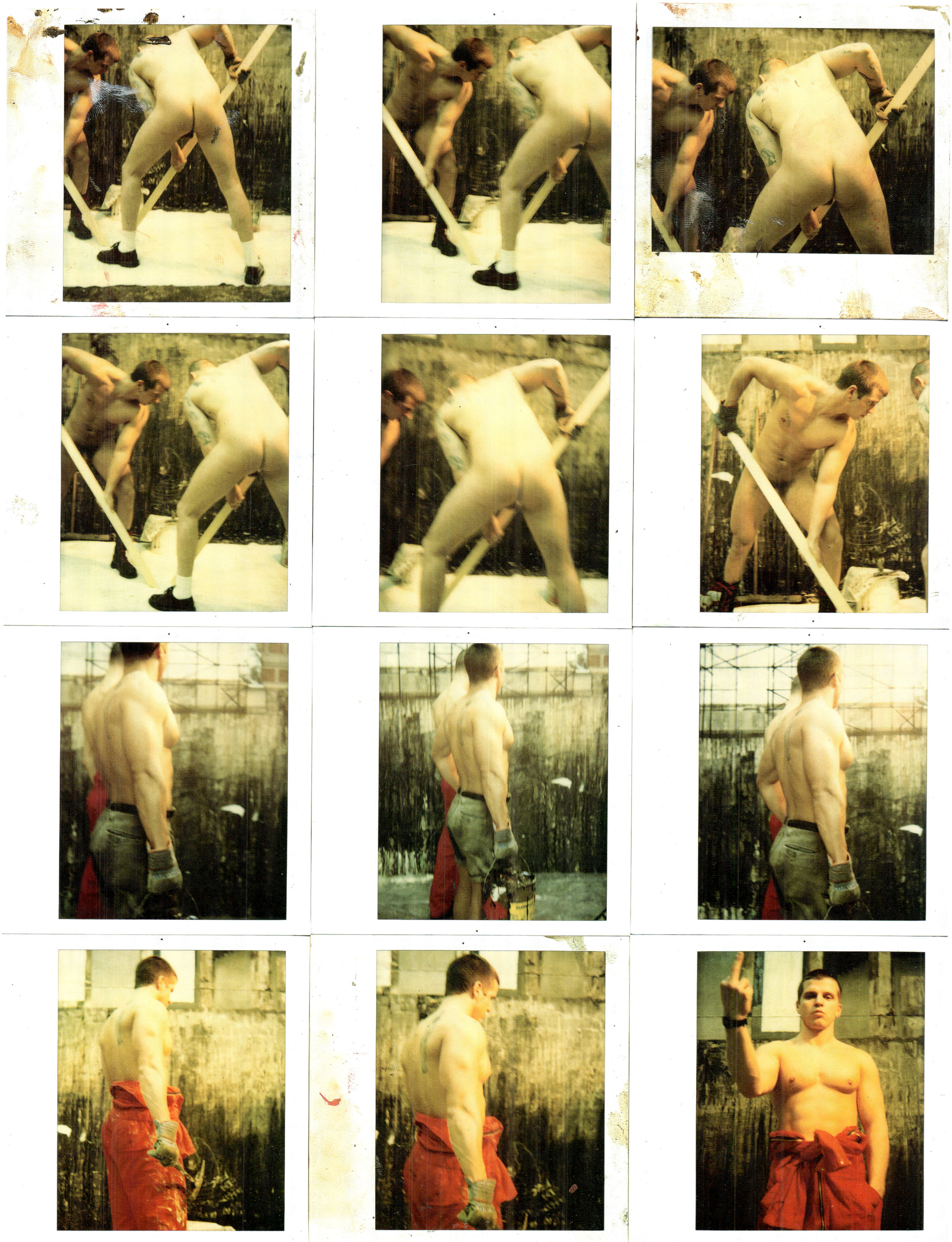

Alex with Tattooed Skin, Berlin, 1990

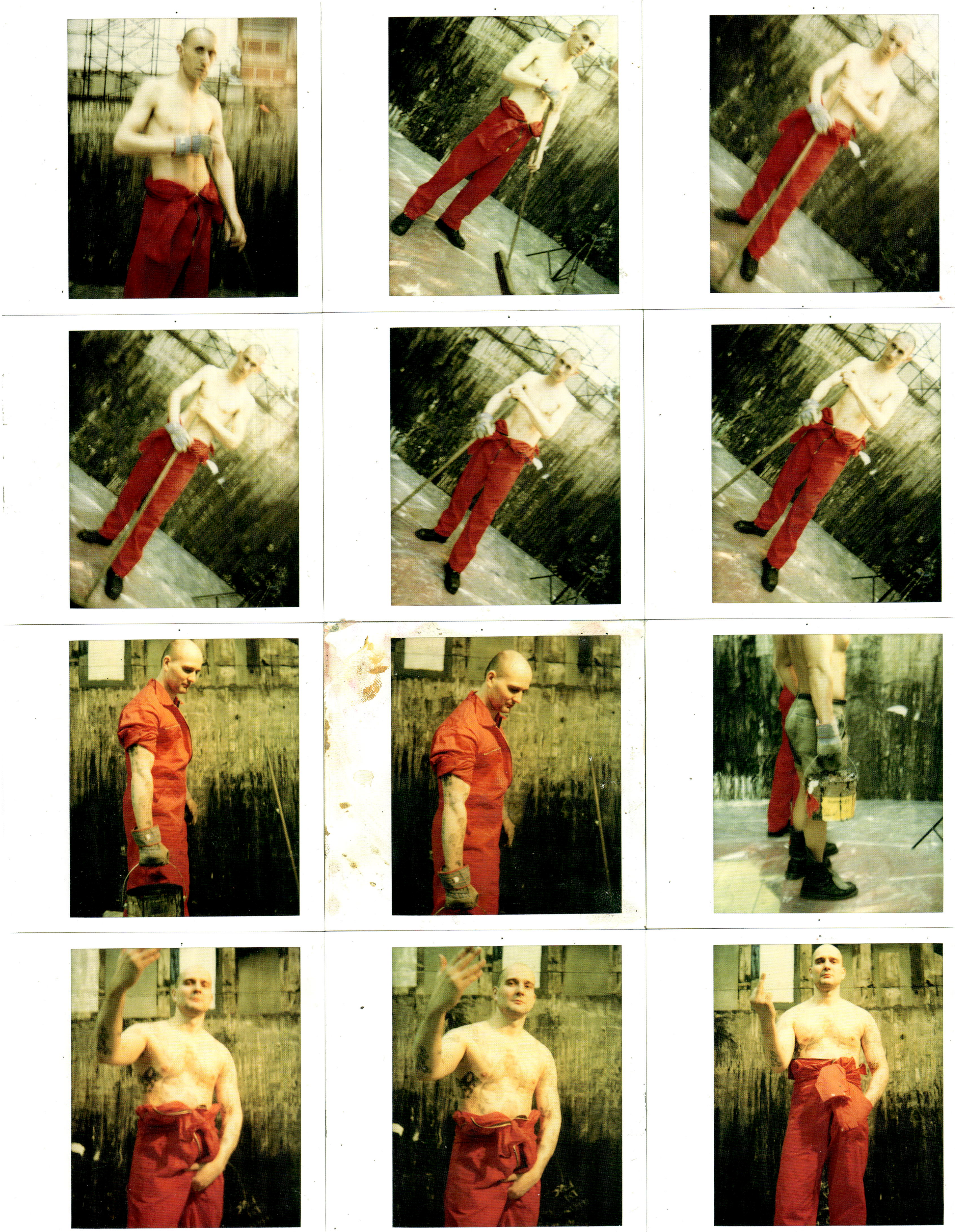

Study for *der Lustgarten* painting, Berlin, 1990

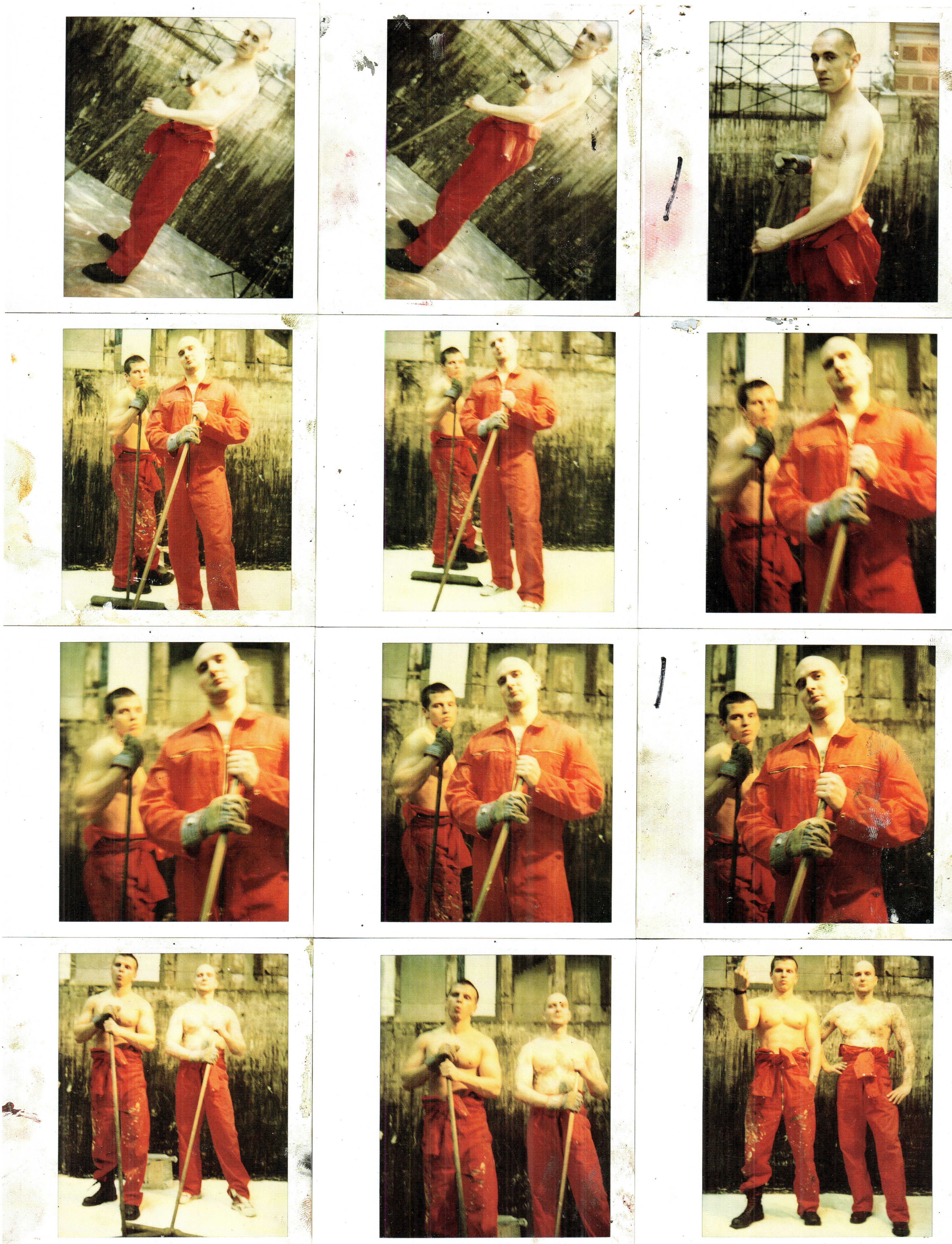

Study for *der Lustgarten* painting, Berlin, 1990

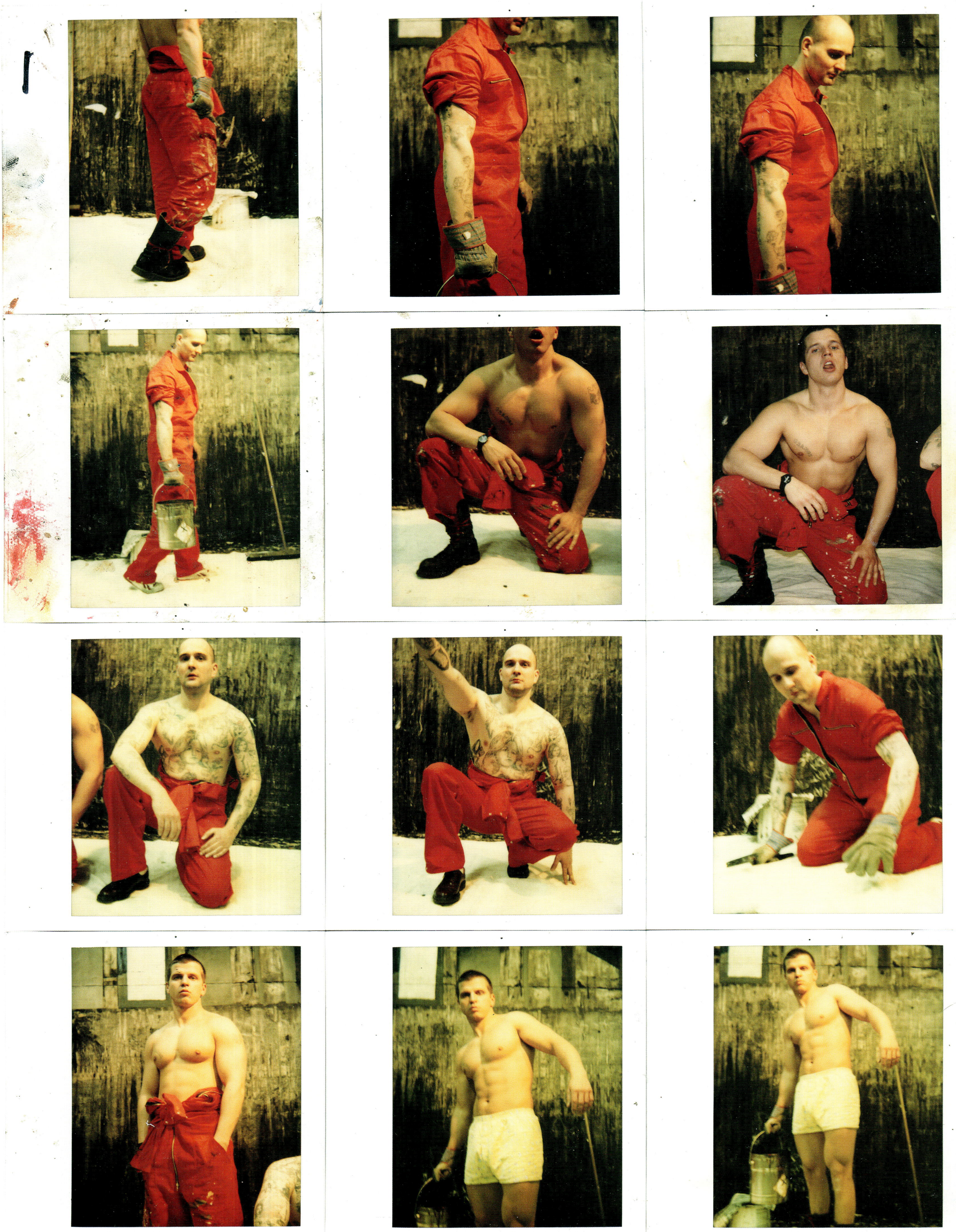

Study for *der Lustgarten* painting, Berlin, 1990

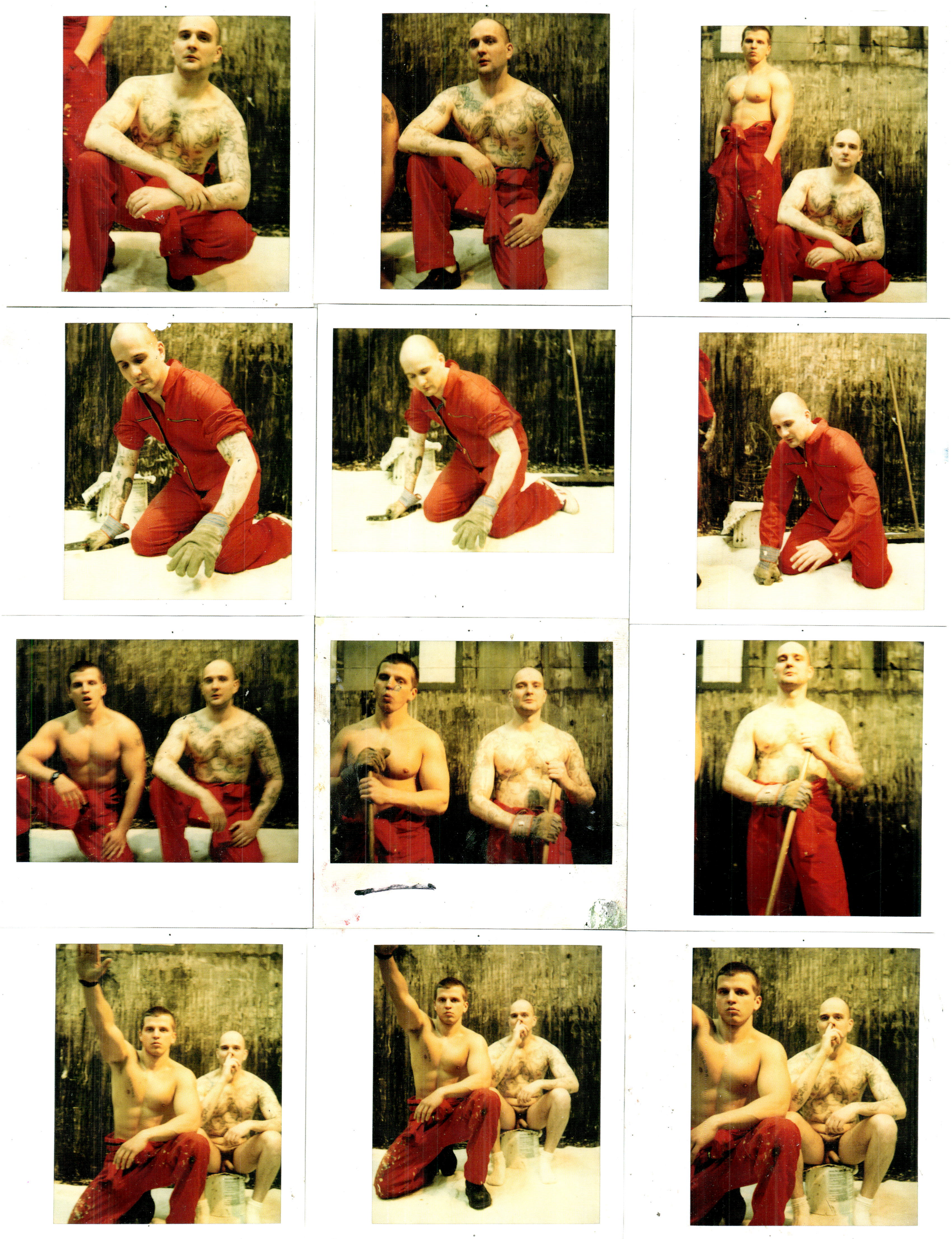

Study for *der Lustgarten* painting, Berlin, 1990

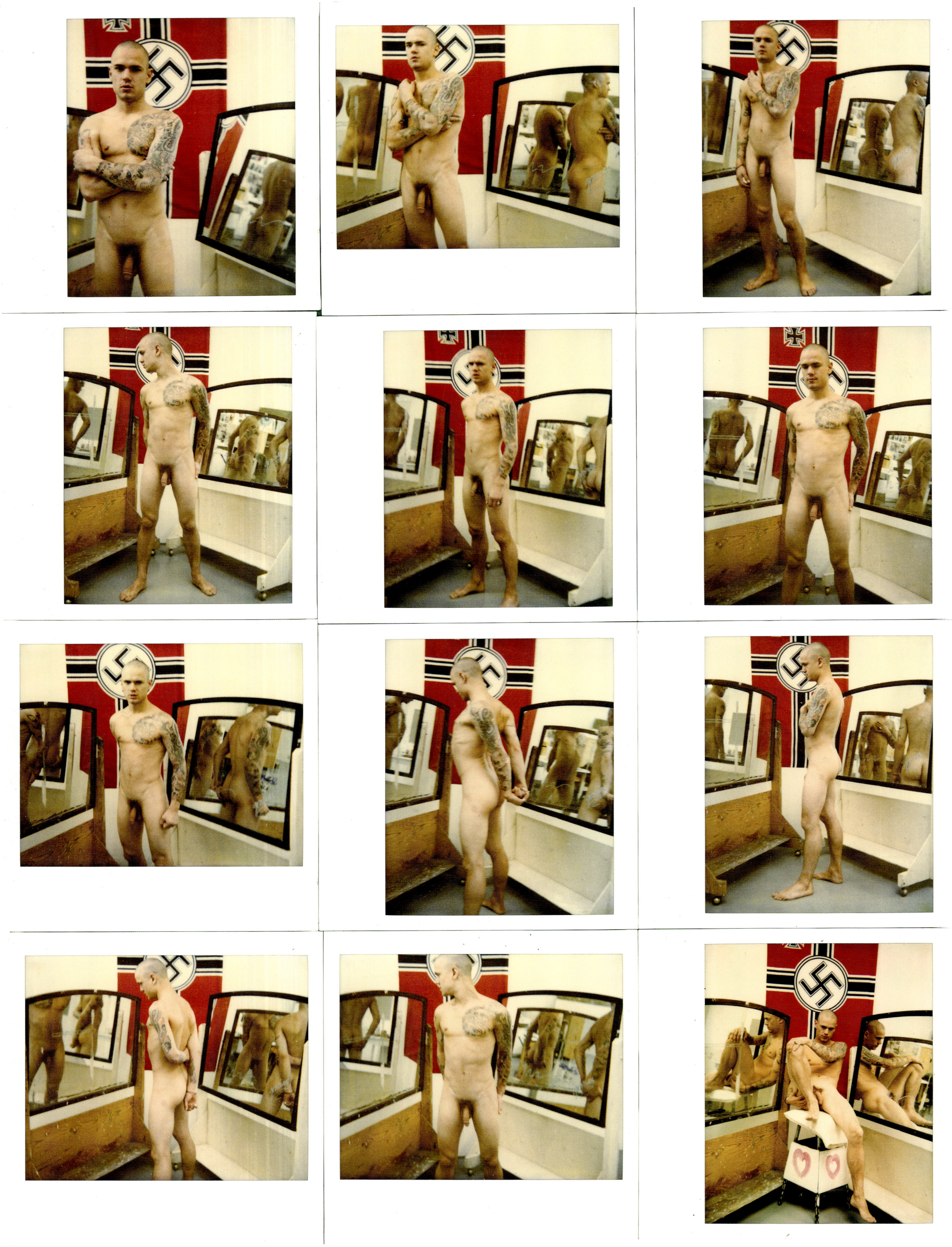

Cameron, Banff, 1990

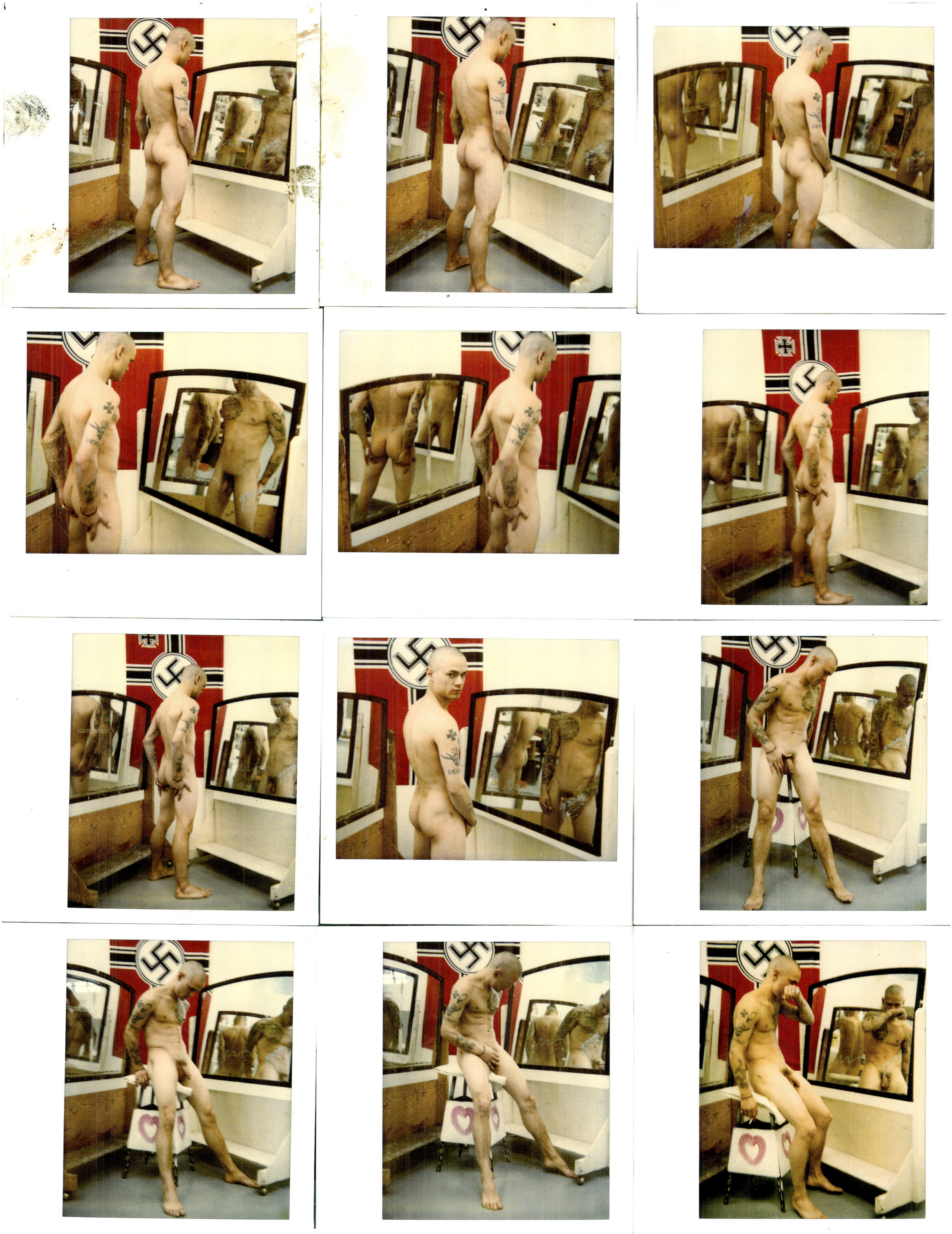

Cameron, Banff, 1990

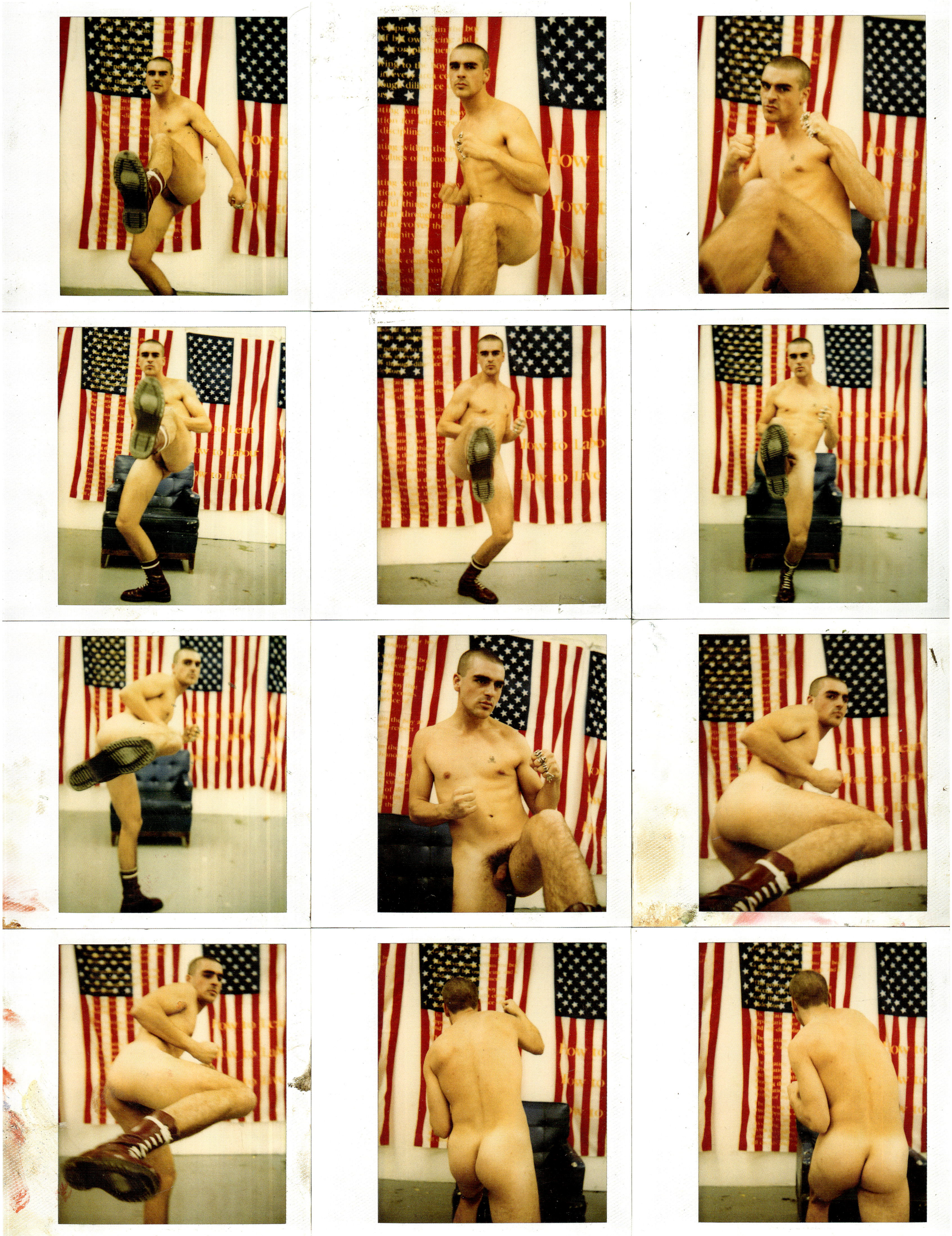

Kickboxing Skin, Banff, 1990

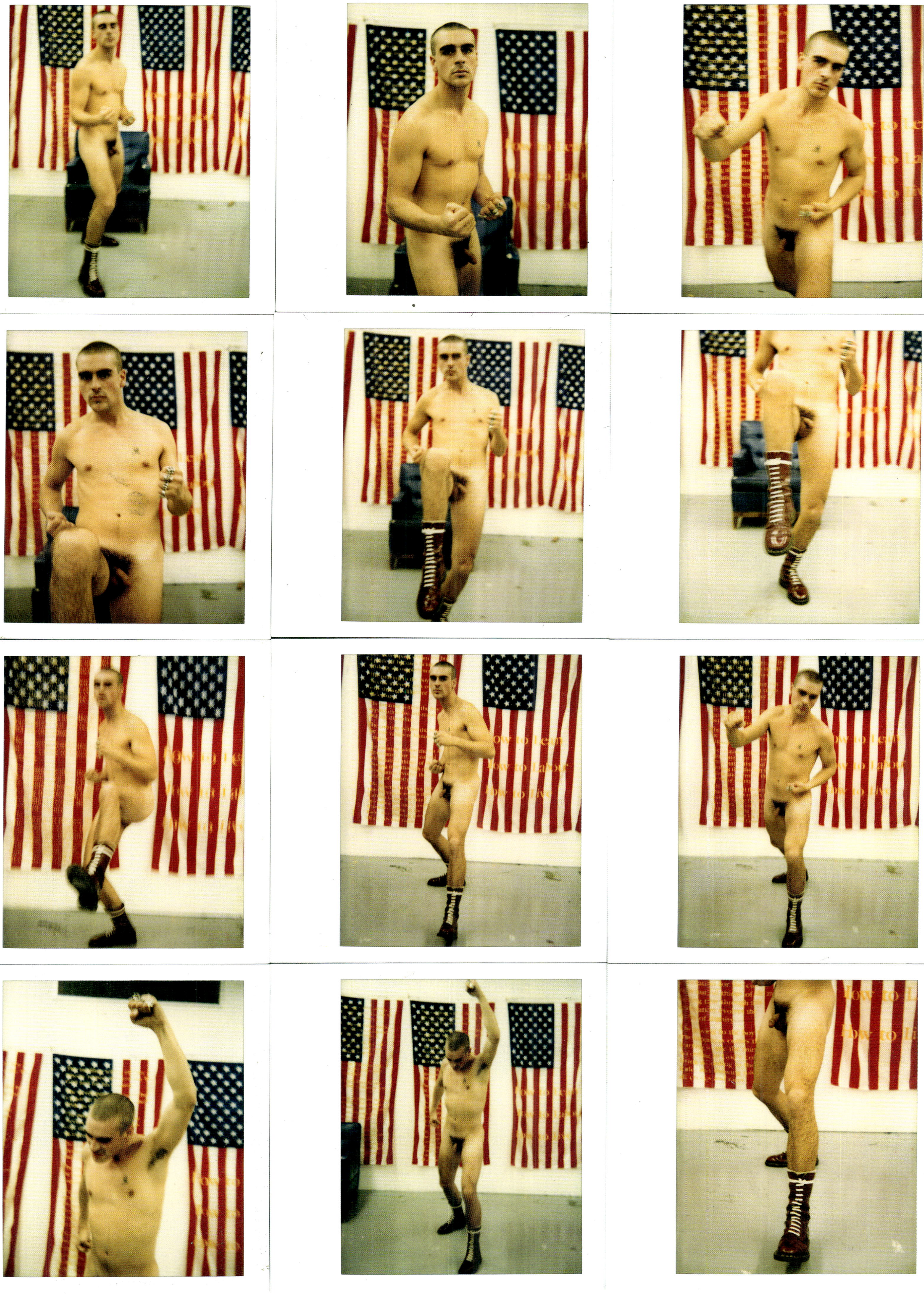

Kickboxing Skin, Banff, 1990

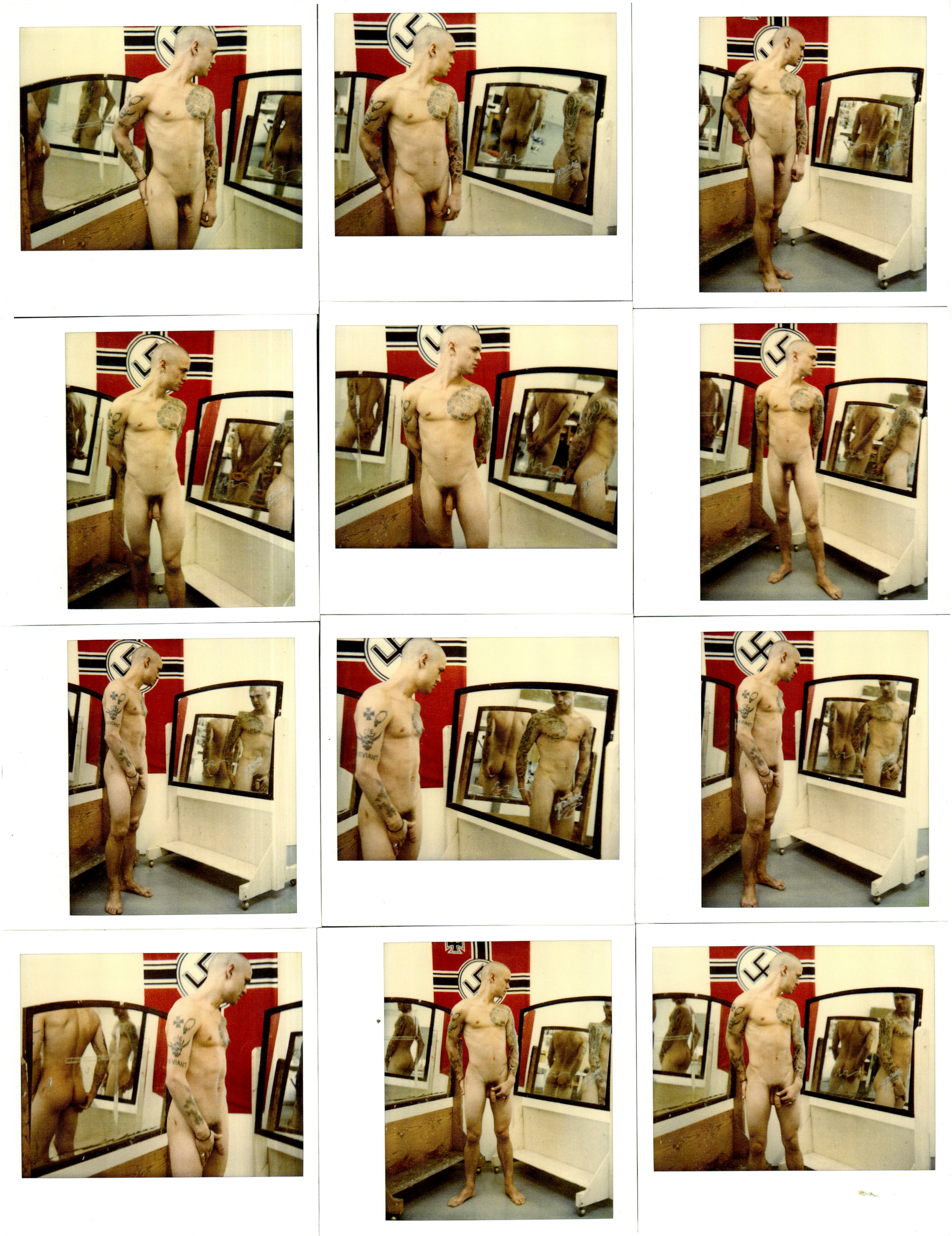

Cameron, Banff, 1990

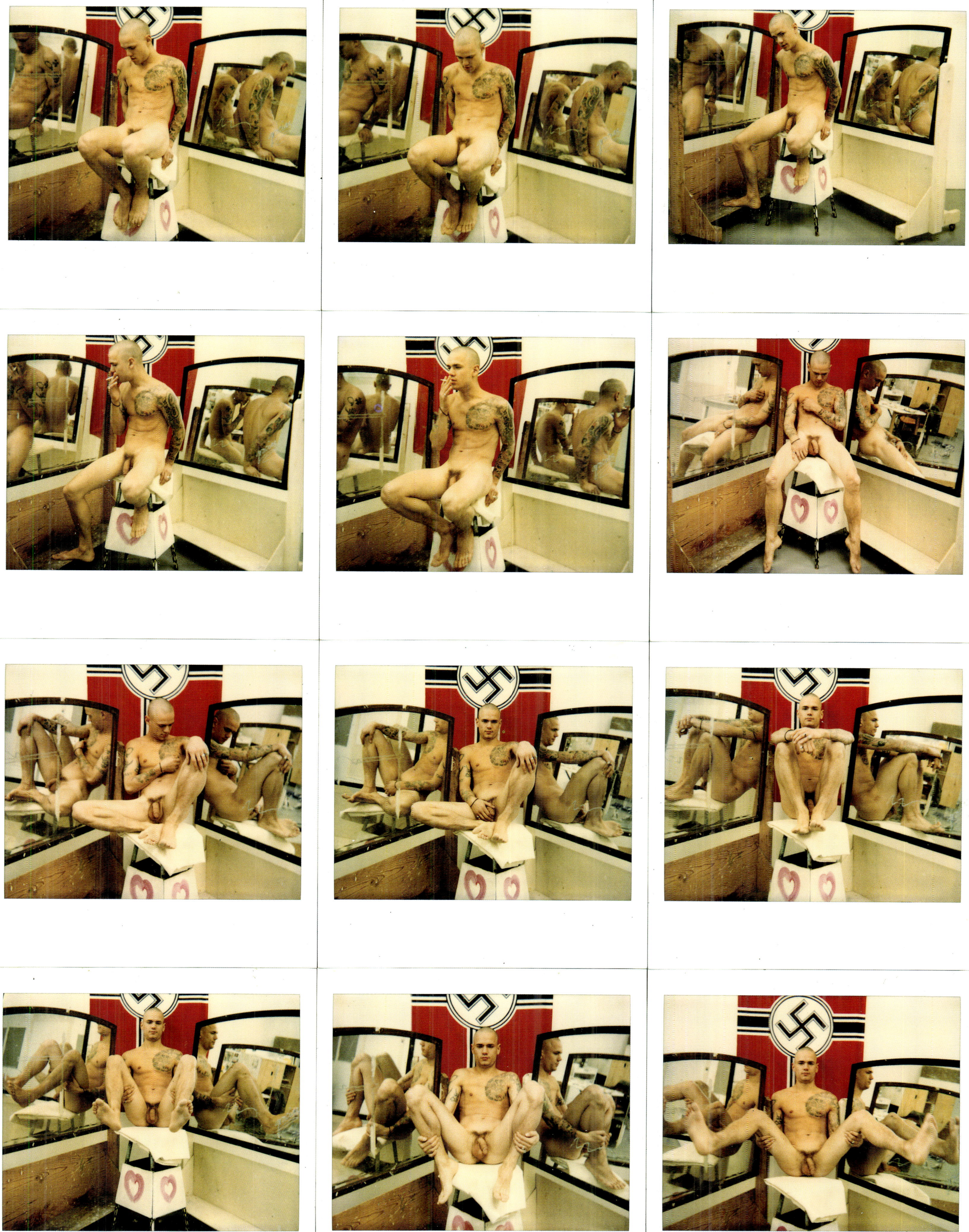

Cameron, Banff, 1990

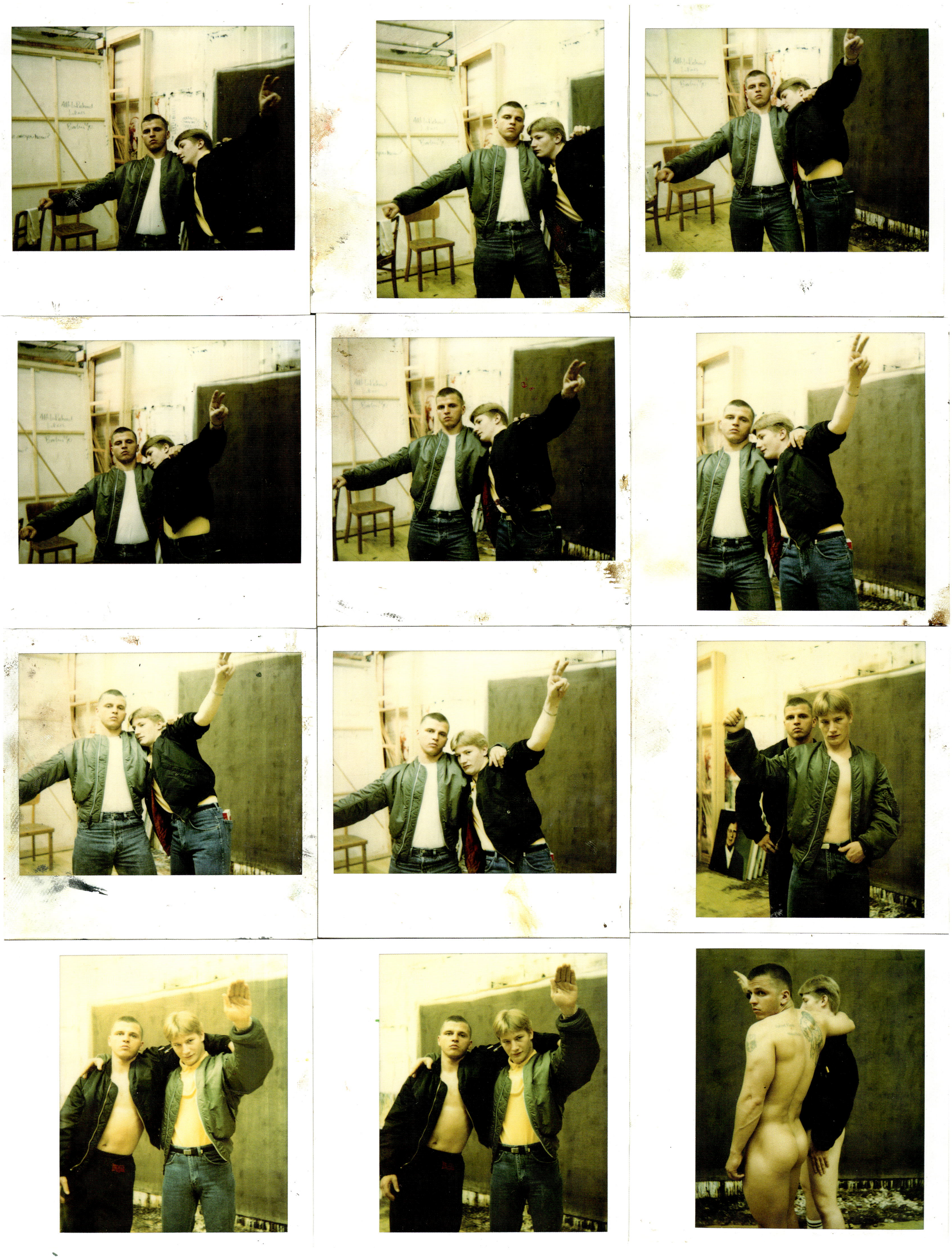

Alex & Zoo Boy, Berlin, 1990

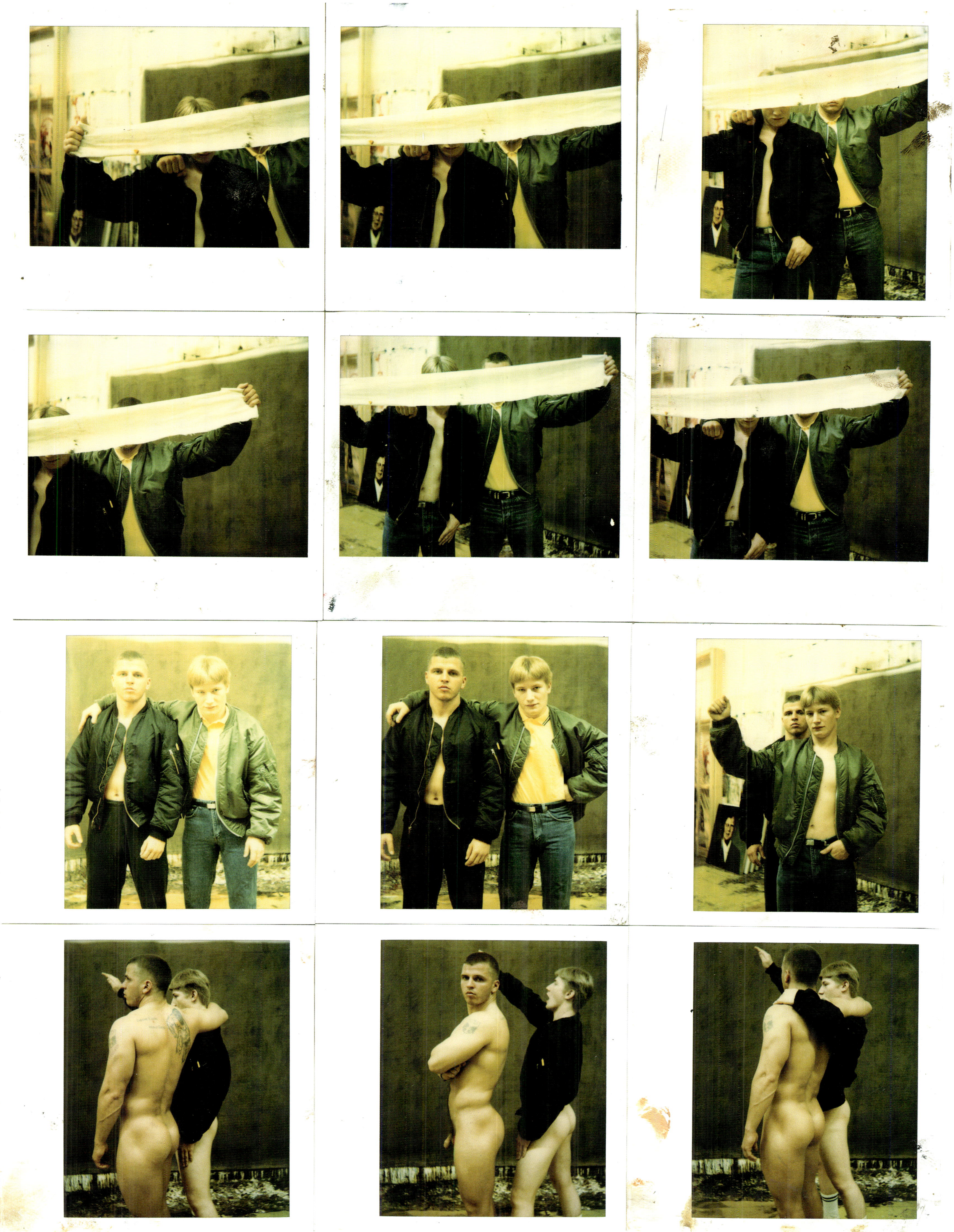

Alex & Zoo Boy, Berlin, 1990

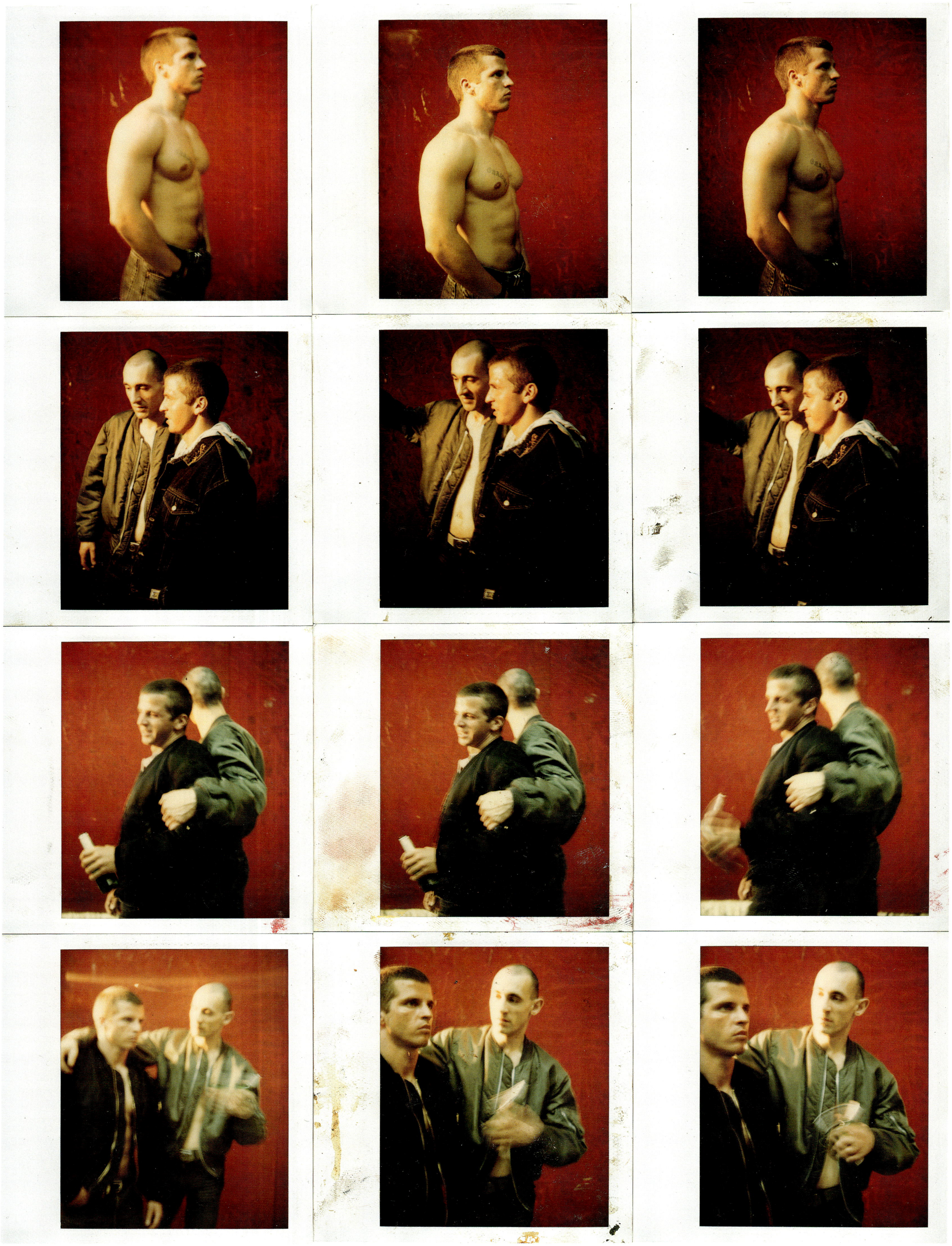

Alex & Roger, Berlin, 1990

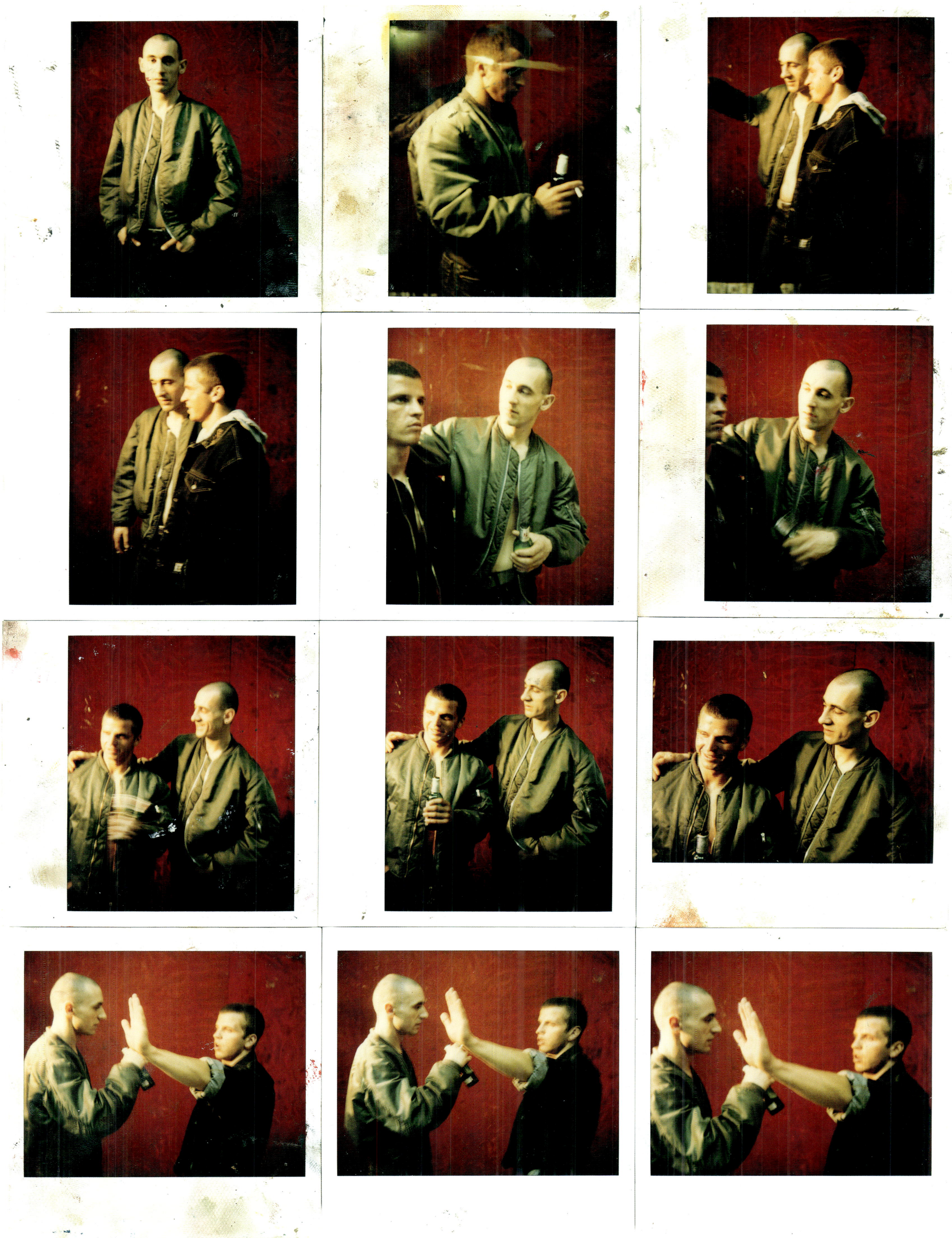

Alex & Roger, Berlin, 1990

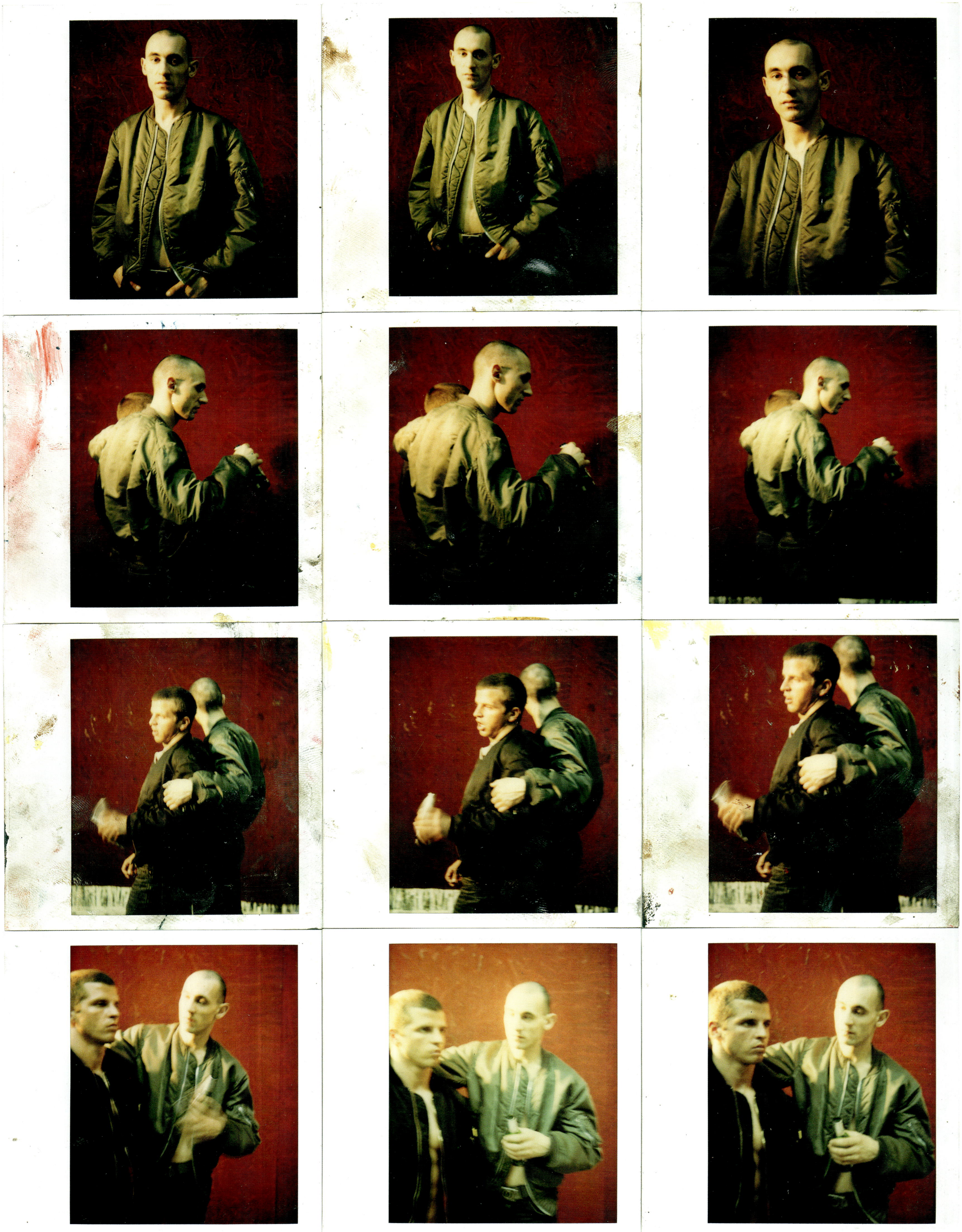

Roger & Alex, Berlin, 1990

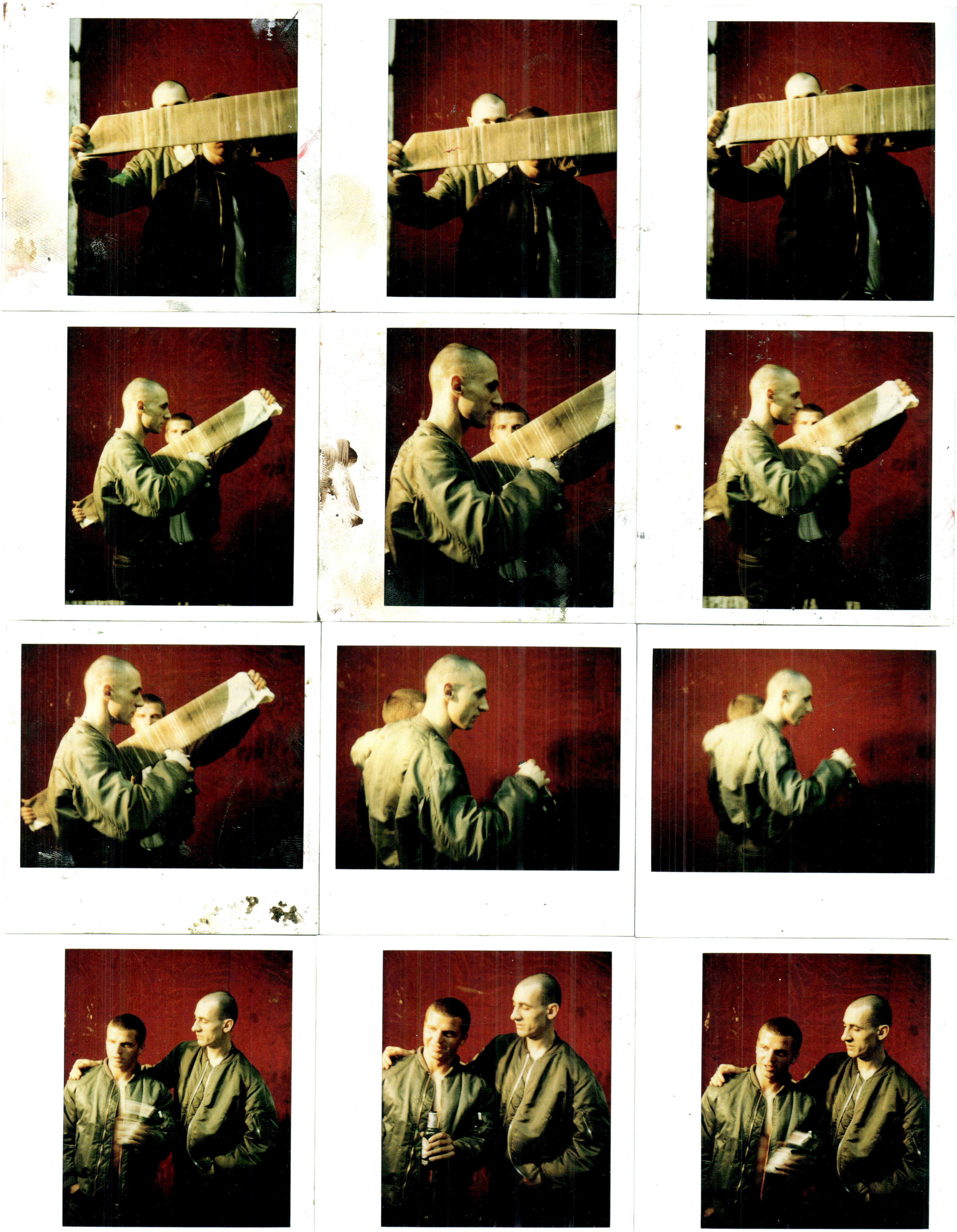

Roger & Alex, Berlin, 1990

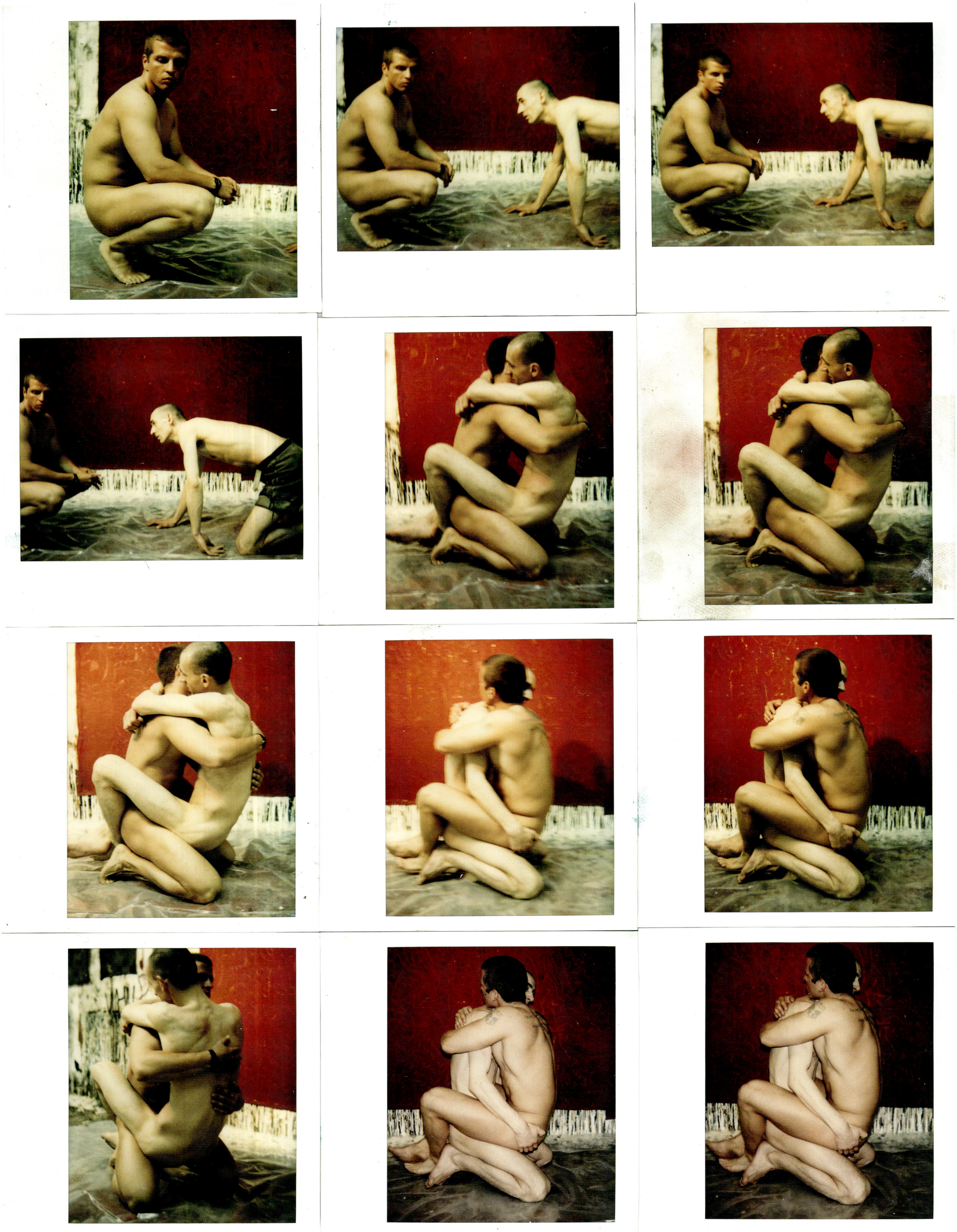

Alex & Roger, study for *Tiergarten*, Berlin, 1990

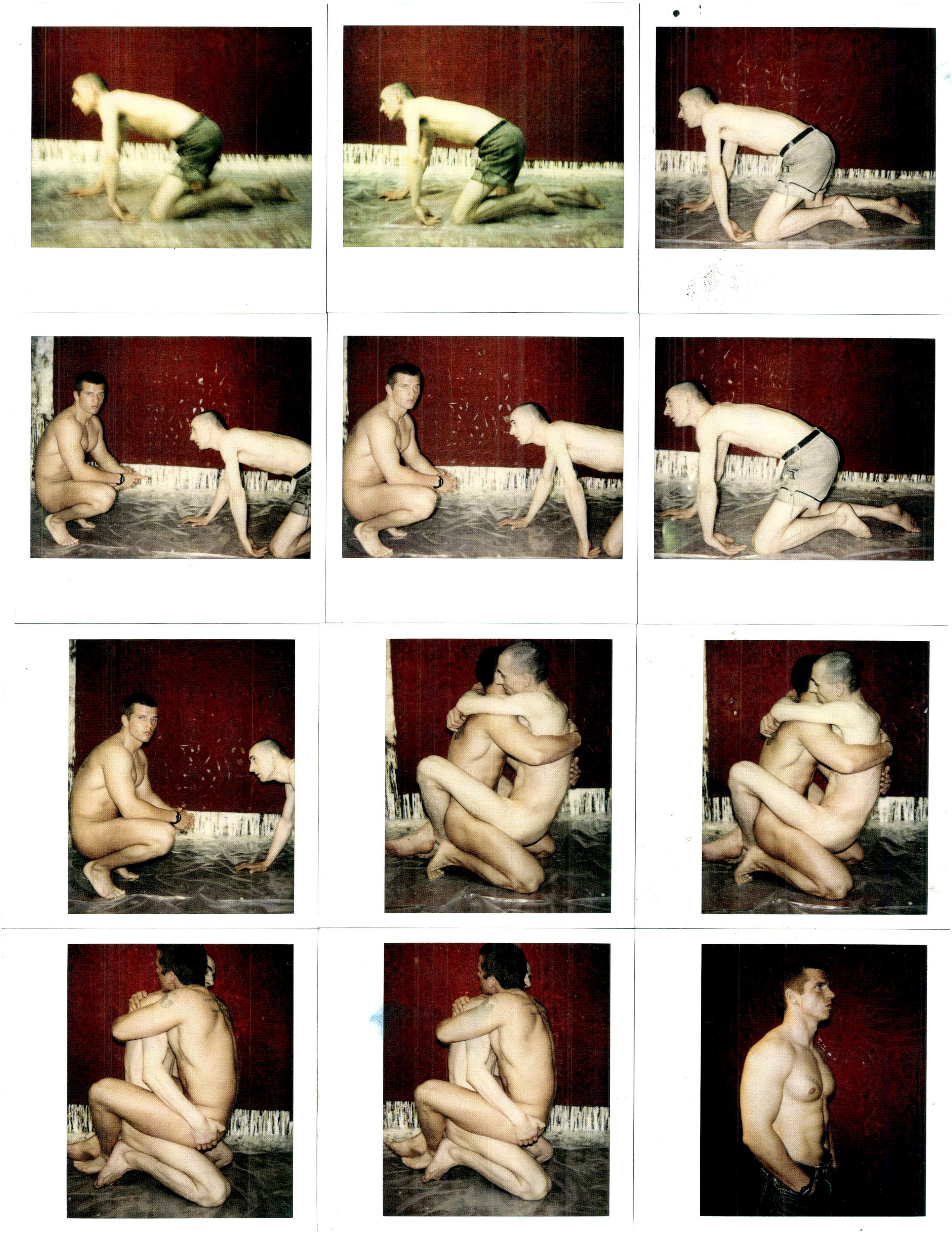

Alex & Roger, study for *Tiergarten*, Berlin, 1990

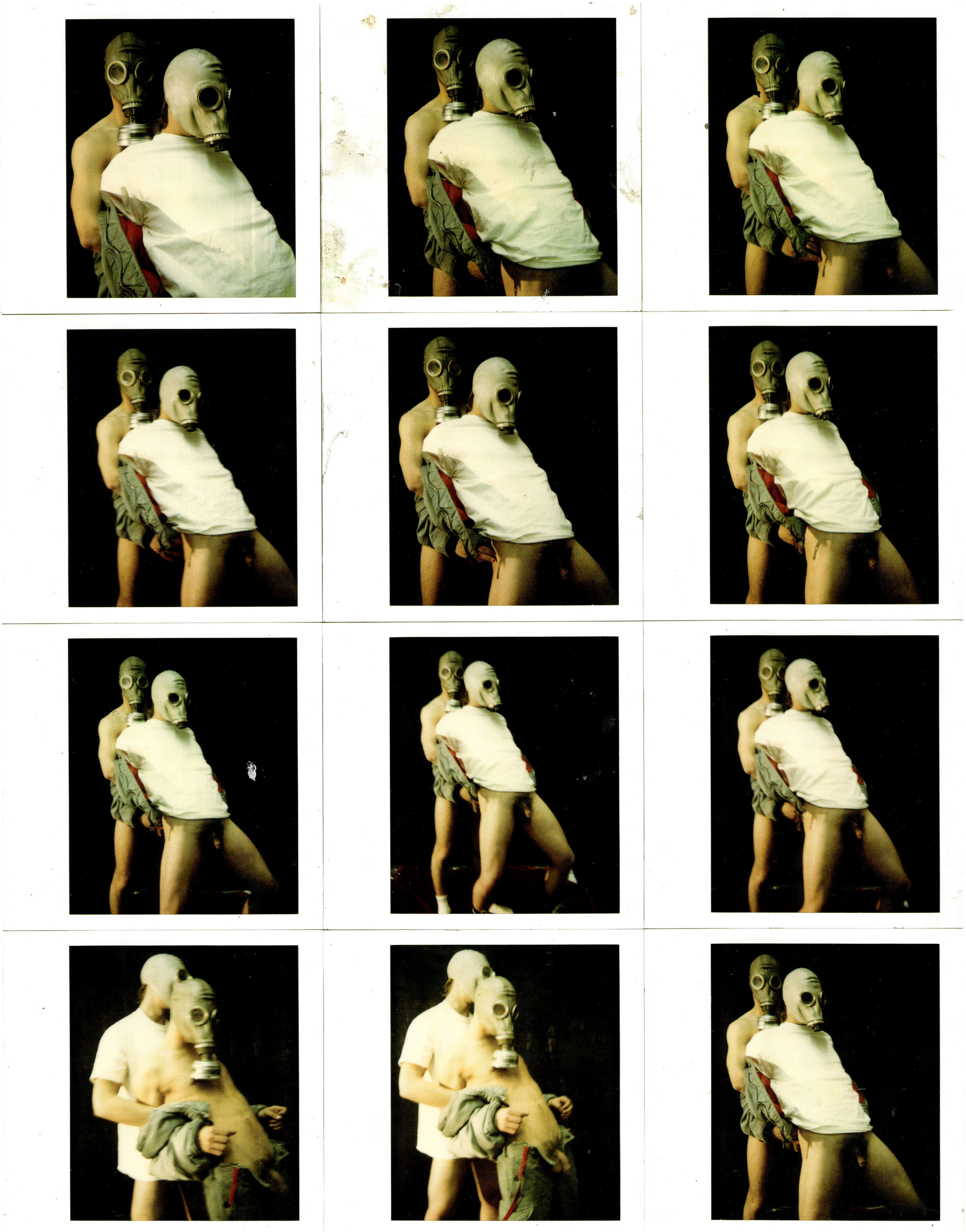

Gas mask study for *Doubting Thomas*, Berlin, 1991

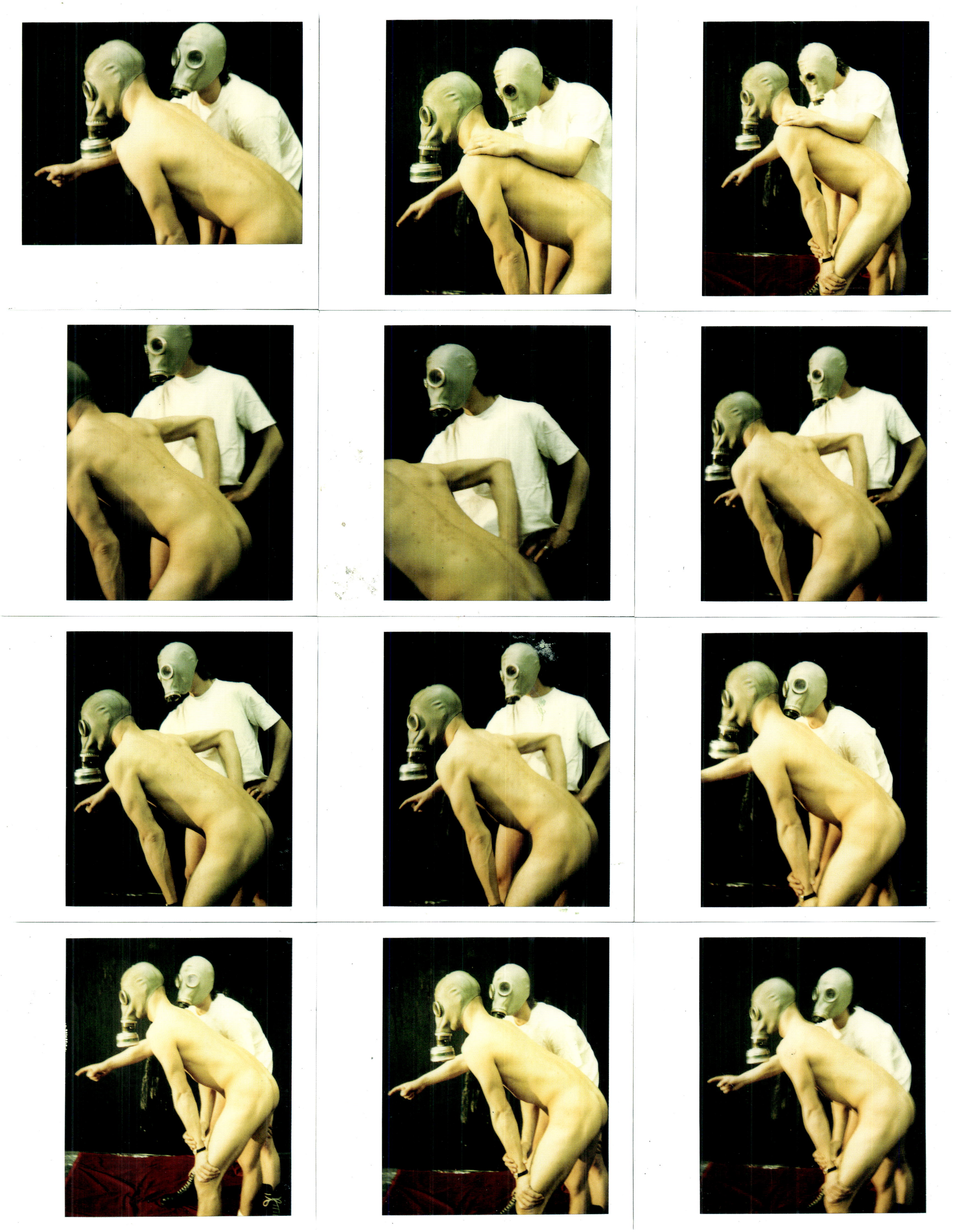

Gas mask stucy for *Doubting Thomas*, Berlin, 1991

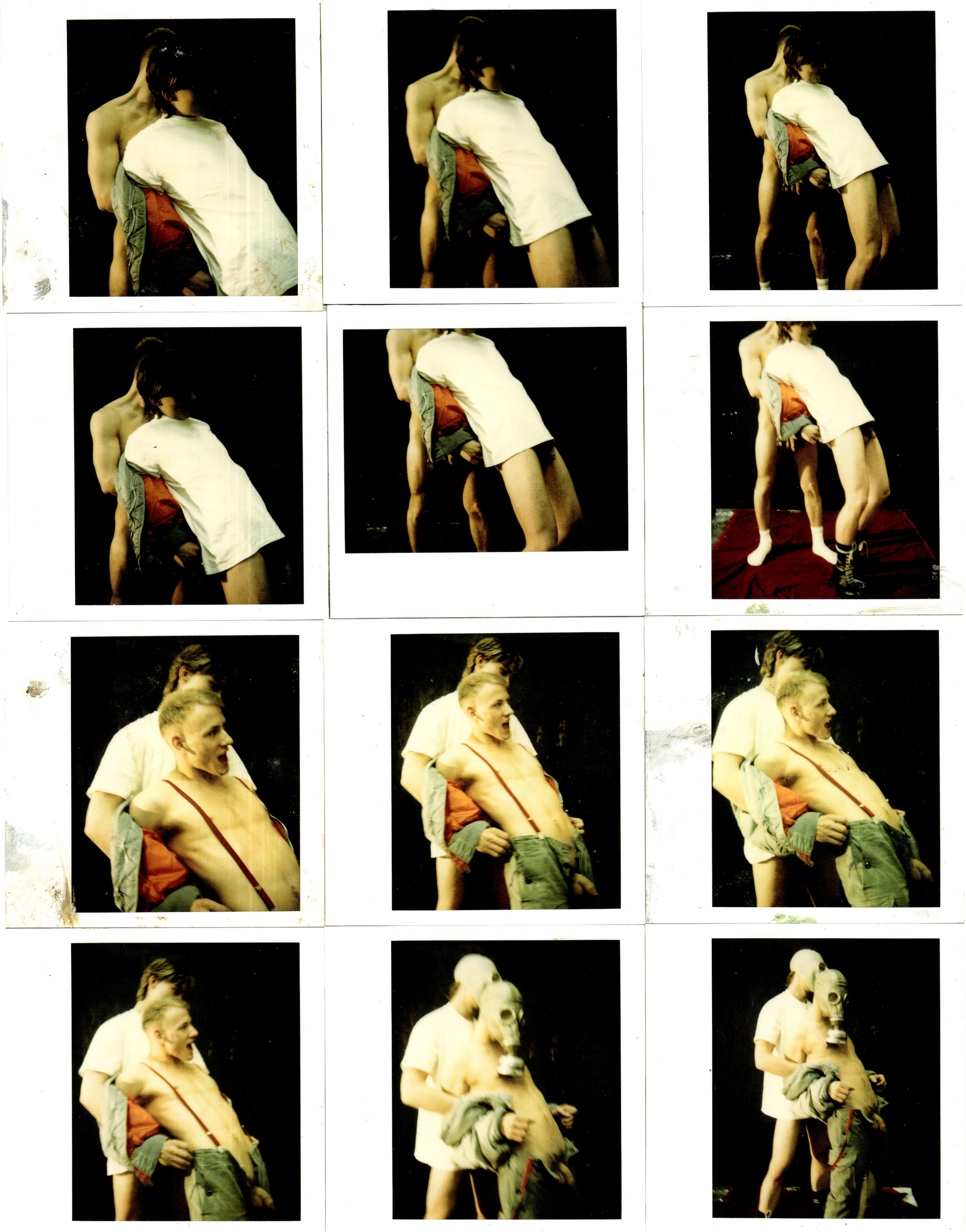

Stephan & Marek, study for *Doubting Thomas*, Berlin, 1991

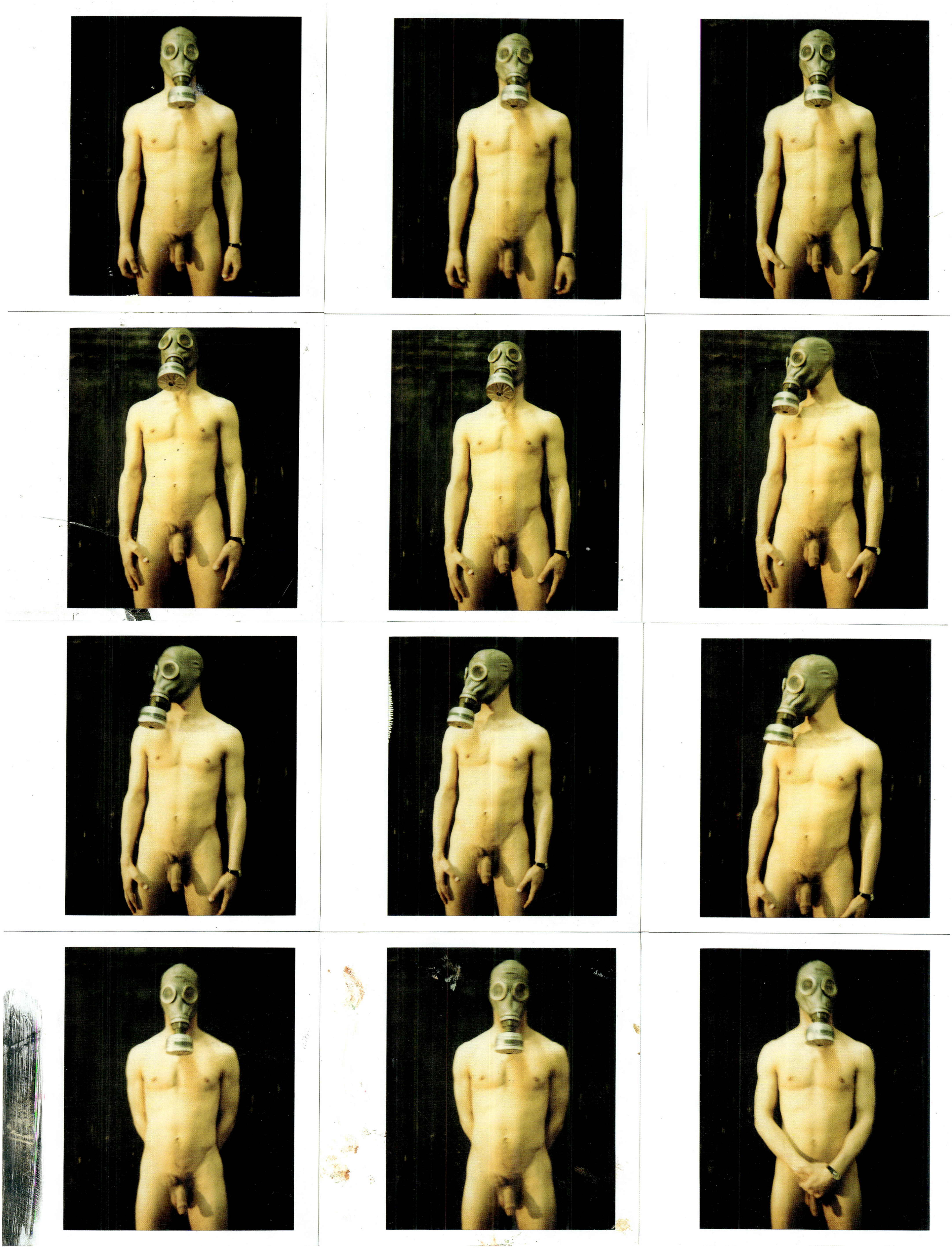

Stephan with Gas Mask, Berlin, 1991

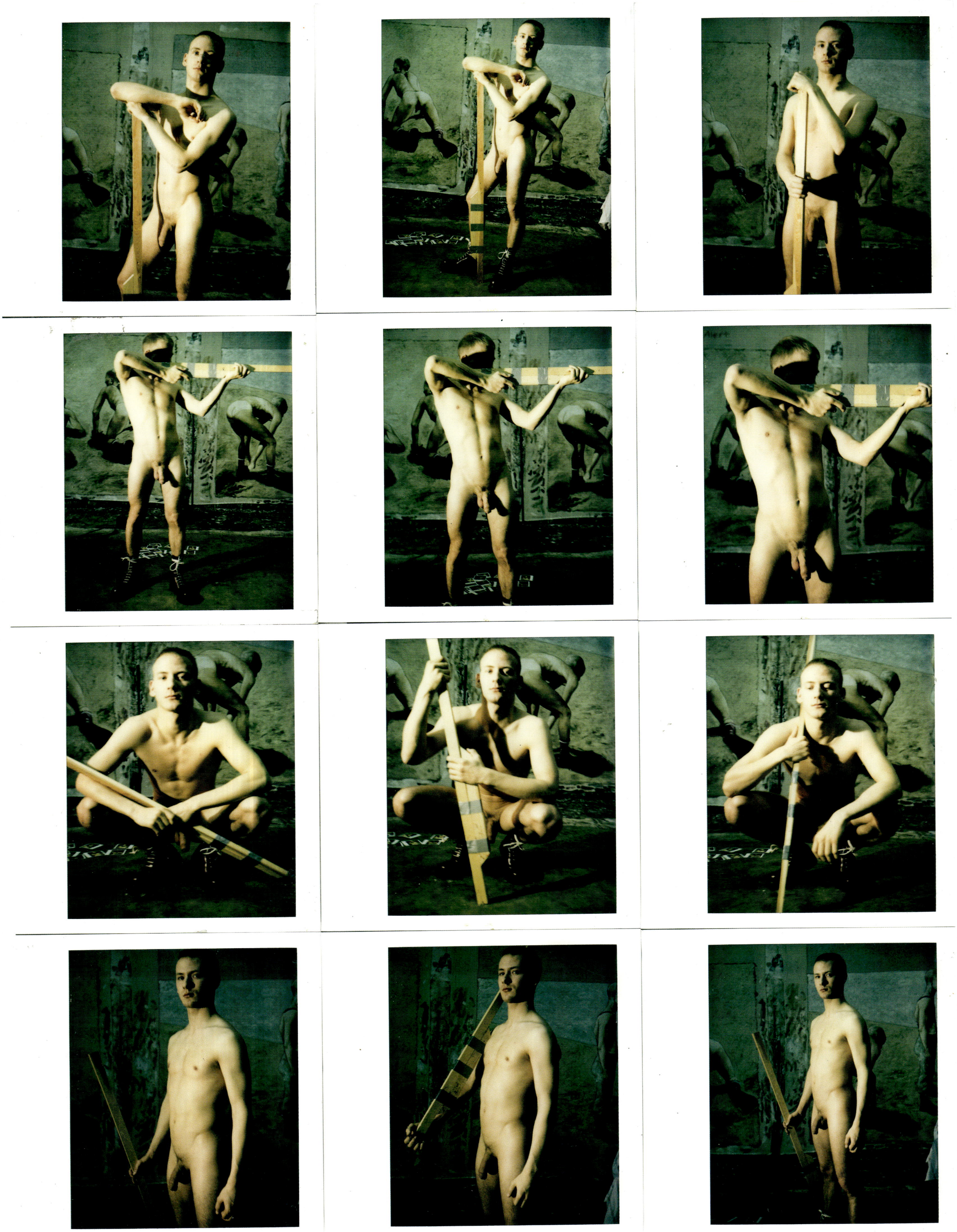

Stephan, Berlin, 1991

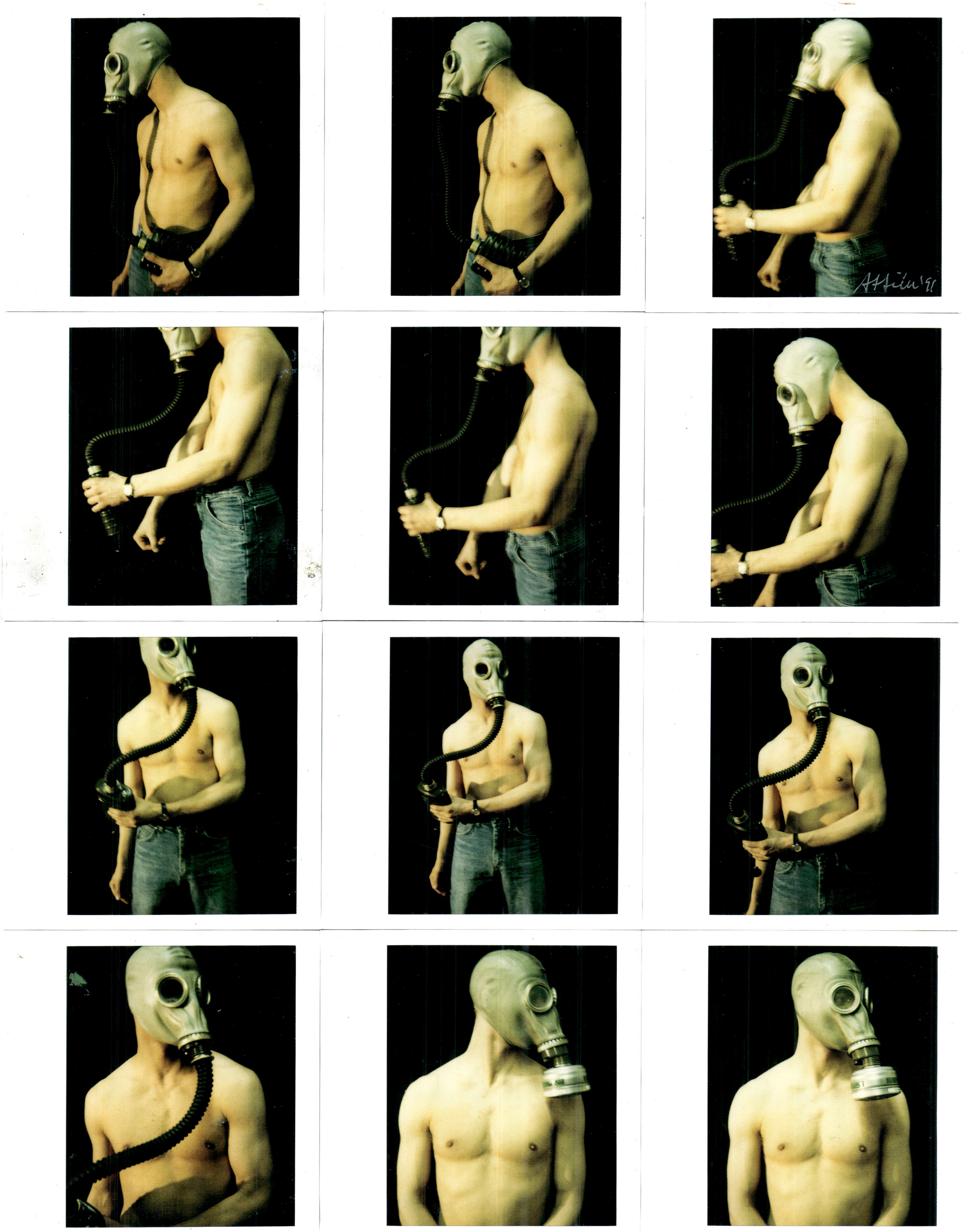

Stephan with Gas Mask, Berlin, 1991

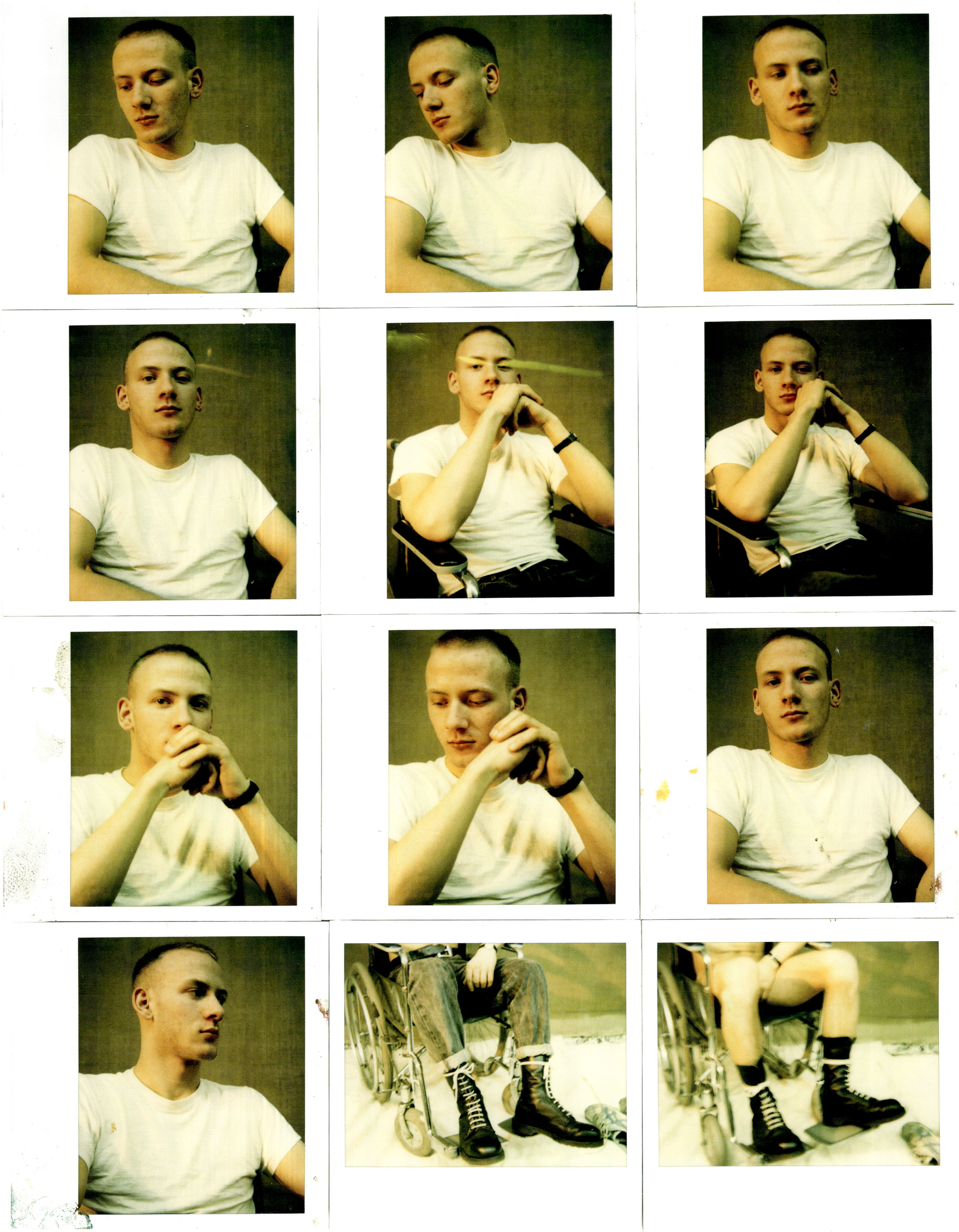

Stephan mit Rollstuhl, Berlin, 1991

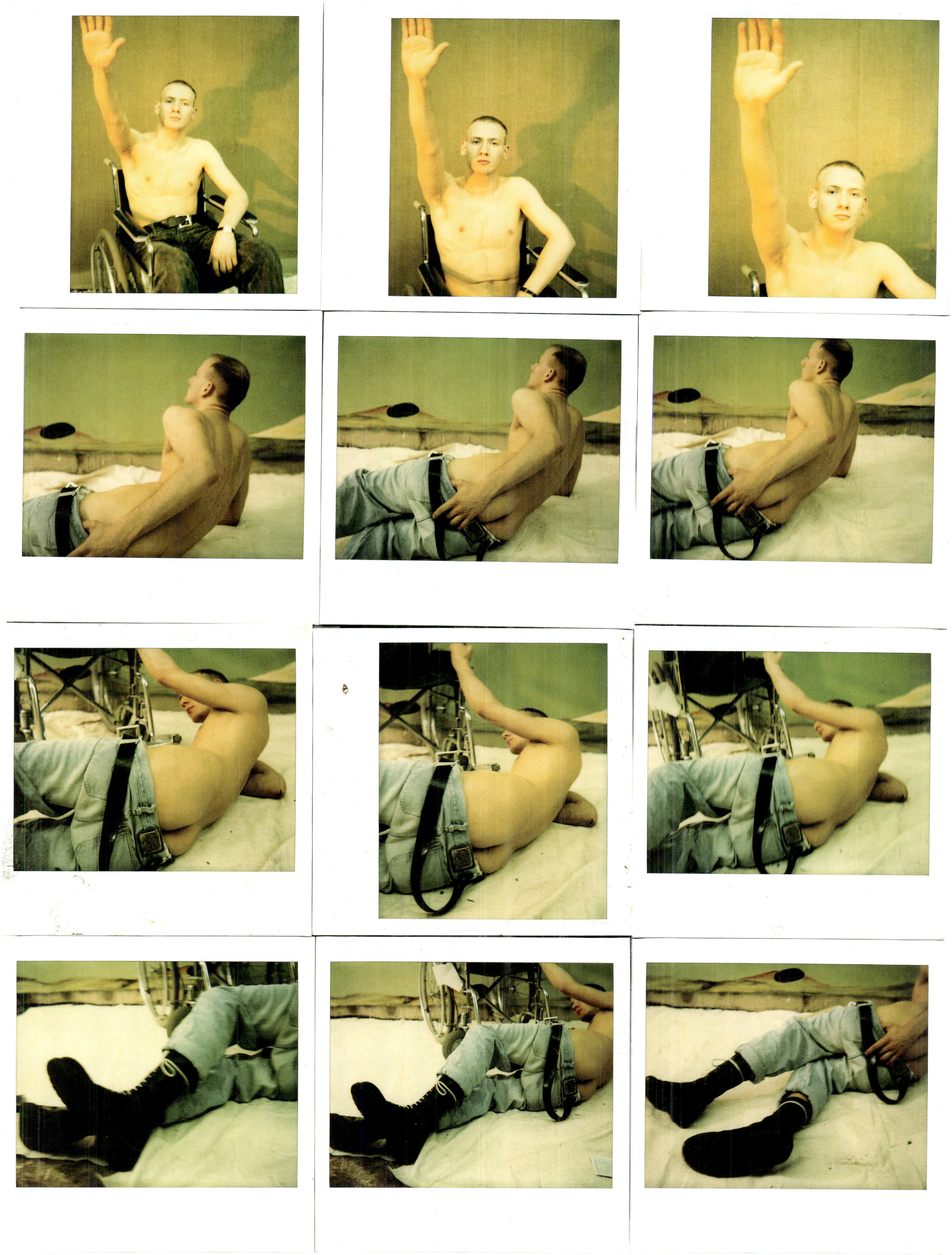

Stephan mit Rollstuhl, Berlin, 1991

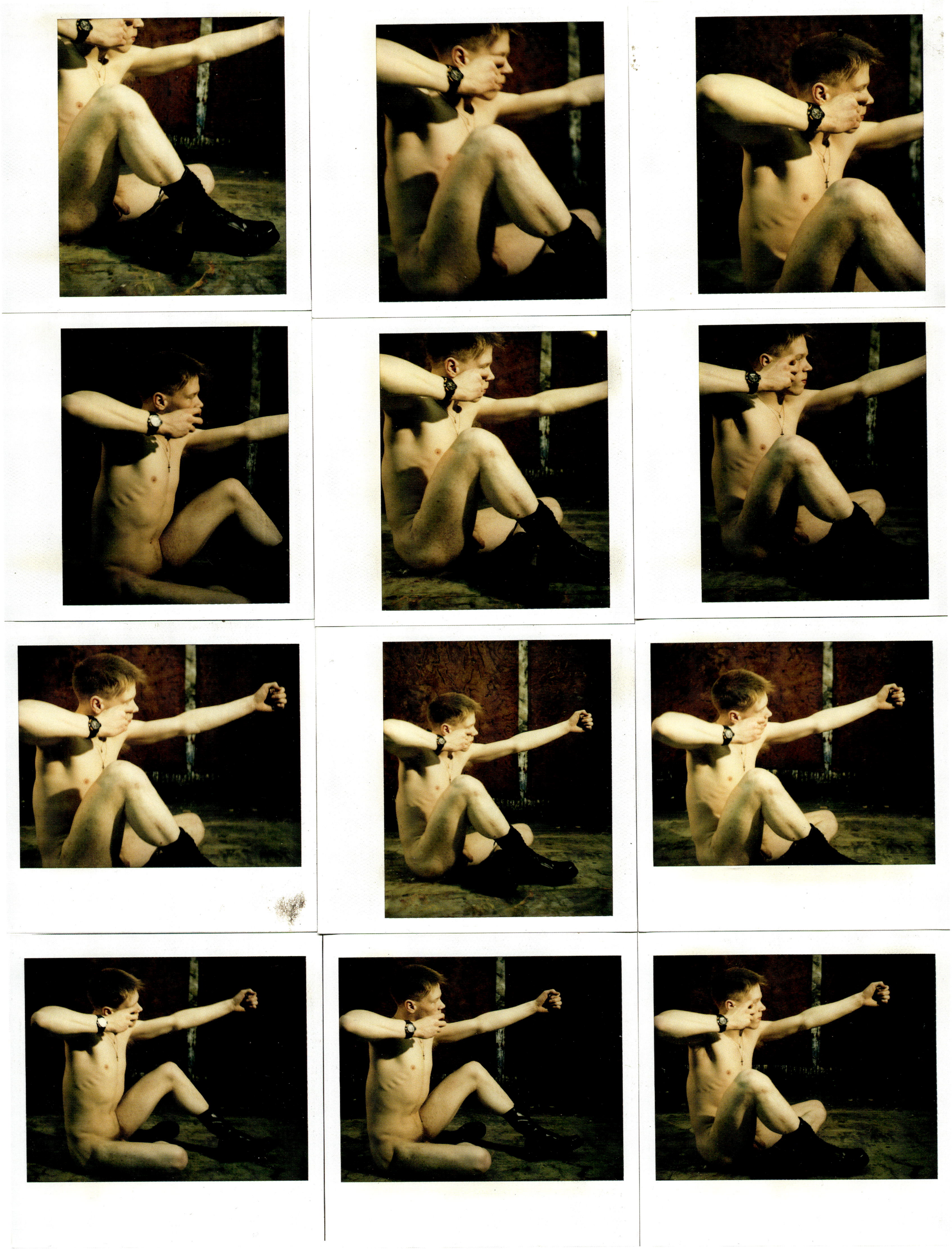

Zoo Boy, study for *Archer*, Berlin, 1990

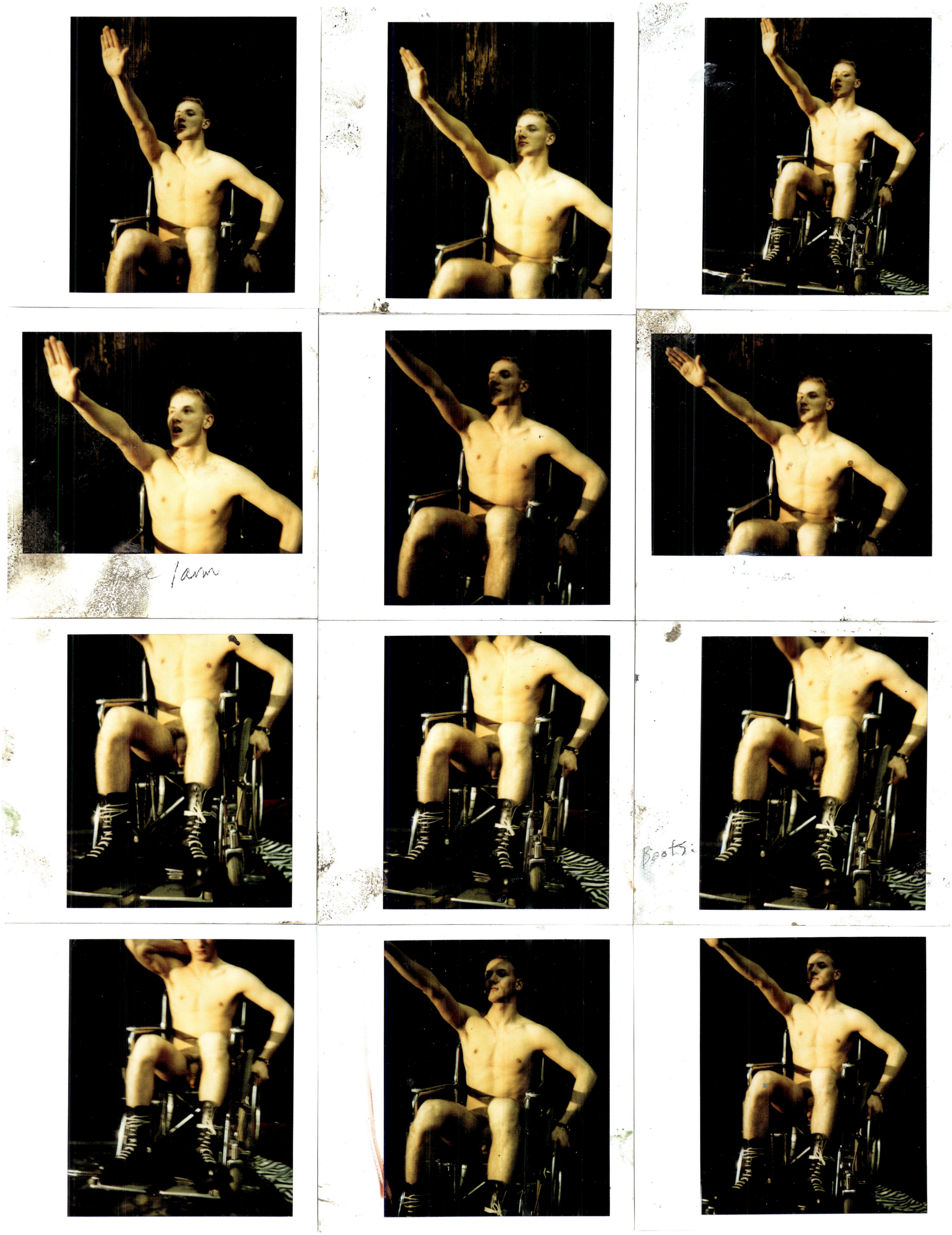

Stephan mit Rollstuhl, Berlin, 1990

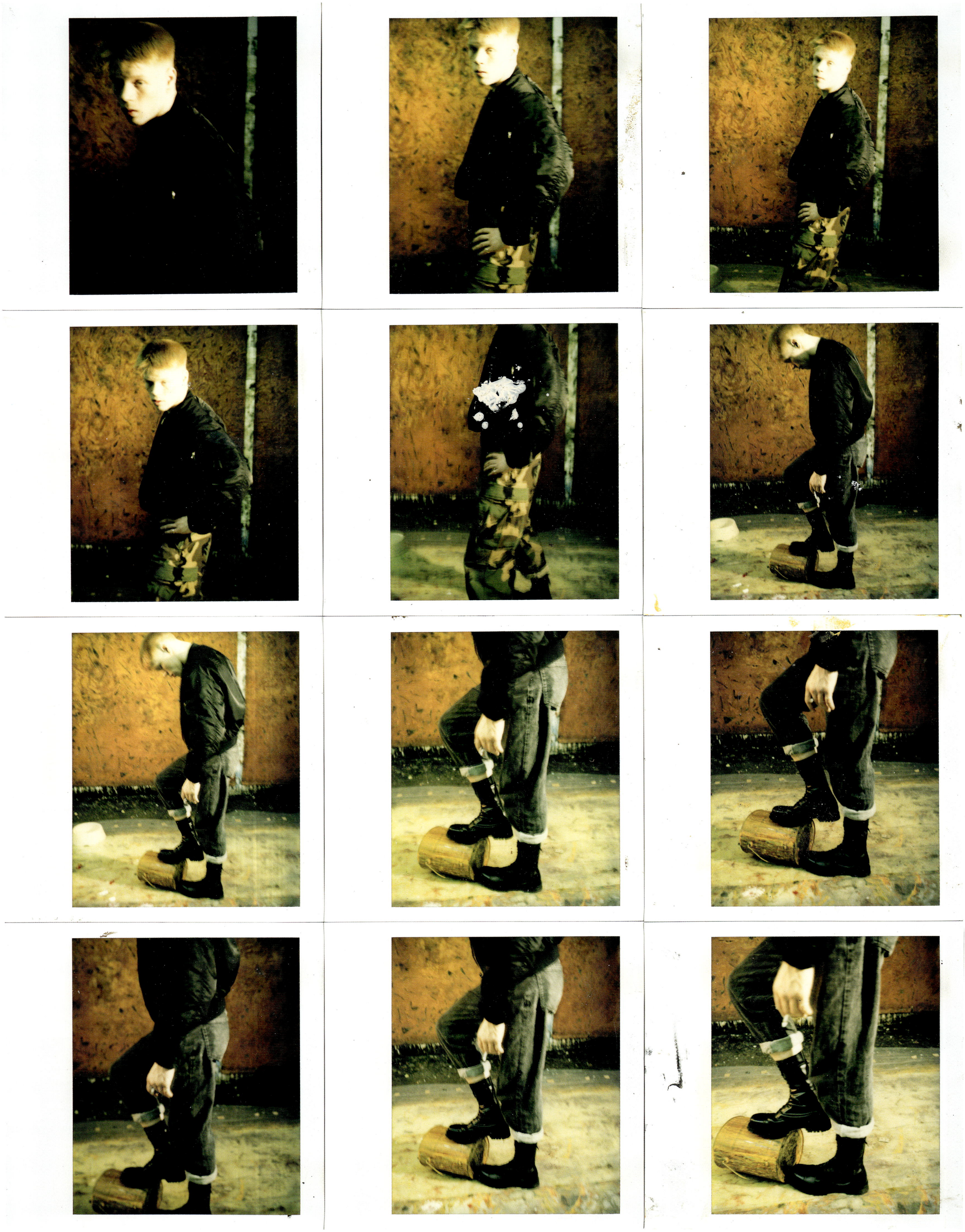

Zoo Boy, Berlin, 1991

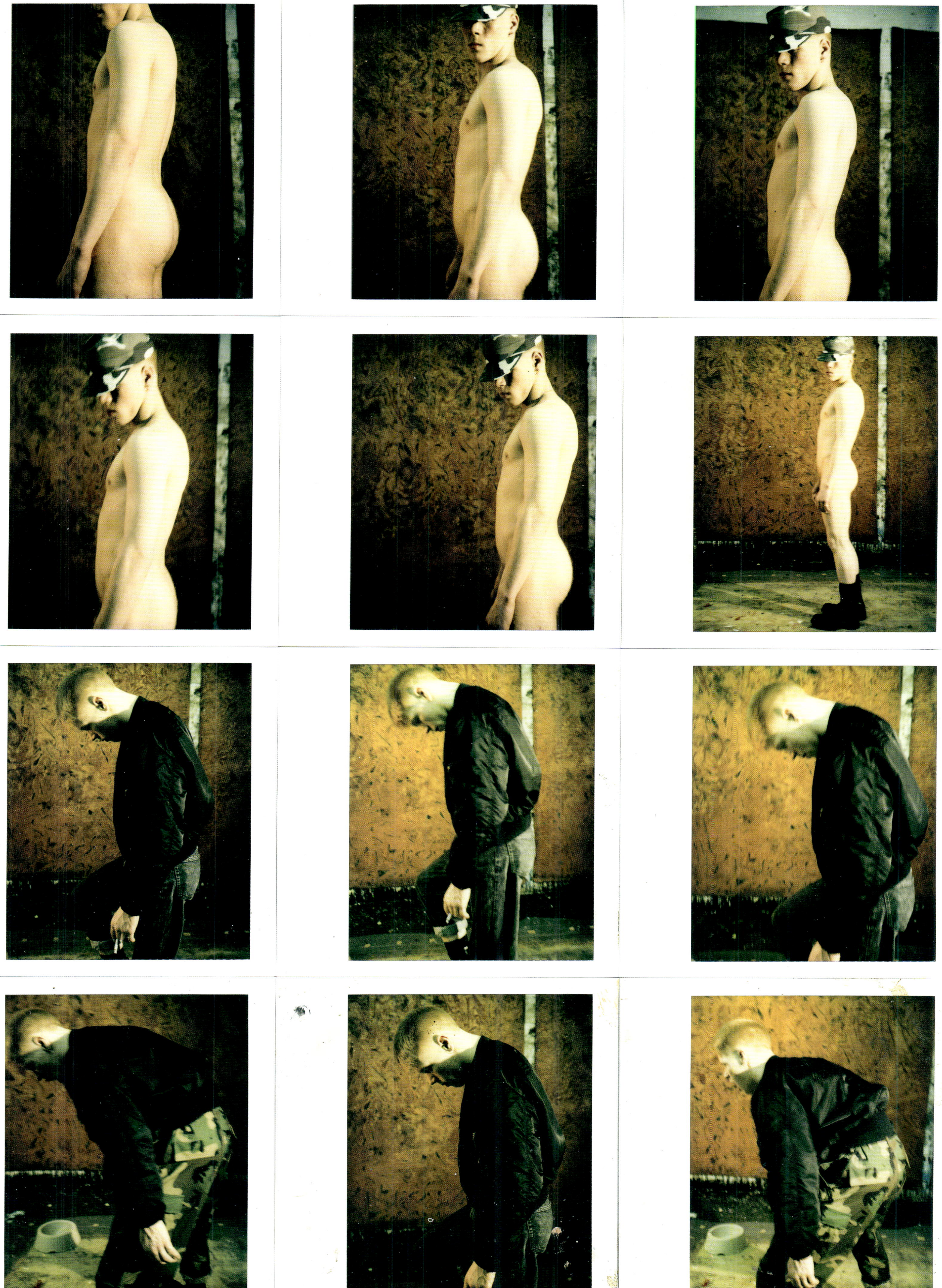

Zoo Boy, Berlin, 1991

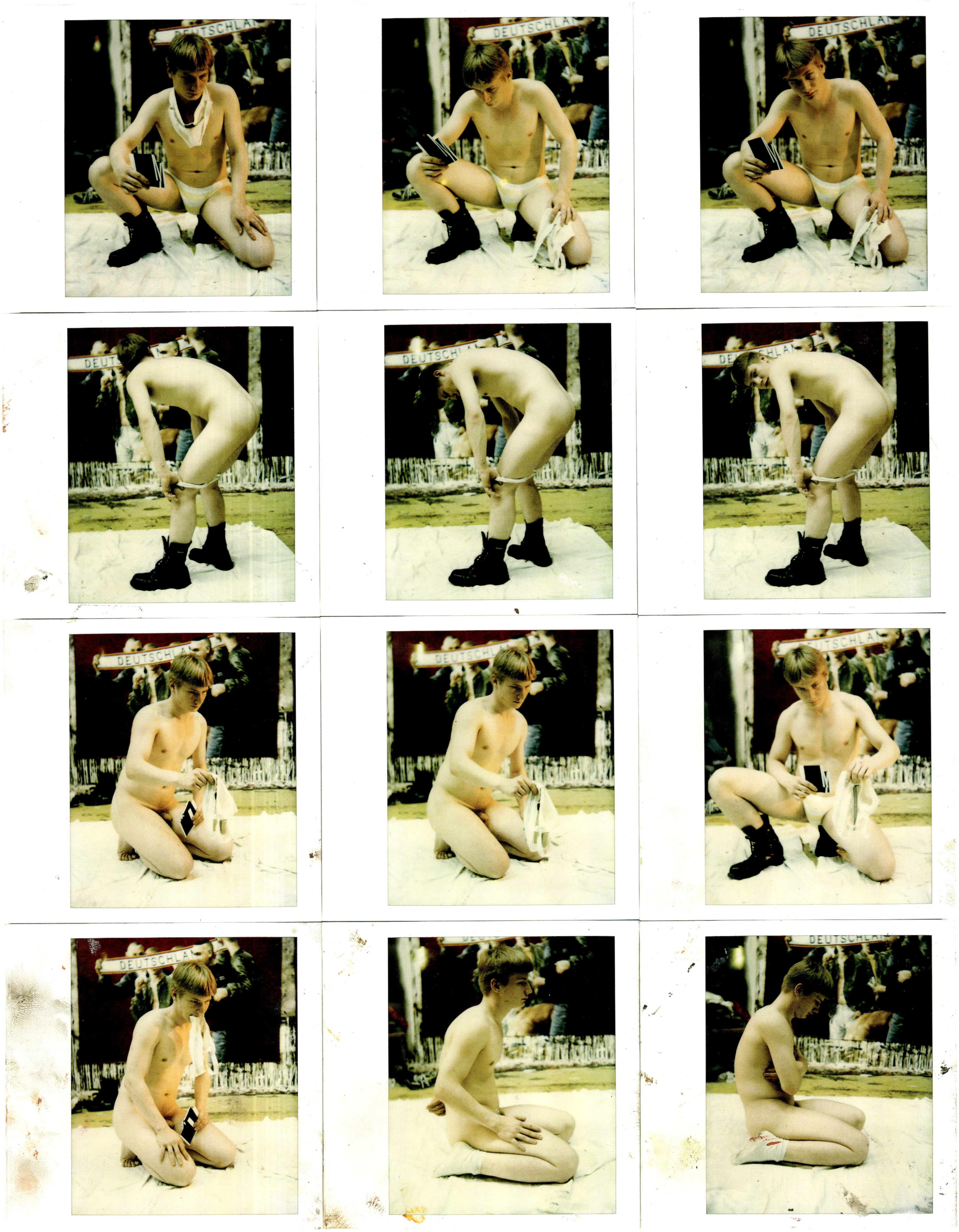

Zoo Boy, Berlin, 1991

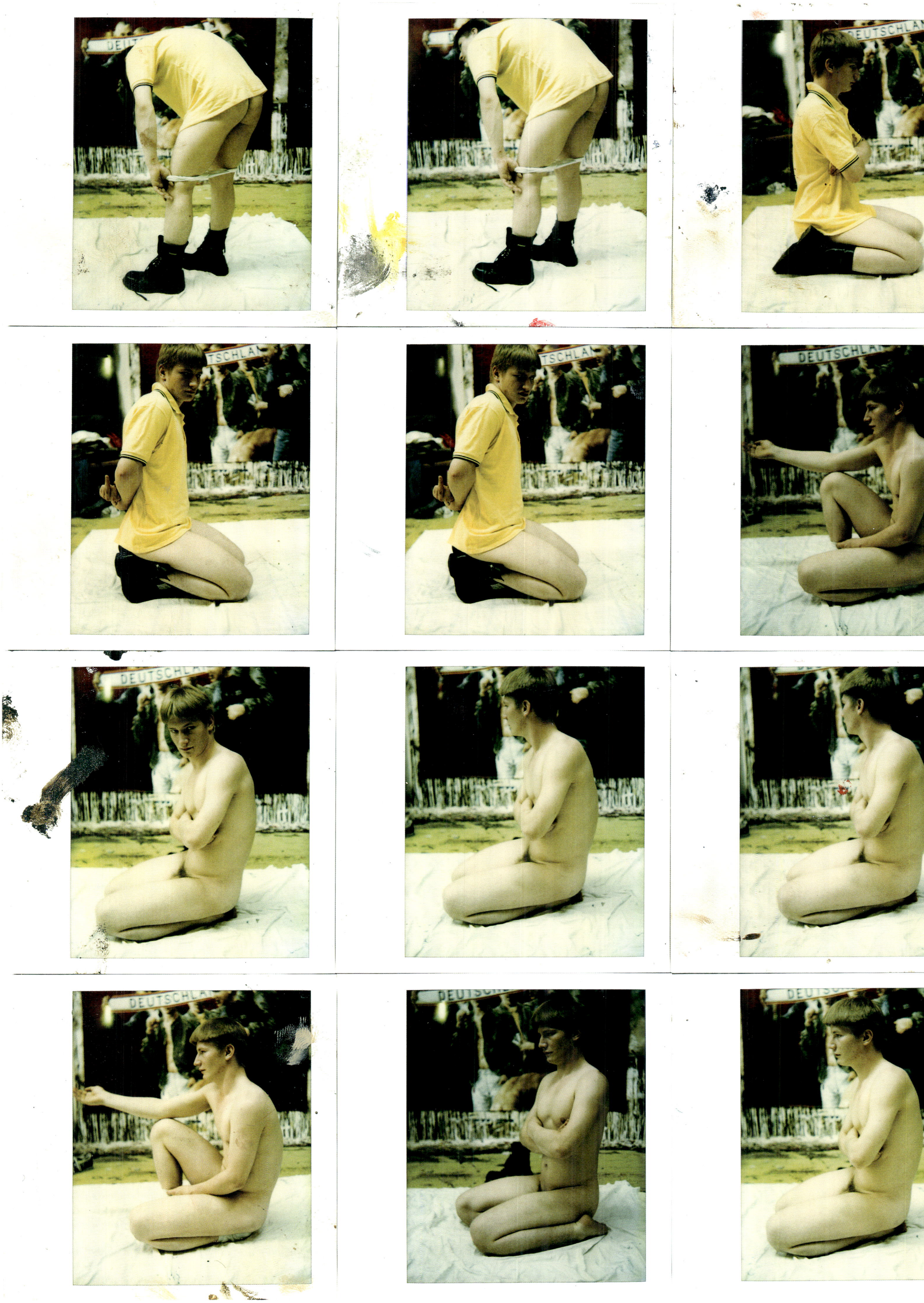

Zoo Boy, Berlin, 1991

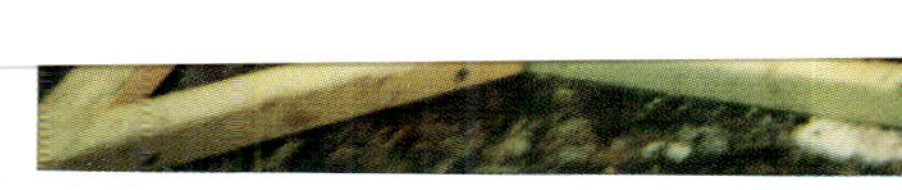

Zoo Boy Bum, Berlin, 1991

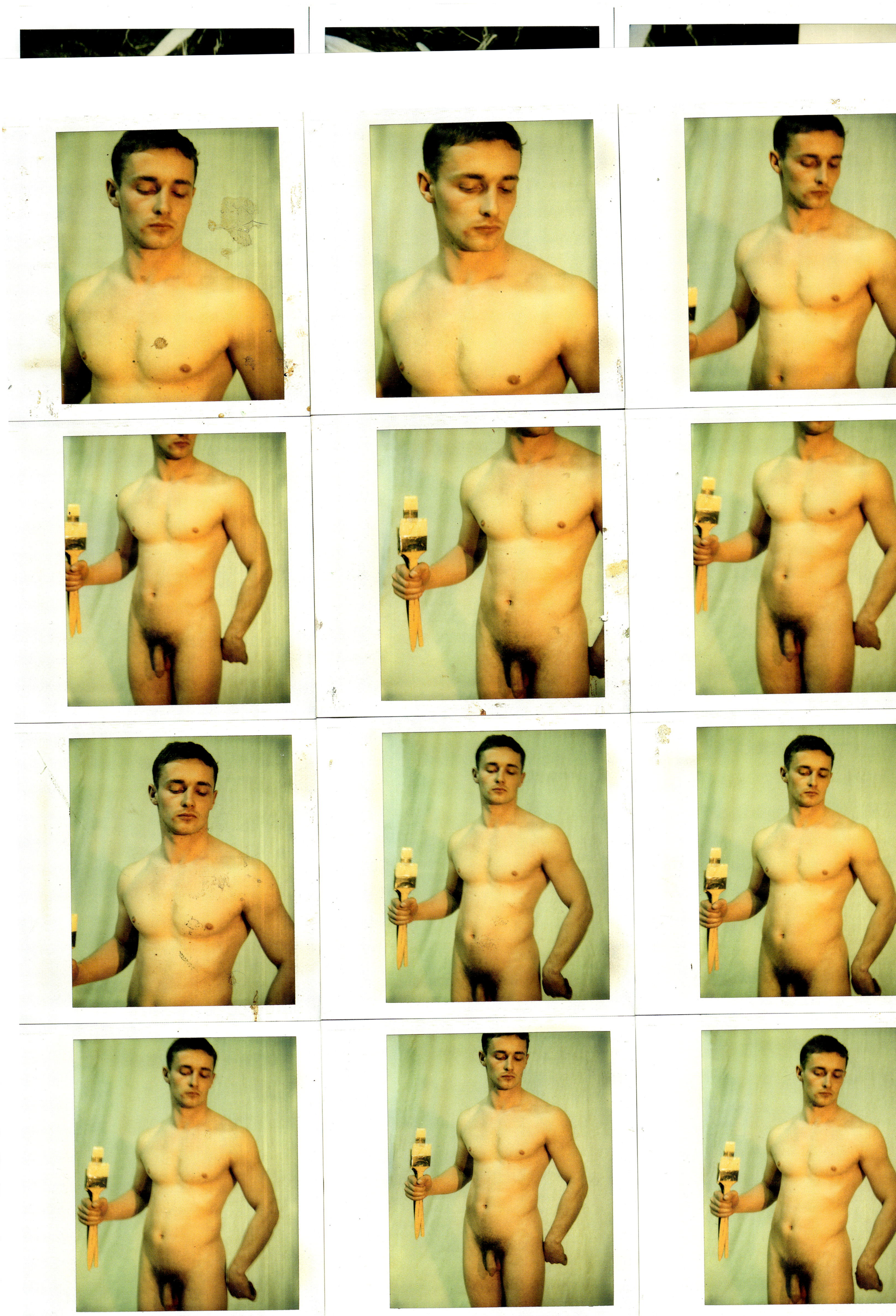

Study for *The Eternal Tea House*, Spring, Berlin, 1991

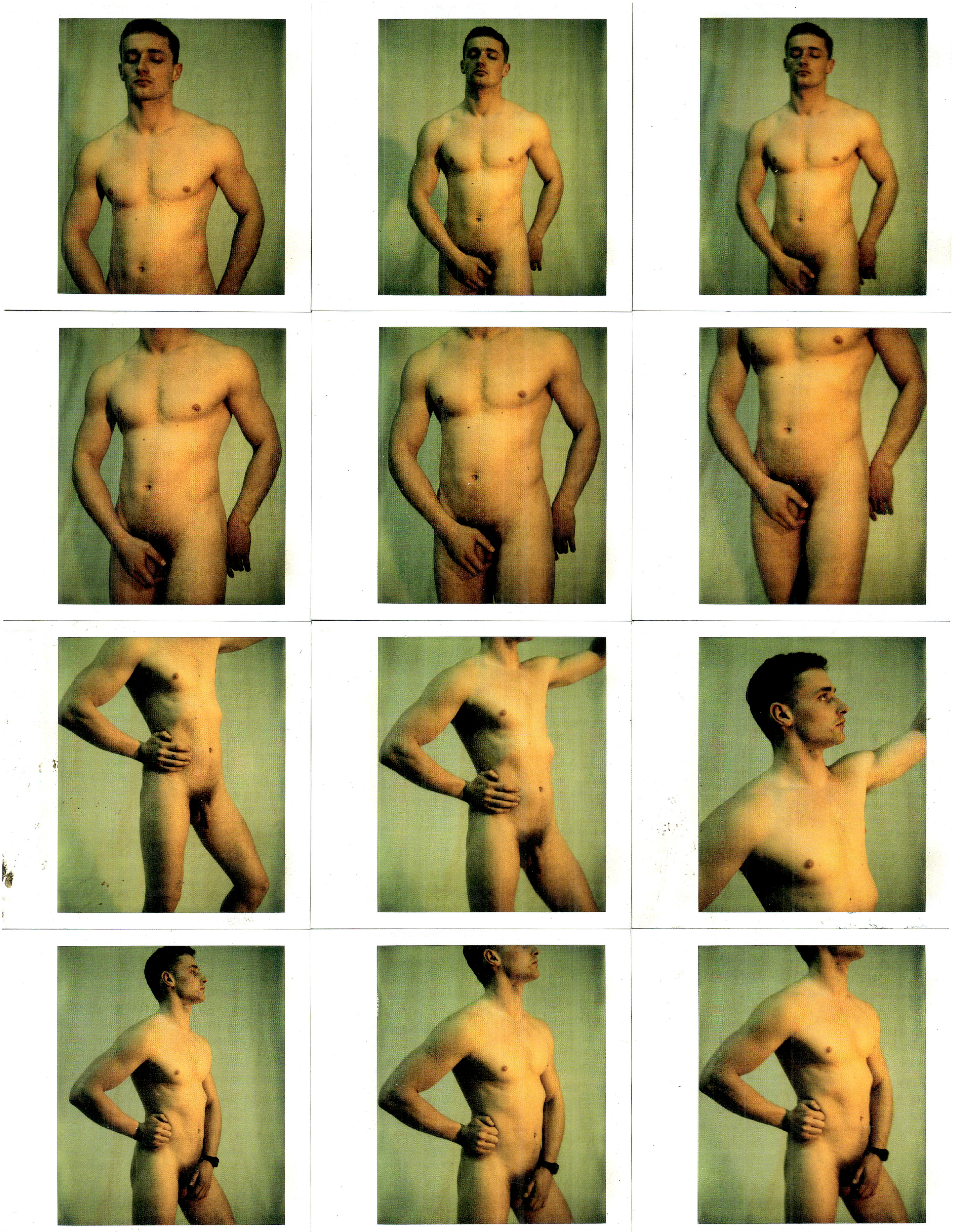

Study for *The Eternal Tea House*, Summer, Berlin, 1991

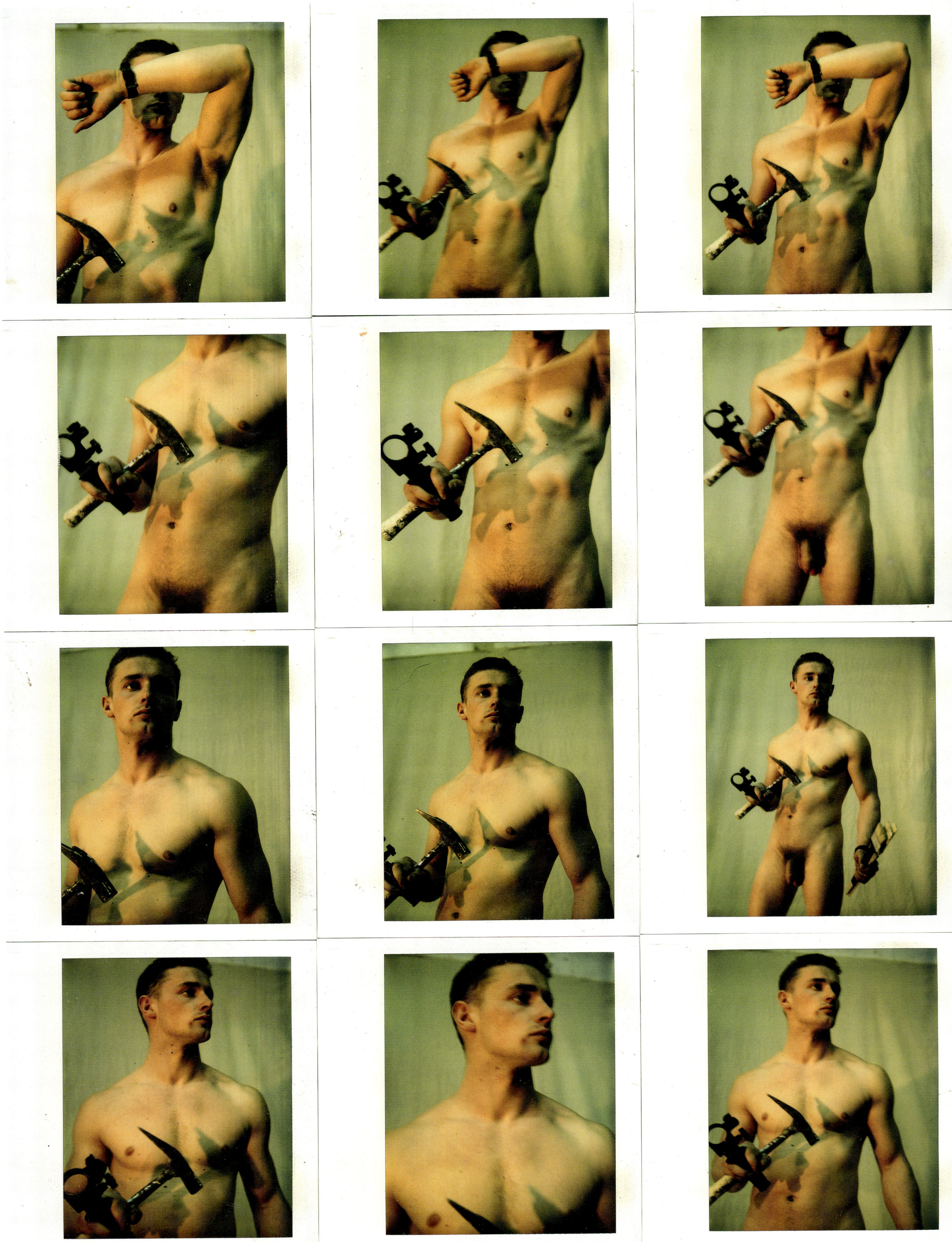

Study for *The Eternal Tea House*, Autumn, Berlin, 1991

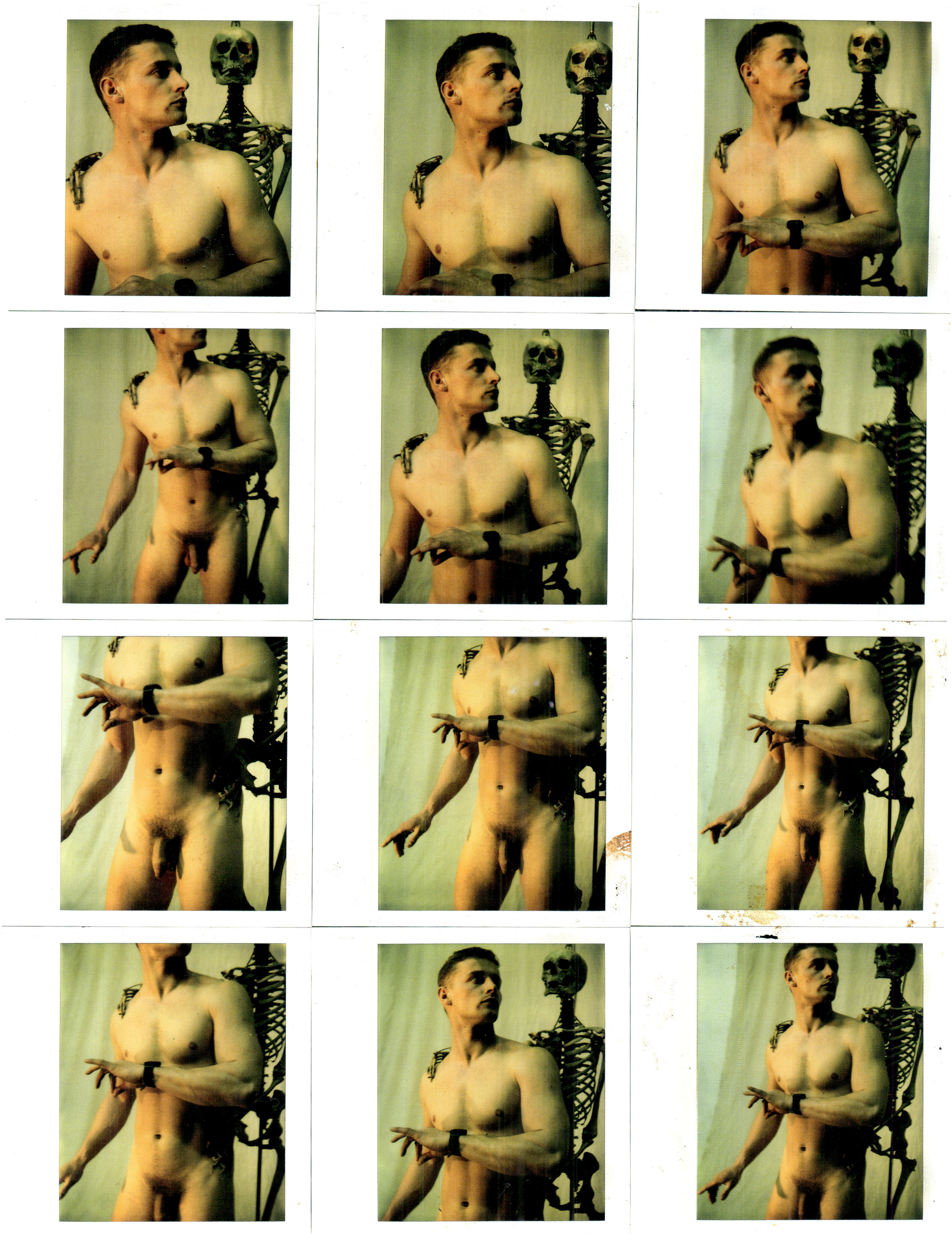

Study for *The Eternal Tea House*, Winter, Berlin, 1991

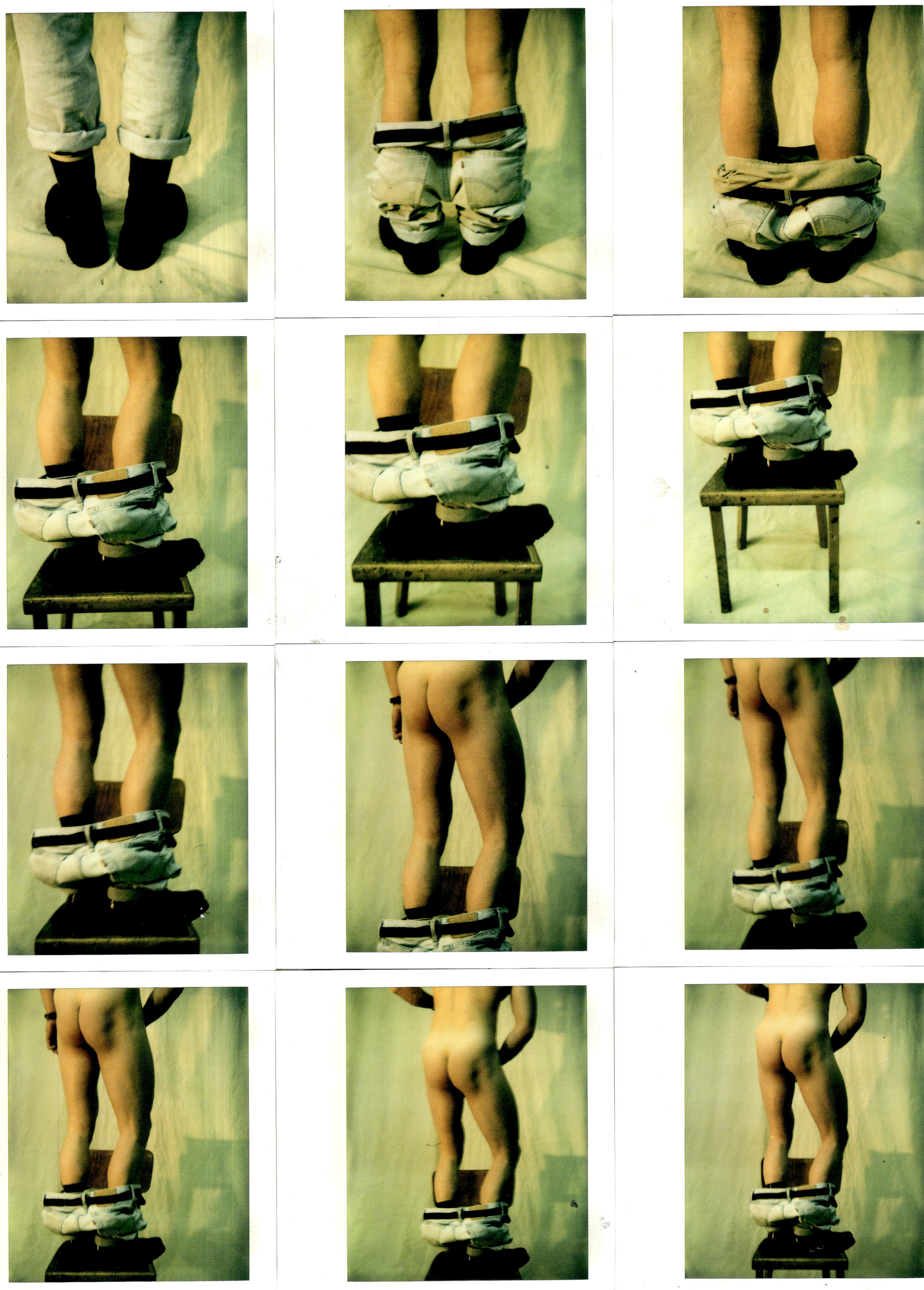

Christof, Berlin, 1991

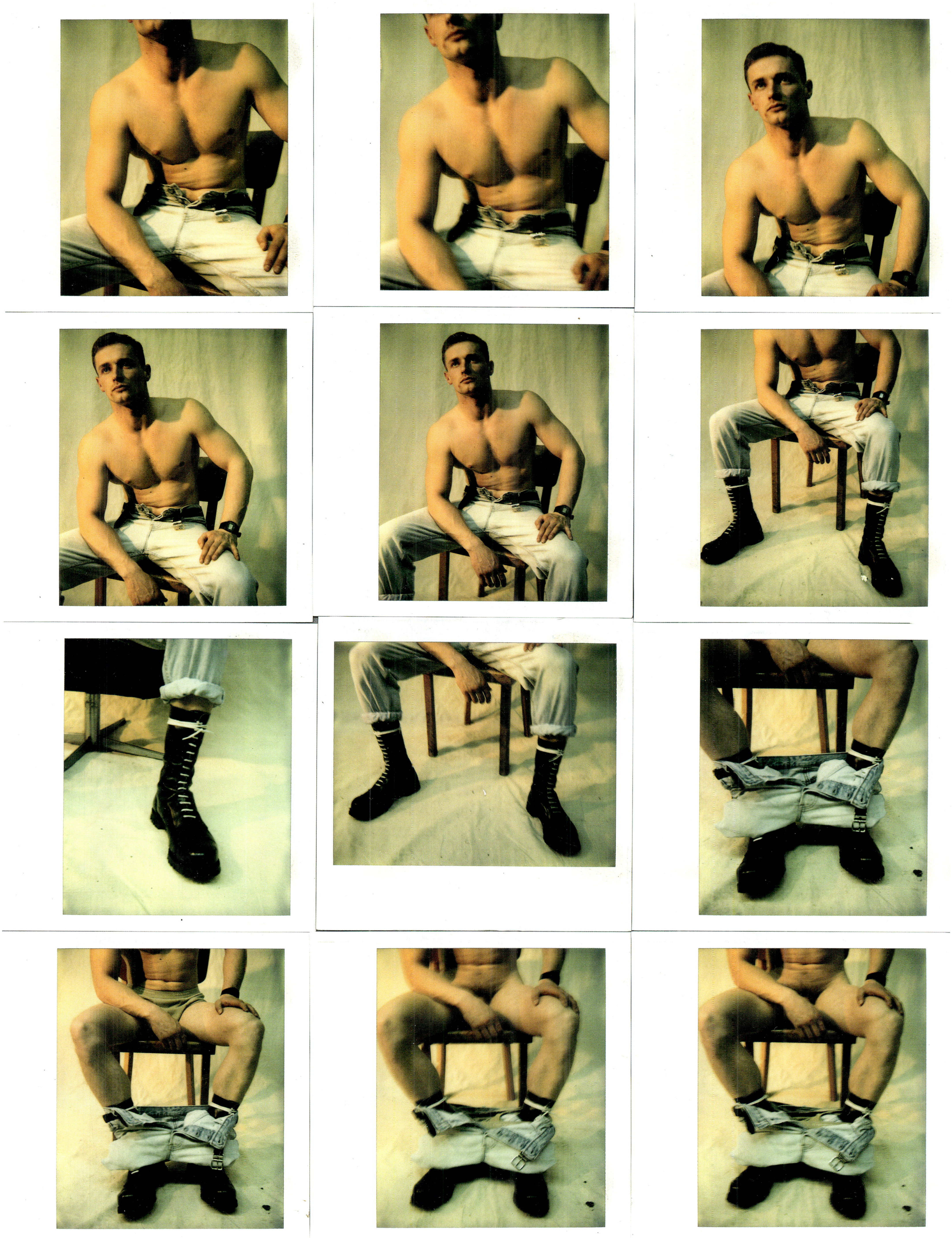

Christof, Berlin, 1991

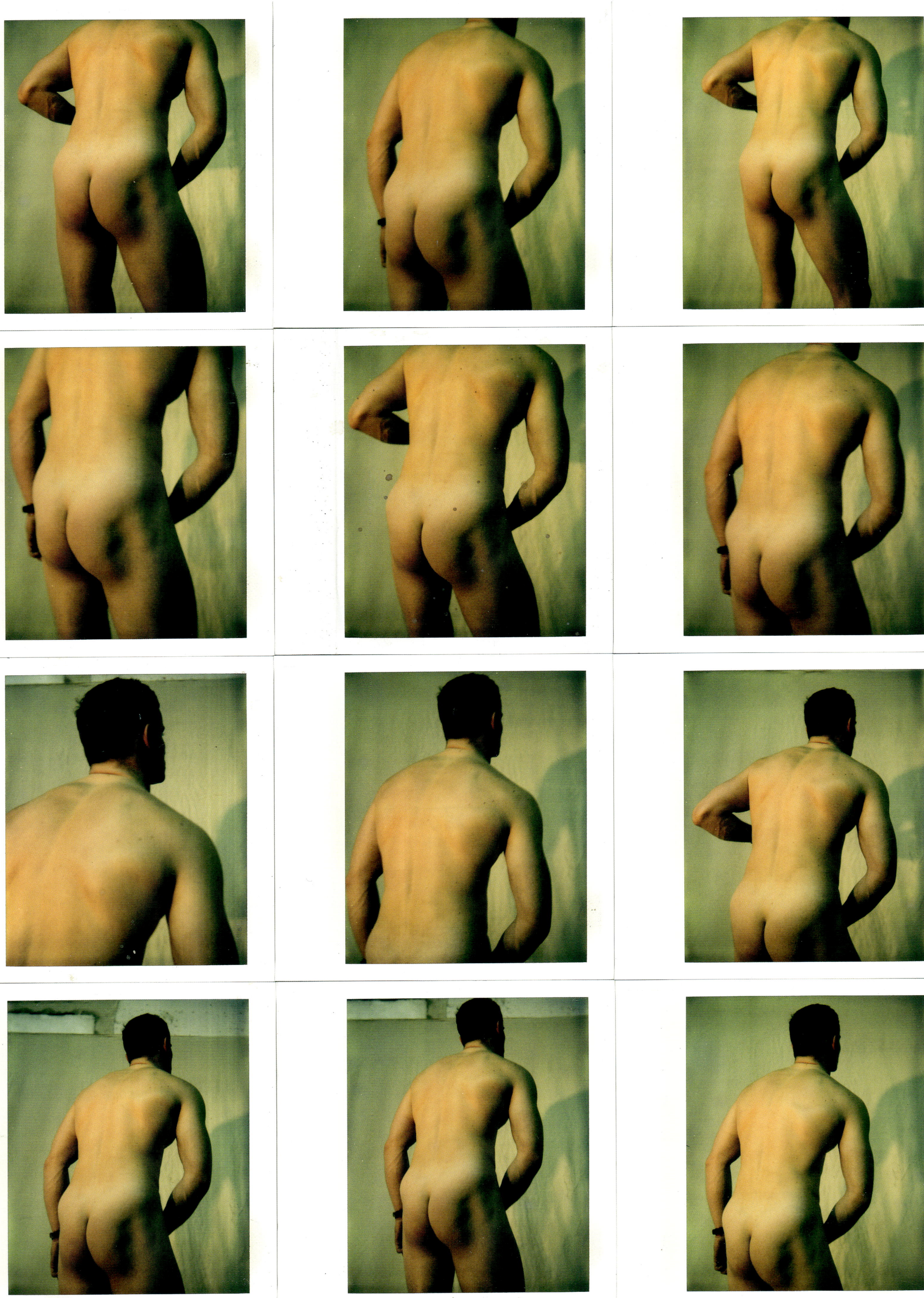

Christof, Berlin, 1991

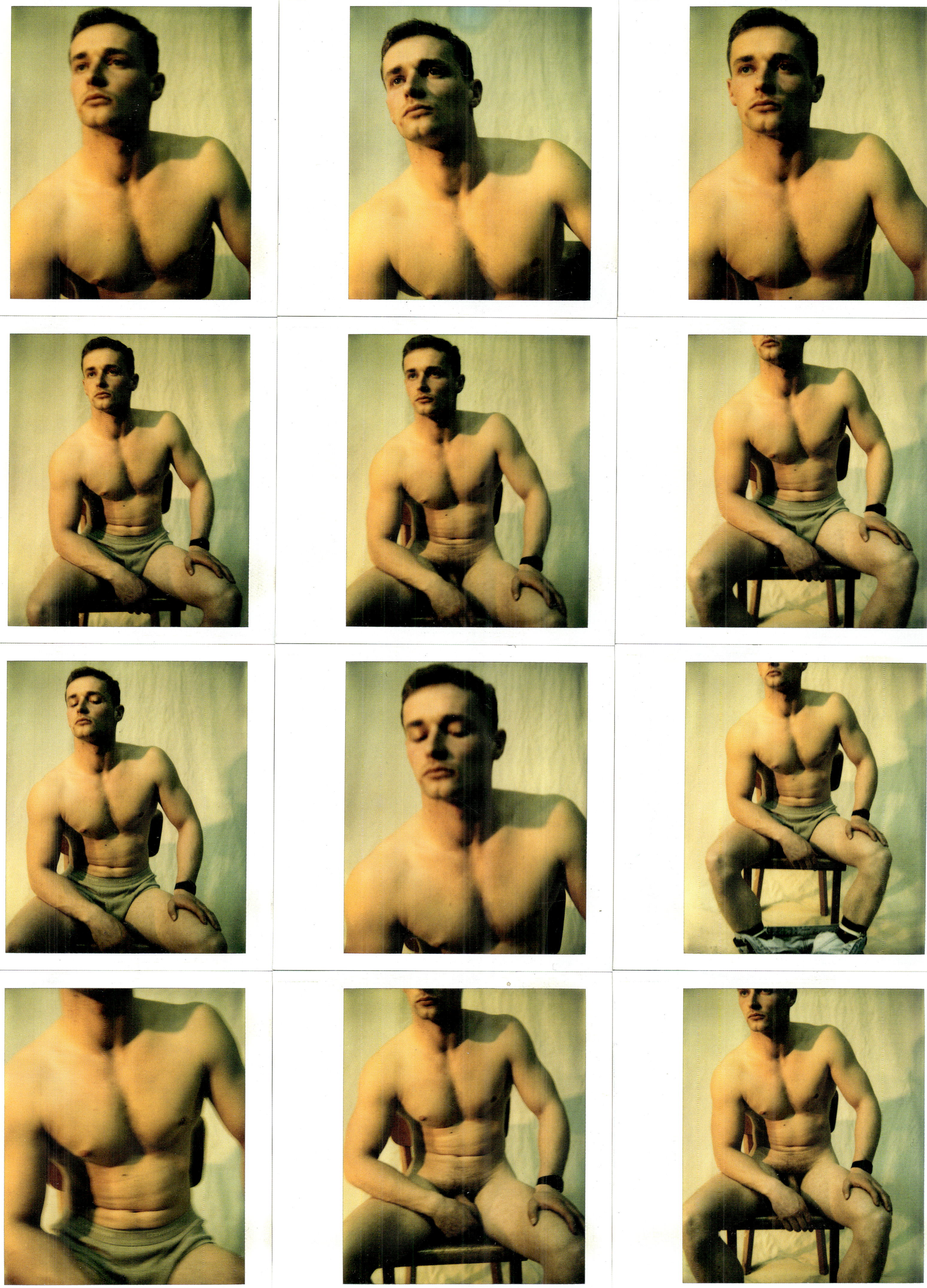

Christof, Berlin, 1991

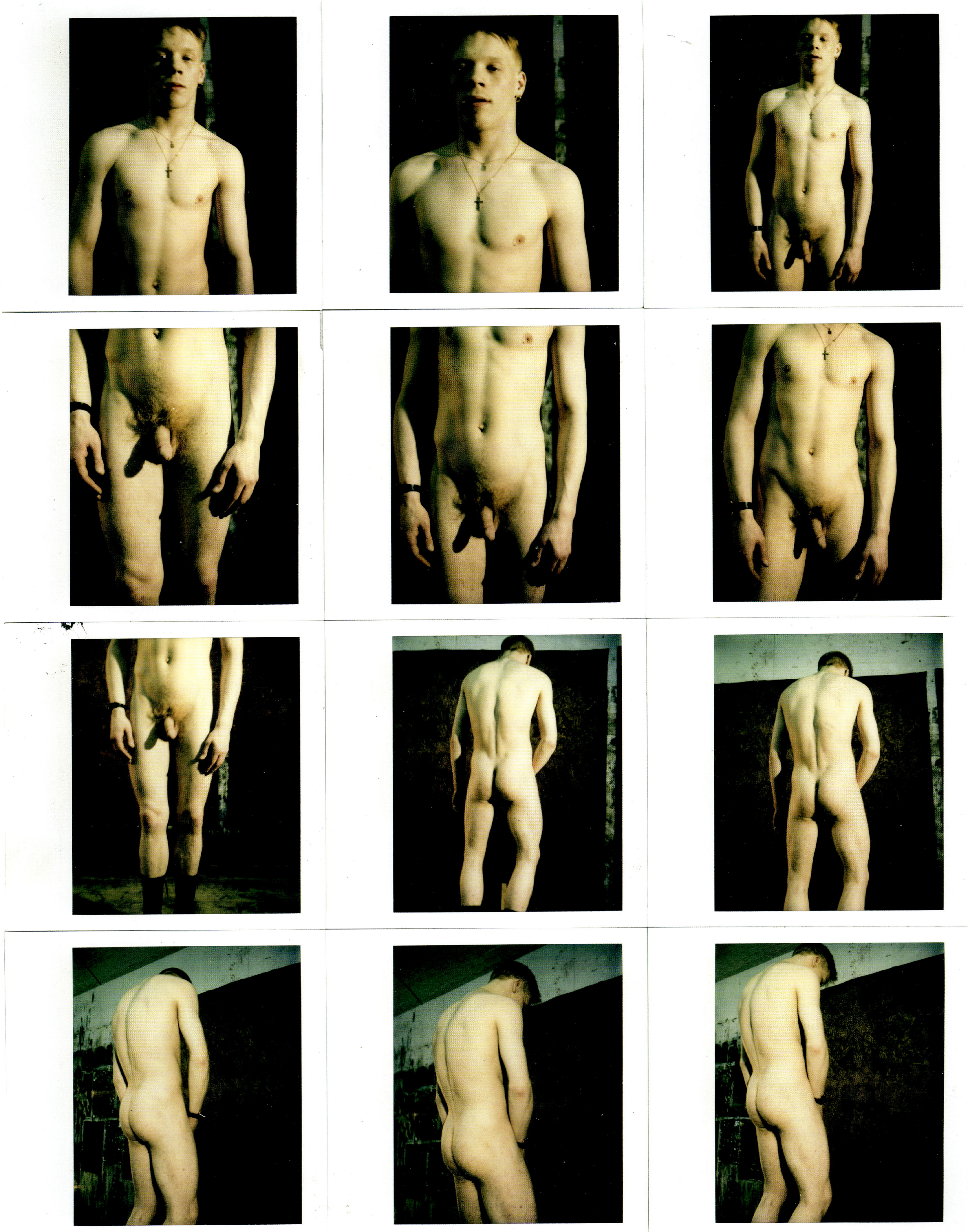

Zoo Boy, Berlin, 1991

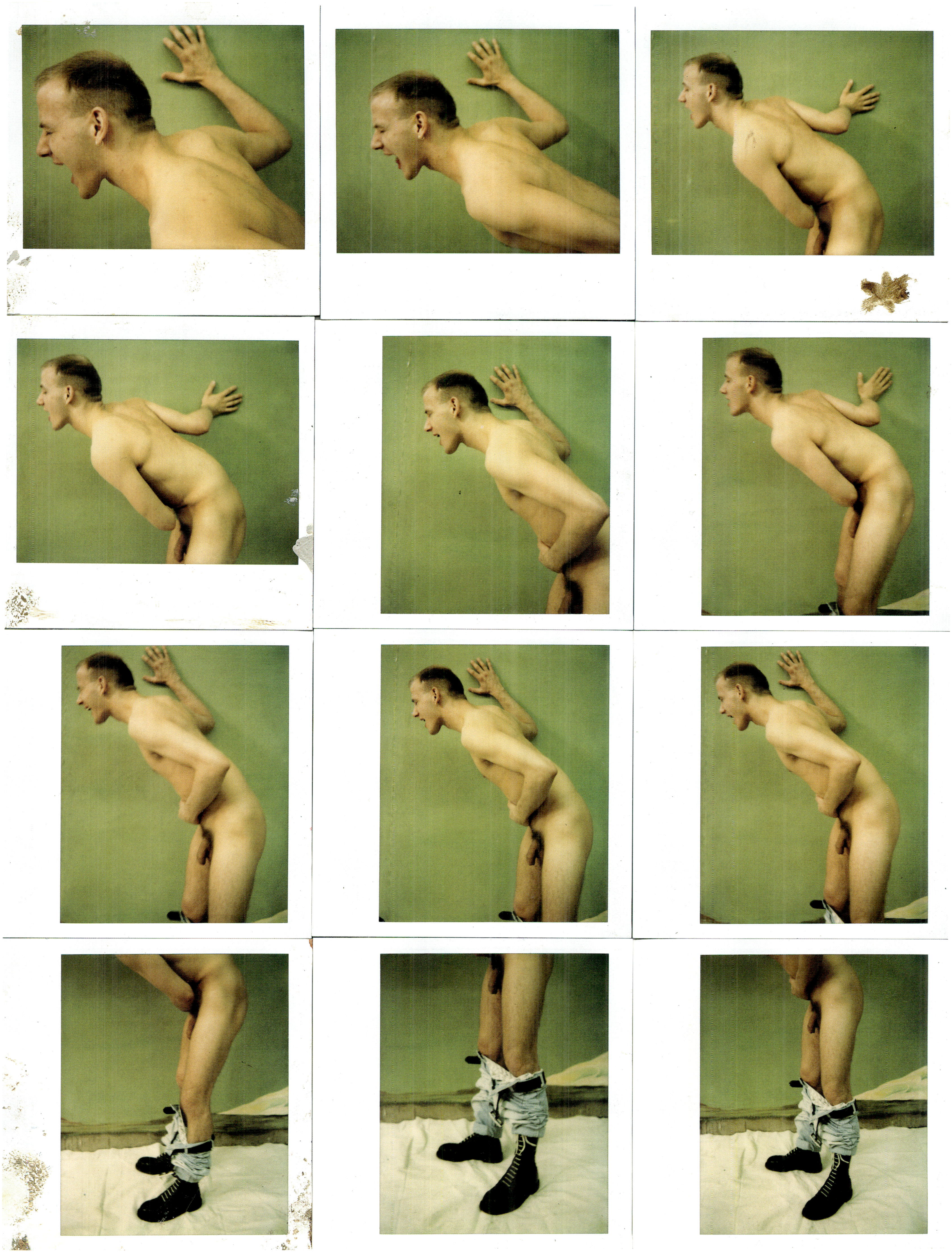

Stephan, Berlin, 1991

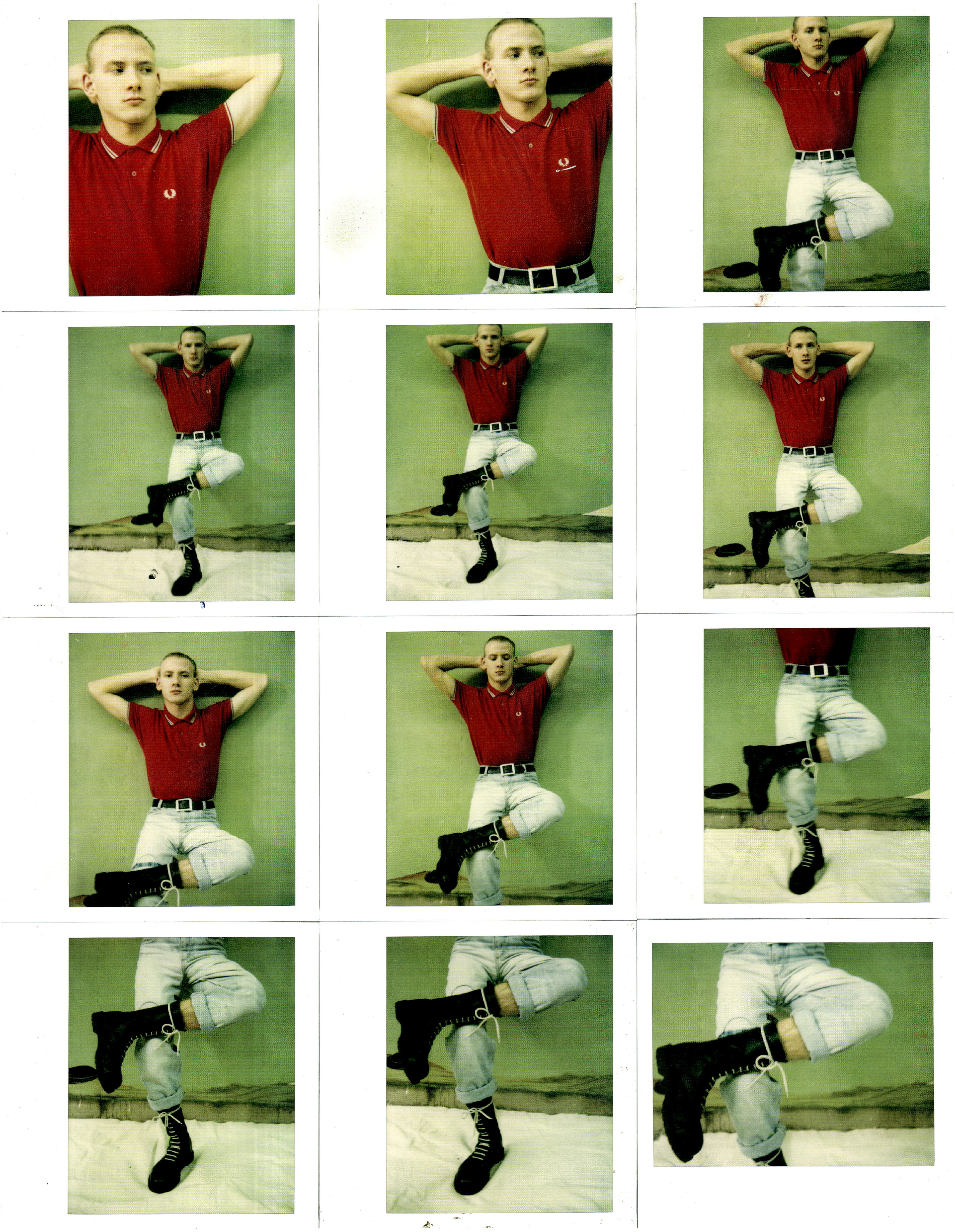

Everybody's Stephan, Berlin, 1990

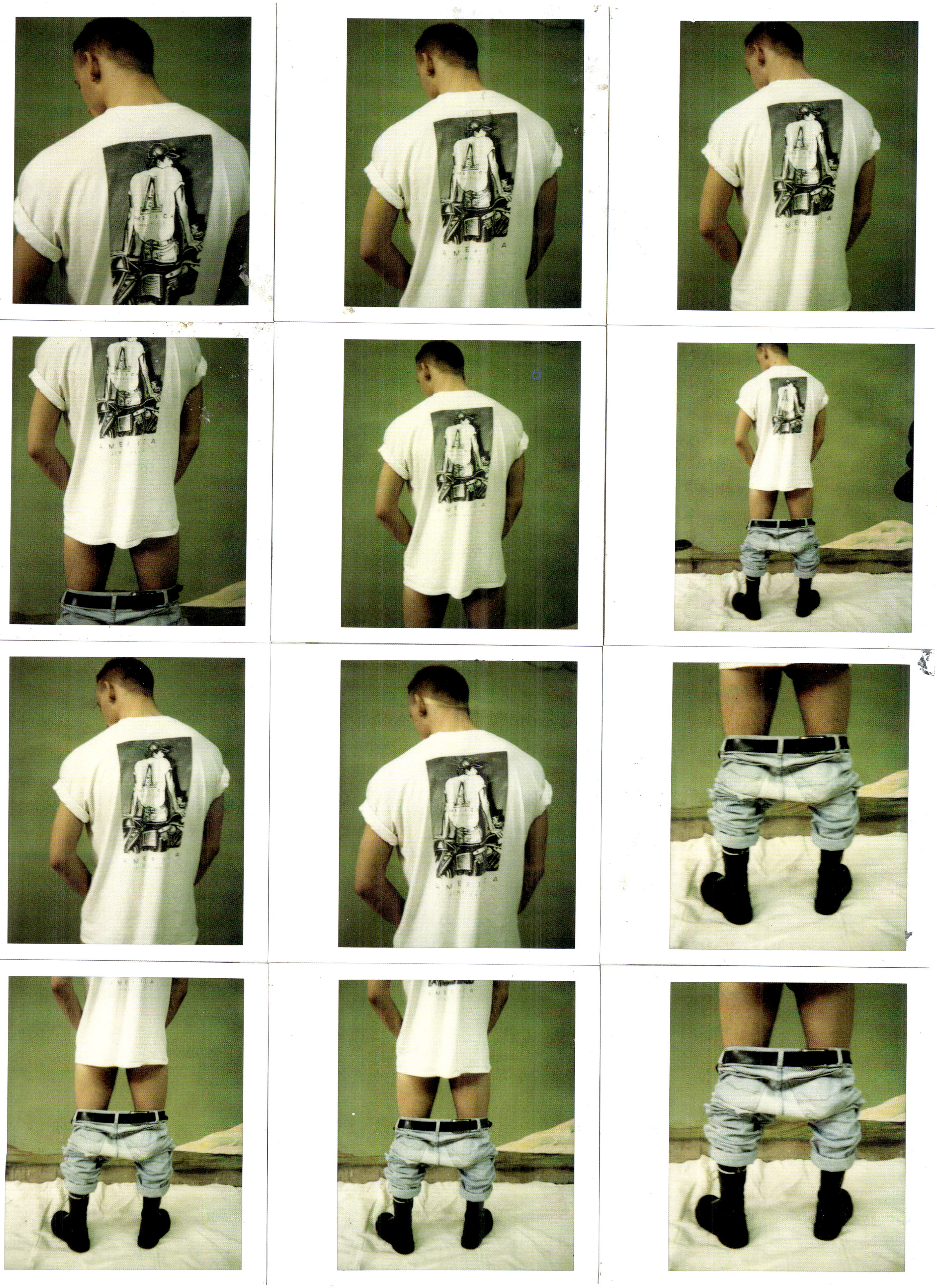

Everybody's Stephan, Berlin, 1990

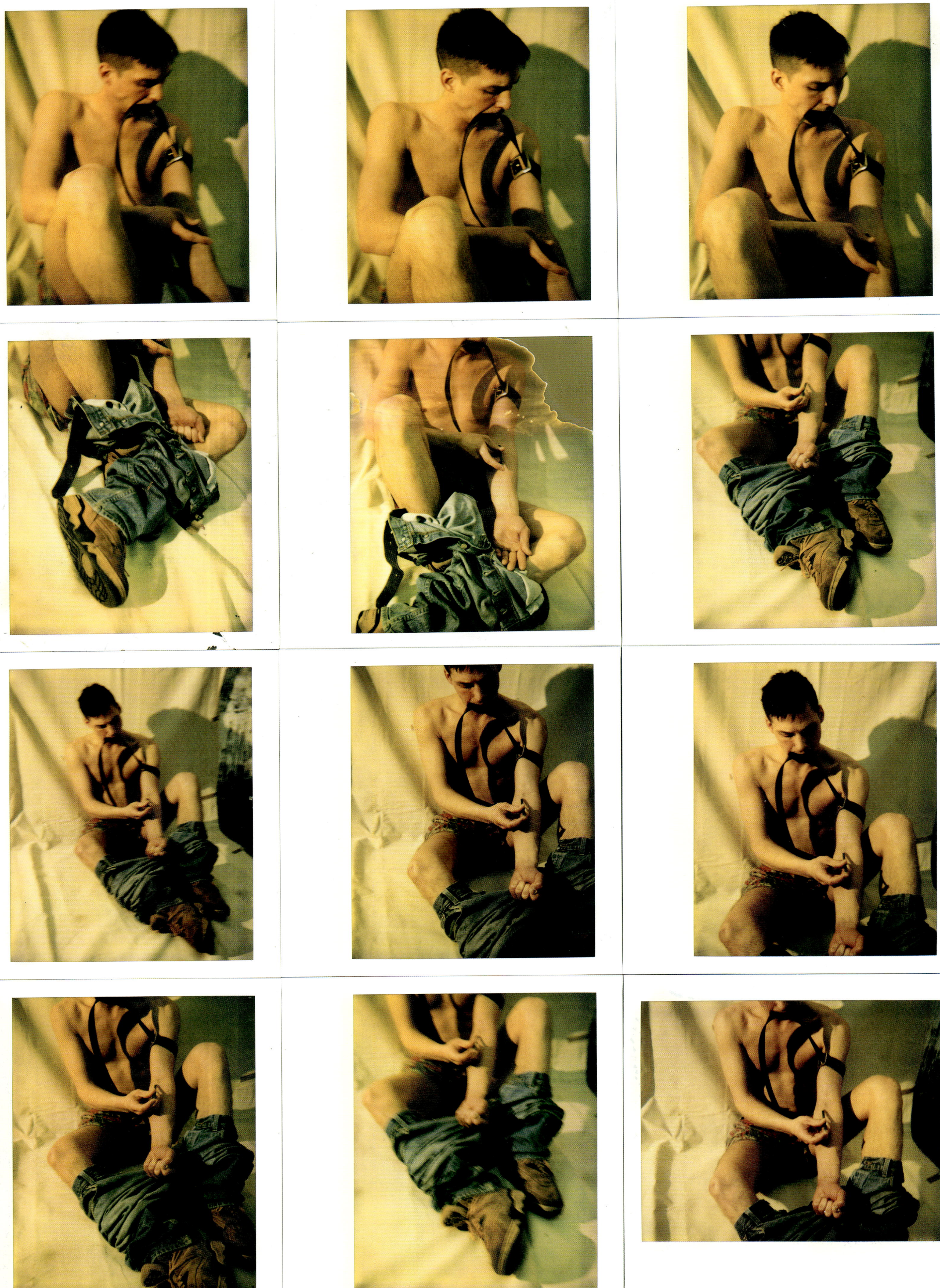

Tyler, Berlin, 1993

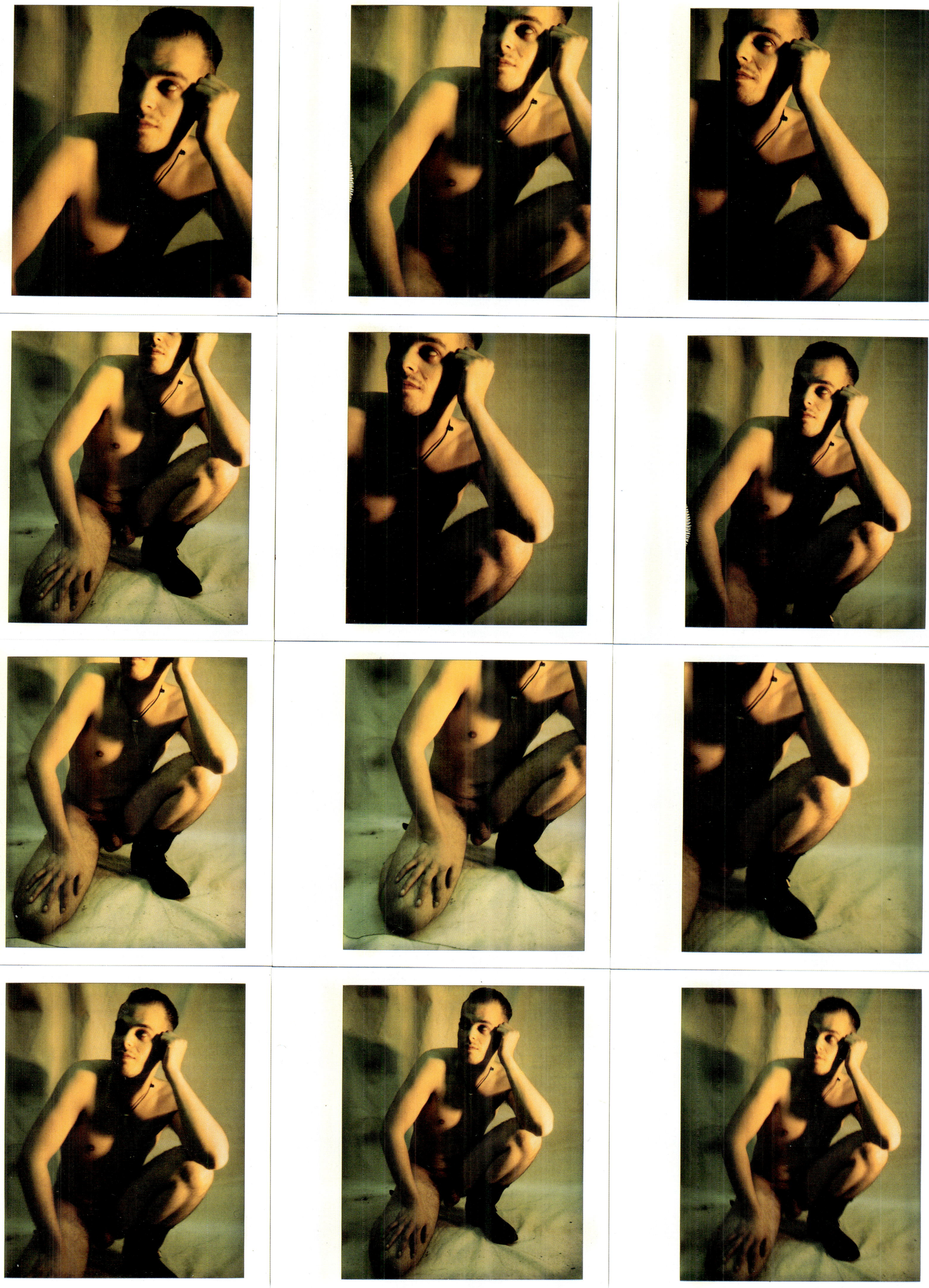

E-Werk, Alex, Berlin, 1993

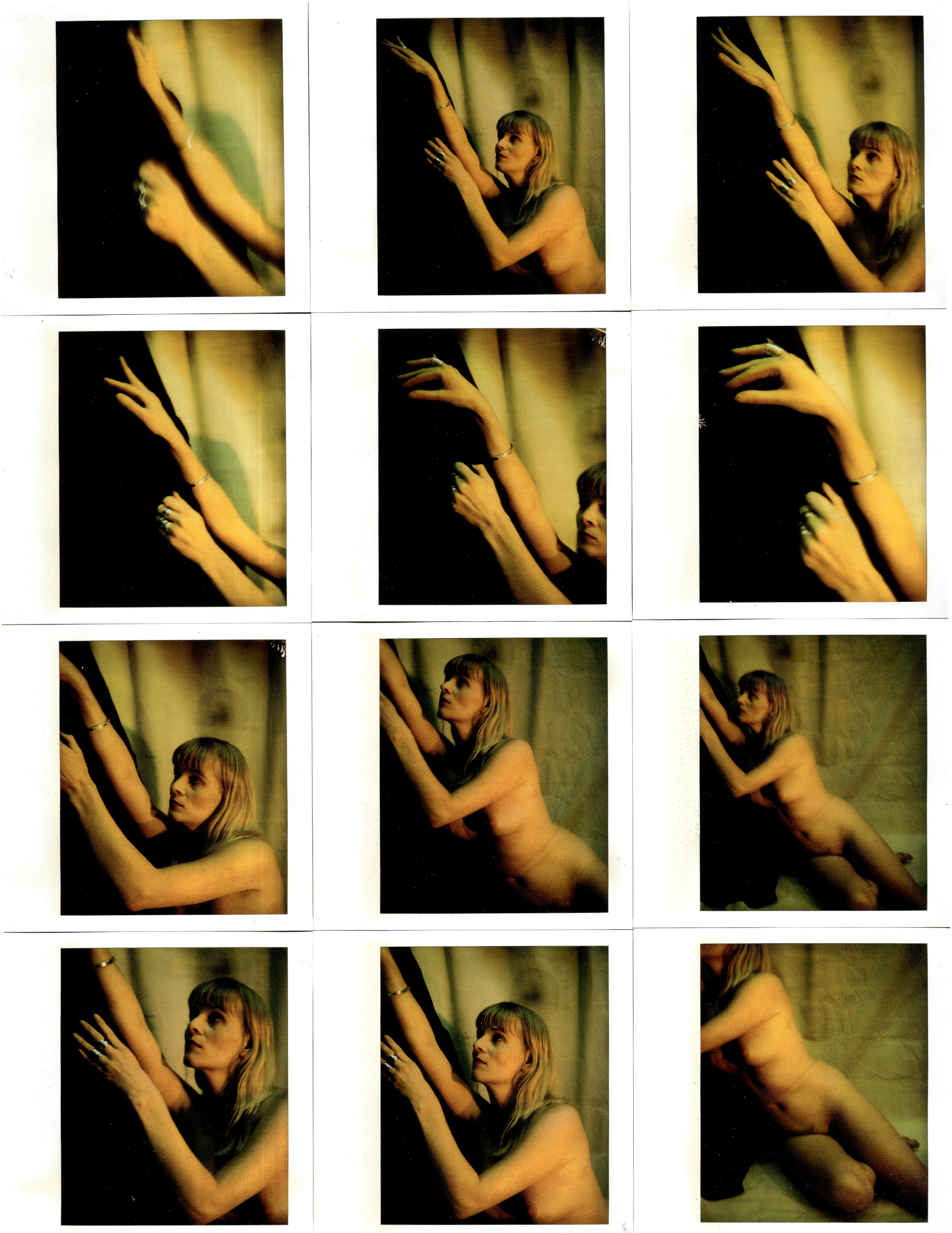

Hille, Berlin, 1993

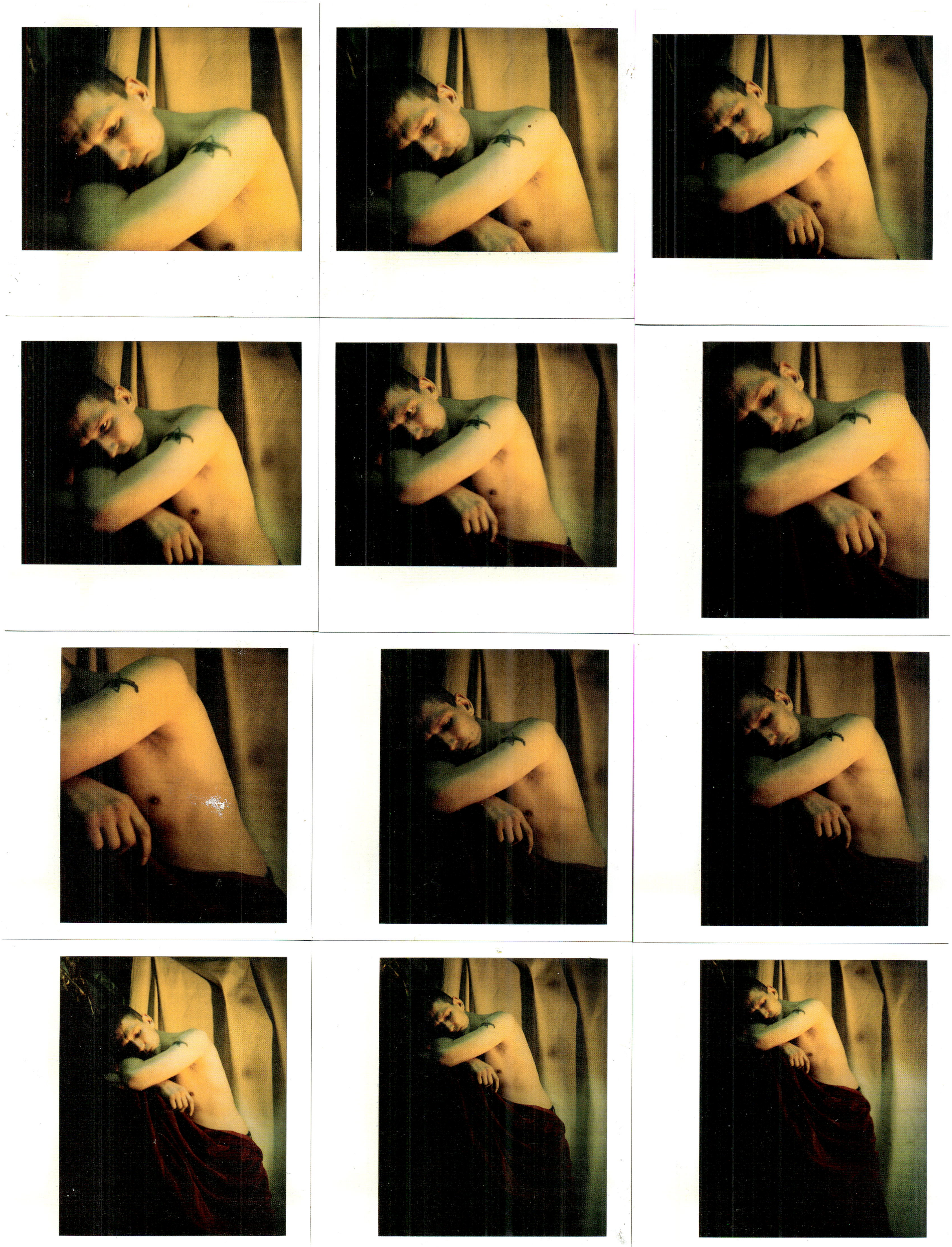

Andreas, Berlin, 1993

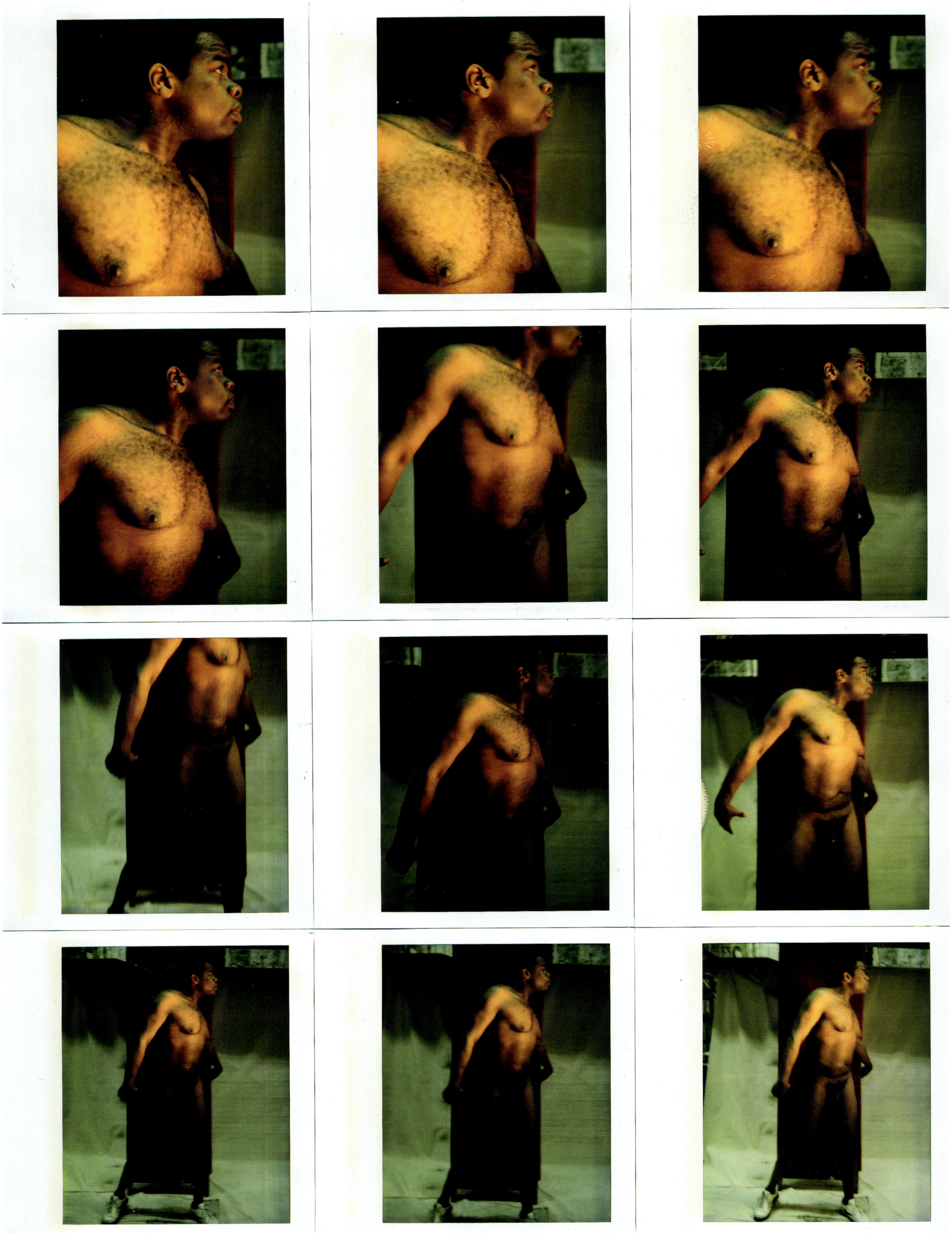

Mac, Berlin, 1993

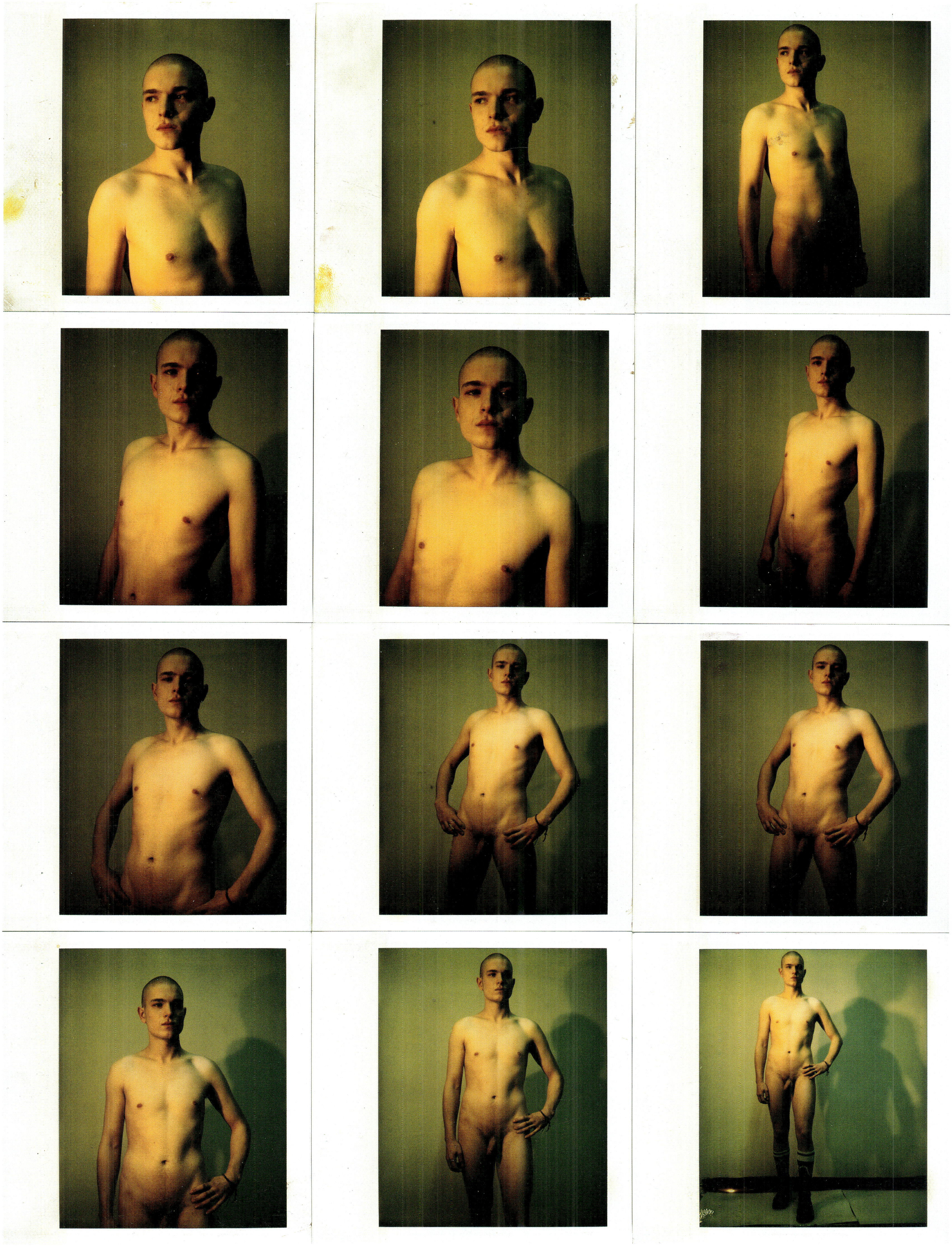

Eric, Berlin, 1993

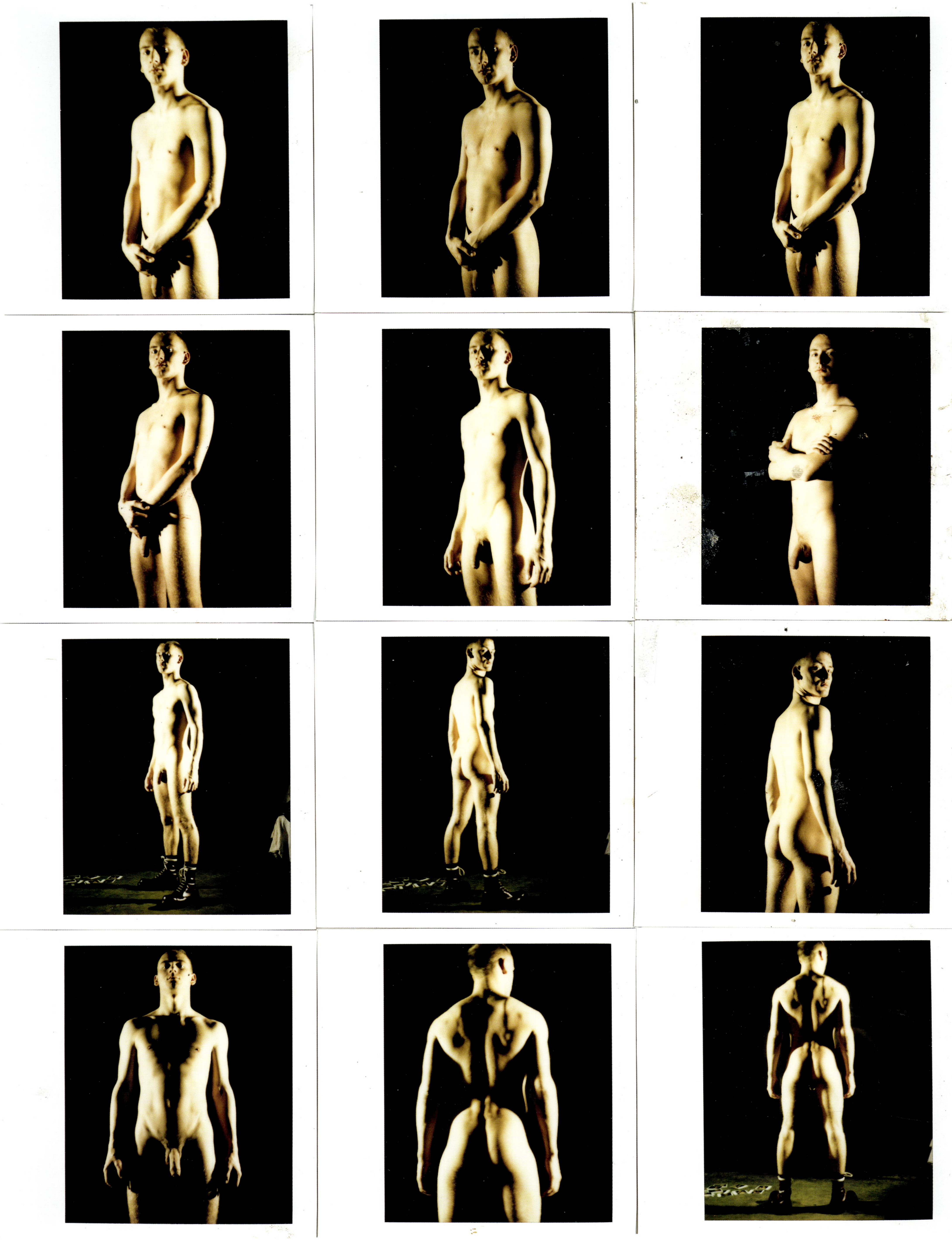

Stephan, Berlin, 1994

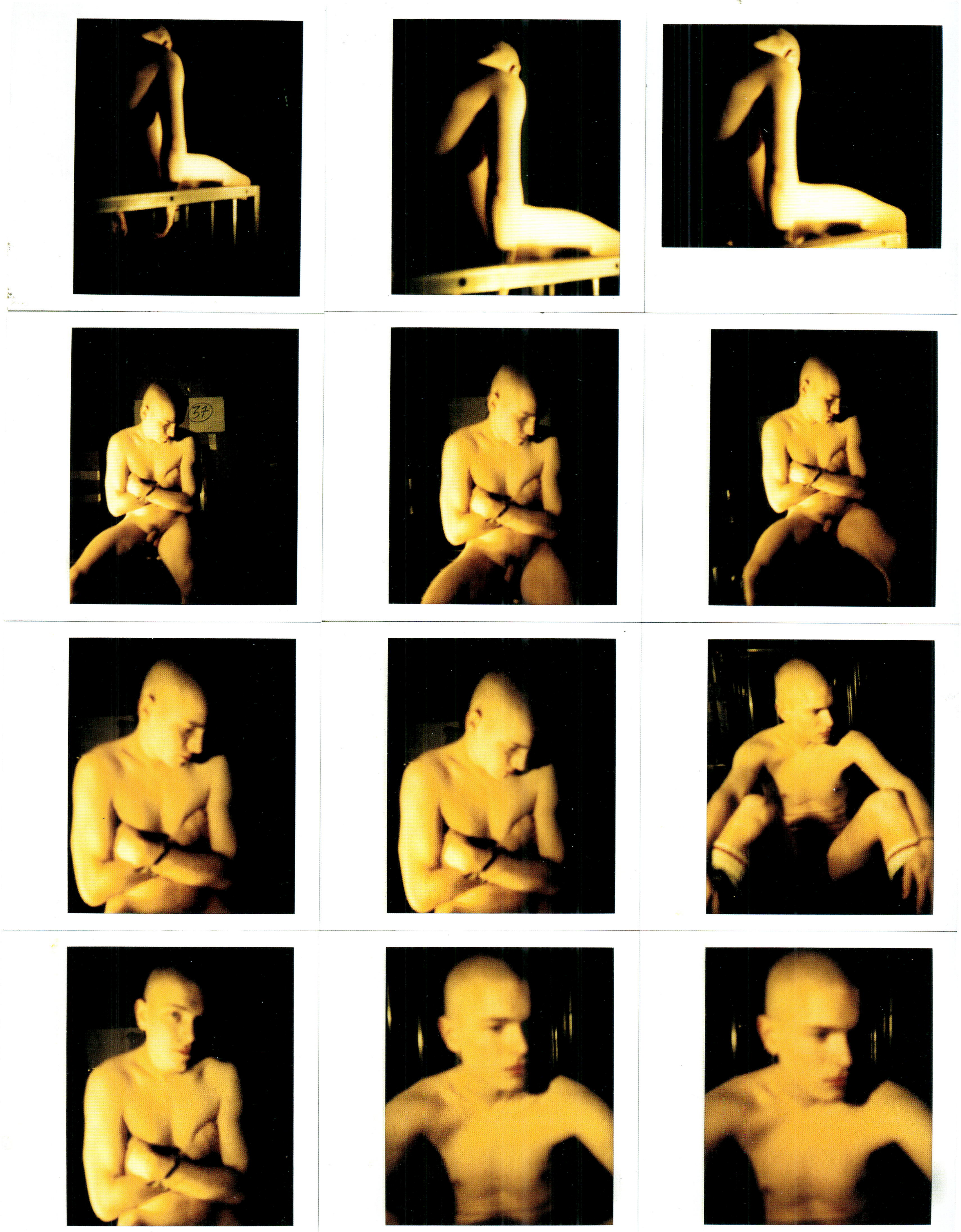

Eric, Berlin, 1994

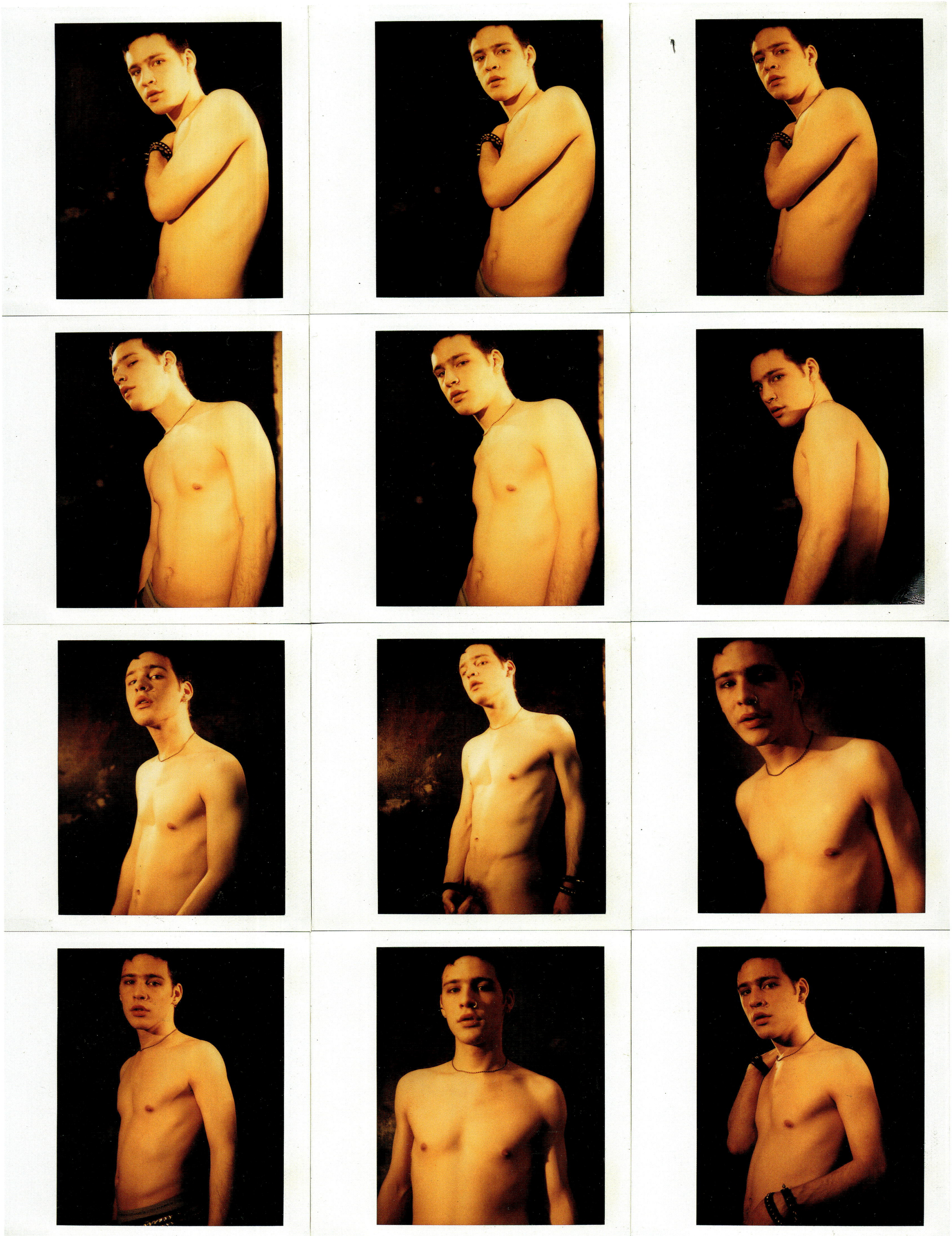

Boy for Bruce LaBruce Shoot, New York, 1998

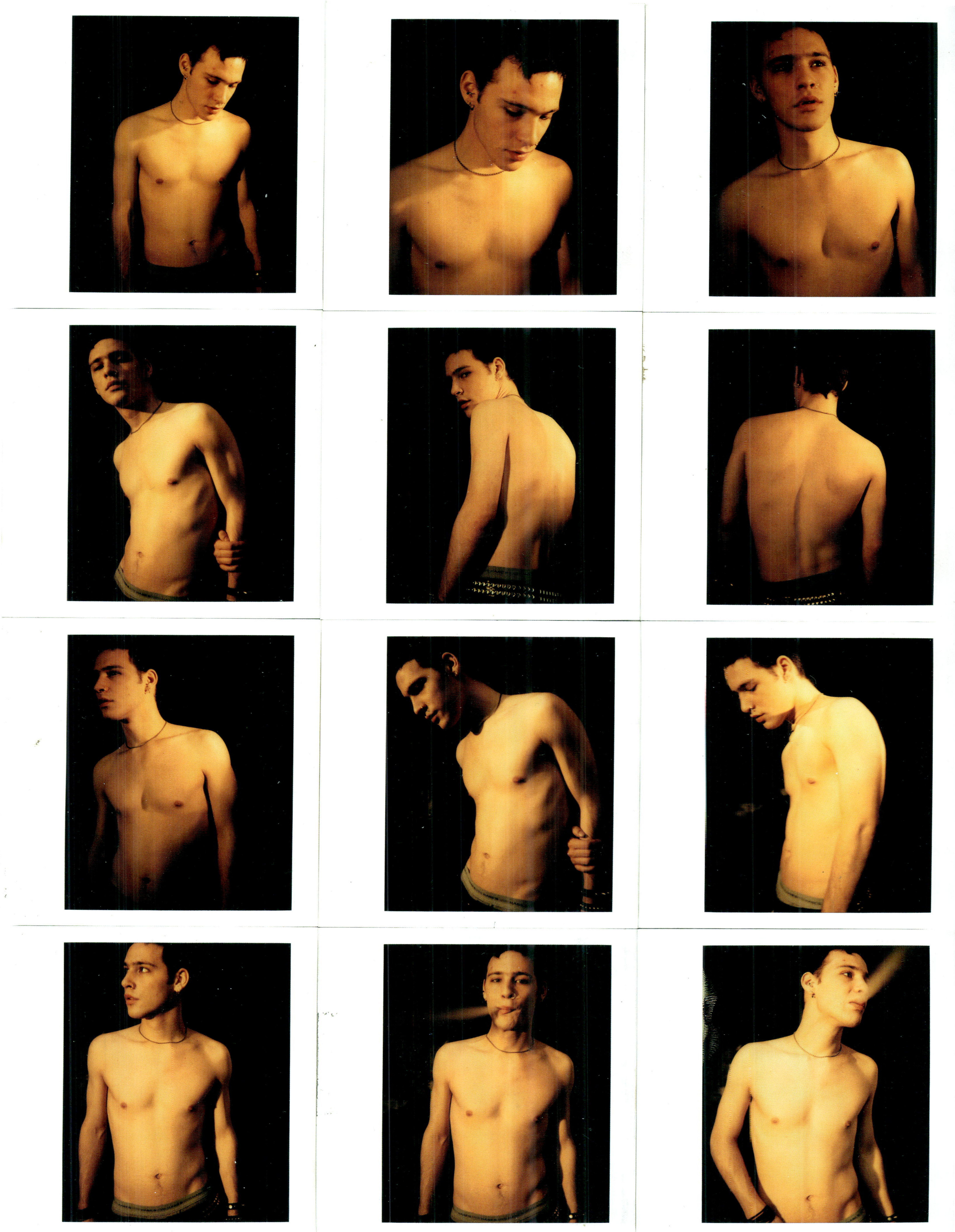

Boy for Bruce LaBruce Shoot, New York, 1998

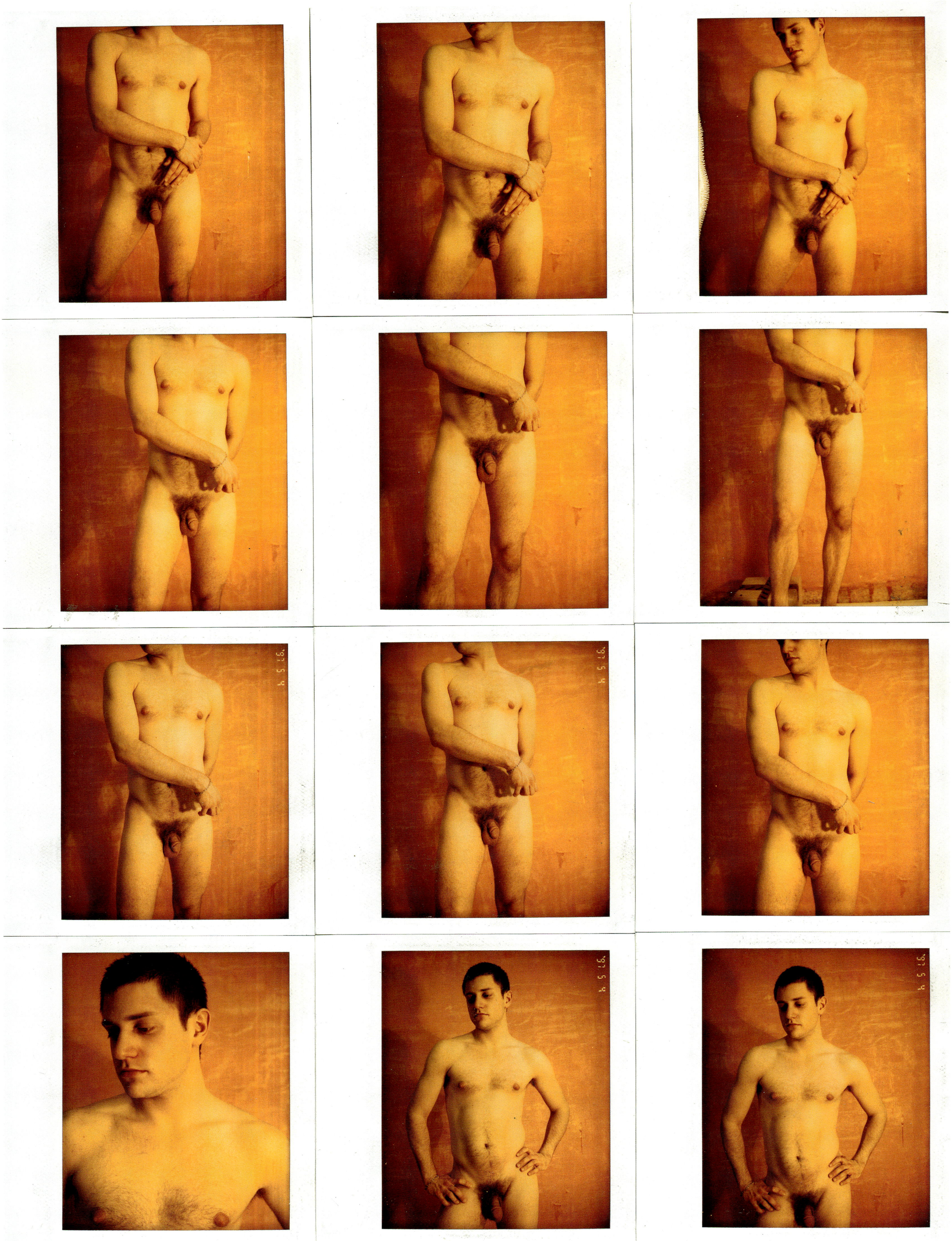

Joey, New York, 1996

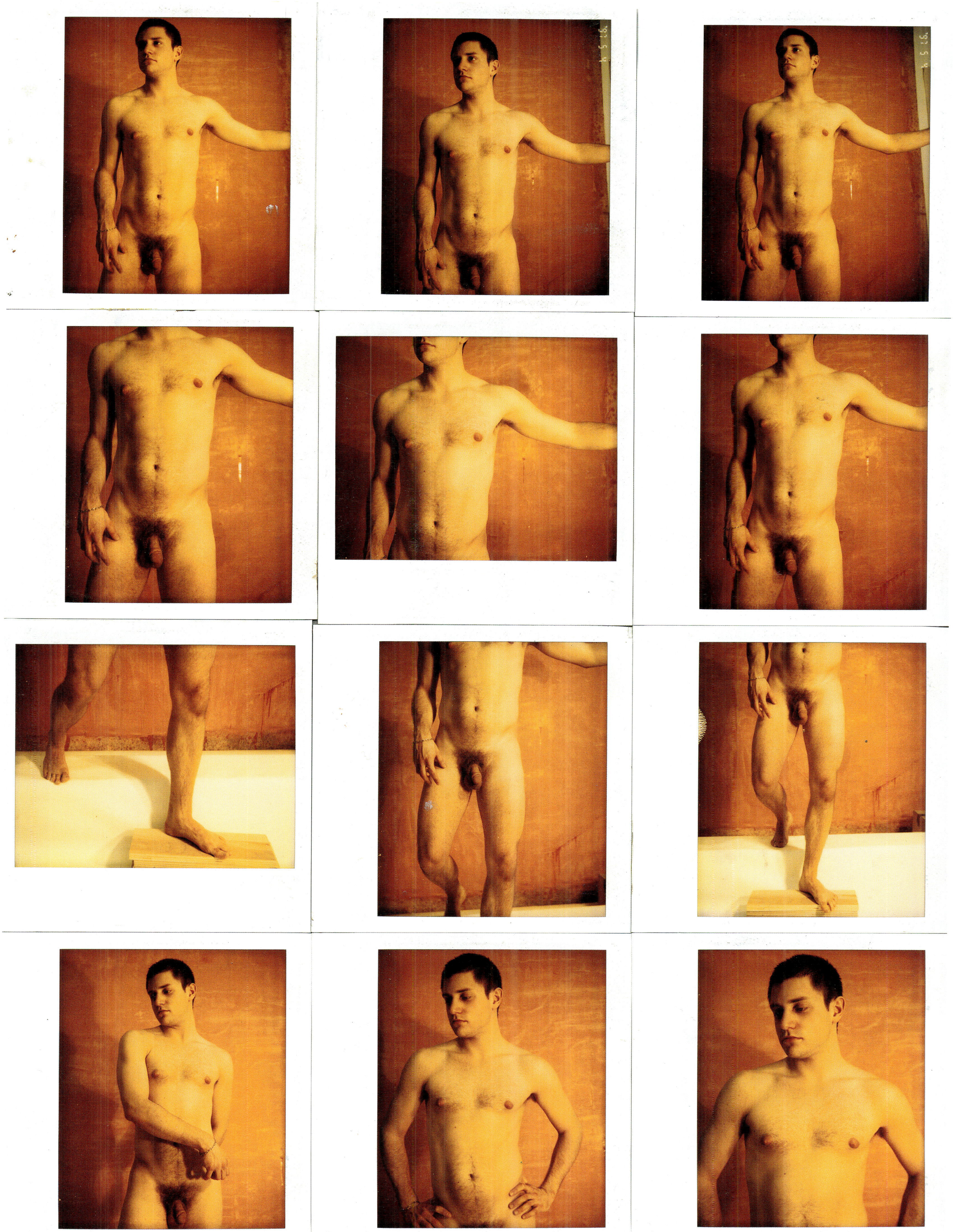

Joey, New York, 1996

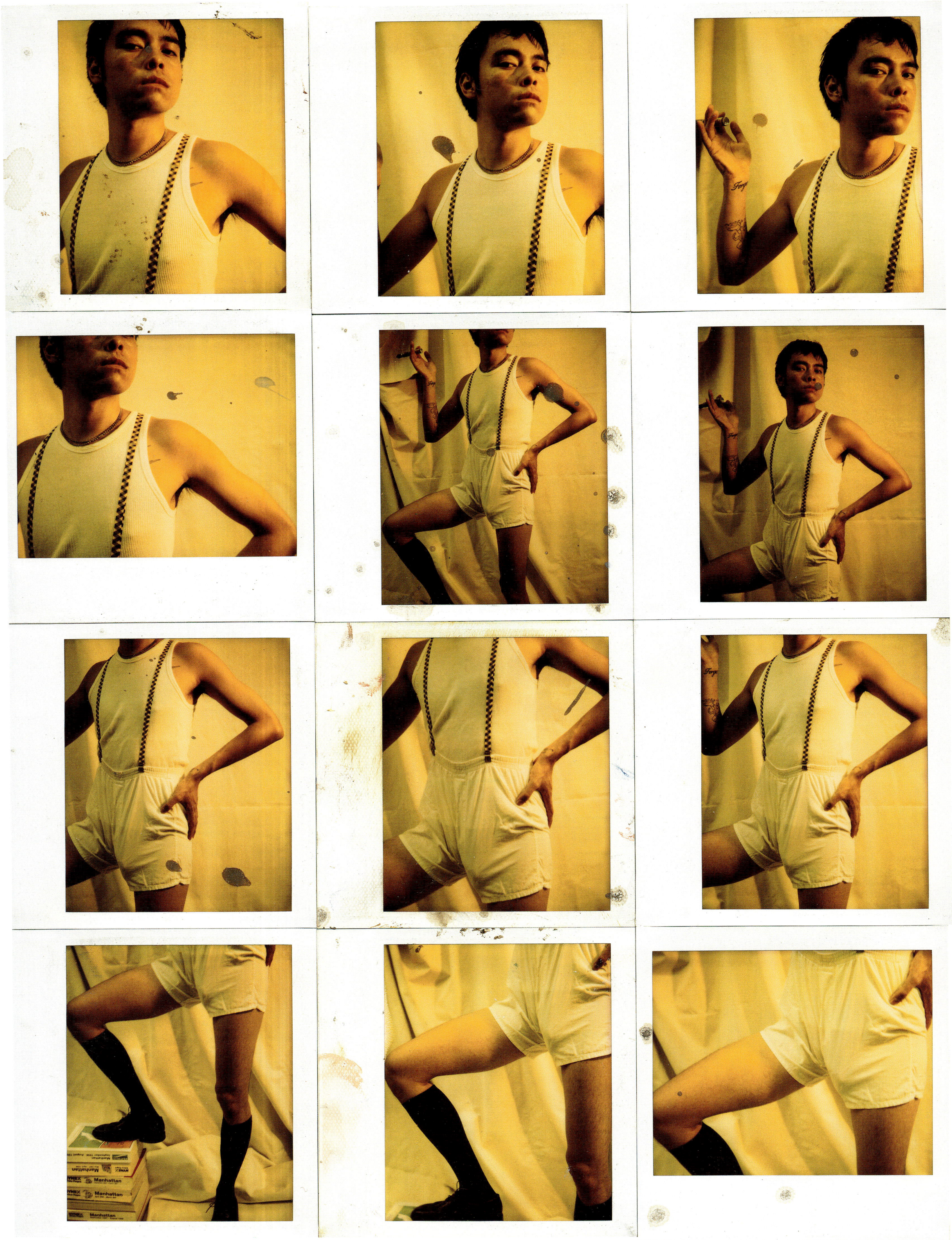

Ted, New York, 1997

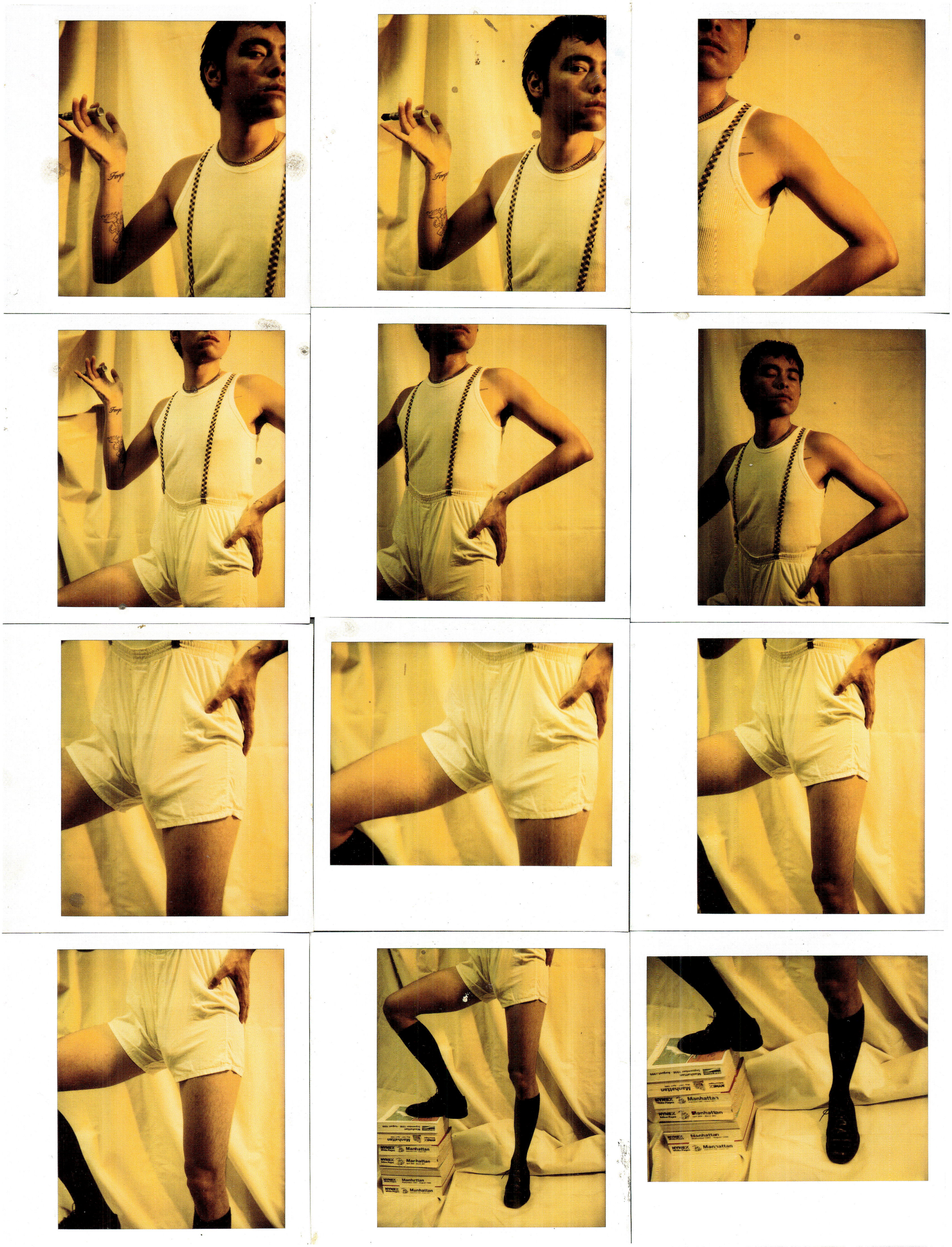

Ted, New York, 1997

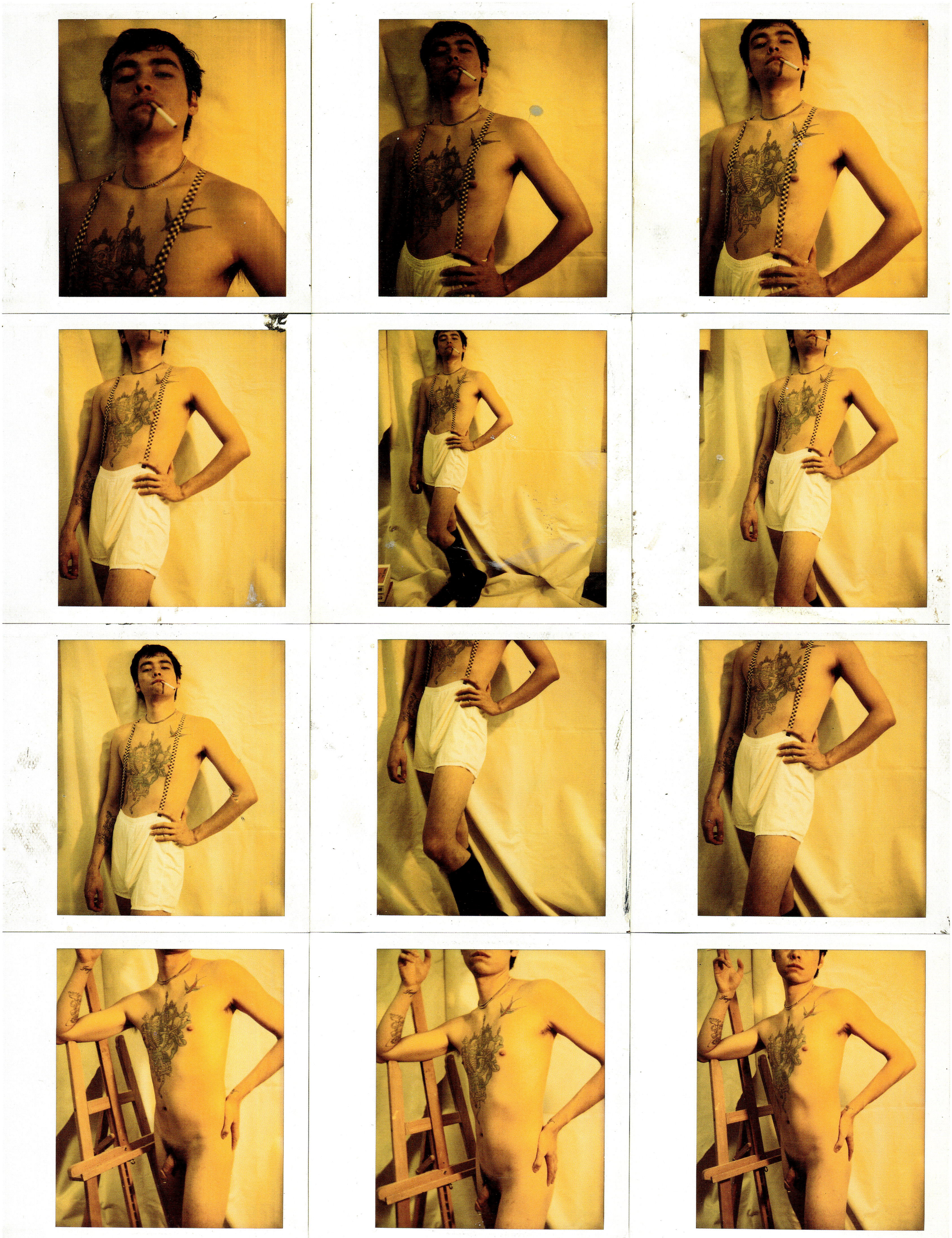

Ted, New York, 1997

An Interview with Attila Richard Lukacs

Vince Aletti

The following interview took place in New York on March 22, 2009, late on a sunny Sunday afternoon. Attila had arrived in New York on an overnight flight the day before and hadn't gotten much sleep because he'd already been out partying with friends. He looked a bit bleary-eyed at first and his voice was a little hoarse, but some green tea helped. Once he settled down, he leaned into the conversation with a mix of earnestness, enthusiasm, and wit that never flagged. Our conversation was frequently interrupted by his rasping laugh and the clinking of a long silver chain that swung from his belt.

V: What purpose did the Polaroids serve for you?

A: The very first time I started to use a Polaroid camera was just after graduating from art school in Vancouver in 1985, when I was looking for models for a painting I was doing. I was looking at art-historical references for those paintings.

V: What sort of references?

A: At the genesis of that project, I was working on a painting by Gustave Moreau. Those were my earliest experimental Polaroids. The Polaroids really got serious when I moved to Berlin in 1986, but my focus had shifted almost one hundred percent to Caravaggio. The Polaroid was good for me and my practice because it was an instant image. I wanted to use my own models, photograph them. But I was never very adept at camera technology, and I didn't like the idea of a waiting period, where you had to take the film in and you didn't know what was going on, and if it didn't work, you were screwed. Polaroid was that instant format, like digital is today; if they had digital then, I would have used it.

V: But wasn't it also satisfying to have an actual image on paper? Something you could handle?

A: Yes, it was perfect. I have to say today that I still feel that way, but I don't know if that's due to twenty years of the same thing. But I think Polaroid is still better; I do use my digital camera once in a while, but (a) it doesn't stay on very long and (b) the camera is precious and you don't want to throw it down on paint. The Polaroids, as you can see, some of them were thrown into the paint and have fingerprints and paint marks on them, and they're used and they're thrown here and thrown there. They're constantly there. If I was to weigh Polaroid twenty years ago and digital today, I'd still choose Polaroid. When I photographed those models with Polaroid, I knew how it was coming out; I knew what was coming.

V: Why did you prefer to use Polaroids—to photograph people—rather than paint from live models?

A: I think I realized that I couldn't use live models because I'd be asking them to do something that they wouldn't be interested in doing. I went to life classes in art school and I saw what the models had to do for an hour, and it's quite strenuous. And if you're going to ask someone to do that for an hour, you can't have every kind of pose, like in some of those art-historical references, which often involve action. It's just too strenuous to hold, unless you're propping them up somehow.

V: But you can do it bit by bit with Polaroids, by putting a model in a static pose and putting those individual pieces together?

A: I started very early on just photographing the whole figure and then sections of the figure—details, like how the hand would go into the elbow and the elbow into the shoulder, the head and neck into chest and the chest into the torso and the torso into the legs. And I'd divide them up that way, going from top to bottom: head, head/shoulder, shoulder/chest, chest/torso, torso/legs. And if you look at the Polaroids, that's kind of how they are, and they also go left to right, too: arm, shoulder, head, other shoulder, and arm.

V: So you have all the details and can piece them all together?

A: Piecing them together is the key part, because I realized early on when I tried to pose models from my art-historical references that it was quite impossible for people to bend that way.

V: Meaning the people in the paintings were in unrealistic or unnatural poses?

A: They look completely natural. The analogy is to a good ballet. The dance seems so easy, but the training part is so fucking hard. Some of those painters, they took a pose and they painted something and made it seem so fluid, but if you actually tried to put someone in that position, you'd almost have to dislocate hips or shoulders in order to get them to do that. So often I would exaggerate—well, not exaggerate—but I'd make them move in the pose to accommodate the movement I wanted in the composition. Like if they couldn't balance with their legs that far apart, then I'd come down to the legs and I'd do that part, where they could take the stance I was looking for. And then I'd put several Polaroids together into the form I wanted.

V: And then you could extrapolate from that Polaroid?

A: No, but I think the funny thing happened with Caravaggio and the Polaroid. Almost from the get-go, back in '86, when I started painting in Berlin and I was photographing my first model, Alex (which are some of the best of the Polaroids), I was photographing for three paintings, *Where the Finest Young Men,* and two other major pieces in that show. Just by coincidence, perhaps, the colour that Polaroid gave me of these models was pretty much identical to the palette of colours that Caravaggio was using. So I started using Caravaggio as a reference and using my Polaroids as a model—Caravaggio for composition, colour, lights and darks, how he would use darks in his background and flesh tones and everything. That was so similar to the Polaroid that the third thing that happened was that I developed my palette. And it took me about ten years to finally figure out my flesh palette. That's an important part because so much of my paintings are about flesh. Or the figure is prominent, as in the Italianate tradition, where the focus of the composition is full-front figurative, and not like the Flemish.

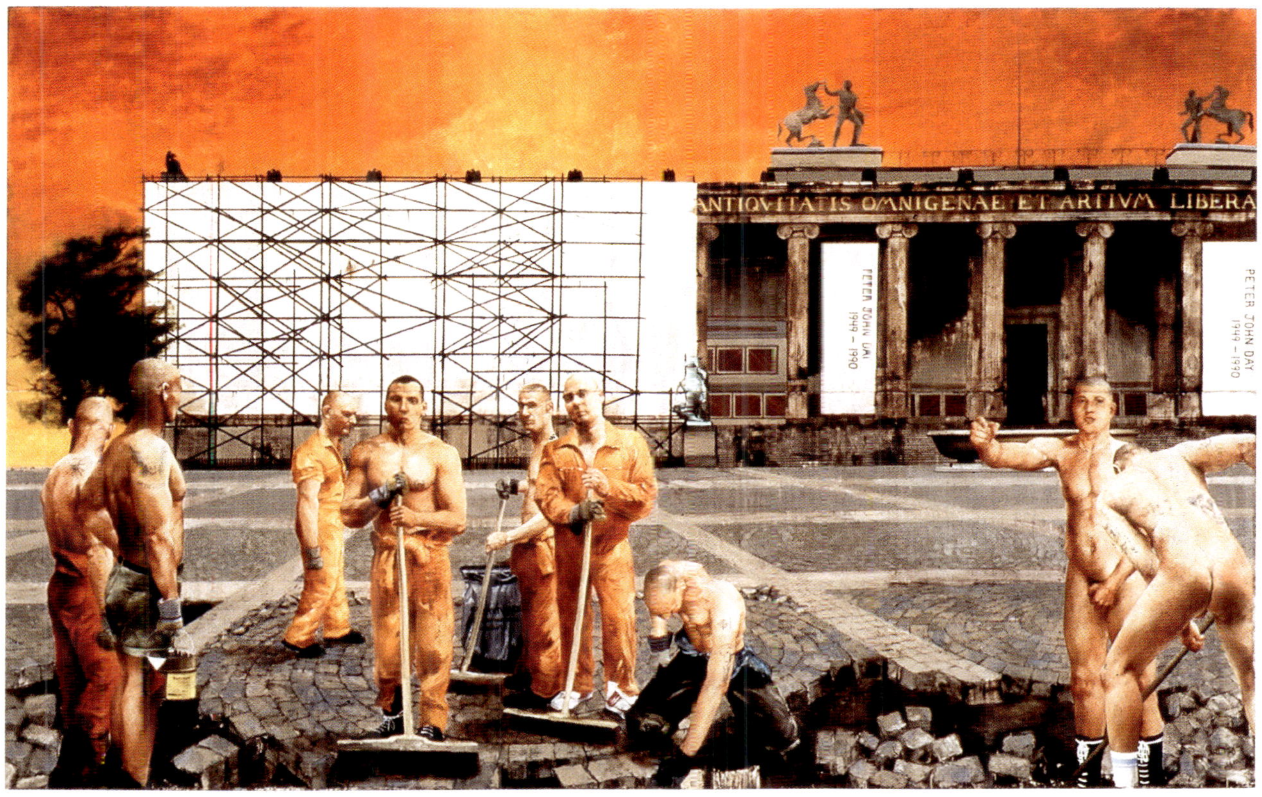

Attila Richard Lukacs, *This Town/Der Lustgarten*, 1990, oil on canvas, 390 x 609 cm, Collection of the Musée d'art contemporain de Montréal.

V: You're saying ten years after graduating from art school?

A: Well, ten years working with the Polaroid, when I was trying to figure out different techniques and how to lay down the figure—what would be most accommodating to the materials I had, the references I had, and my working pattern. What would work best: which kind of layering; what kind of materials, enamel, oil, varathanes, tints. First, because I was poor, living on a grant in Berlin, I started using hardware-store paints, enamels and stuff, things that would go far. When you can afford paint, you have to change over your materials, so you're constantly changing.

V: As you were able to afford better materials, you would change your approach?

A: Yes. As I was working more with oil paints instead of house enamels and varathanes, which a lot of those earlier paintings were made from. Like *Where the Finest Young Men*—there's very little actual artist's oil paint in it. I also started to expand my palette, get to know the colours, get to know the browns. And not just use them in the way I was using the paint previously, but I started to work with putting down a green undercoating to the figure. And that came about the time I moved to New York. Just before I left Berlin for New York, for about a year there I was experimenting with the transition, going from laying down a classical under-painting, either an ochre, burnt sienna, or a green. I used chrome green—that's what I settled on. This was about the ten-year phase.

V: You were in Berlin for how long?

A: Ten years. Then I came to New York for five years. During those five years I was really working on still figuring out how to paint that material. But the point is my palette had developed according to the Polaroid, the lighting of the Polaroid.

V: That's really fascinating—that you were able to combine the old master colouring that you had started with and the colour of the Polaroid that had become more and more important to your working process.

A: Which wasn't always so easy, because sometimes you'd get a bad batch of film, so sometimes it would be too green, too yellow, or too orange. Too orange happens a lot. But somehow you work it all out.

V: I would imagine that it would all become so familiar that you could adjust in your head what you're looking for.

A: Yes, it's just filters.

V: I was curious about how you used the Polaroids as raw material.

A: The Polaroids were the practical end of it. The models were the other end of it.

V: Clearly you had a very strong idea of how the models should look and how that would affect the outcome of the pictures.

A: The interesting thing to me about Caravaggio is that he was probably the first modernist. He was the first artist to populate his paintings and depictions of martyrs and Biblical scenes with the people of his time. It's like they were off the street. If you look at those paintings, the guys had dirty fingernails and they were just wearing street clothes. His contemporaries were still painting scenes with Greco-Roman robes and drapery and lots of marble everywhere and all these fancy settings. But Caravaggio just kept it very plain and simple and he made it seem like those scenes could have been happening out in the street. My models—I kind of focused on skinheads. Since I was referencing Caravaggio, I thought, I'm going to try and reference what he would do today. Who would he be looking to on the street? And how would he be dealing with it? He would probably be doing photography, not painting, so it's a bit of a moot point, so I had to always swallow that. But, I thought, at least he'd be combing the streets and looking for his type. And you know what, that was probably the greatest thing: the hunt for my model. I used to have great fun, even if it could be very frustrating. I'd go through stints or weeks of handing out cards and getting nothing.

V: What sort of cards? How did you do it?

A: It was in Berlin with not even broken German. In the beginning, I had to introduce myself and make myself clear. I had just gotten a studio in Künstlerhaus Bethanien four months after arriving in Berlin, and starting these new paintings. And across from Künstlerhaus Bethanien, there was a park where they were having a festival of some sort. Outside my window, I spy three adorably gorgeous skinheads. So I go down there, I introduce myself, I invite them up for a beer. They come up, they take their shirts off for a few quick Polaroids, and they're gone again. But half an hour later, they're back, ready to beat my face in. "We don't know what went on here! We don't like it, and we want those photos!" So I said, "I'll destroy those photos," and I cut them up in four pieces in front of them. That seemed to settle them and they walked out. The act of cutting them up actually helped, but those were my first two Polaroids taken in Berlin and I was still able to paint from them.

V: The cut-up ones?

A: Yeah, yeah, yeah. It's in the paintings. But then after that, I had no luck giving out cards. My boyfriend, Micha, whose real name was Michael Danger, found me my best model. Micha owned a bar in Berlin called Oranienbar; it was one of the legendary gay bars. He came home one night and said, "I found a model for you. He's perfect for you." And when this guy Alex showed up, I was beside myself he was so beautiful.

V: What did he look like?

A: Perfect. Skinhead, straight, from East Germany.

V: What was he wearing?

A: All German boys wore tight pants. Tight jeans, T-shirt, bomber jacket, and shoes or boots. That didn't really matter because I'd just make him dress up anyway. I'd have several changes for my models back then. I always tried to have a few different

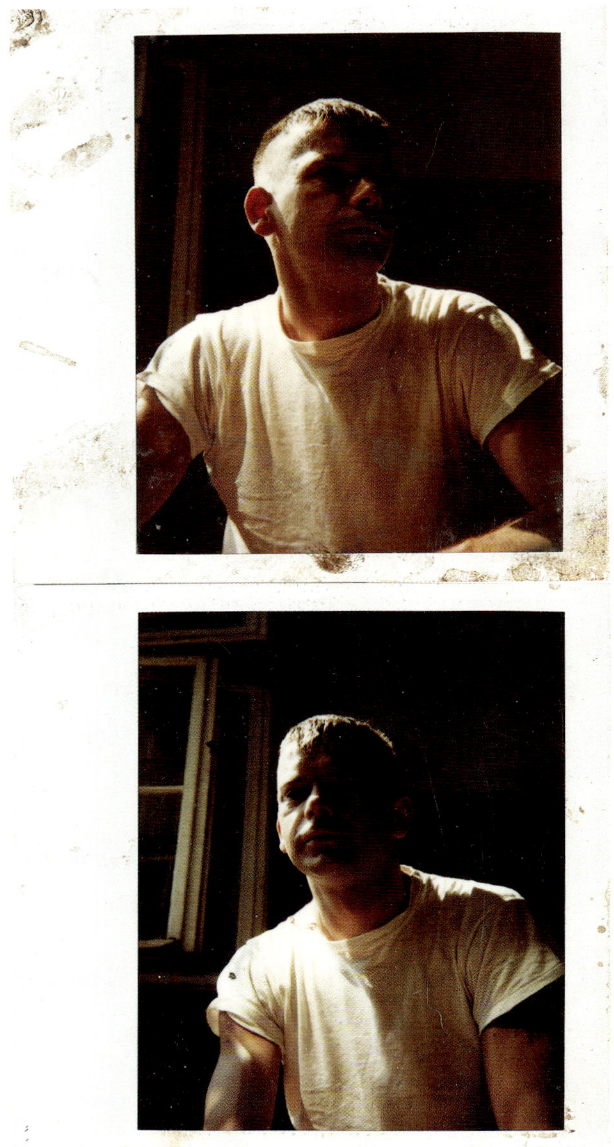

Michael (Micha) Danger, Oranienstr., 1998

scenarios set up. "We'll start half dressed and work down to nothing and then we'll put this on."

V: What kind of stuff did you have for them to put on?

A: The classic was a jockstrap. And in a way, because the jockstrap is so American—not German, not European—that changed things. It was so American so they weren't used to it. The German boys have really bad taste in underwear. Other than that it was boots. I was also looking at the art-historical references. Caravaggio would build up a pattern in red, whites, blacks, in his figures. You see that in a lot of his paintings, like *The Calling of Saint Matthew,* where there's a rhythm. And that's one of the paintings that I did reference identically. The painting itself is called *The Young Spartans,* based on a painting by Degas called *Young Spartans Exercising.* I put two paintings together, the Degas and the Caravaggio. I photographed models in identical poses. The Degas poses are all nudes, and the Caravaggio were nude and clothed. If the Caravaggio figures were wearing, let's say, a black, billowy-sleeved shirt—well, those were very much like bomber jackets in the cut. Which was a uniform. So it was very easy to put a bomber jacket into a Caravaggio blouson shirt.

V: I didn't realize there were such direct connections. But let's go back to the model search. After you met this guy Alex, was he able to introduce you to other guys or did you just keep looking?

A: I kept looking. Alex introduced me to one of his friends a few years into it when I needed somebody else. But it's never worked when I've asked a model to bring a friend by, because they never really have the same aesthetic. But I did sometimes arrange for two models to be there, and Alex was easy—I had an ongoing relationship with him for ten years, solidly; he was my main staple, he was fantastic, him and Stefan. When I had another boy over, I would introduce them and get right into it: "I want both of you to get undressed and go over there and ..." And Alex was great about it. I mean he was completely straight, he was a football hooligan—a real hooligan, loved to fight. Got arrested a lot for fighting. He was the real thing. From East Germany. Got bought out by the West.

V: What do you mean?

A: Before the Wall came down, the best way to get out of East Germany was to try and escape, get caught, and be put in jail. You'd have to do about a year in jail, in an East German prison, and then the Western government would buy you because you were an attempted escapee. Those who got caught trying to escape were bought by the West German government, which paid about 100,000 marks per person, what the East was asking.

V: The West thought they were potential good citizens?

A: I think they were just bought, regardless. I mean, Alex wasn't potential anything. He turned out to be more of a liability for the West than anything, because he was a radical hooligan.

V: So Alex worked with you during the whole ten-year period you were in Berlin. Did you use many other models during that time as well? Were you always looking for the ideal model?

A: I was constantly looking. It might just come down to ten or twenty different models, perhaps. But I was always looking. I'd search Bahnhof Zoo everyday for the perfect model. Bahnhof Zoo is a train station in downtown Berlin. It's right beside the zoo, which is a part of the Tiergarten, which used to be the royal hunting grounds, and that's where all the cruising happens. So you can be cruising in the Tiergarten and hear the elephants roaring while frolicking between the rhododendrons. And there was the train station—a notorious train station where all the hustlers hang out. Quite the scene. My route from home to the studio was by bike everyday and I had two routes. One was the classic Berlin route: along the wall, Checkpoint Charlie, Brandenburg Gate, the Reichstag, and then my studio was right there. Or I would go through downtown, through Fürstendamm, Bahnhof Zoo, see what talent was about. Because if there was any talent, it was a fifteen-minute walk to my studio. A lot of my models came from Bahnhof Zoo, hustlers that I picked up, and we'd just walk to the studio.

V: And how many of them actually turned out to be good models?

A: Only two or three. Three that there are lots of Polaroids of, at least.

V: How did this whole process change your way of painting?

A: I liked having the physical Polaroid there, because I don't do a drawing for my paintings—it's all in my head.

V: You don't sketch out a painting in advance?

A: No. I do now, but with those works I never made preliminary sketches per se. Back then I would just start on a canvas and throw in a figure where I wanted to. But I was still looking at art-historical references and trying to build my compositions based on what I thought was a successful composition. With Caravaggio, I liked the way he put something together; I liked his dark spaces and I drew upon that. In some of his paintings, it's really just dark space: there's no decoration, it's just dark space and these few figures carrying so much drama that they hold all of it together.

V: Did working with Polaroids change the nature and look of the work?

A: Sure. I don't think the paintings would have happened without the Polaroids, and the Polaroids wouldn't have happened without the paintings. So they're symbiotic. And I think they became more and more a part of each other. Every time I used it, the Polaroid became more and more a part of the process. Of course there's some disturbance today because of the fact that Polaroid is now ... extinct. And my palette has aligned itself so much with my source material. Going back to those twenty years of developing a palette for skin or flesh, the first ten years were spent just learning; now I know how to do it, but it's a matter of making it right. Once you learn how to do it, you have to learn how to not do it again.

V: I'm not sure what you mean by that. You mean you need to unlearn these things in order to be more natural?

A: It goes back to something I think Picasso said: It took my life to learn to paint like a child again.

V: Ultimately, the Polaroids are just raw material and elements for a larger composition and a larger idea, right?

A: The first time I had Alex in, I didn't have very much film. And I quickly learned that I have to have lots of film around. Sometimes I got very obsessive—I don't know why. Sometimes it's not working and you're just pushing and pushing the button for something to pop out that's going to look nice.

V: It's interesting and surprising to me because your final result is not the Polaroid. What were you looking for in those individual frames? Was it the pose or did the Polaroid itself become more and more important, so it had to be just right?

A: No, no. It was about focus, lighting, pragmatic concerns. But I have to say that after those first couple sessions with Alex, when I had masses of Polaroids laying down on the floor and three photo shoots behind me, it came into my head that they looked great, and that one day I would show them. As I amassed more and more and more, I got off on each set. It was fantastic seeing them all on the floor. I'd line them all up and go through them. Out of a hundred, I'd use ten, or five, or whatever.

V: But you kept all one hundred?

A: Oh yeah. As those sheets were laid out on the floor, they looked fantastic. And I just loved how obsessive they were. Because they were really obsessive. Hand, hand, hand. Head, head, head. Crotch, crotch, crotch. Foot. And I was getting an idea of the format of the camera and framing that body part nicely. But I still liked to shoot fast, so usually one Polaroid would shoot the previous one out of the camera and just land on the floor like that. I didn't like to wait too long. But I started to think about showing them one day. And I think at that point Michael Morris was there. He got me set up in Berlin. Michael's the reason I went to Berlin, in a way, because I had met him in Vancouver and he said, "If you come to Berlin, look me up." So I was there that fall, and he was my contact. Michael hooked me up with the studio at Künstlerhaus Bethanien, or he got me the right intro and I got accepted. Michael was my mentor in terms of my painting, too. And he was feeding me every night, cooking dinner for me and introducing me to people and the scene.

V: He's been an important part of your life for a long time then?

A: Yeah, yeah. We went to openings—but he also came down [to the studio] at the drop of a hat if I was having a painting problem. "Michael, I can't figure this out."

V: So he was a good person to exchange ideas with?

A: Yeah, exactly. "Can you see what I'm trying to do? What should I do? Dark? Light?" But I'd also quite proudly display my Polaroids and he completely got into them. And there is a great reason for Michael to be on the case with these now because he's familiar with all the shots except for the New York period. He'd been there and seen the paintings that they were used for, so when it came to organizing them, he was able to sort them out into the shots as they were shot, and he was able to reference the paintings they went into, sometimes better than I could.

V: Exactly what kind of camera were you using?

A: It was always a Polaroid Spectra.

V: Is it the same model you're still using?

A: I would if I could.

V: So will you start using a digital camera?

A: Well, yes. I don't want to be like Latin and die because I can't keep up with the times. So yes, if I'm worth anything as an artist, I'll have to accept the fact that digital is now in.

V: I'm curious to know whether anything changed when you moved to New York.

A: My palette changed. And my way of painting figures. I had gone off from using the house paint so much. In those five years in New York, there was a lot of figuration going on in my canvases, and not all of it was good. That was a period of struggle for a lot of my painting. I'm not satisfied with a lot of what I did then. In the end, where I've come to today, I'm glad I was able to take that step because now it allows me to move further instead of still being back there.

V: What did you put behind you, then?

A: When I left New York, I put the palette behind me in a way. Because I stopped painting. Stopped. I said, That's it, I'm not going to do any painting now for a year. It was combined with a drug spiral, midlife crisis, downward spiral. But I did say to myself, I am going to paint the black male now. I've painted enough white boys. I got my palette down. I need a new challenge. But it's not as simple as that—you also want to get to know your subjects. One of the reasons I enjoyed painting figuratively

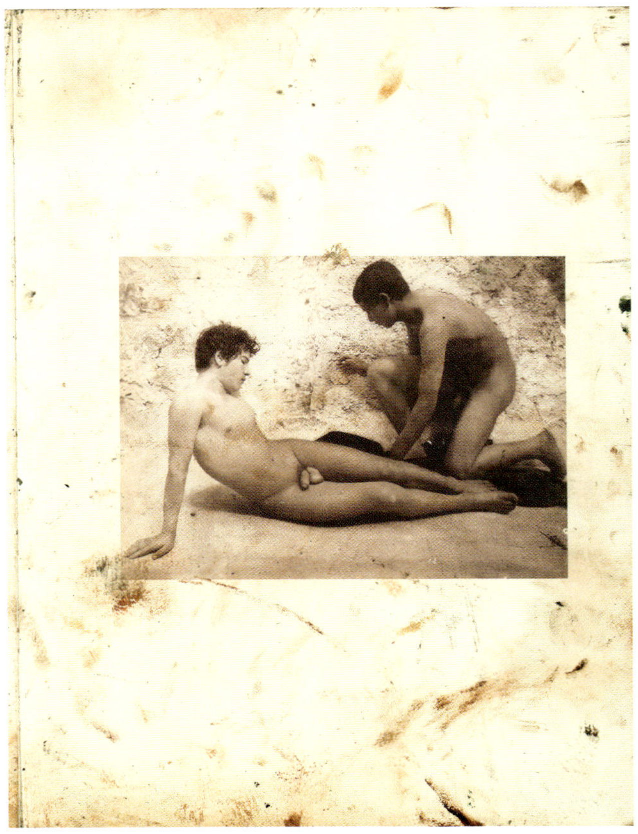

Page of *Taormina* by Wilhelm Von Gloeden, San Francisco: Twelvetrees Press, 1986, from the collection of Attila Richard Lukacs.

so much is you can really get yourself into those paintings. I don't mean to sound so romantic or anything, but you know where that thigh is, you can associate smells with certain ... whatever. I did a few attempts of painting the black male...

V: From Polaroids or from life?

A: From some poses from von Gloeden. Using the photos themselves but changing the skin palette. Which I didn't find quite worked because one always needs to get to know one's subjects. If you look at my paintings now, they're about fifty/fifty. So with that [black] portrait series I did, I spent two years every Saturday and Sunday painting a portrait. Every weekend—two days out of seven—were devoted to portrait painting and working on my palette and different variations of the browns.

V: And working from photographic material? The material I saw in your studio included some Polaroids but also a lot of pages torn from magazines.

A: Media images. Sure, I rely as much on, or even more on found imagery than my old Polaroids because the photography I do is only to set a figure into a place.

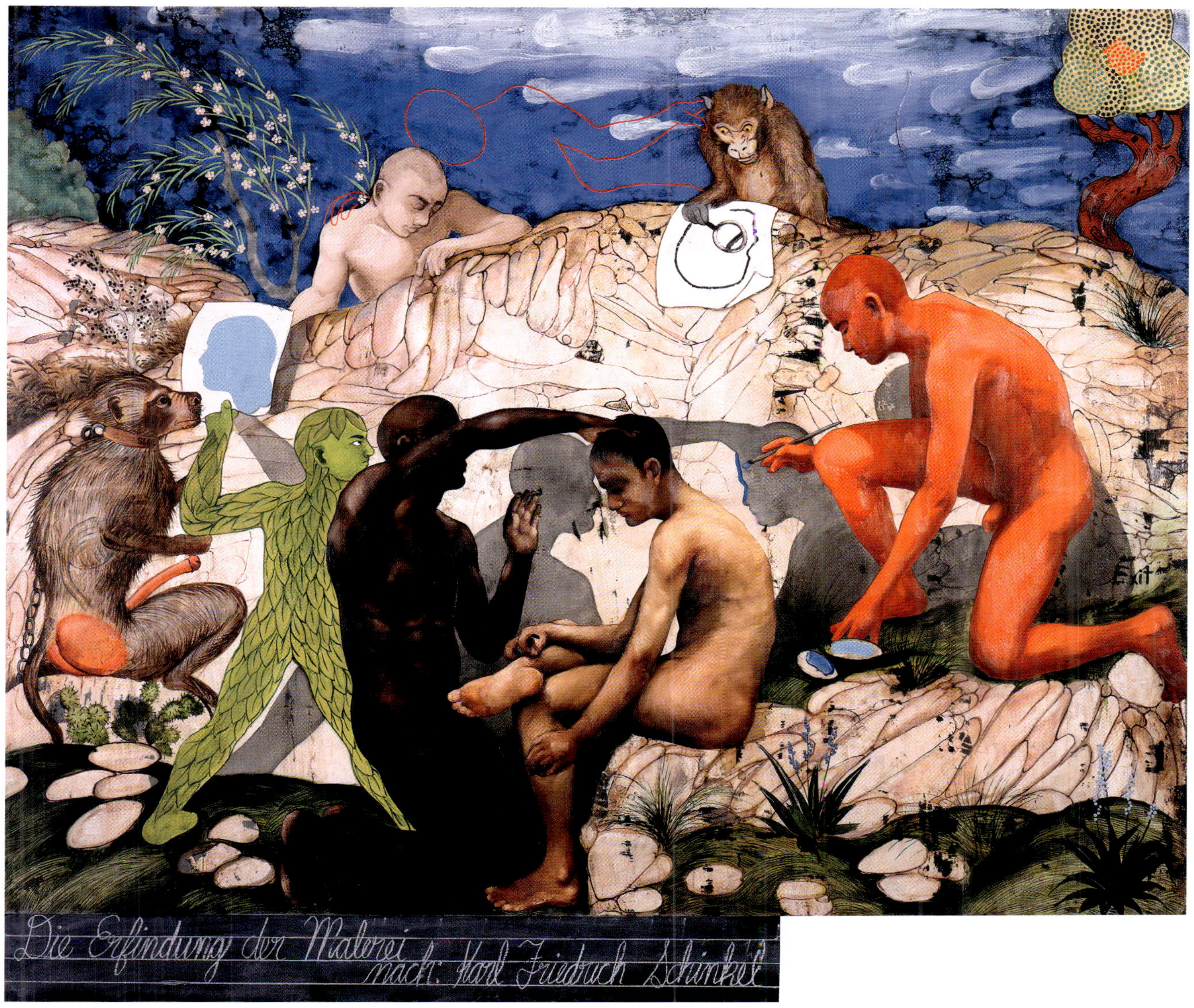

Attila Richard Lukacs *The Discovery of Painting*, 1999, oil on canvas, chalk on board, 239 x 282 cm, Collection of Michael Healy.

V: For the black portraits, it seemed you were using a lot of hip-hop magazines.

A: The muse is my friend Jermaine, the dreadlock guy. And so far there's about thirteen [paintings] of him. I met him just as I was leaving New York, and I took some Polaroids of him when I was coming back and forth. I had to fly in from Canada to do community service, and I met him on one of those trips. Anyway, we became tight, and I got some Polaroids of him and said, this is going to start a portrait series where I wanted to start practising a darker, browner palette instead of all those whites.

V: Which, I imagine, created a need to rethink your approach to the figure.

A: Yes, because the black figure, first of all, sits differently in space. Quite practically, I was used to setting a composition with all bright, white figures, like in the Italian sense. The main focus is the figure in the foreground, populated by those figures that build a story around him or her. Those compositions would be quite different if they were all black males, in terms of those dark brown Caravaggio backgrounds. Black on black.

V: Could be interesting.

A: Could be quite interesting.

V: Most of what I saw of the black portraits were single heads, without a sense of space or location.

A: I was simply practicing portraiture and trying to get it down as fast as possible. Trying not to make it too laboured. Although some of them I spent more time on than I should have. Or, perhaps, less time? But I really did focus on trying to change my palette. Because it's not that easy to change your palette: you're dealing with a whole different set of colours, and they react differently, and the composition reacts differently, so your focus on the composition is different. Now instead of white, white, white, you can actually set up a very nice rhythm: black, white, black, white, half white, half black.

V: Have you also put these figures into larger compositions?

A: Yes.

V: And still based primarily on Polaroids or Polaroids and the sort of mass-media photos I saw in your studio?

A: Up until today, yeah. Polaroids and mass media. The mass media will always be there because it's fantastic source material. The body of work I've been working on in the last three years is war, and wars are fantastic source material for artists. And as artists we also want to document our times. Depending on what I'm doing, mass-media imagery is very important. Sometimes it's web sites. Some of the sources for my war paintings came off of soldiers' personal web sites.

V: And some of these paintings are based on news images, if I remember correctly. And are you still combining them with classical framing or compositions?

A: Sure. It's a combination. The painting I'm working on right now—I'll use that because I have it in my head—I'm working on a composition by Botticelli, *Venus and Mars*. So Botticelli's Mars figure, I had that photographed on Polaroid—I did that in New York, and that set is in the show. But I've been working from those Polaroids because I've always wanted to make a painting out of them. I knew I wanted to do this image, and I photographed that pose, not necessarily for the painting I'm doing today, but for something back then. Anyway, so I have that art-historical reference and I have references of soldiers in uniform from newspapers and magazines.

V: In action?

A: It's a very calming composition, so it's not really in action. So I have art-historical references, re-photographed in Polaroid, several mass-media references, and then about a dozen other secondary art-historical/mass-media references or referencing back to other paintings.

V: Of yours?

A: Yes, that are going to be built into this composition. Clues are set out on a table and around me, but the composition is really stuck in here [points to his head].

V: Meaning it's a quite elaborate collage that's processed in your brain?

A: It takes months to develop, and it sometimes it takes an effort to hold. It's a bit like memory on a computer. You always have to clear a space for it.

V: And get rid of other things that are crowding it out?

A: In a way, yeah. It takes up a certain chunk of space. I notice that now.

V: A number of the paintings I saw were enormous. Is that still the scale you're working in?

A: Well, yeah. I'm starting to wrap up this series that's going to be eight paintings of that scale, about ten by twelve feet on average. During the week, I'd be dealing with the large canvases, organizing a whole bunch of source material and imagery to coordinate. When you're working on these paintings, you know it's like a three-month process and you have all the steps planned out, or at least you know what the steps are from previous experience and previous paintings. So you know when you have to lay this in before you can start laying that in. You have to keep the balance going. And because of the regimen of the studio, phone calls coming in and other distractions, Saturdays became my portrait days because... the opera. No assistants, no friends coming in, the opera [playing], and somehow I just painted a black boy to every opera I was listening to for two years.

V: Kind of a disconnect, no?

A: I know. How the hell did I associate these guys with opera? But you know, in a way, it's just like practicing your voice. I want to get away from the problems and just want to do something that's meditative. Really about painting and not about bigger worries. I just want to concentrate on a head and the problems within the confines of that head. And there's enough there. Without having to worry about the background and everything. Of course, that's all part of the consideration, but it's basically like when I do the prep time to get myself there and I do the preliminary drawing, I paint in the chrome green undercoat and that would all dry, and come Saturday, I'd take a couple of hours to prep myself. I'd put down the brown tones and I knew exactly how much time I needed for that paint to dry. And even though it was oil paint, sometimes fifteen minutes or half an hour makes quite the difference—the difference between a good day and a bad day. I was timing it, and then I'd go in and finish off the portrait in the second act. Just like that! And usually, if it was a good day, the applause [on the record] would come just as I was laying down my brushes.

V: I'm curious about the range of material you used for that series of black male portraits. If you were still taking Polaroids, where did you find your models for that group?

A: The portraits are mostly mass media. Jermaine was the muse for the series. [Of the few Polaroid subjects], a couple are friends, a couple are models. But most are from mass media.

V: And where did the wooden signs and other plywood painting surfaces come from?

A: The plywood's been sourced from all over the place, from India to Maui, from New York, Berlin, East Coast of Canada, West Coast of Canada. I just brought back some from Maui. I was collecting those boards for about three years prior to starting the project. Now I'm almost done, almost at my magic number sixty-nine, and I'm hoping to show them all together as a group.

V: When you're looking for images to base these portraits on, what exactly are you looking for? Is there an ideal, and if there is, how would you describe that?

A: There is an ideal, because I would only tear one or two pictures out of a magazine, or often I wouldn't find any.

V: So what is that?

A: I don't know. Something that I can articulate? A face that I like? Something that has the right light—that I can paint from?

V: Does the figure need to be handsome on some level?

A: He has to be handsome, yeah. But once again, that's a relative thing. For me what is handsome or cute is how I interpret it. There's also factors in terms of how it's lit, how it's shot. Is it airbrushed? If it's a celebrity or not, that never bothered me, but actually the more anonymous they are, the better they are. However, I did go on a bit of celebrity tangent with this.

V: Including who?

A: Some of your regulars: DMX, The Game, Tupac, and T.I.

V: I wanted to return to your use of Polaroids for the larger paintings. Did you continue using Polaroids after you returned to Vancouver from New York?

A: I did go back to using Polaroids again back in Vancouver once I started painting again on canvas. The process didn't change, but it was short-lived because it was only about 2004 that I started shooting again.

V: Had you really stopped painting completely?

A: I stopped for the year 2000. And the years 2001 to 2004 were consumed with my recovery and trying to find myself after so many nervous breakdowns. And I was also fairly transient in those years, living between Vancouver and Maui, although I was working feverishly, doing a lot of work.

V: What kind of work?

A: Mostly on paper, drawings and paintings on paper, because I was going back and forth between the two locations, so canvases are not very convenient. I was working in an eight-by-eight-feet format at the largest—papers put together so I was creating my own surfaces, really, and I could roll them up. They were paintings, but paintings based on going back to drawing and experimenting with material again. I didn't need the Polaroid reference because I was just working out of my head. I wasn't using any art-historical references; I wasn't using any mass-media references, really. Maybe one out of thirty was a mass-media reference—a photograph. But basically it was just off the top of my head. I was just learning new materials.

V: What were the subjects for the most part?

A: Figurative. I wasn't working on canvas because I was so transient and I didn't have a large studio, which becomes a kind of anchor. It costs money to maintain and set up.

V: And you wanted to be loose?

A: Yes, I wanted to be loose. So finally in 2004, I decided I was ready to root myself again, and I started with small studios, working out of my home in Vancouver.

V: Did the Polaroids become less interesting for you at some point or were they always a useful tool?

A: It's a useful tool. And sometimes it was less interesting when I wasn't really getting any magic out of the camera—or myself. The same thing happens with the painting.

V: I assume at some point along the line that you threw things away. Or did you keep everything?

A: No. I kept everything.

V: And what percentage of those Polaroids are being used in this book and the show that you and Michael Morris put together?

A: It probably represents about a quarter or a third of all the Polaroids.

V: The grid format of the work I saw exhibited in Vancouver—was that Michael's idea or was it something that you had thought of? How did that come about?

A: Like I said, back in Bethanien, when I was laying them out on the floor and Michael would come over, he had indicated then that, down the road, this was something I should consider doing something with. And when I settled back in Vancouver again in my first canvas studio in 2004, Michael and I were both there when my stuff started coming out of storage—the archives and the Polaroids. I brought out all my reference material and source material, and I started shooting again. And Michael was there and he said, "This is the time when we should talk about those ideas we had about doing something with the Polaroids. If you don't mind, I'd like to take this on." I said, "Michael, there's boxes over there with ten thousand Polaroids, all messed up. Go ahead! Sort your heart out." So he began the process, and it was great because he knew the models and he knew in which sequence they were shot. There were several sessions with Alex and other models, but Michael was able to tell which ones were from this period of time and that period of time and which paintings they went with. He knew the art-historical references I was using. If I had to do all the work he did, I don't think the show would exist. The format started, as with sorting anything, with laying them all out. And for a good year, Michael was really just shuffling them around, working on different formats. Laying them out, marking them, putting them in piles, coming back, laying it out again, cutting it down. Once it came down to designing the show—how is it going to look on the wall? How are they going to look framed? After about two years, we came down to the three-by-four grid, with variations. In this show [one of the exhibitions on which this book is based], there are 250 of those grids, but we've got at least that many put together that are not in the show. Some are bigger, some are smaller. Some are groups of four, or like a couple together, and there are some really nice individual ones. But there are still volumes to be put out, and there are still at least a couple of shows coming out of that archive. My original idea was just to show them all on a big wall. I'm glad I didn't do that, because so much would have been lost.

V: It would have been overwhelming.

A: But that's how I would have done it. I couldn't have taken the time that Michael took. He worked on it for four years, and I'm glad he did.

V: Initially, though, you took the Polaroids as studies and source material for paintings. It doesn't seem to me that you intended to be a photographer.

A: But about five years into making the Polaroids, I said, at some point I'm going to have a show of these. And I kept it as source material. I kept it hidden. I didn't make it part of the way I presented my work or let it be known. I didn't do side shows of it. I wanted it as a big show sometime to back up the paintings.

V: And as the older work becomes historic, the Polaroids inform them.

A: Sometimes the reasons why I was taking them one after the other is that's how the best shots happen. Lots of times, if I went for a second version, it became like a laboured movement in a painting. Or sometimes, you could take your time, frame it, and then just go from there: click, click, click, and keep going. The Polaroid is a medium of chance, in a way. The film itself has variables in terms of colour. I think I got pretty good with the framing; I got a good feel for that. Sometimes I'd just shoot for the sake of shooting. I didn't always have a direct reference. And I knew that I was using like one in every ten, one in every twenty, realistically. So there was lot of extra there. But I still wanted to maintain and expand that extra [material] for perhaps future use.

And that's another reason why I built up such an archive, because I was always thinking about the next painting.

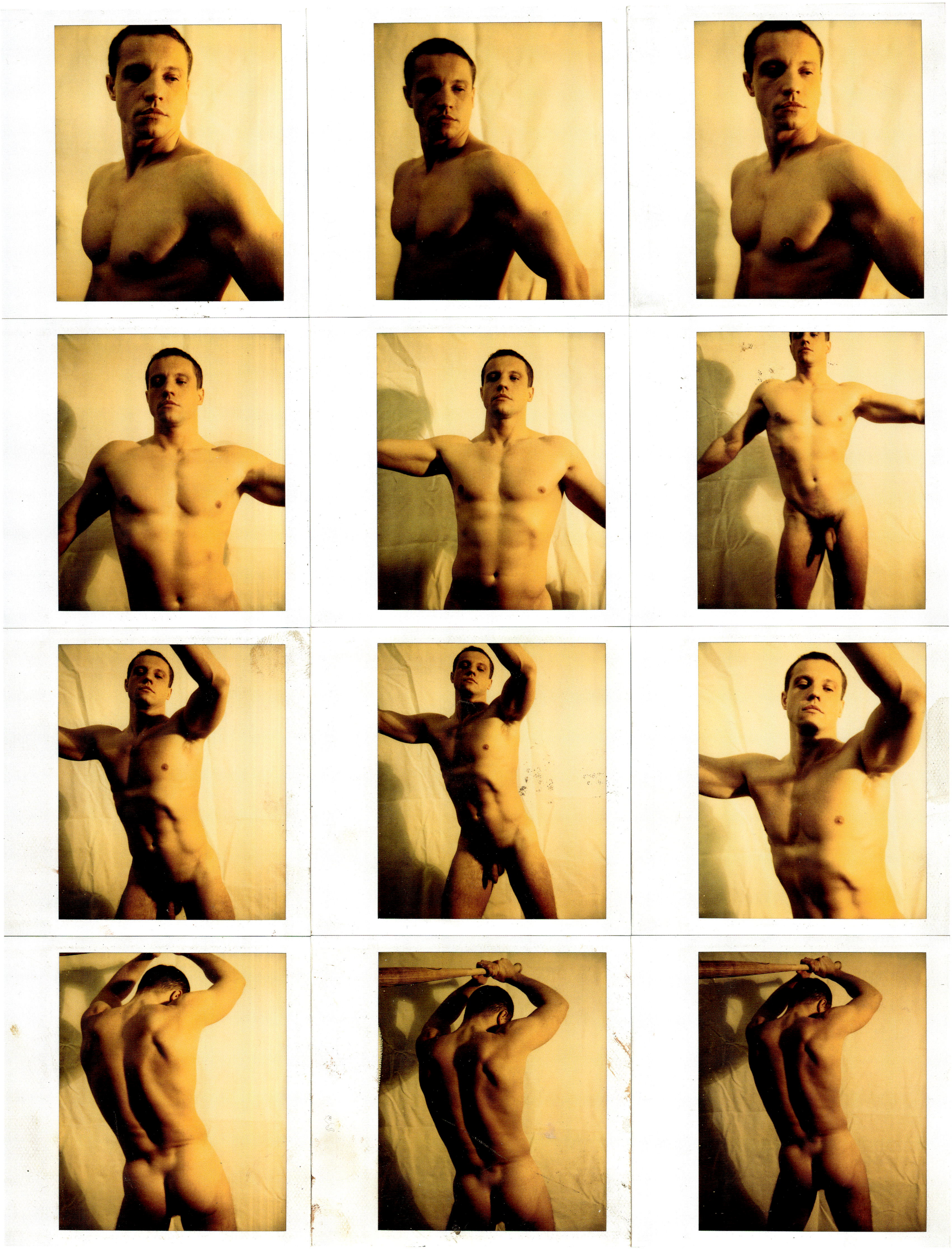

Dariusz, New York, 1998

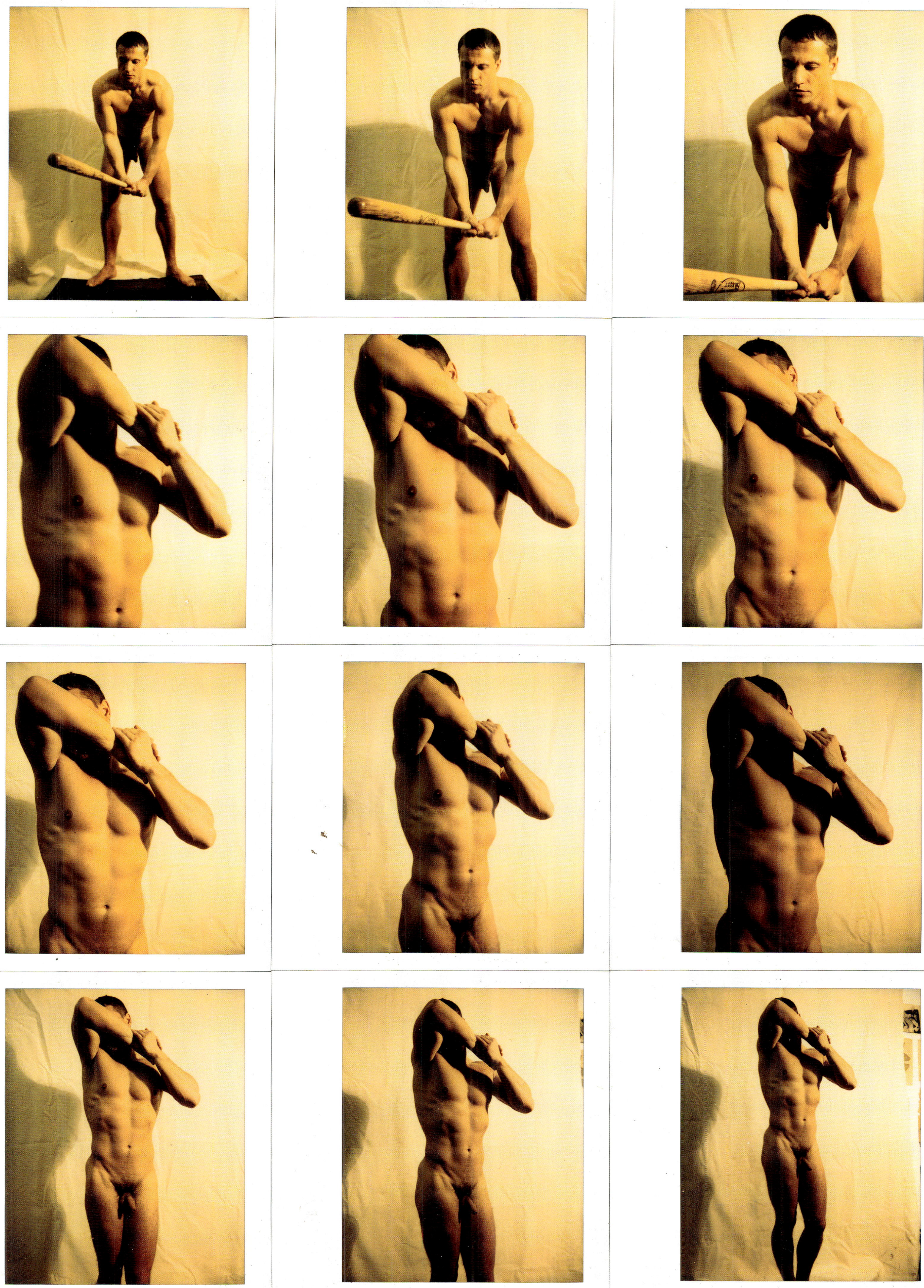

Dariusz, New York, 1998

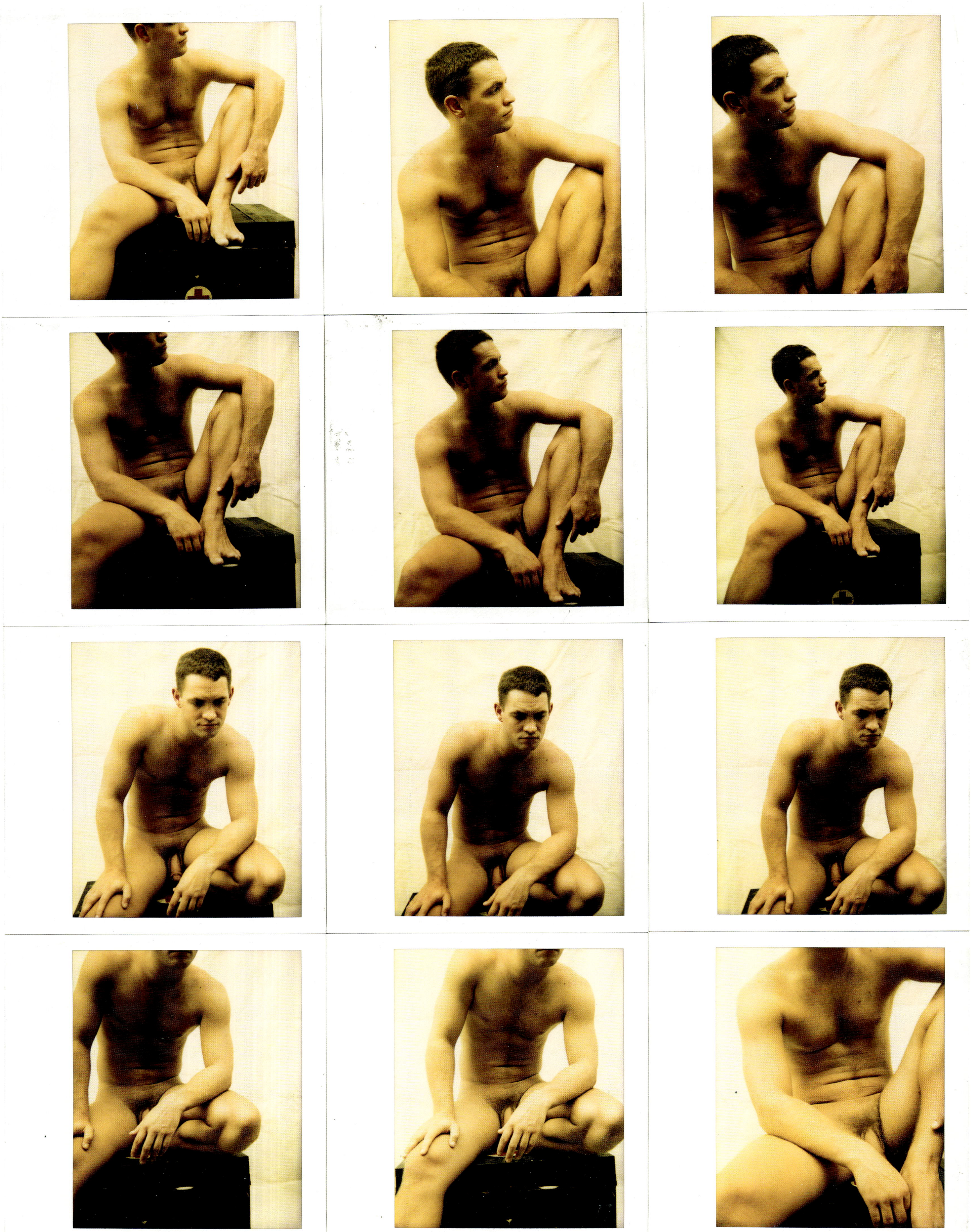

Bar Back, *The Lure*, New York, 1998

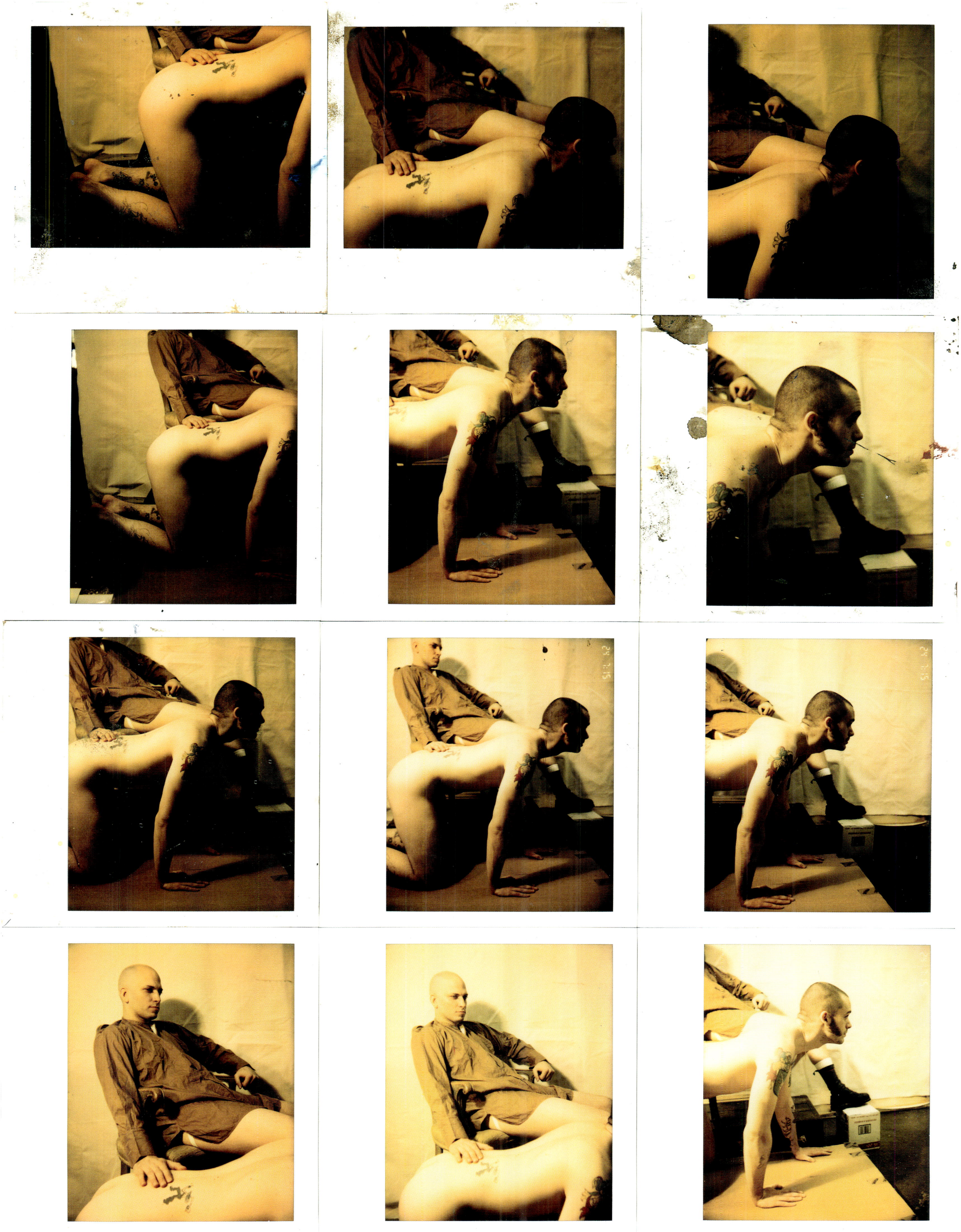

New York Skins, New York, 1998

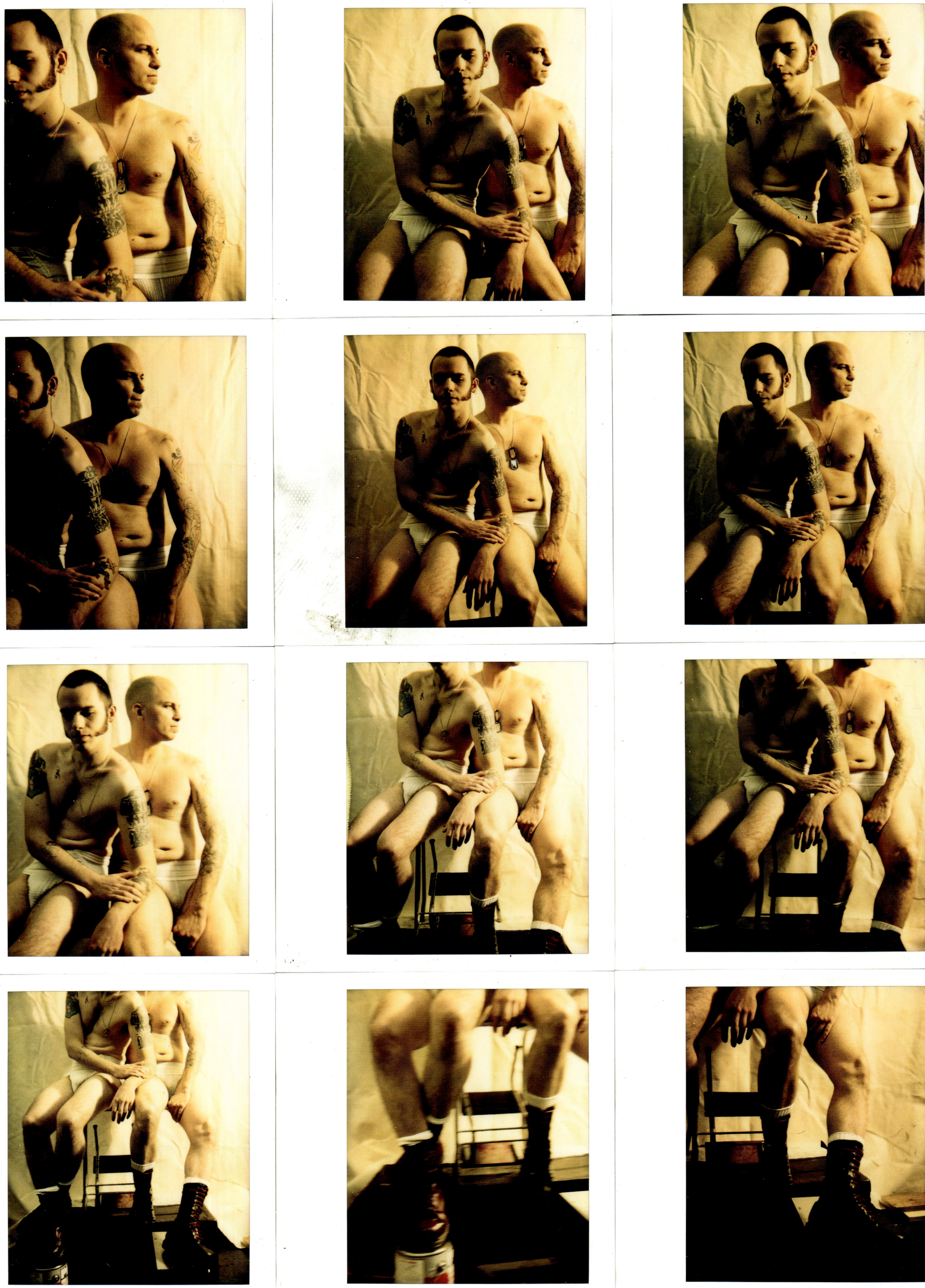

New York Skins, New York, 1998

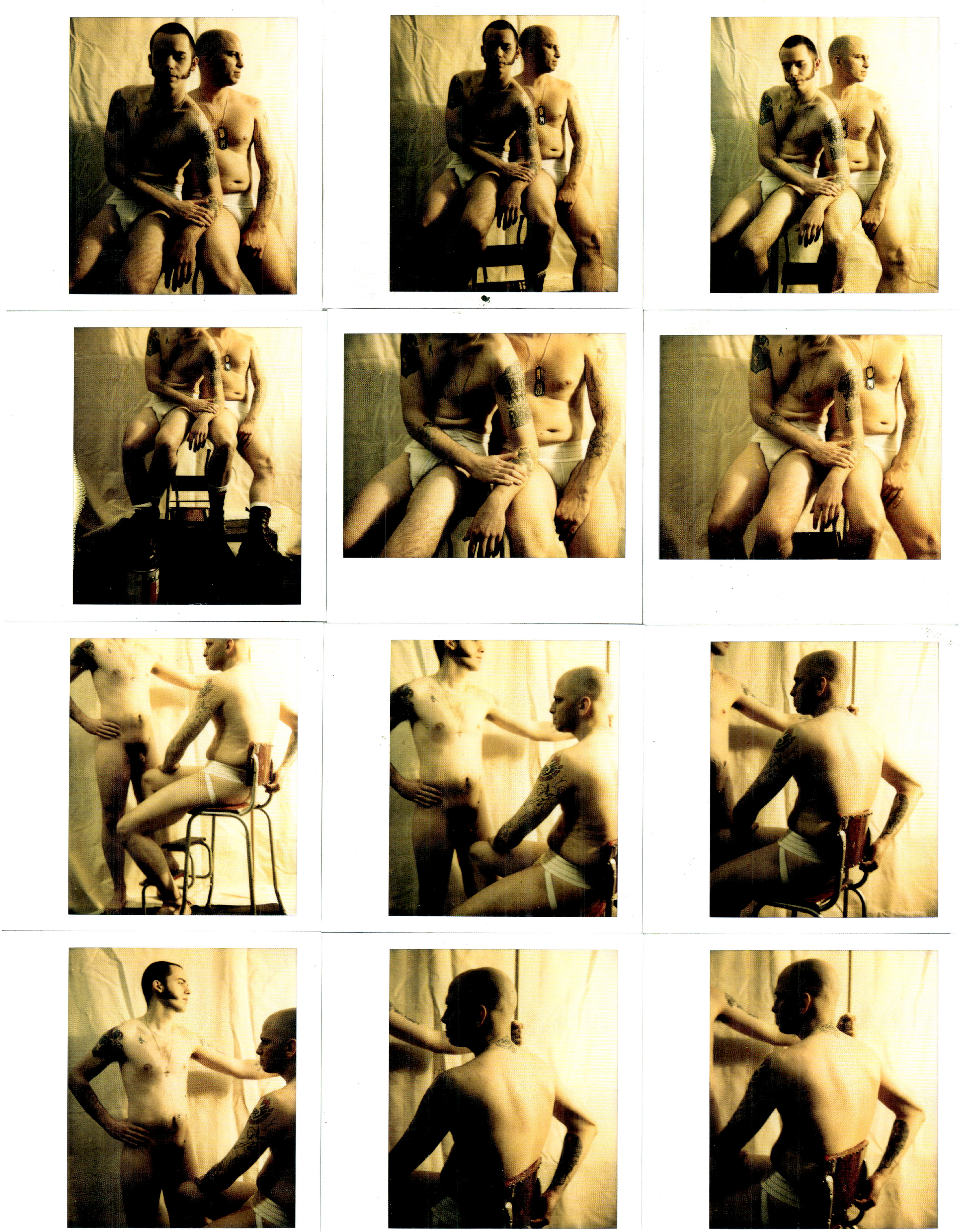

New York Skins, New York, 1998

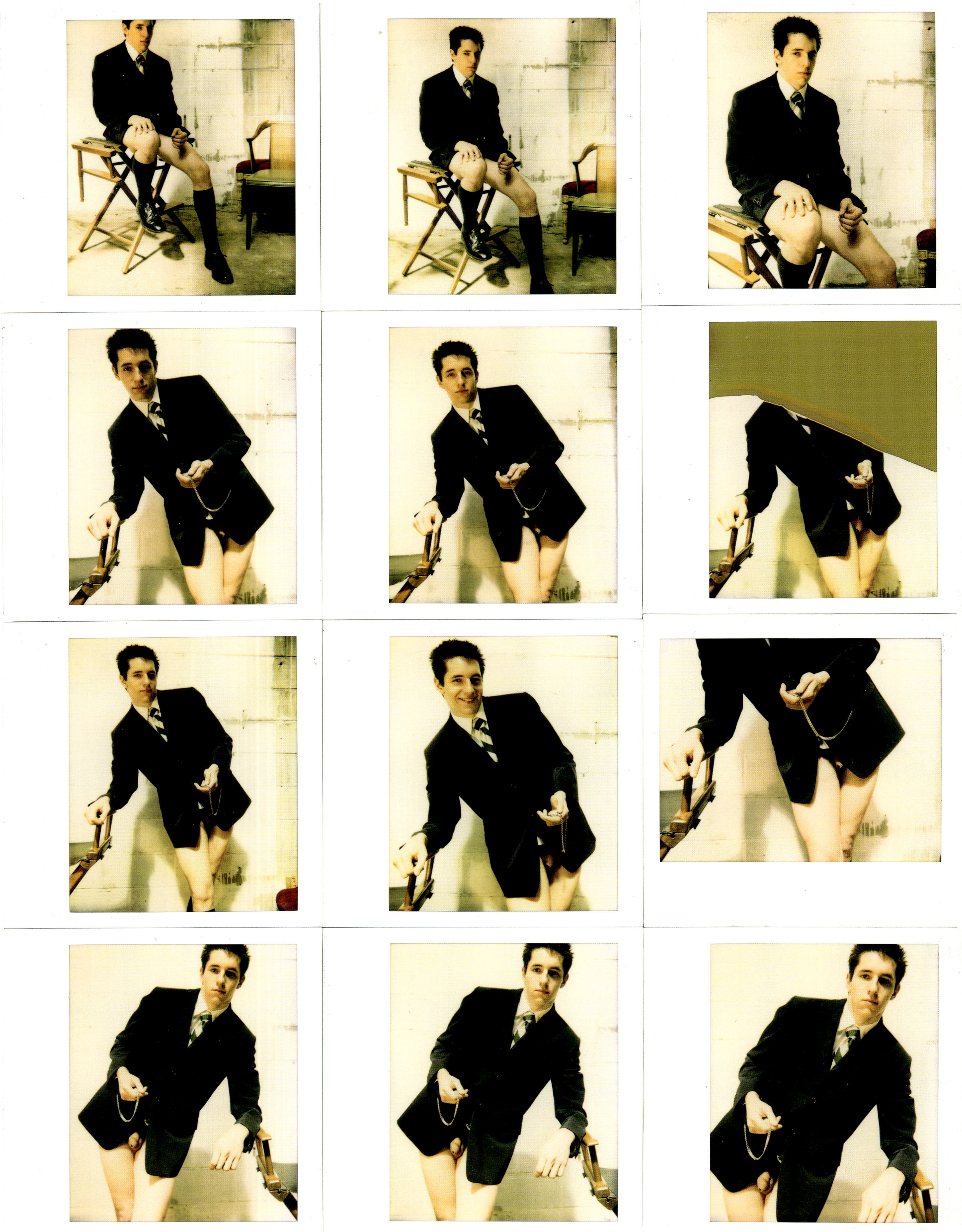

Michael, New York, 1998

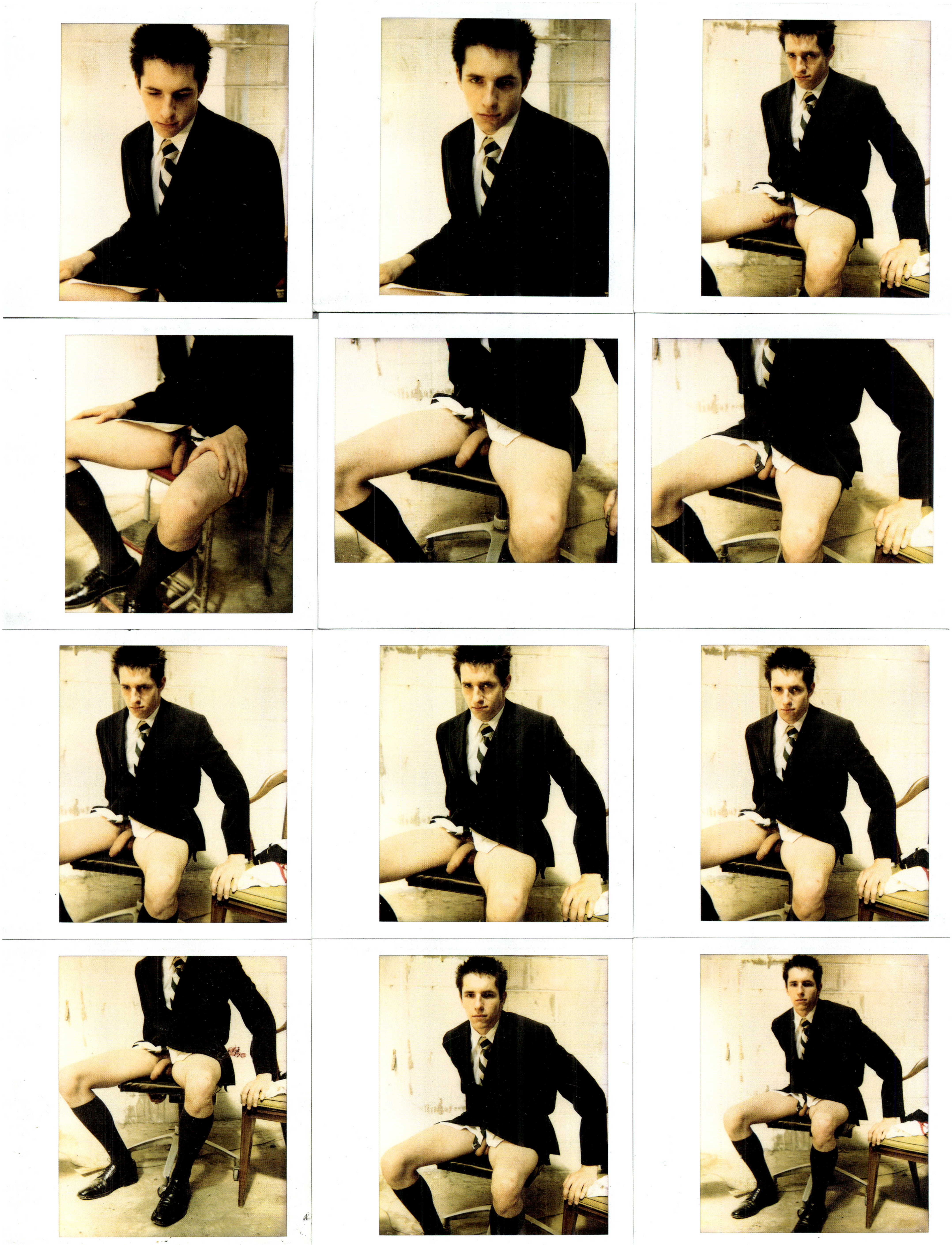

Michael, New York, 1998

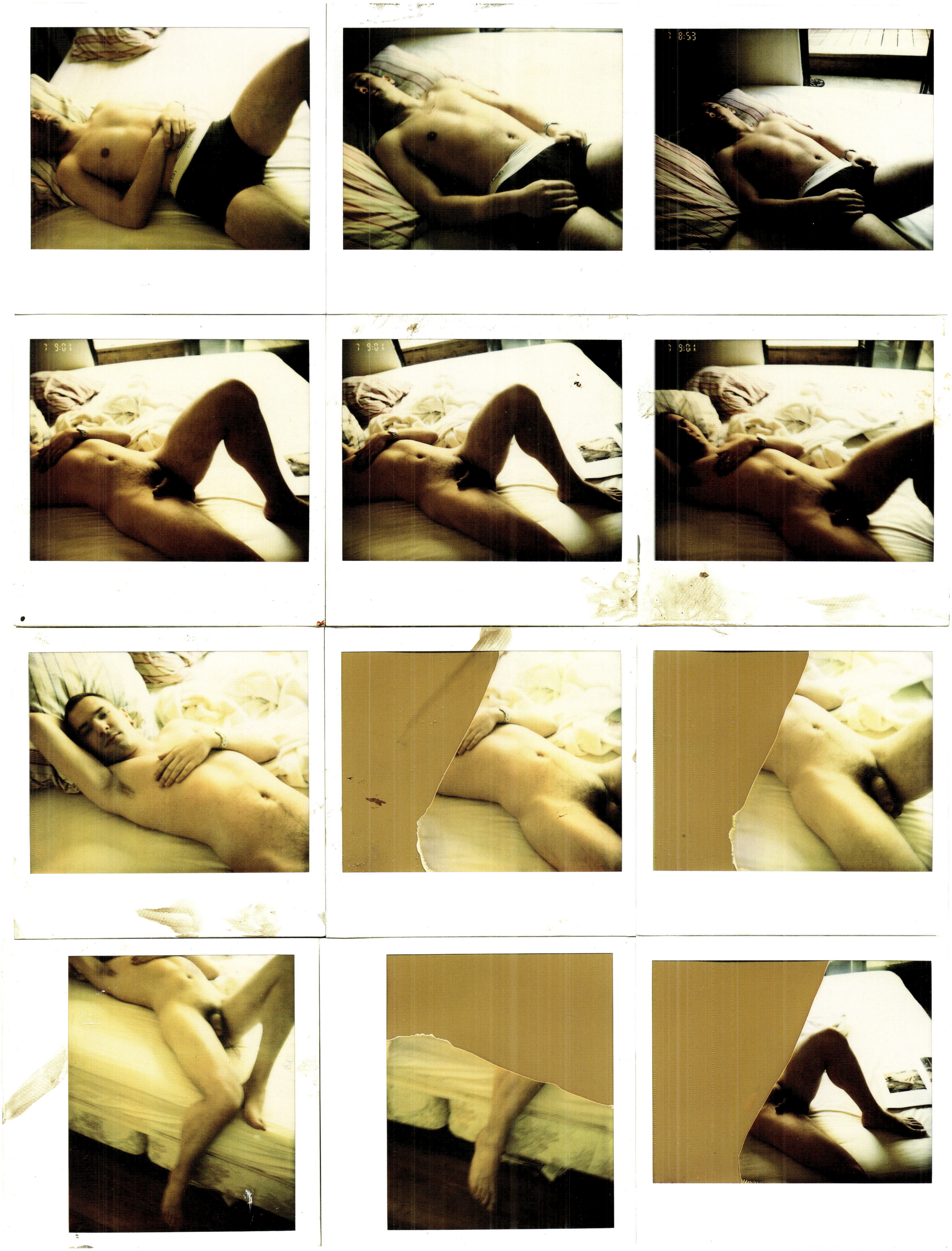

Claus, New York, 1998

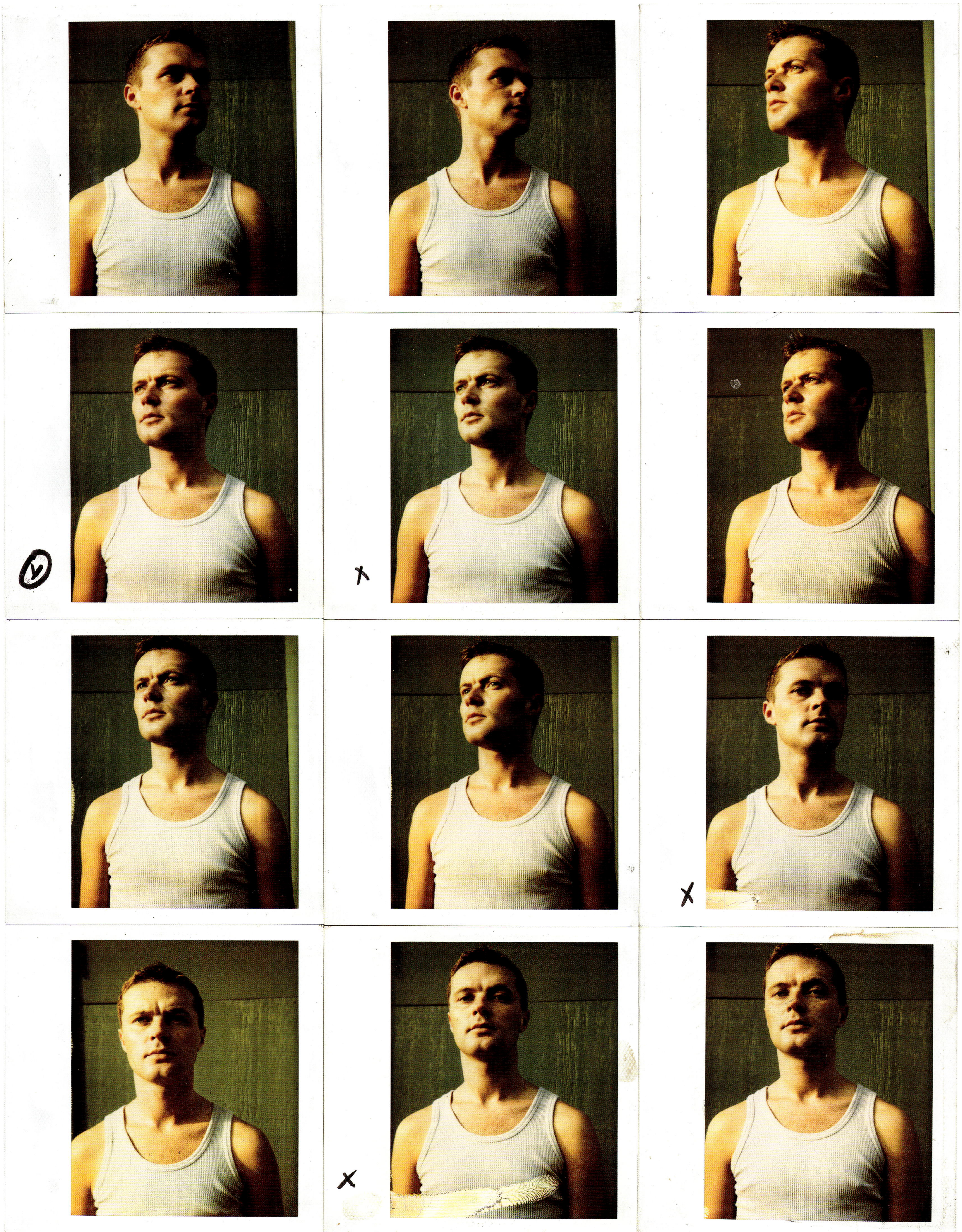

Morton, New York, 1998

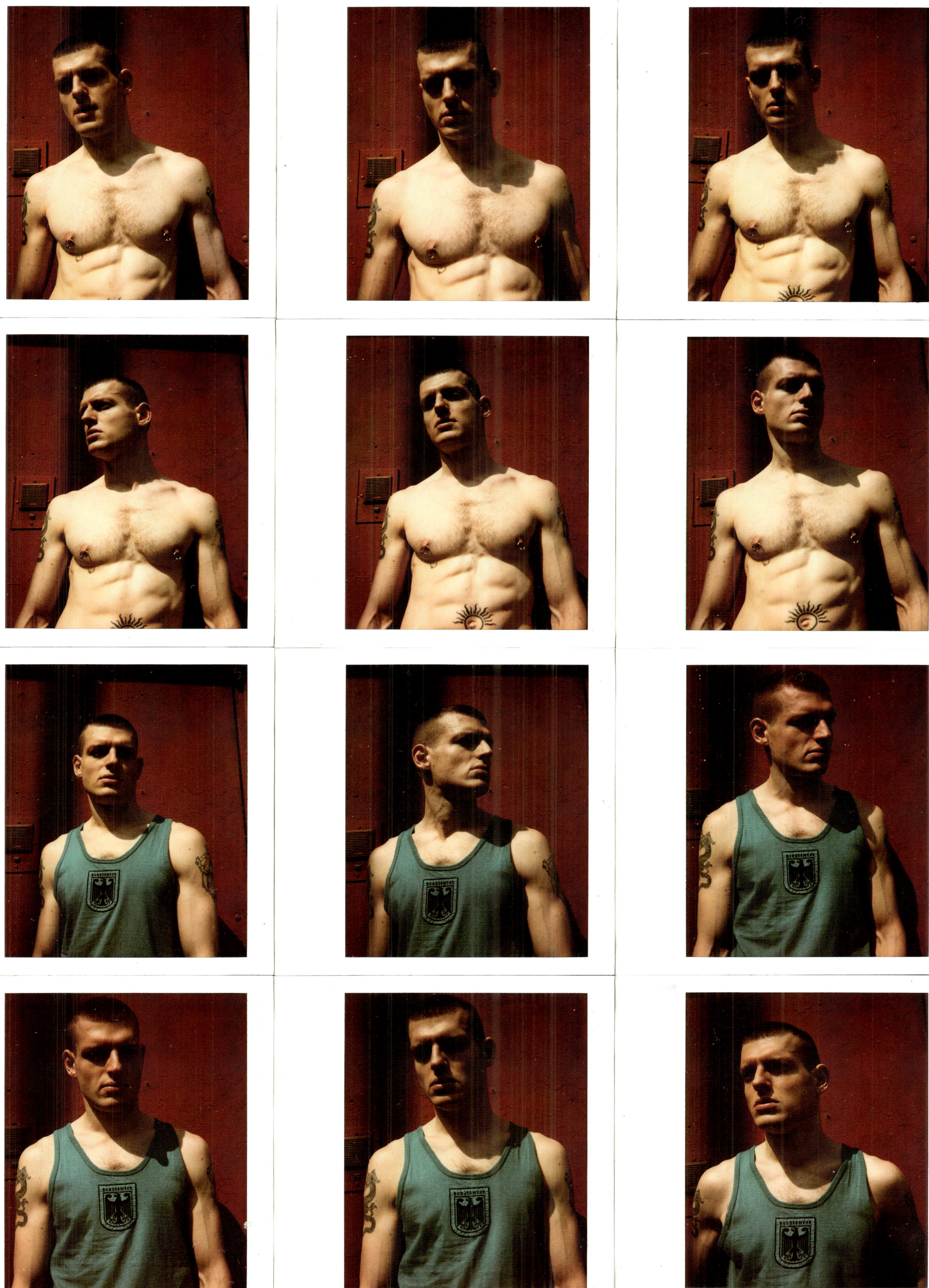

Slava, New York, 1998

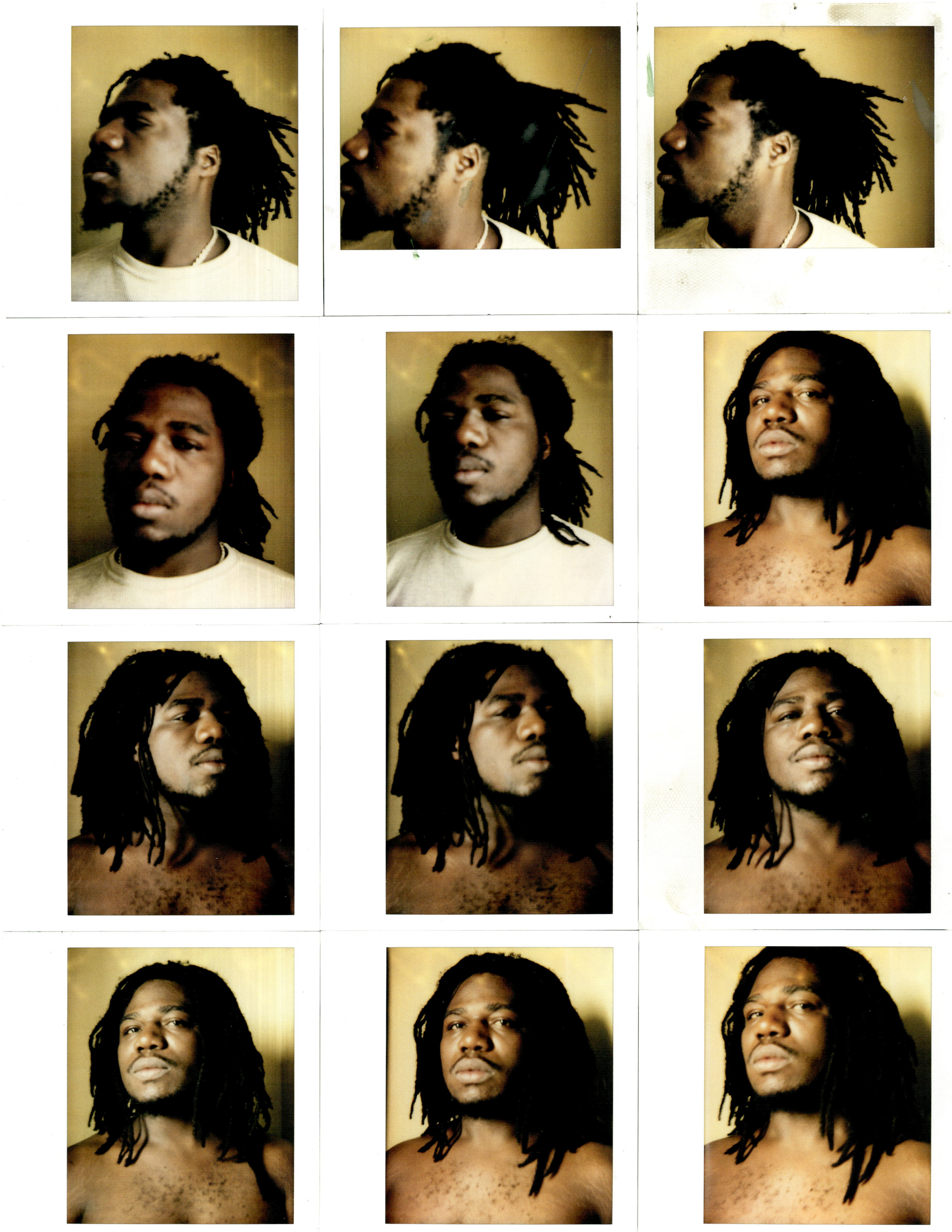

Jermaine, New York, 2004

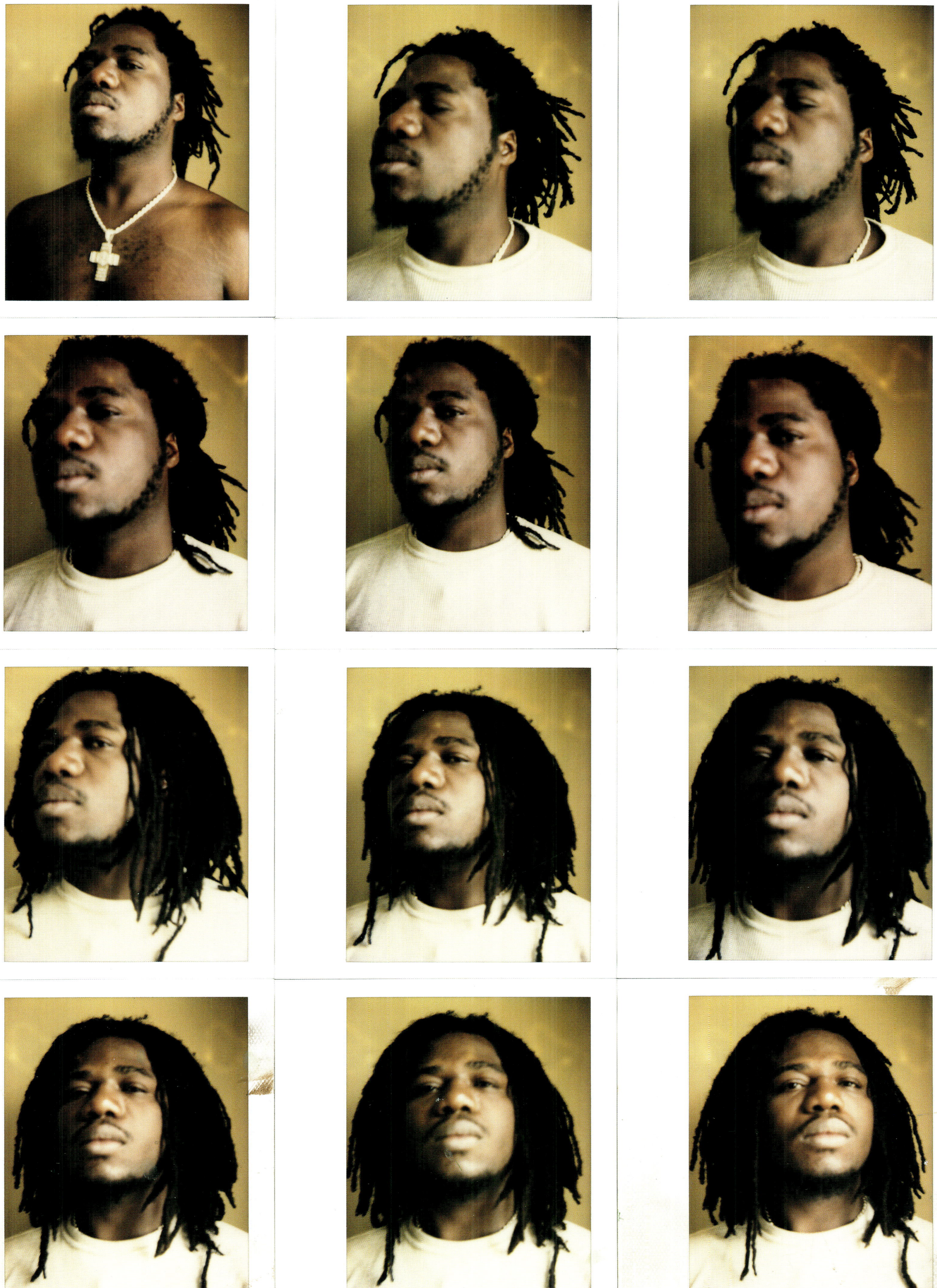

Jermaine, New York, 2004

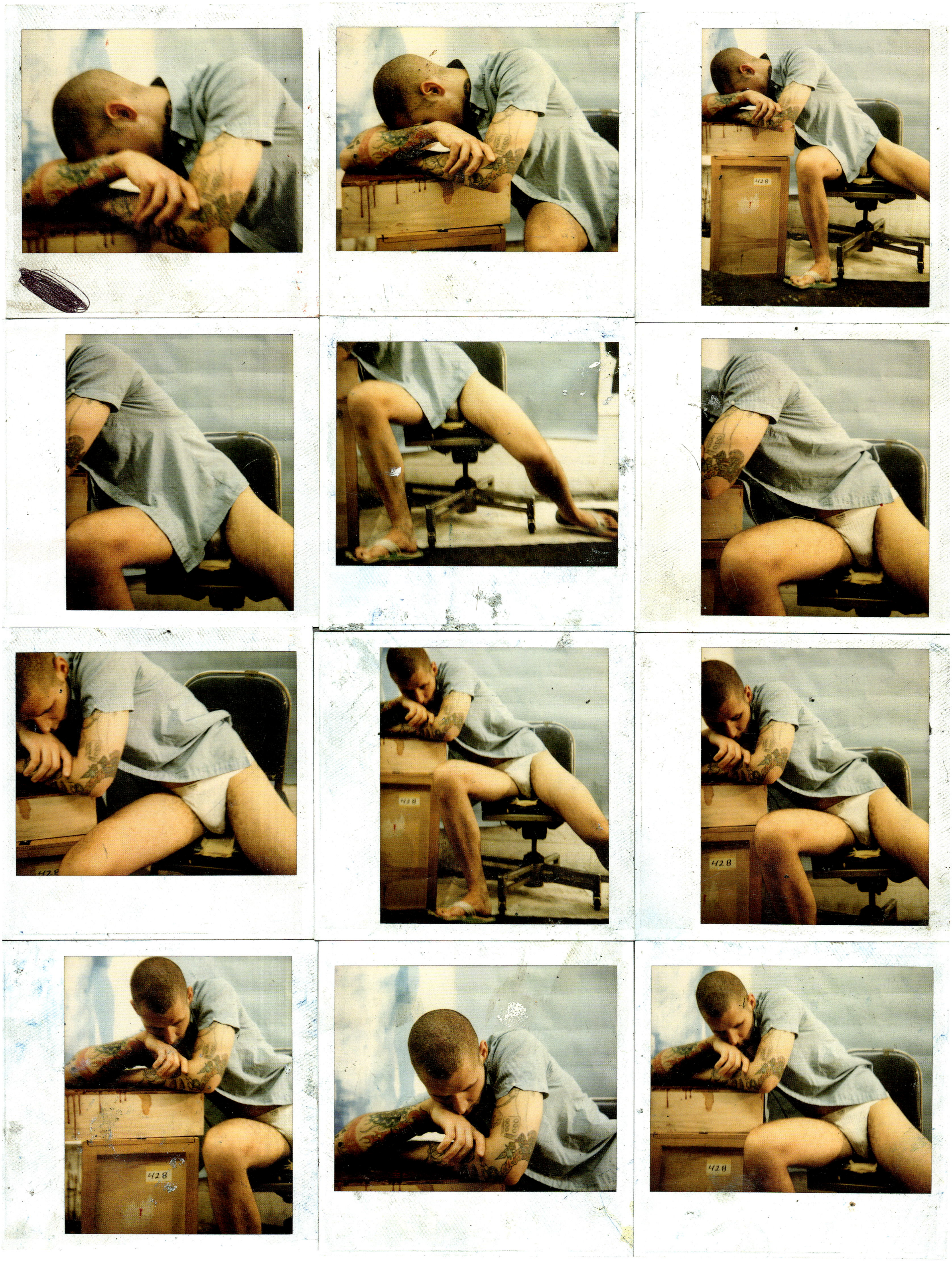

Phil, study for Goya's *The Sleep of Reason*, New York, 1999

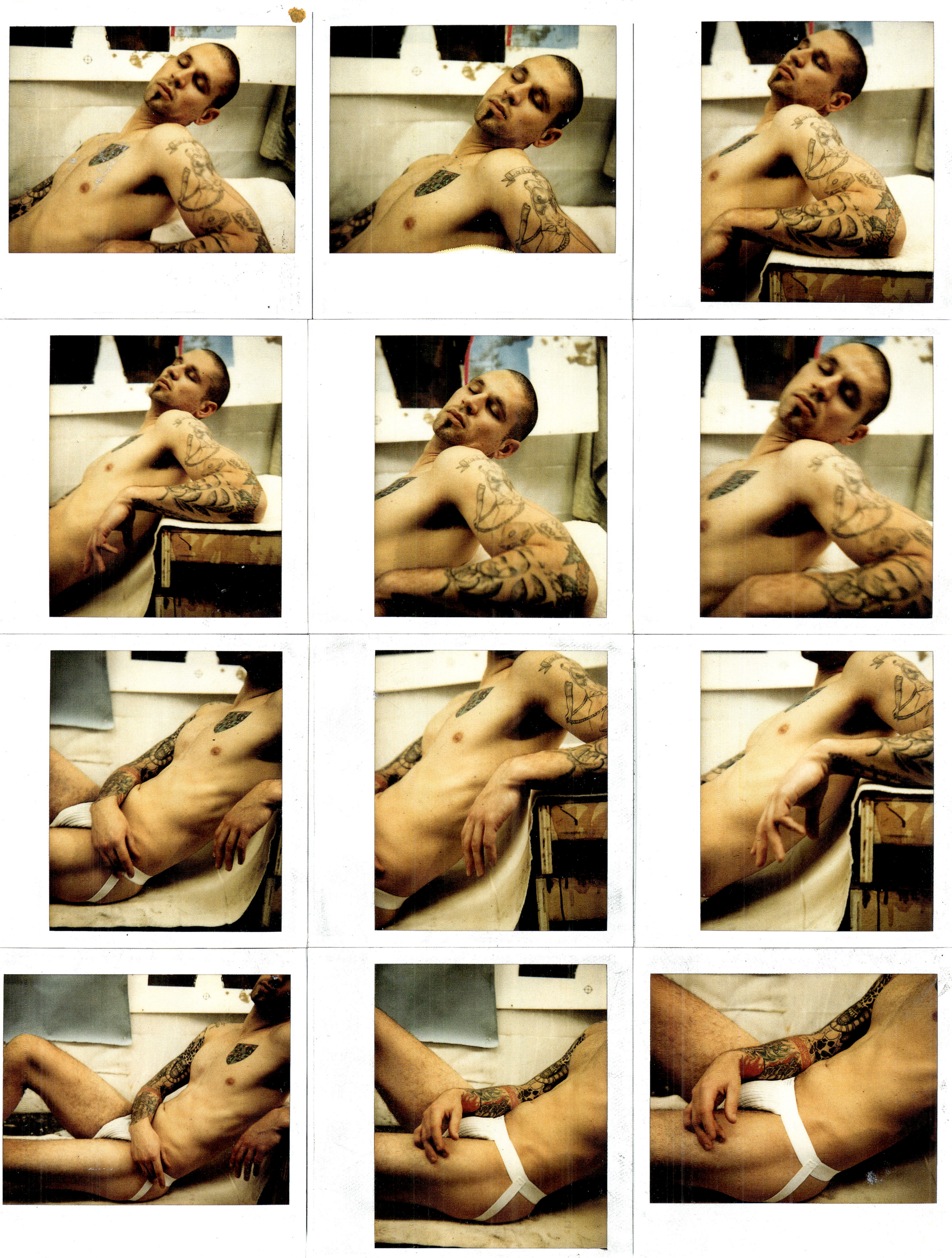

Phil, study for Mars, *Mars and Venus* Botticelli, New York, 1999

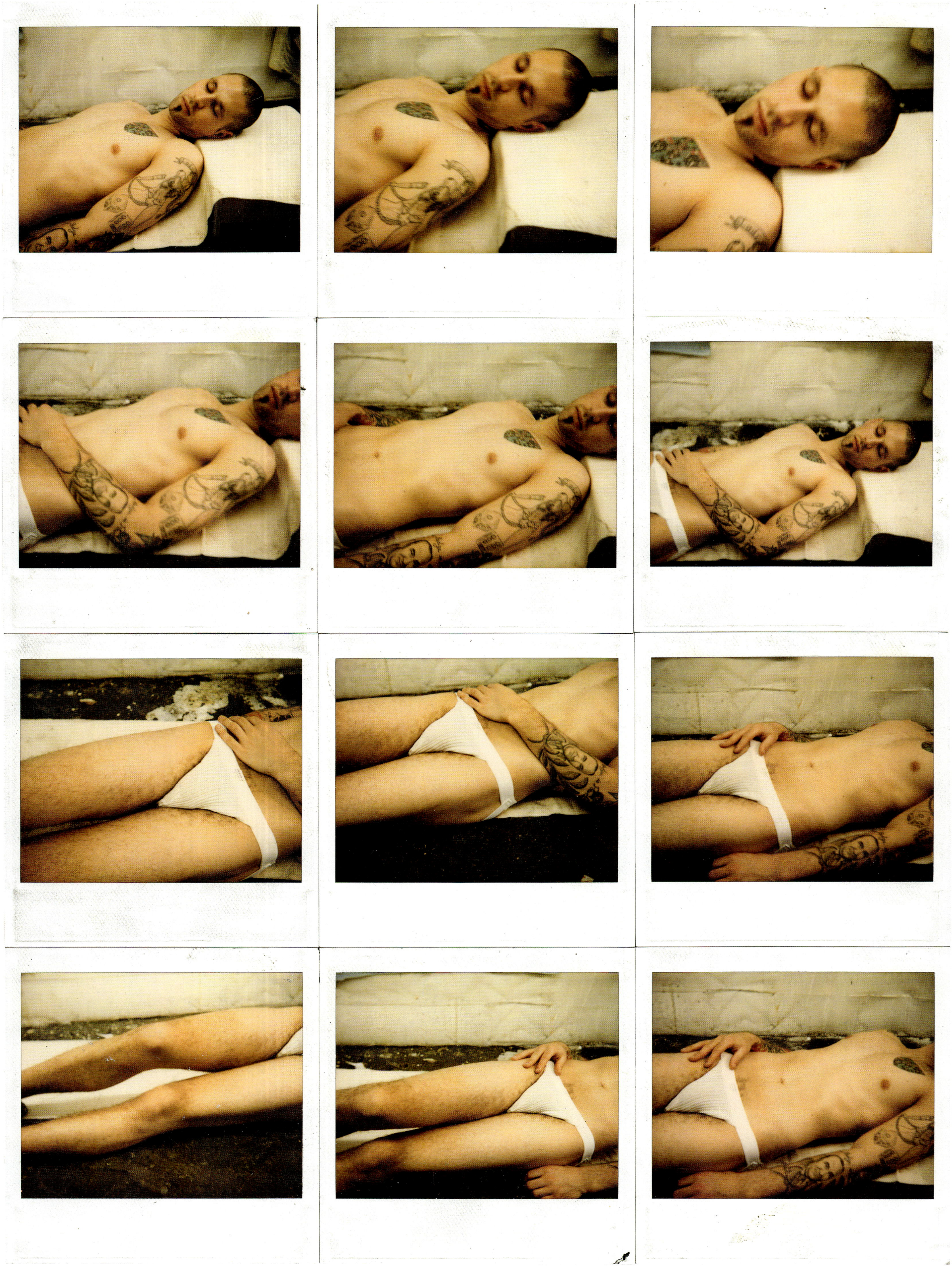

Phil, study for Mars, *Venus and Mars and Cupid*, Piero di Cosimo, New York, 1999

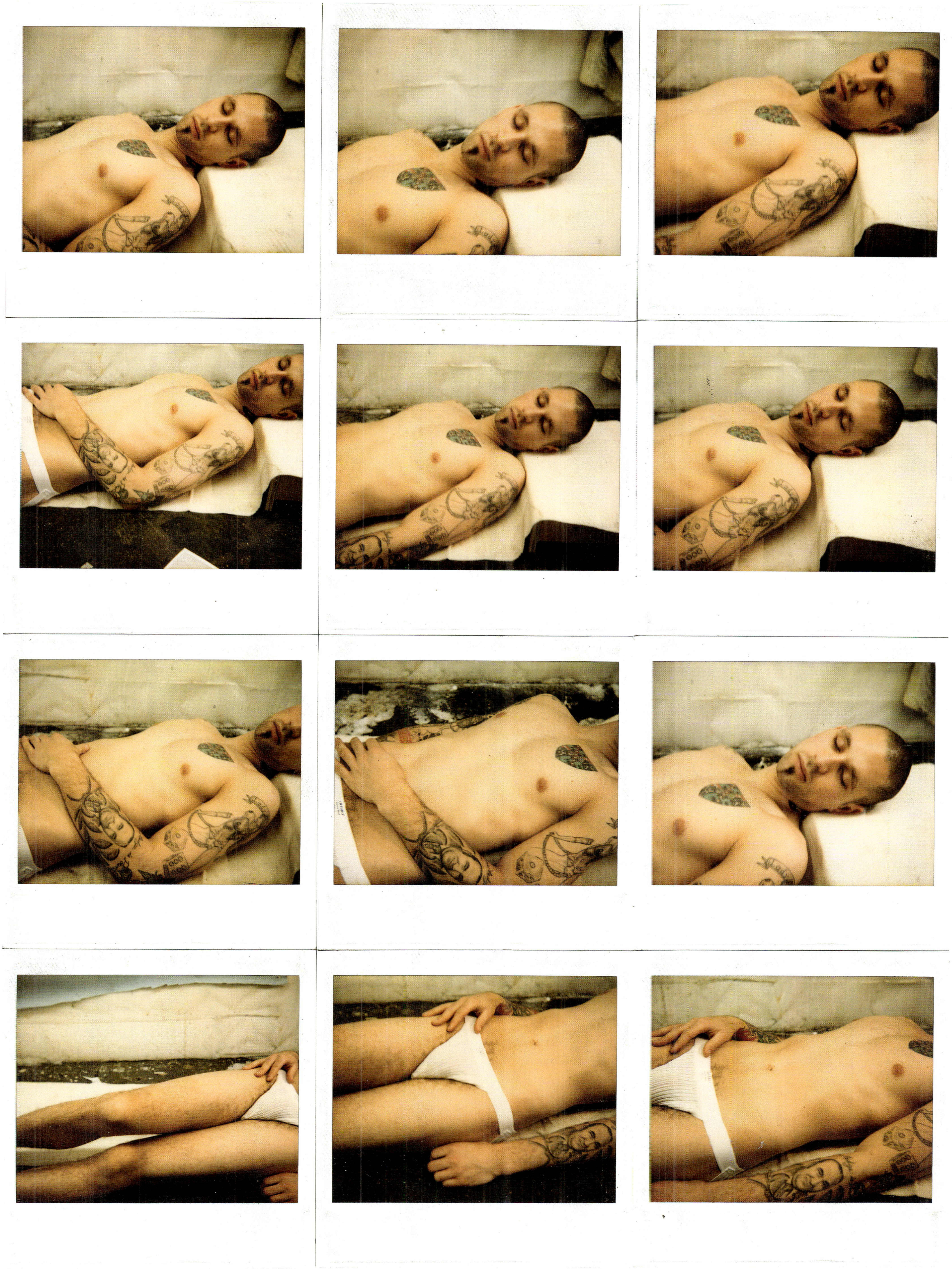

Phil, study for Mars, *Venus and Mars and Cupid*, Piero di Cosimo, New York, 1999

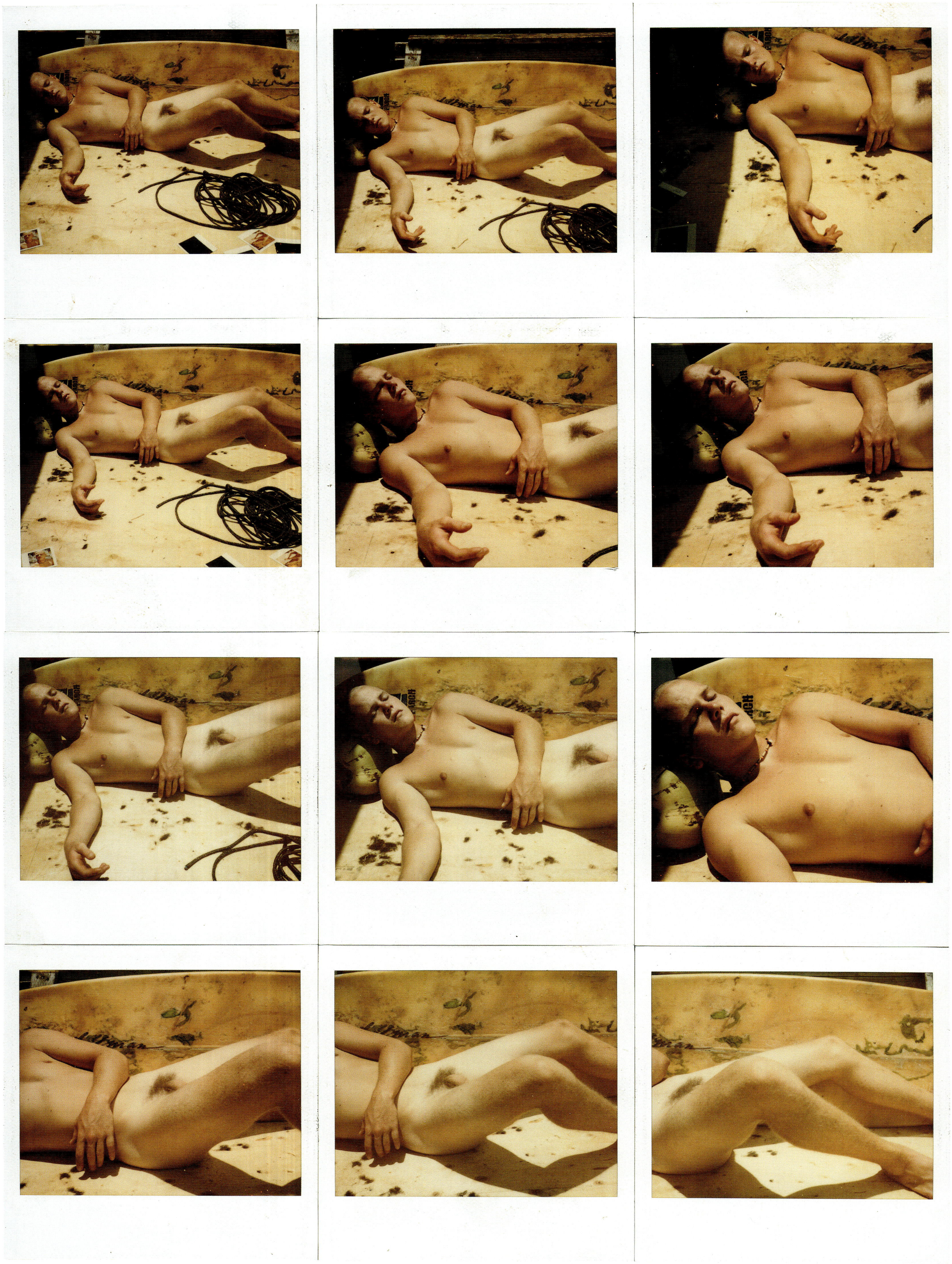

Royce, Paia, Hawaii, 2003

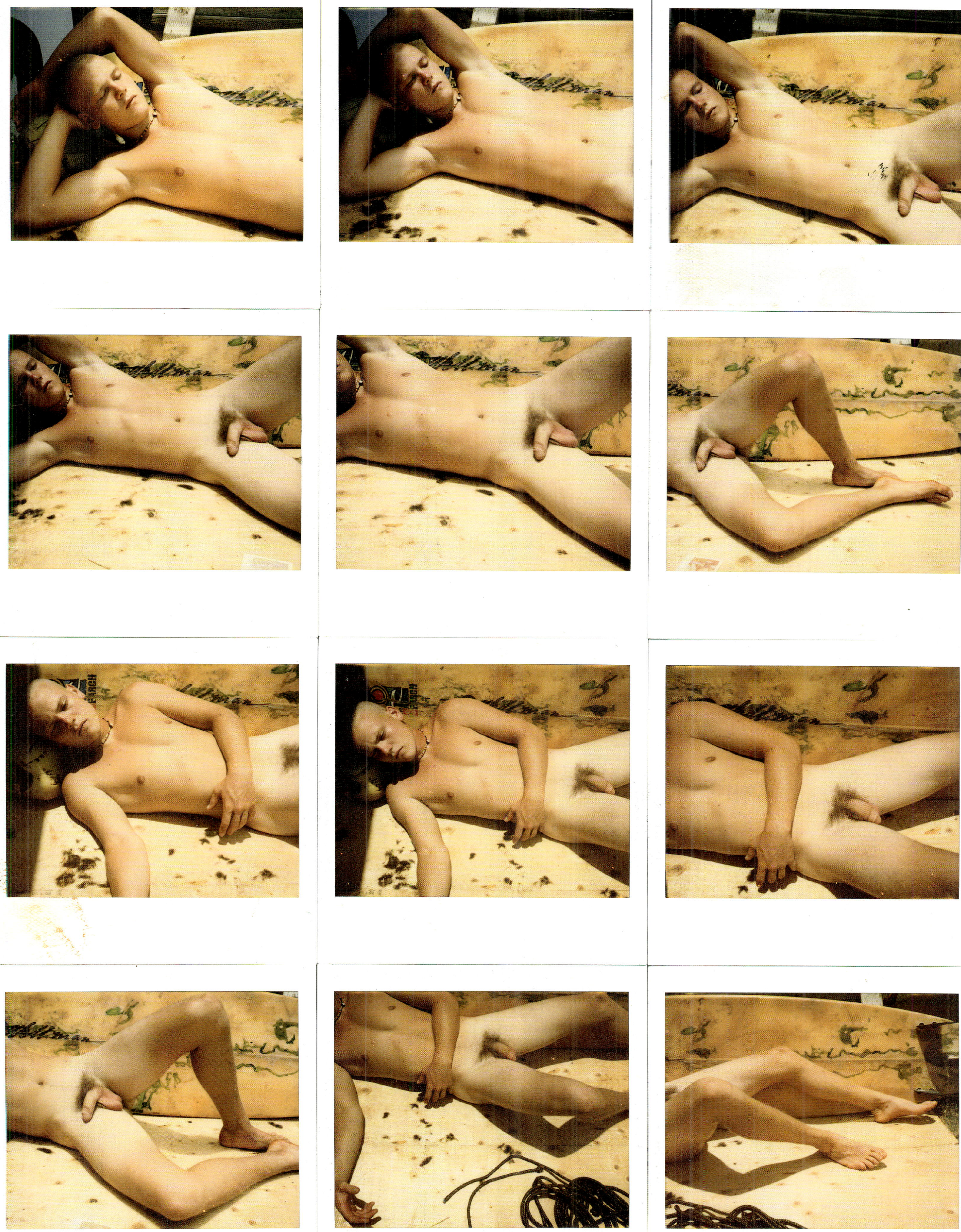

Royce, Paia, Hawaii, 2003

Attila Lukacs's Skinheads: Ciphers of Cold War Twilight

Scott Watson

In the early summer of 1986, the so-called *Historikerstreit* began to take hold as the dominant topic of public intellectual life in West Germany. This public "history dispute" was inaugurated when Jürgen Habermas, Germany's most eminent philosopher, responded to a newspaper article by historian Ernst Nolte in which Nolte argued that, in the larger scheme of things, the Third Reich was "on side" in the twentieth century's defining battle against Communism, and that Hitler's campaign to exterminate the Jews was the result of a comprehensible fear of Bolshevism. In the ledger of history's judgment, claimed Nolte, Soviet Communists committed greater atrocities than the Nazis. Furthermore, he compared the expulsion of Germans from Poland and Czechoslovakia after the War to the expulsion of Jews from the same countries during the Third Reich, as if they were commensurate historical crimes. (Does the reader need to be reminded that the dispossessed Germans lived, while the Jews did not?)

A circle of conservative historians began to represent views more or less like this in public—breathtaking in their revisionist audacity—insisting that Germans needed to reclaim pride in their history. Some of them were close to then-Chancellor Helmut Kohl, whose dream of a reunified Germany, seemingly on an impossibly far horizon, was actually only a few years from becoming reality. Thus, several years before German reunification, a great ghost had reappeared … that of the Old Empire, a Germany that included the *Bundesrepublik*, the DDR, the Sudetenland, and East Prussia.

Habermas attacked these views. He argued that they threatened to undermine the very foundations of liberal democracy in West Germany by trivializing the Holocaust and halting the process of reckoning that was West Germany's greatest cultural challenge and the *Vergangenheistbewältigung*, which was the basis of its post-war rehabilitation.

The history debate penetrated daily life through newspapers and television and came to the fore around any project involving restoration, civic planning, or public monuments, especially in divided Berlin. As one example, a proposal to make a permanent memorial of the Gestapo torture chambers next to the Martin-Gropius-Bau (where the outdoor museum Topography of Terror is situated) elicited an official response that the site was not fit for German history, as if the Third Reich and its crimes could be passed on to another nation (i.e., the Soviet Union) to bear.

Attila Richard Lukacs arrived in Berlin in mid-October 1986; he remembers an eclipse of the moon (October 16), which marked an auspicious arrival. Through the connections of Canadian artist Michael Morris—who had lived in Berlin since 1980 when he arrived as a guest of the DAAD, a German academic exchange service, Attila secured a studio in the Künstlerhaus Bethanien, an international artists' residence located in an old hospital in Kreuzberg, Berlin's district of discontented Germans, foreign misfits, and much of its Turkish population. He soon fell in with the young crowd that frequented the gay bar Oranienbar, whose owner became his lover. In the late 1980s, the Kreuzberg art scene was dominated by the nihilistic bricoleur group End Art, whose gallery was just doors away from Attila's apartment, and the performance art/music group Die Tödliche Doris.[1] End Art, and Kreuzberg art at its best during those years, was an all-out assault on liberal German values and the sacred cows that forty years of being "good Germans" had wrought. It must have struck the young Canadian artist just how public the enactment of battles with private demons was, and how much they had to do with history in a place like Berlin in the twilight years of the Cold War.

In this studio and in a subsequent one in Moabit, a few convenient blocks from a youth detention centre, Lukacs began his monumental "history" paintings of Berlin's skinheads, many of whom also lived in Kreuzberg. I'm not sure if Attila was a follower of the history debate as it appeared in print, but its symbolic effects certainly caught his eye. Berlin was, before the collapse of the East, a city obsessed by History. It was a place where the Second World War had not yet come to a close, literally an occupied city, where Soviet soldiers stood guard at the monument in the Tiergarten. Yet there were two versions of history, the Western and the Eastern, each explaining the present and each obliterating the other. The result was a special field of forces whose dominant chords were melancholy, perversion, and perseverance. Berlin saw itself as the European modern metropolis *par excellence,* cut in half and frozen in aspic. Walking past the bullet-scarred buildings on a grey winter's day, the air acrid with the smell of coal, or through the corridors of Greek and Roman statues in the Pergamon Museum, it was easy to imagine Heidegger by one's side, extolling the German language ("to think, one must think in German") or advancing the claim that Enlightenment Germany, so vividly a ruin, was the heir to ancient Greece. The vibrations and transhistorical connections between the Nazis and Greeks are epitomized in Karl Friedrich Schinkel's Altes Museum (completed around 1830), whose façade was the template for the future architectural work of Albert Speer. But more melancholy than

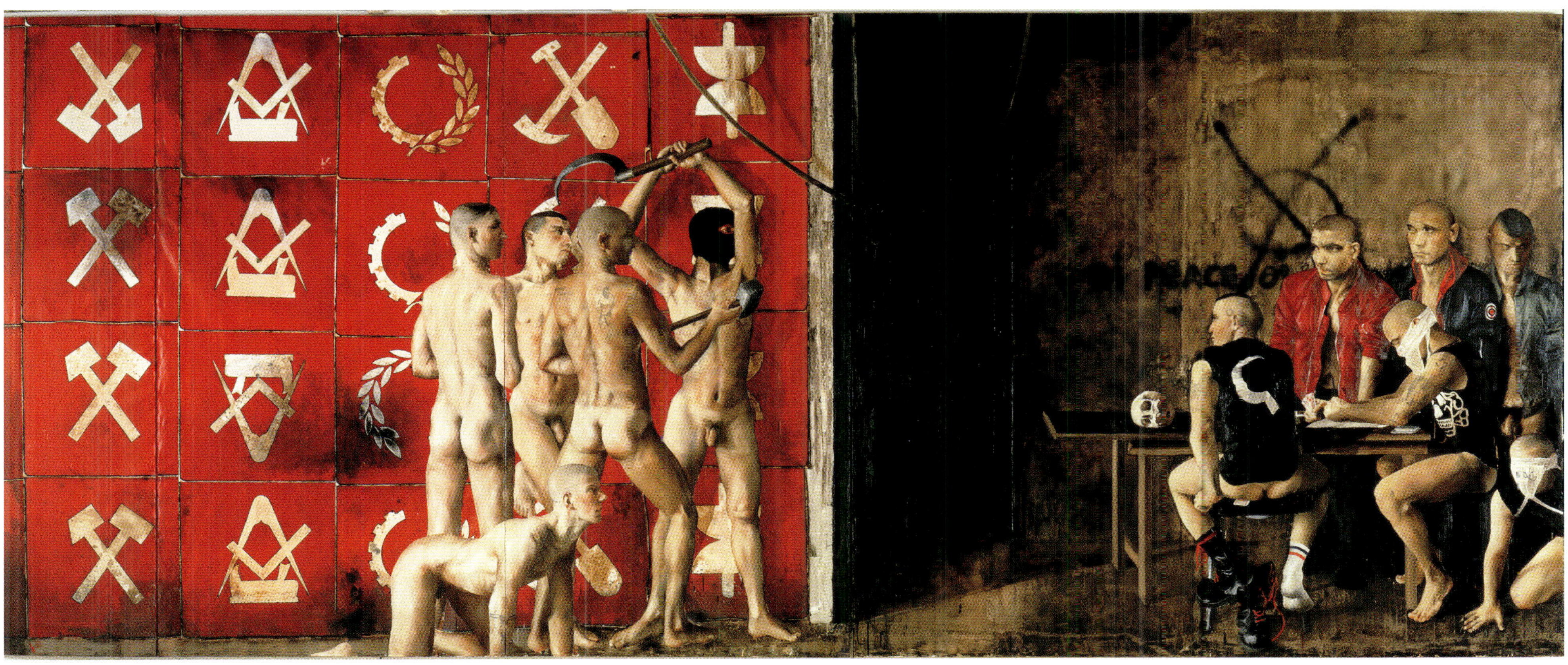

Attila Richard Lukacs, *The Young Spartans Challenge the Boys to Fight*, 1988, asphalt, oil, enamel on canvas, 279 x 673 cm.

all of the ghosts, both good and bad (some very bad), was the general feeling that the prosperous *Bundesrepublik* and the lazy Western Allies would simply tire of supporting Berlin and that it would eventually be ceded to the drab police state that surrounded it. Without an economy, West Berlin sustained its population by offering exemptions from compulsory military service to the young people who agreed to live there. The Germany of the Economic Miracle resented these subsidies. "A million marks an hour," groused one famous curator, "Berlin costs a million marks an hour!"[2]—the implication being that it was hardly worth it.

Into this historical endgame appeared the skinhead. The skinheads were united by fashion, adopting a uniform of Dr. Martens boots, Fred Perry polo shirts, and dangling red suspenders; their hair was buzzed, shaved, or mohawked. This conformity of look belied their division into factions, the most notorious and perhaps numerous being the self-styled neo-Nazis who beat up Turks and gays. But there were also Communist, Turk, and gay skinheads. These, and the uncategorized majority of skinhead youths (hooligans), became Lukacs's models. His painting, *The Young Spartans Challenge the Boys to Fight* (1988), shows a face-off between neo-Nazi and Communist skinheads; the left (Communist) side of the painting is based on Edgar Degas's *Young Spartans Exercising* (1860) and the right side on Caravaggio's *The Calling of Saint Matthew* (1599–1600). The face-off echoes the East/West divide, layering it with a confrontation between Communists and Fascists. The figure of Christ has been removed from the Caravaggio composition. Instead, the "apostles" gaze into an ever darkening shadow … a Heideggerian void, a penumbra of dread about the future that caught the mood of Berlin before *Wiedervereinigung*, in a painting that seems, on the other hand, to auger reunification.

Probably half of the writing on Lukacs from the 1980s was an anxious encounter with these young men through the medium of Lukacs's work, even though he removed them from the streets of Berlin and put them into the space of painting. But a bourgeois anxiety about Lukacs's engagement

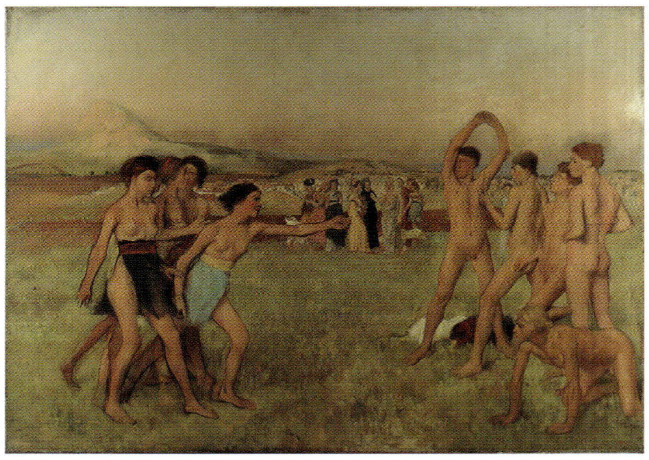

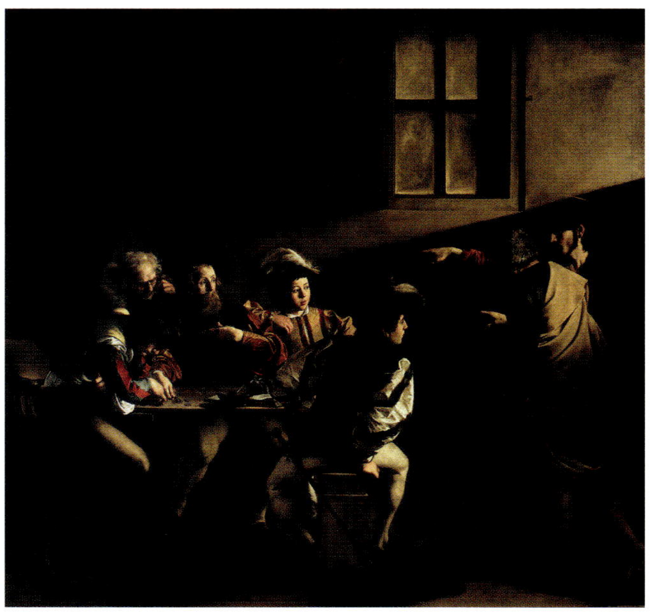

(Clockwise from top left): Edgar Degas, *Young Spartans Exercising*, 1860, oil on canvas, 109 x 155 cm, National Gallery, London (courtesy of Art Resource). Film still from *Salò, or the 120 Days of Sodom/Salò o le 120 giornate di Sodoma* (1975, Italy). Directed by Pier Paolo Pasolini, © Zebra, courtesy of Photofest. Caravaggio, *The Calling of Saint Matthew*, 1599–1600, oil on canvas, 322 x 340 cm. San Luigi dei Francesi, Rome (courtesy of Alinari Archives).

with the models persisted even as the bourgeoisie embraced the paintings themselves. In his world, the skinheads are a Benjaminian type, a version of his "Parisian Apache," upon which much could be projected. His boys dressed up, not only in military gear and the street uniforms of the disenfranchised, and they hung out at the decrepit baronial hunting lodge in service of some unseen aristocratic leader. There are notions of the Sadean retreat (conflated with the Göring *Jagdschloss*) in the skinhead paintings, isolated from the urban world and having a lost, "aristocratic" relationship to nature. But the skinheads were also, importantly, as they appeared in both real life and in history, the true face of Reagan-Thatcherism's thuggish ideology. Lukacs was not the only artist to notice the skinheads in the 1980s; they populate the work of Gilbert and George, the films of Derek Jarman, and later, the photographs of Wolfgang Tillmans. As violent, loathed outcasts, they were perfect candidates for both saints and angels. One of Attila's favourite models, Alex, was a skinhead of no particular political persuasion. He had been born in the East and "bought" by the West; that is to say, he was caught (rather than killed) trying to escape the East, sentenced and imprisoned, then "bought," as was the custom, by the West. (In such a world, just how do we expect people to behave? Like "good" citizens?)

It would be fair to say that just as a skinhead's devotion to his look transcended his politics, Lukacs's interest in the skinhead as a type was a cathexis, a projection onto an erotically charged semiotic field. The political nastiness of the young men is not withheld. Instead, the more extreme and further from the normal progressive views that artists like Attila hold, the more exciting they became as sexual possibilities. Irrational, loutish, violent, and full of hate, especially for homosexuals, the skinheads provided Lukacs with the major inspiration and subject during the years he painted in Berlin. He dwells on the homosociality of the all-male world of skinheaddom, sometimes segueing into other worlds that produce a similar excess of masculine signs—the military academy, the mine, the factory—turning them into a homosexual orgy with much of the erotic focus directed to the artist's surrogate, the tormented sexual toy of the skinhead.

Lukacs tends to see the paintings of the 1980s that feature skinheads as prophetic—in a fashion sense. That is, he tells the future that it will embrace this look … or that the gay world will. Of course, he is right. The gay world, whose European capital is no doubt Berlin, eventually did accept the skinhead into the great fetish index of masculine signs. But it didn't always. The artist recalls being asked to leave the leather bar Knast (by two men dressed as Gestapo officers) as his skinhead look was "not appropriate." The artist considered it a great triumph when his 1988 Künstlerhaus Bethanien exhibition was the cover story not of *Artforum* or *Wolkenkratzer*, but of *Disziplin,* a magazine devoted to publishing an up-to-date gay fetish/S&M contact list. (The magazine and others like it have long been eclipsed by the Internet.)

The Sadean *mis-en-scène* has often been used to critique Fascism before, most notably in Pasolini's terrifying masterwork, *Salò* (1975). It's possible to lodge one's view of Lukacs's history paintings in this same critical realm, especially if one follows

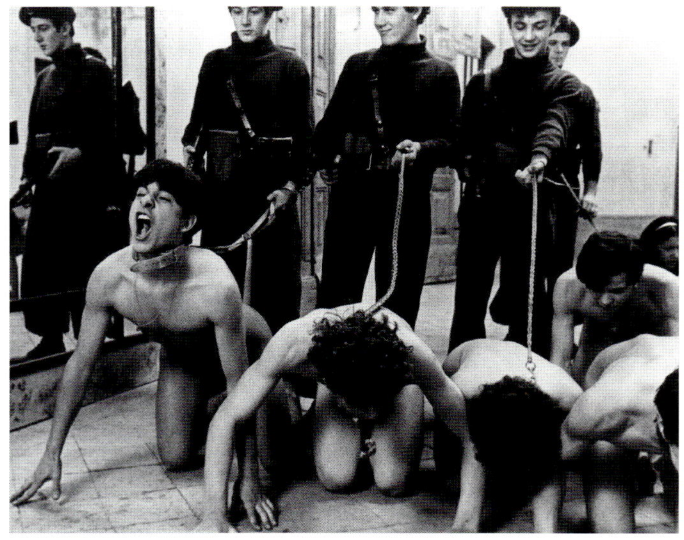

what he has been doing recently. But it is their sheer aestheticism that interests me. To make an absurd comparison, Lukacs's young men inhabit a world somewhat contingent to Burne-Jones's world of somnolent, hunky knights. It's also useful to remember that Lukacs's Berlin paintings are contemporary to the 1980s work of Robert Mapplethorpe and that at the same time, there was a crusade against sexual variety, which was countered by adopting S&M as style. And as the worlds of Lukacs's young men progressed from skinheads in Sadean retreats to a series on their "twins," cadets in a military academy, and then to the most accomplished of these series, a re-imagining of the world of Indian and Persian miniatures (*Varieties of Love*, 1991–92), they became more ethereal. Perhaps this change of tone had something to do with the artist's growing familiarity with the work of Michael Büthe, who appropriated von Gloeden photographs in paintings sourced in Moroccan decorative art. Yet the idea that sexual signs should be inscribed in nature, that they are fundamentally Edenic, became more pronounced.

One of the most interesting of the *Varieties of Love* paintings, *Amorous Meeting* (1991), was selected for curator Jan Hoet's *Documenta IX* (1992) but ultimately not exhibited.[3] The painting depicts two skinhead, homo comrades embracing. Across a field of poppies they greet a rising sun, which is a swastika. One salutes, while the other fingers. The one who salutes has a hard cock; one imagines that he's going to fuck the one who fingers. This is in fact a history painting. We know this because Jan Hoet would not allow it to be hung even though his associate, Pierre Luigi Tazzi, had chosen it. The artist was told the paintings were "too male." Not "too

Nazi," but excessively male, as if somehow the cosmologies of Jean Genet and Tom of Finland were not born of war. Thus the work became embroiled quite literally in the history debate. Today, the image is crystal clear. Two lovers look, across a field of narcotic dreaming, at the future. One salutes, one resists. They are the same gesture, overridden by an erotic prior command that represents nature itself.

In the world of *Salò*, the aristocrats have sold out to Fascism (in fact, the co-option of the aristocracy to Fascism is central to Facism's sentimental narrative). In the world of Lukacs's paintings, the real masters are not there (except perhaps in the military academy works, which are very much aimed at daddy and daddy types).

From the very beginning of his career, the scale at which he worked, the scouring of contemporary media for images, the looting of Renaissance and Mannerist paintings, and the particular poignancy of his models—young men who seem lost in history but who might flourish in nature—Lukacs's paintings have been shadows of a future that can only be read through a system of signs that connects war, work, uniforms, and sex between men. If the Berlin paintings are becoming (and slowly but surely they are) a great artistic witness to a massive historical hinge, Lukacs's New York works (1996–2002) witnessed the turning gyre of the politics of masculinity in the US, and his current work is even more pronounced in its focus on that terrible place where History devours beautiful young men.

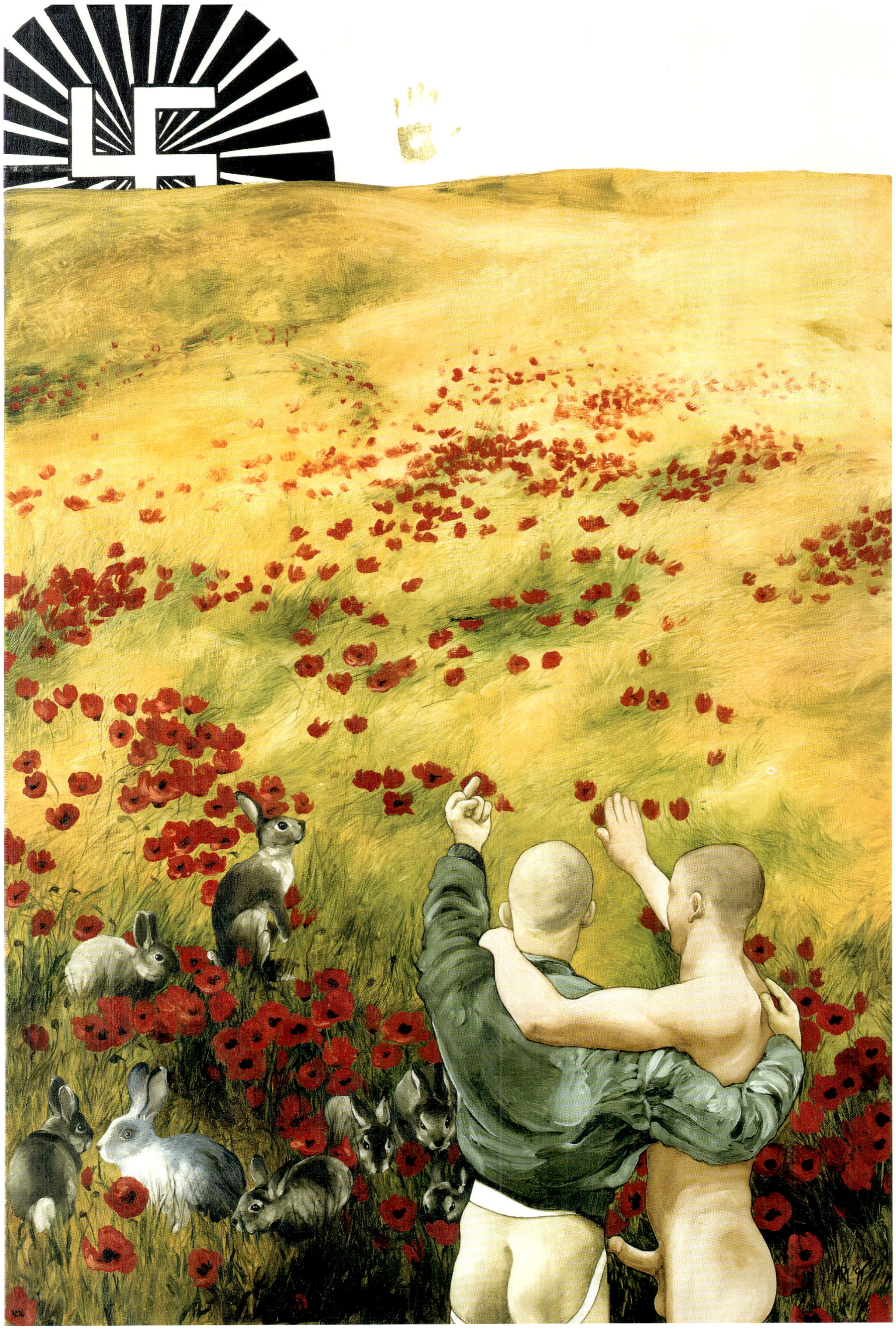

Attila Richard Lukacs, *Amorous Meeting*, 1991, oil and enamel on canvas, 297 x 199 cm, Collection of Sammlung Jurgen Wolff.

NOTES

1. The Deadly Doris was Wolfgang Müller, Käthe Kruse, and Nikolaus Utermöhlen.

2. In 1987, in a restaurant on Kantstrasse, to the writer and several other assembled art world types.

3. The painting was shown in Frank Wagner's The Eighth Square exhibition in 2006 at the Museum Ludwig, Cologne.

Attila Richard Lukacs, Michael Morris, Berlin

Stan Persky

1.

Upon arriving in Berlin in spring 1990, the first piece of "visual art" I saw, or perhaps the first that I actually *looked at*, was in the apartment of Canadian artist Michael Morris. The work was a set of twenty Polaroid photos, placed in a single frame. They were of a nude young man, about nineteen or twenty years old, taken by Attila Richard Lukacs, then a twenty-seven-year-old Canadian painter also living in Berlin. I had come to the former (and future) capital of Germany as a freelance journalist, just months after the fall of the Berlin Wall in November 1989, to cover the first post-communist "free" election in East Germany. I wasn't at the moment especially focused either on seeing art or thinking about erotic matters (although both of those things are always lurking, at least at the back of my mind).

I knew who Lukacs was, having seen the paintings of the Alberta-born artist in the *Young Romantics* exhibition curated by Scott Watson at the Vancouver Art Gallery in 1985, an exhibition that became instantly legendary for its declaration of the resurgence of figurative painting in Canadian art.

Michael Morris's apartment was located on Mommsenstrasse just off Ku'damm, the main median-divided, tree-lined boulevard of what was then West Berlin. It's an elegant corner of the Charlottenburg district, whose five-storey, weighty, Jugendstil apartment buildings had been accidentally spared the bombings of World War II. Those bombings, as I'd already observed on the bus ride in from Tegel Airport, had destroyed half of the former capital of the Nazi Reich and necessitated the postwar construction program of drab, but functional, plaster frontages that filled in the gaps of the cityscape.

The familiar figure of Michael Morris was waiting for me at the Ku'damm bus stop across the street from the tiny, triangular GeorgeGroszPlatz. I trudged alongside him, luggage in hand, to Mommsenstrasse, where we passed through his building's enclosed courtyard and climbed the circular tower staircase to his third floor studio apartment.

I'd known Michael since the late 1960s in Vancouver, where he was a prominent Canadian painter. He was perhaps best-known for formalist abstract works ("stripe paintings," we called them) and a variety of minimalist sculptures (dubbed the "Colour Bars" project). He was also influenced by the international Fluxus movement, which led to work in performance, video, and a vast collection of images that appeared as "Image Bank," a collaborative project with fellow Canadian artist Vincent Trasov. A further strand of his work included a voluminous set of homoerotic drawings that made an obvious connection to contemporary gay consciousness and, as well, there were many photo albums documenting his life in Berlin. For any Canadian passing through Berlin even vaguely connected to the art world, the instruction was to "Call Michael" (which also happens to be the title of one of Lukacs's more notable paintings, in which Morris appears). Apart from all else, Morris was an astute guide to the intertwined historical strata of the about-to-be reunited city, as well as a person with an unrivalled historical knowledge of the arts.

But for the moment (that crucial first moment), he was simply a gracious host putting on the kettle for tea and dealing with a disoriented, jetlagged writer from home. When he ducked into the cramped, combination pantry-library he casually called out to me: "Come and have a little shriek at this."

On a wall inside the room was the set of Lukacs's Polaroids. In them, a naked youth was photographed in a variety of postures, taken from different angles, including several shot from above. In many of the images, the poses suggested scenes of submission, bondage, and a vulnerability beyond the subject's nudity, all pointing to a transgressive underworld of eros.

The reason for putting "visual art" in quotation marks when referring to these photos was because the intent of the piece seemed variable to me—that is, they could be seen as a playful gift from a young artist to an avuncular mentor—not necessarily a "work of art" in the "serious" sense of that term, although clearly from the process of art. As a viewer, I saw the pictures of the boy, with his hands locked behind him as if tied or spread-eagled on the ground, as images of desire that momentarily jolted me out of my dazed traveller's state. At the same time, I consciously filed that response or "shriek," as Michael described it, into more practical terms: "So this is Berlin, too." This, in the manner of Christopher Isherwood's declaration: "Berlin meant Boys" (from his memoir *Christopher and His Kind* of 1976). Whatever else I would see in Berlin over the next few days—mostly politicians, the still-functioning checkpoints of the Berlin Wall, first impressions of a city destined to become the post-communist new centre of Europe—those images of Lukacs's Polaroids remained as an erotic underlay to the larger historical tableau.

2.

During the almost three decades (1961-1989) when it was walled in, West Berlin had been a city of political and artistic fantasy. Heavily subsidized by the West German government, it was meant to be a "showcase" of freedom to its East German counterparts. Its odd status as an ideological projection, and its substantial cultural funding from the West, were among the things that made it possible for artists like Lukacs and Morris to live there in the years before the Wall came down. It's what permitted young people in West Berlin to play at revolution in the political movements of "squatters," the self-declared "autonomous" groupings, and other leftist groups of the period; it brought young West German males to the city, since they were exempted from the military while living there; and it permitted the disenfranchised to play at neo-Nazism. But if its politics and art were in one sense a fantasy, it was a fantasy from which real life and desire, with its un-playful dangers, could also break out, and its "look" could be authentically captured in the work of a remarkable artist like Lukacs.

Lukacs had come to Berlin in 1986 and Morris helped to obtain a place for him at Berlin's Künstlerhaus Bethanien. The Künstlerhaus was an artists' residence and studio space in the Kreuzberg district, a neighbourhood, as Morris recalls, "known for its bohemian community, working class population, Turkish immigrants, artists and skinheads," figures that Lukacs drew on as models for his work. Here, Lukacs energetically embarked on a succession of large paintings of youths, often involving the use of his Polaroid studies. These monumental paintings featured gangs of skinheads in clubhouse scenes of ritualized sexual initiation, set within underground and abandoned industrial settings. They, along with a series of portraits,

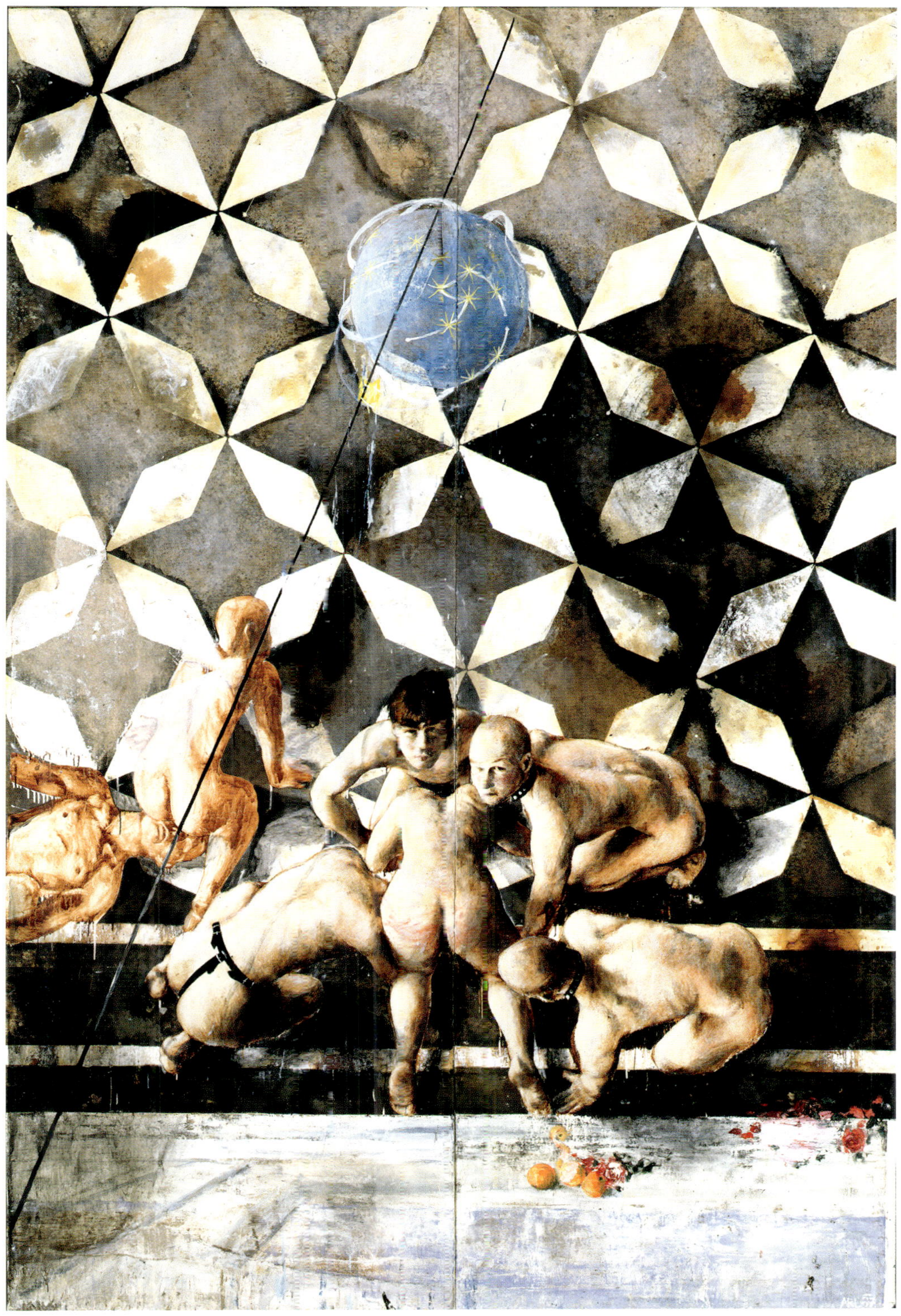

Attila Richard Lukacs, *Down*, 1987, asphalt, oil, and lacquer on canvas, 421 x 287 cm, Collection of the artist.

were shown in a solo exhibition at Künstlerhaus Bethanien in spring 1988.

When I returned to Berlin in the spring of 1991, Michael introduced me to Attila and took me to his studio. It was a large vaulted space under the S-Bahn railway tracks at Lüneburger Strasse 370, in the Moabit district north of the city's central Tiergarten park and within range of the Reichstag and Brandenburg Gate, two of the city's iconic architectural images. Lukacs's earlier works, as well as paintings produced after the fall of the Berlin Wall, now filled the walls and storage racks of the studio, over which the trains periodically rumbled.

Berlin in 1991 was a city in transition, under the gaze of what the German social critic and essayist of the Weimar era, Walter Benjamin, famously identified as "the angel of history." Benjamin tells us that the angel's "face is turned toward the past. Where we perceive a chain of events, he sees one single catastrophe which keeps piling wreckage upon wreckage and hurls it at his feet. The angel would like to stay, awaken the dead, and make whole what has been smashed." If the dead can't be awakened, or the wreckage made whole, the painter at least can work as a recording angel.

And, while the angel of history would like to stay, "a storm is blowing from Paradise; it has got caught in his wings with such violence that the angel can no longer close them. This storm irresistibly propels him into the future to which his back is turned, while the pile of debris before him grows skyward. The storm is what we call progress." This debris of "progress" could literally be seen throughout the reunited city in the form of hundreds of yellow construction cranes at building sites. The wastelands created by the former Wall were being noisily filled with a new, often commercially-driven, utopian vision, not the first time in the city's catastrophic history that it had undergone a "reinvention" of itself.

With the official unification of Germany and the reconstruction of unified Berlin underway in every district of the city (one film of the period, set in Berlin, was titled *Life Is a Construction-Site*), visitors like myself could turn their attention from politics to art and desire. And as before, I turned to Michael and Attila for guidance.

Together, we went to the "Metropolis" show at the Martin-Gropius-Bau museum. It was a gigantic survey of contemporary art that provided a rough idea of what leading artists, such as Sigmar Polke, Anselm Kiefer, Gerhard Richter, and others, were up to and provided a context in which to locate the images of the time. We also went to smaller exhibits by painters like Rainer Fetting and Salome, who were part of the resurgence of figurative painting in the mid-80s, and thus closer to Lukacs's work.

It is important to note that in addition to the milieu of art, Lukacs was also immersed in Berlin's pop culture, and its well-known gay scene, a subculture now beleaguered by the plague of AIDS. At the same time that the city's gay community responded to its health crisis, it continued to be a European centre of *Toleranz*, signalled by the annual Christopher Street Day parade, which wound through the city, attracting several hundred thousand participants.

When I asked Attila for directions, he said, "Well, there's Tabasco, but that's the worst, you don't want to go there." Naturally, the next evening, I was at Tabasco, a rent-bar in the Nollendorfplatz area, the centre of West Berlin's gay subculture. It was home to some fifty or so gay bars and clubs. What's more, it was a part of a century-old history of gay Berlin that began in the 1890s with sexologist Dr Magnus Hirschfeld, who founded the Scientific-Humanitarian Committee to oppose Germany's anti-homosexual laws.

The British gay writers W.H. Auden, Stephen Spender, and Christopher Isherwood all met Hirschfeld at his institute in the 1920s, and Isherwood memorably depicted the bohemian and gay scene amid the incipient rise of Nazism in *Goodbye to Berlin* (1939). Just around the corner from Tabasco, at Nollendorfstrasse 17, there was a plaque outside the five-storey apartment building commemorating the years Isherwood had lived there, and from whose top-floor window he had proclaimed, "I am a camera with its shutter open, quite passive, recording… Some day, all this will have to be developed, carefully printed, fixed."

There is also a history of actual cameras to be discovered in Berlin, of which Lukacs's Polaroids were becoming a part. While the photos he made had the practical function of being "studies" for his paintings, they also are rooted in an artistic tradition, well-known to Lukacs and frequently explicated by Morris, of the more than century-old succession of German homoerotic photography, one of direct transmission from Wilhelm von Gloeden to Herbert List to Herbert Tobias, the latter two of whom had worked extensively in Berlin, photographing the same sort of models as Lukacs was now recording in the 1990s.

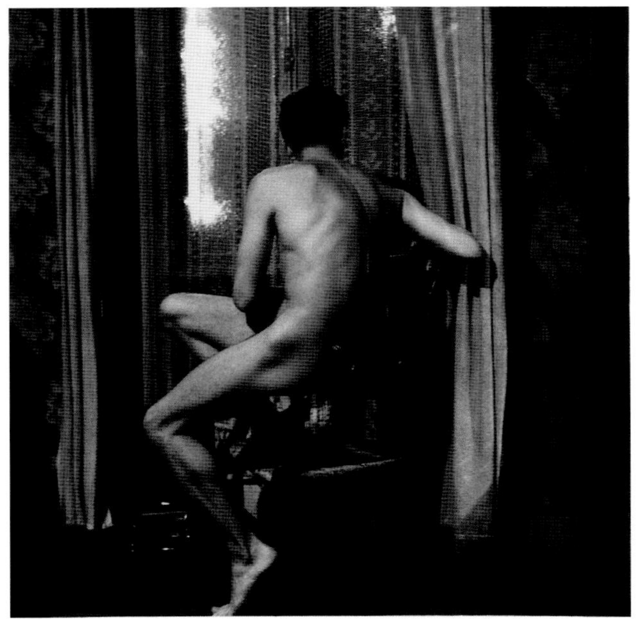

Herbert Tobias, *Dirk in Front of the Window, Paris*, 1952, Berlinische Galerie, Landesmuseum für Modern Kunst, Fotografie und Architektur.

With Germany reunited and the borders between former Soviet bloc countries opened, an influx of people from the former East Germany and other eastern European countries entered the newly amalgamated Berlin. The repertory company of those photographed by Lukacs in his Polaroid studies expanded with the new arrivals but, as before, included casual pickups, designated muses, lovers, old friends, and various participants in the Berlin "scene." In his vaulted studio under the inter-urban railway tracks, there were scattered piles of those photos that visitors could casually flip through, occasionally identifying one of the models as a figure in the paintings on the studio walls.

Amid this large body of work, I eventually found the boy I'd first seen in the Polaroids at Michael's apartment. He appears in a 4 x 3-metre 1987 canvas titled *Down*. Its balcony perspective looks down on a cluster of a half-dozen, naked, kneeling or grovelling youths, one of whom looks plaintively up toward us, set against a background of a marble, patterned, palace floor, its white diamond pattern occasionally merging with the flesh to give the effect of wings attached to submissive angels.

3.

Angelic or not, the model in the first Polaroids I saw was to have, unbeknownst to him, a further adventurous career. A couple of years ago, long after Morris and Lukacs had moved on from Berlin, Michael called. This time, it wasn't a "Call Michael" occasion, but a call to me as a long-time member of the British Columbia Civil Liberties Association (BCCLA) board. In a sort of nightmare of errors, the details of which can be skipped, the Vancouver police had entered Morris's apartment, and had seized the set of Lukacs Polaroids, as part of an investigation into the possibility that they were "child pornography" under Canadian law. A BCCLA lawyer was soon on the scene. In short order, it was pointed out to the police that the model was clearly of age, and that the set of Polaroids was, equally clearly, a twenty-year-old "work of art" (now in the "serious" sense of that term). In due course, the art was returned to the owner, and the investigation closed.

A few months later, I was visiting Lukacs's Vancouver studio, a former auto garage, looking at a new array of his visionary paintings about the wars of the young twenty-first century, and others depicting present-day life in Vancouver's grim Downtown Eastside. I noticed a framed set of Polaroids. That first set of Polaroids I'd seen in Berlin so long ago had resurfaced. Looking at the photos once more, I asked Attila who the young man was, and he offhandedly recalled that the model was a rent-boy he'd picked up at Bahnhof Zoo, which was at the time the main train station of West Berlin, and a well-known gay cruising site. Attila added, with a characteristic chuckle: "So, it was a two-for-one deal"; in addition to the usual services, the young man also became a model for his Polaroid studies.

At first sight the Polaroids are, of course, homoerotic pictures, part of the extensive image repertoire of our times, one that ranges from private photos, cruising websites, queer magazines, all the way to widely available commercial porn. The other, more obvious, sense of the photos as intimate sources resides in the subjects of the photos themselves. Lukacs's choice of persons to photograph is of course idiosyncratic. As Michael Morris reminds me, citing a sentence I had once written, "Desire orders itself with ruthless tyranny." So, we don't ask, Why that one?, or, Why skinheads?, or whatever else, but rather, Who is he? The answers range from the casually encountered boy from the Bahnhof Zoo to people who inhabited Lukacs's life. When I look at the set of photos of a young man injecting himself with heroin, eponymously labelled "Tyler," I recall someone both Michael and I knew and spent an occasional afternoon with, one of Lukacs's oldest friends from Canada. And I also recall the moment a year or two later when Michael told me that Tyler, who had been living/dying with AIDS, had fatally overdosed.

Just as raw canvas receives an underlying primer coat, the content of any given painting, whether historical, utopian, or simply the particularity of a portrait, is underlain by the implicit relationships in the photos. The Polaroids, rescued from boxes and scattered piles, now reappear as their own form of art. But after seeing them, I want to go on to the paintings. If desire is often the artist's first epistemology, as these pictures demonstrate, the knowledge to which he ultimately aspires is the finished story, revealed in the painting. But the sequences of Polaroids tell their own interesting stories, short-stories perhaps, but ones that preserve desire, untouched by the ravages of time and aging.

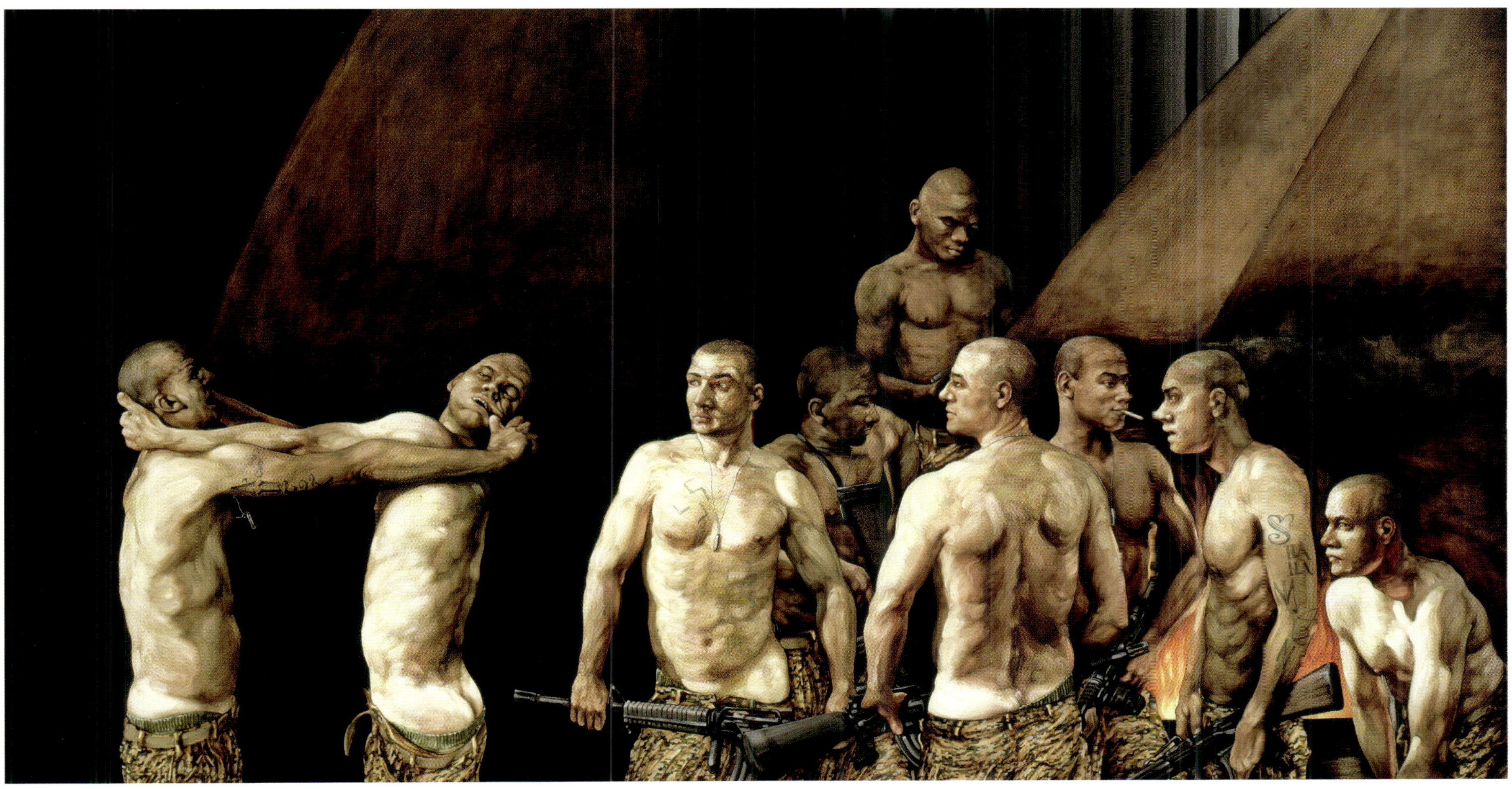

Attila Richard Lukacs, *The Forge*, 2007, asphalt, oil on canvas, 195 x 366 cm.

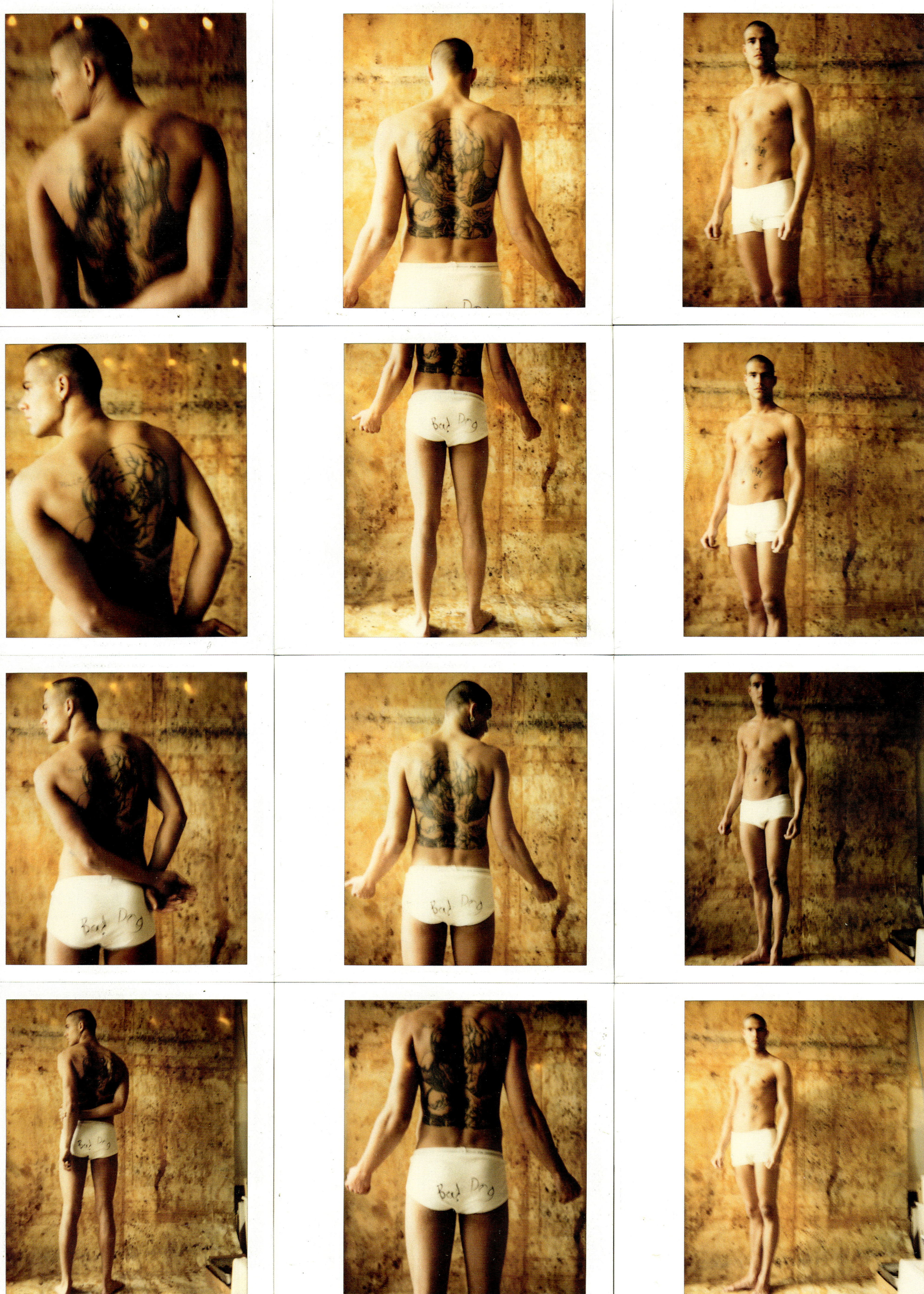

Study for *Saint Francis in Ecstasy*, Bellini, Vancouver, 2002

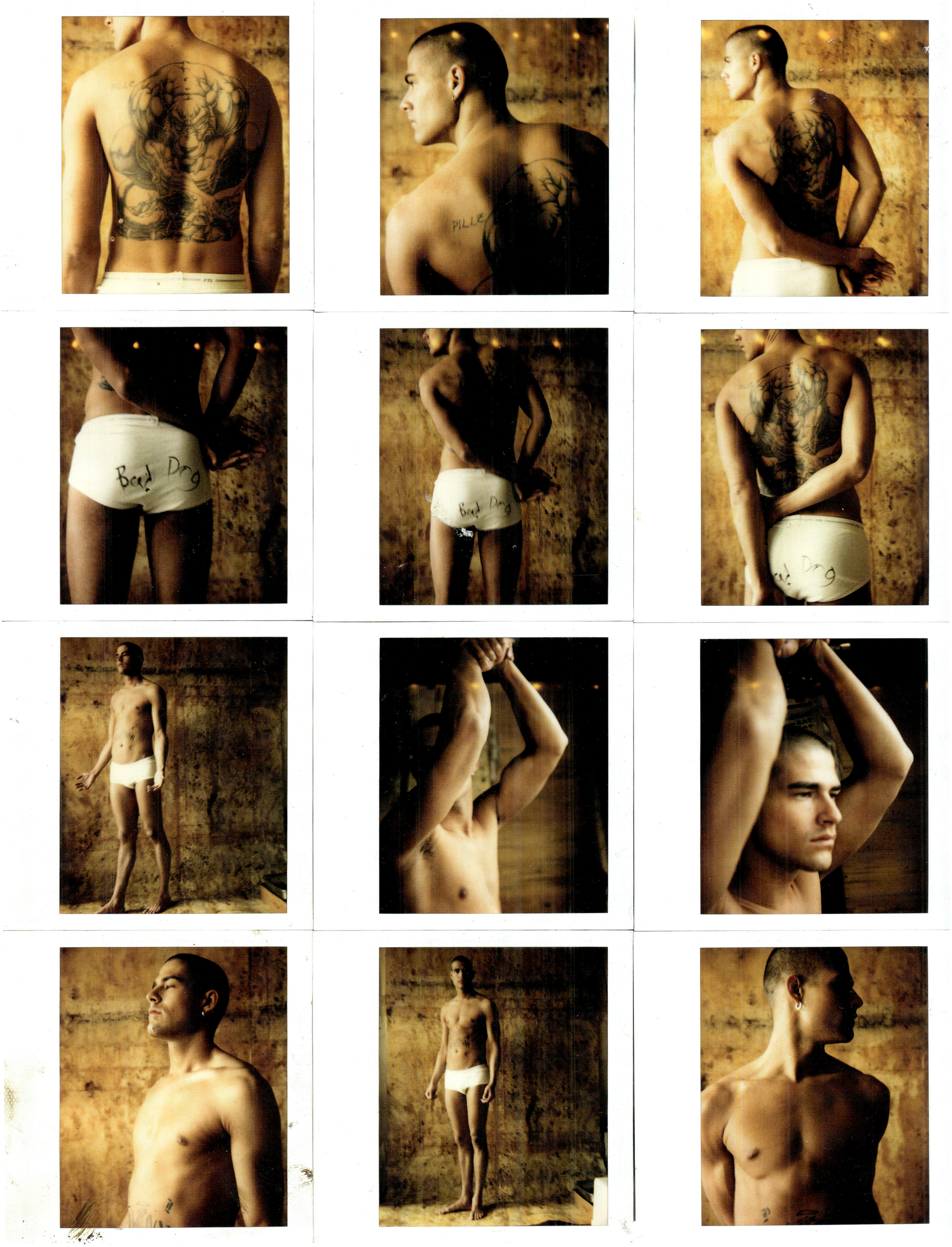

Study for *Saint Francis in Ecstasy*, Bellini, Vancouver, 2002

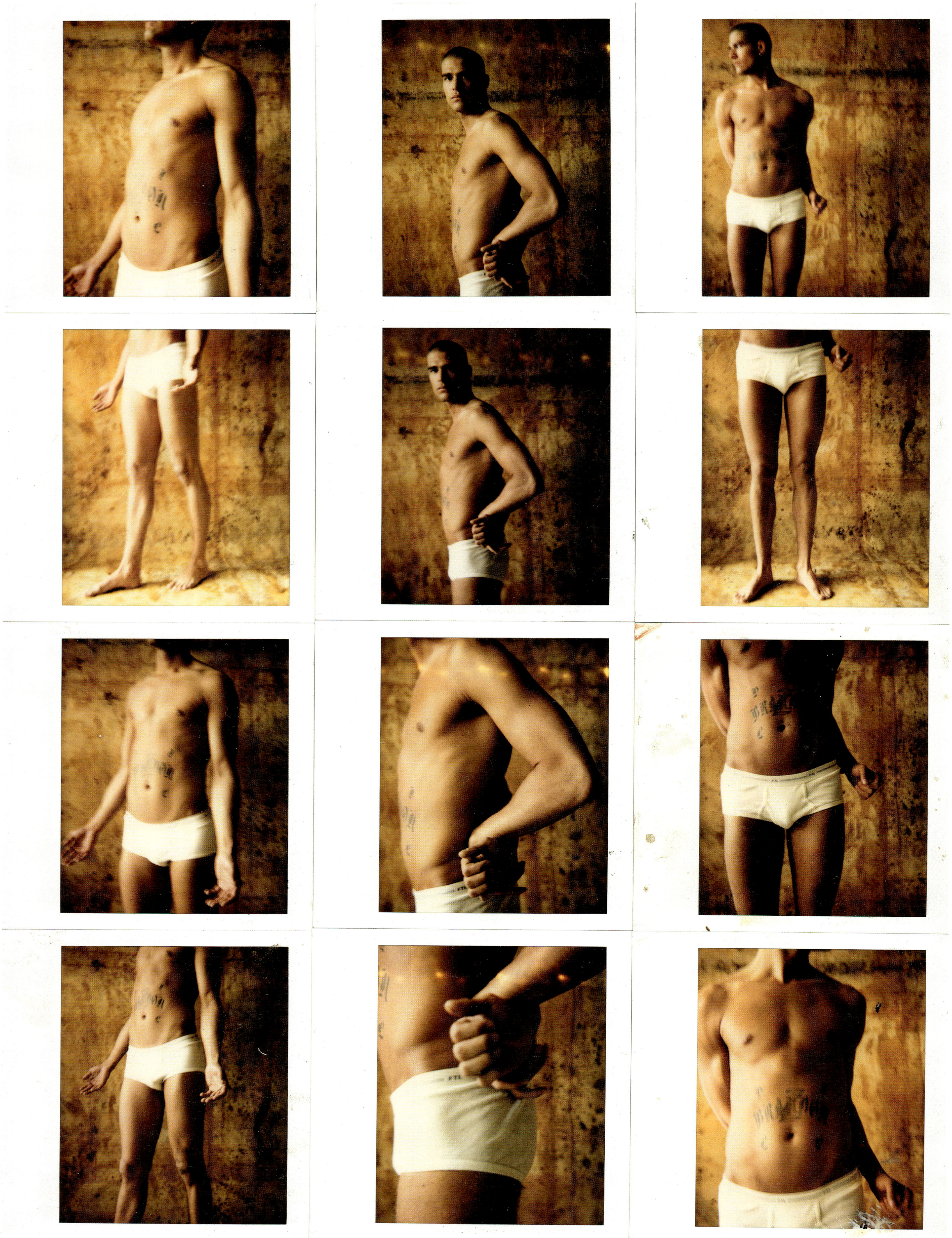

Study for *Saint Francis in Ecstasy*, Bellini, Vancouver, 2002

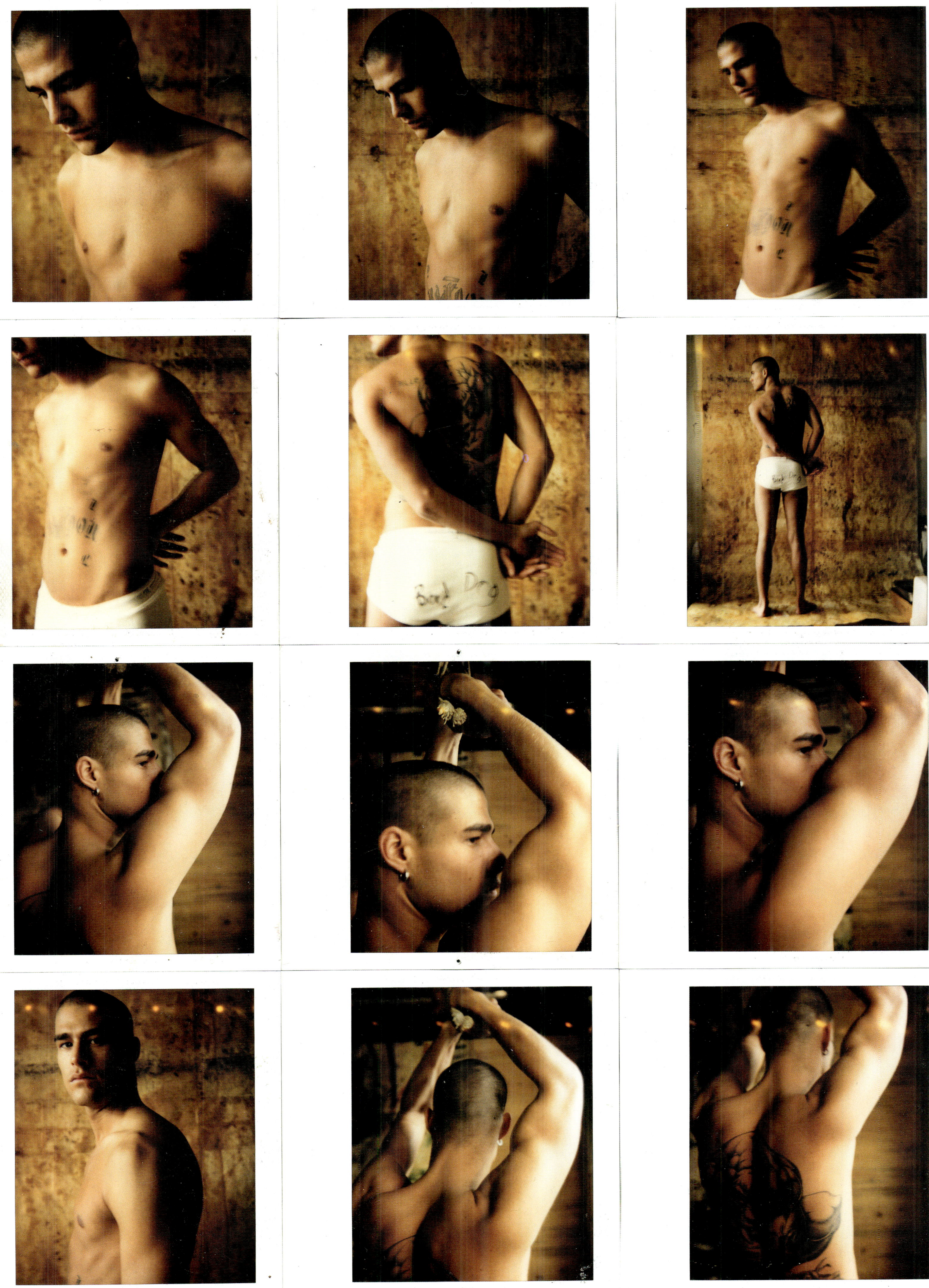

Study for *Saint Francis in Ecstasy*, Bellini, Vancouver, 2002

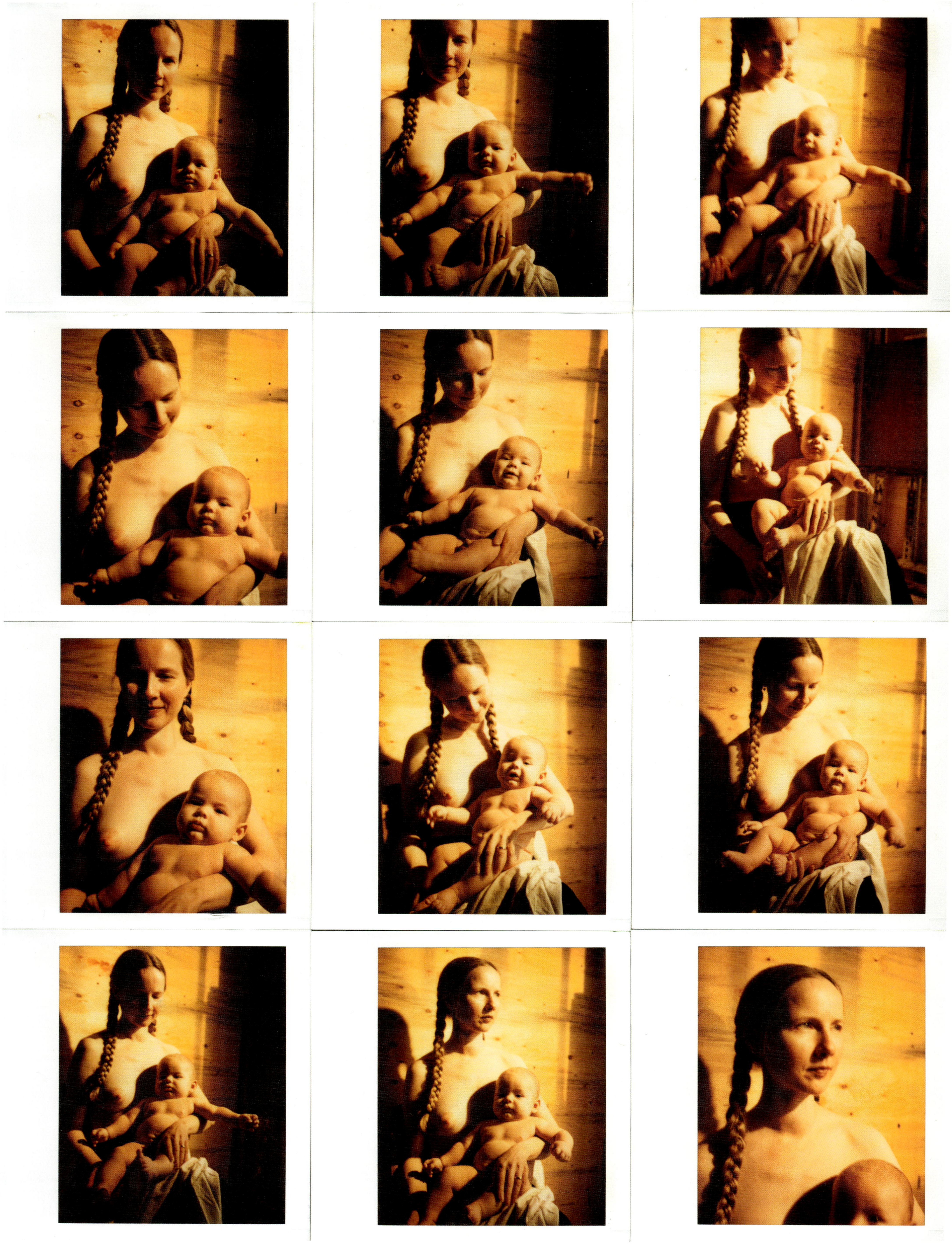

Laurie & Francis, Vancouver, 2002

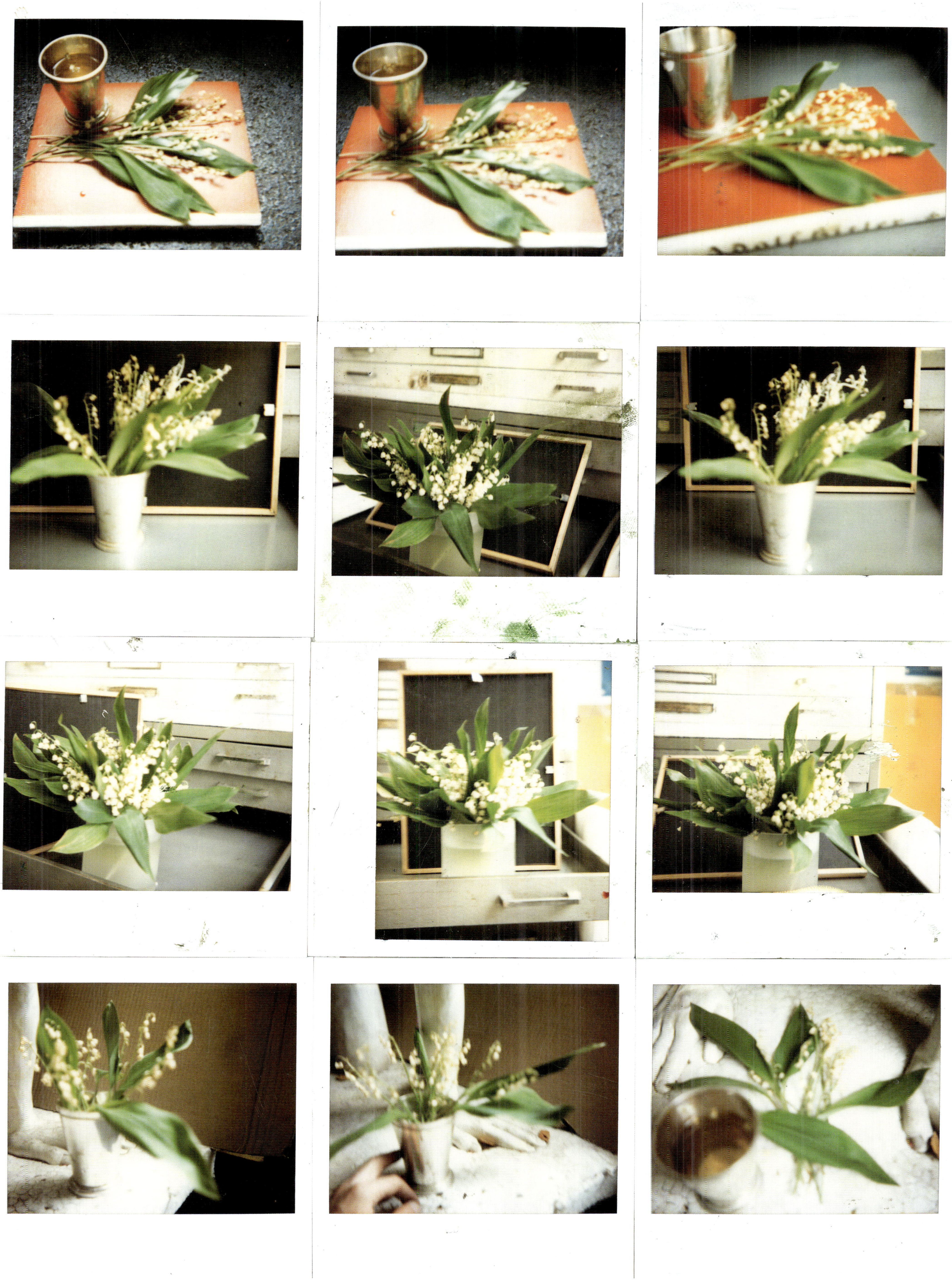

Lily of the Valley, New York, 1998

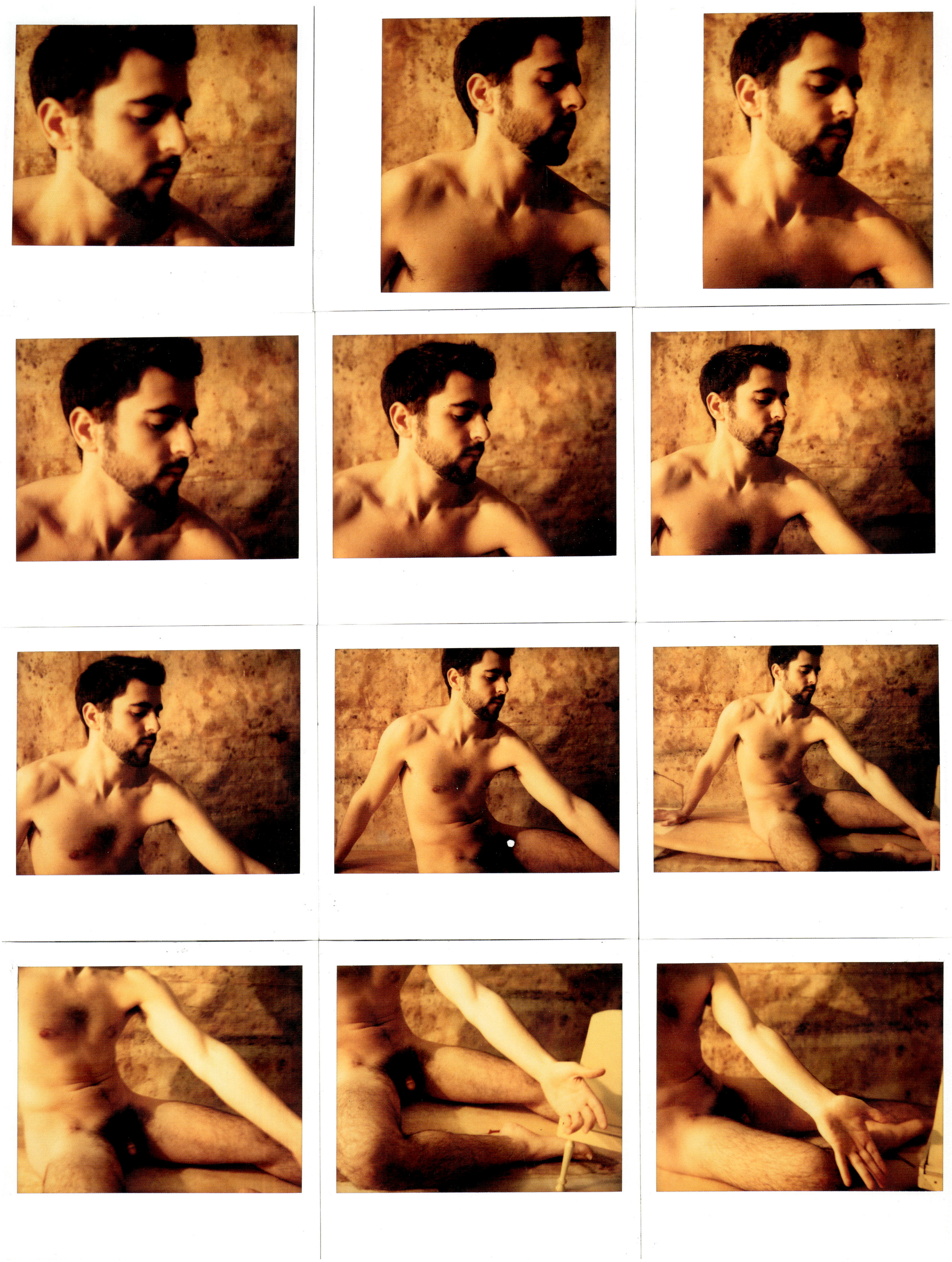

Ophir, study for *Saint Jerome*, da Vinci, Vancouver, 2005

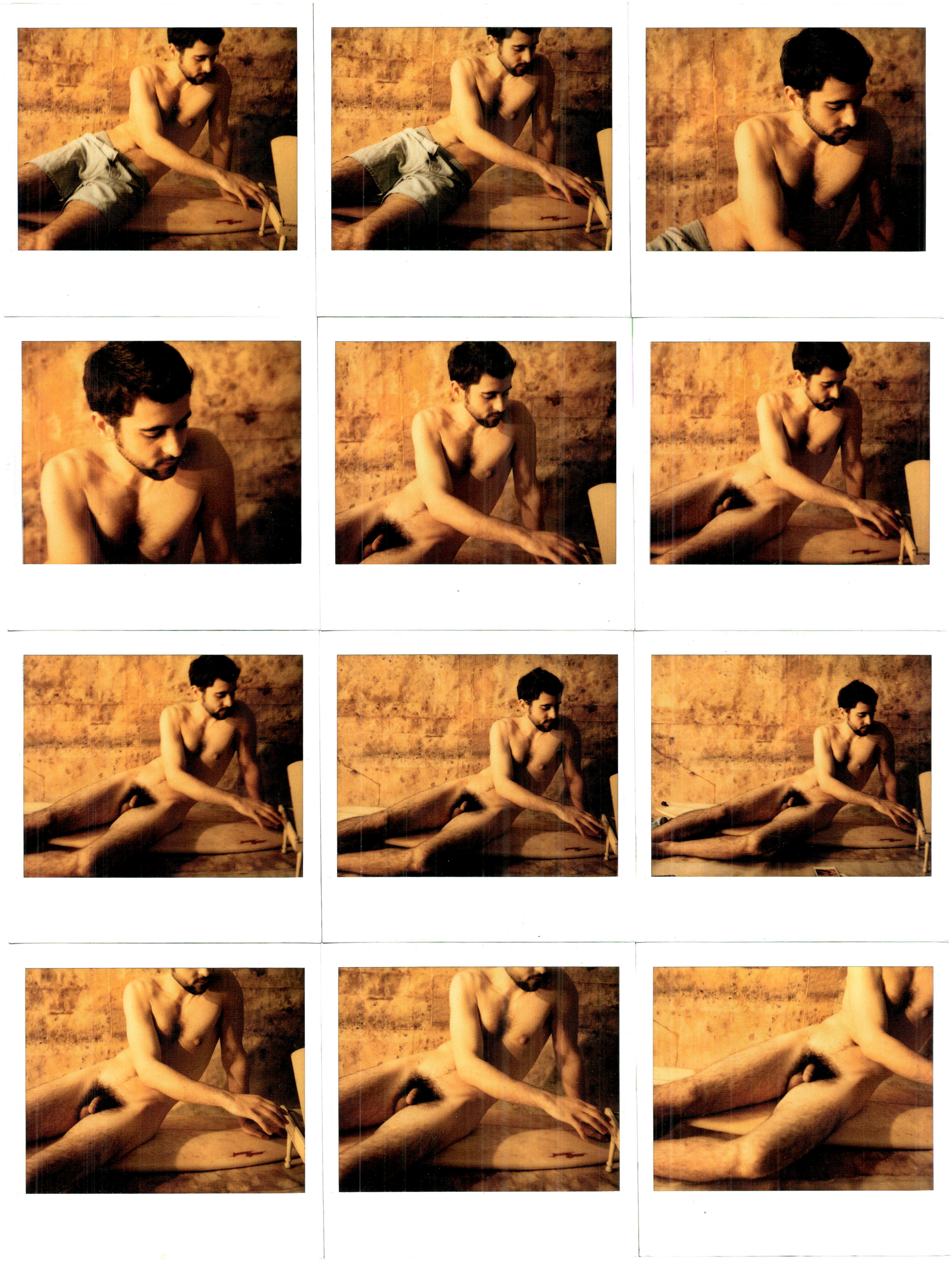

Ophir, study for *Saint Jerome*, da Vinci, Vancouver, 2005

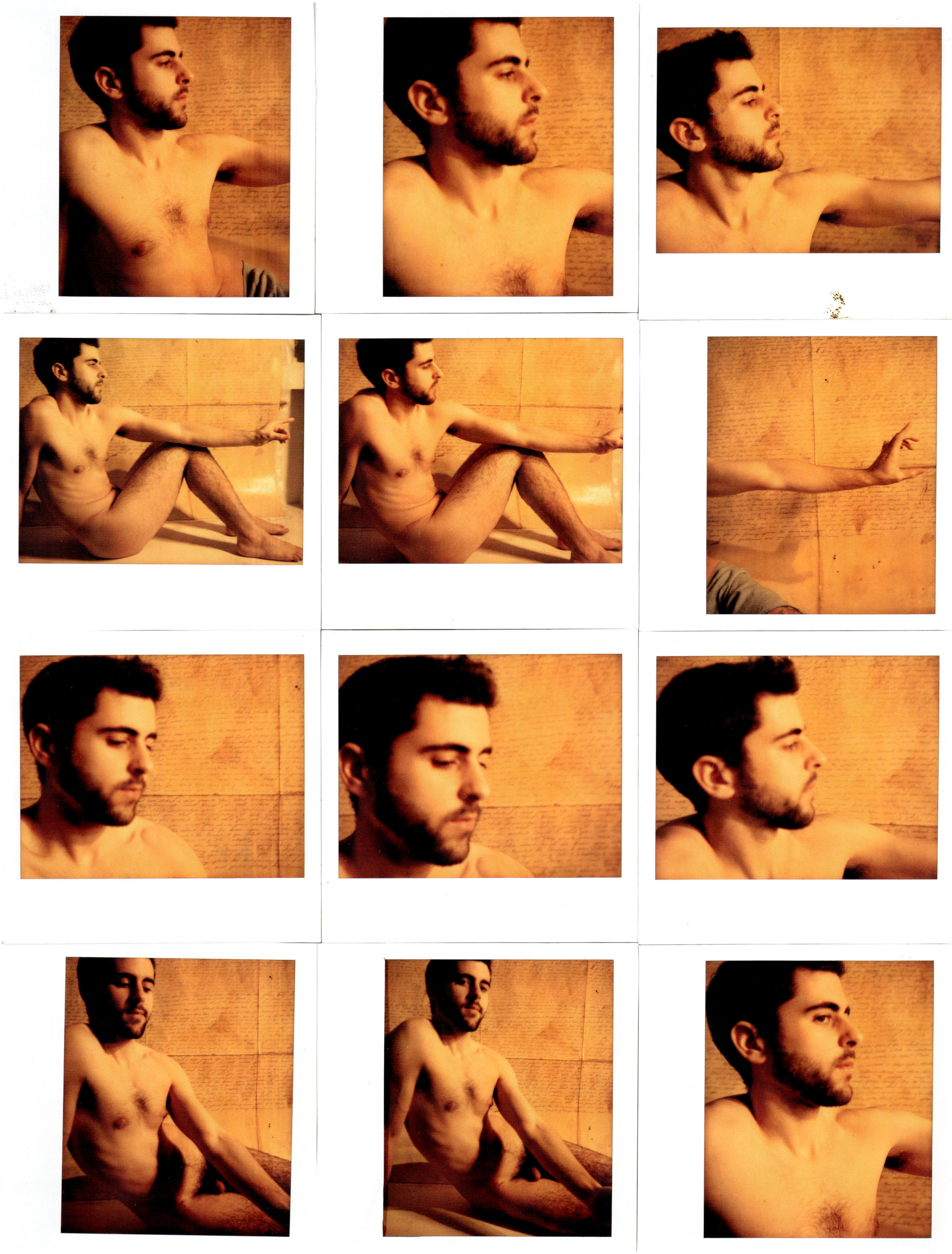

Ophir, study for *Saint Jerome*, da Vinci, Vancouver, 2005

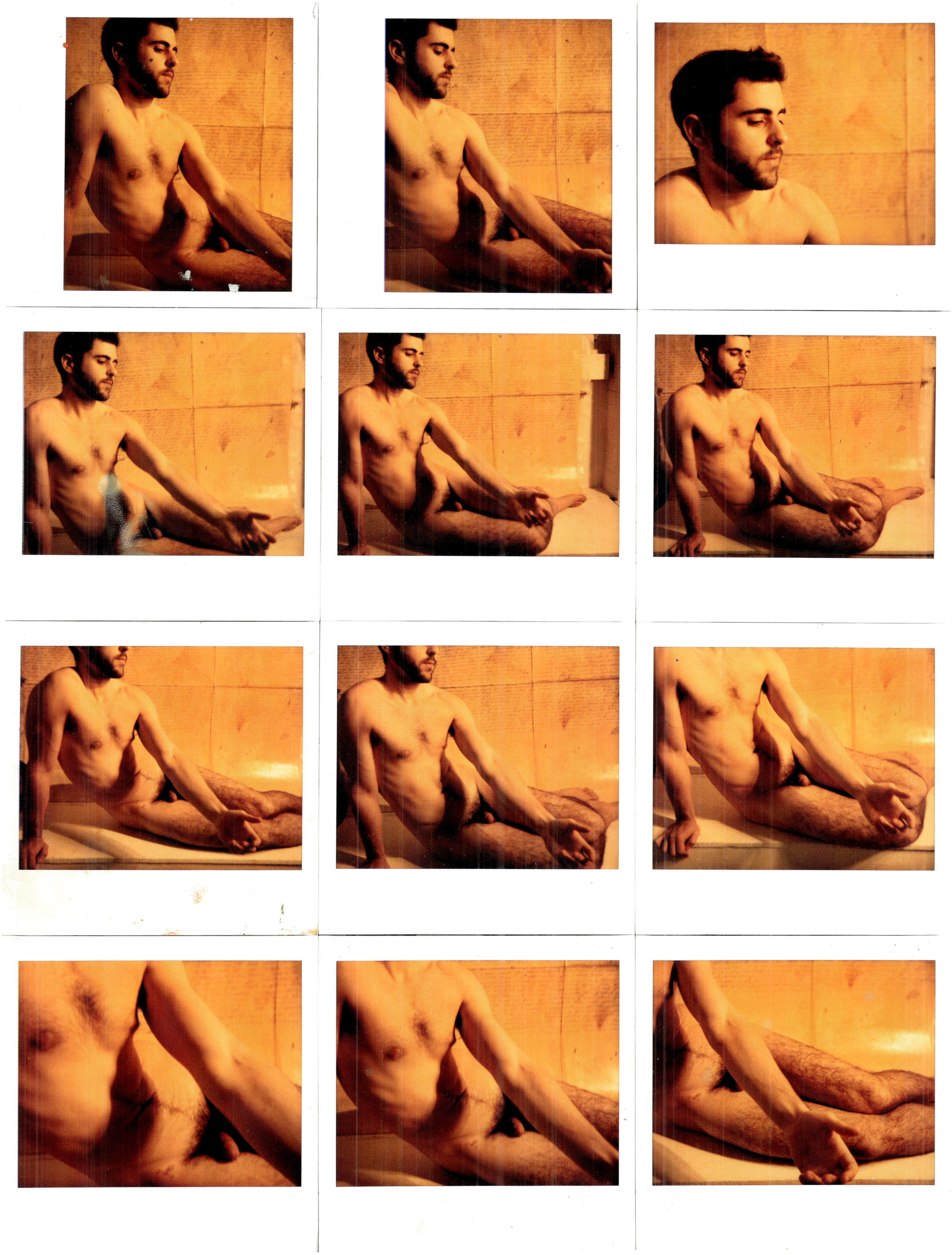

Ophir, study for *Saint Jerome*, da Vinci, Vancouver, 2005

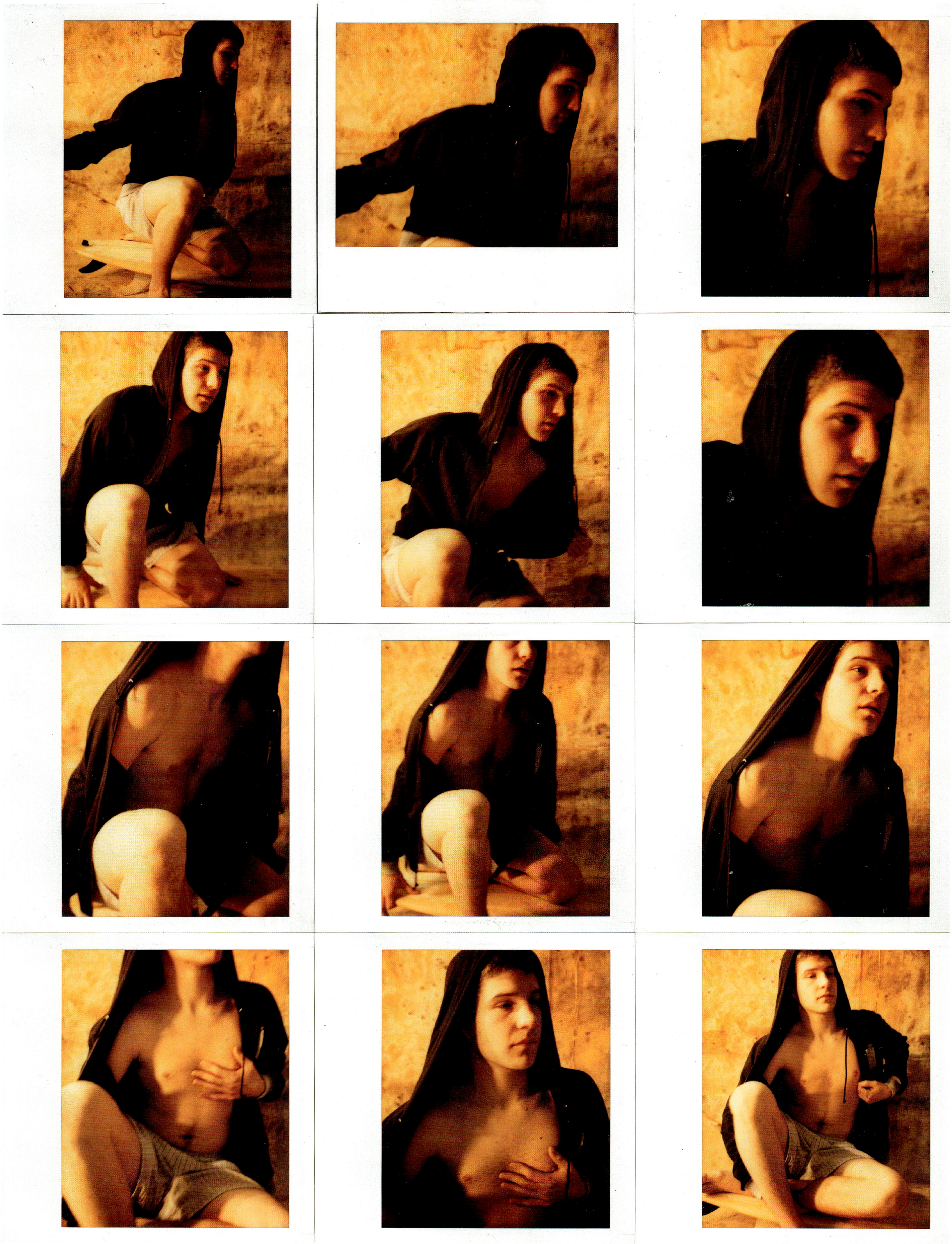

Study for *Saint Jerome*, da Vinci, Vancouver, 2005

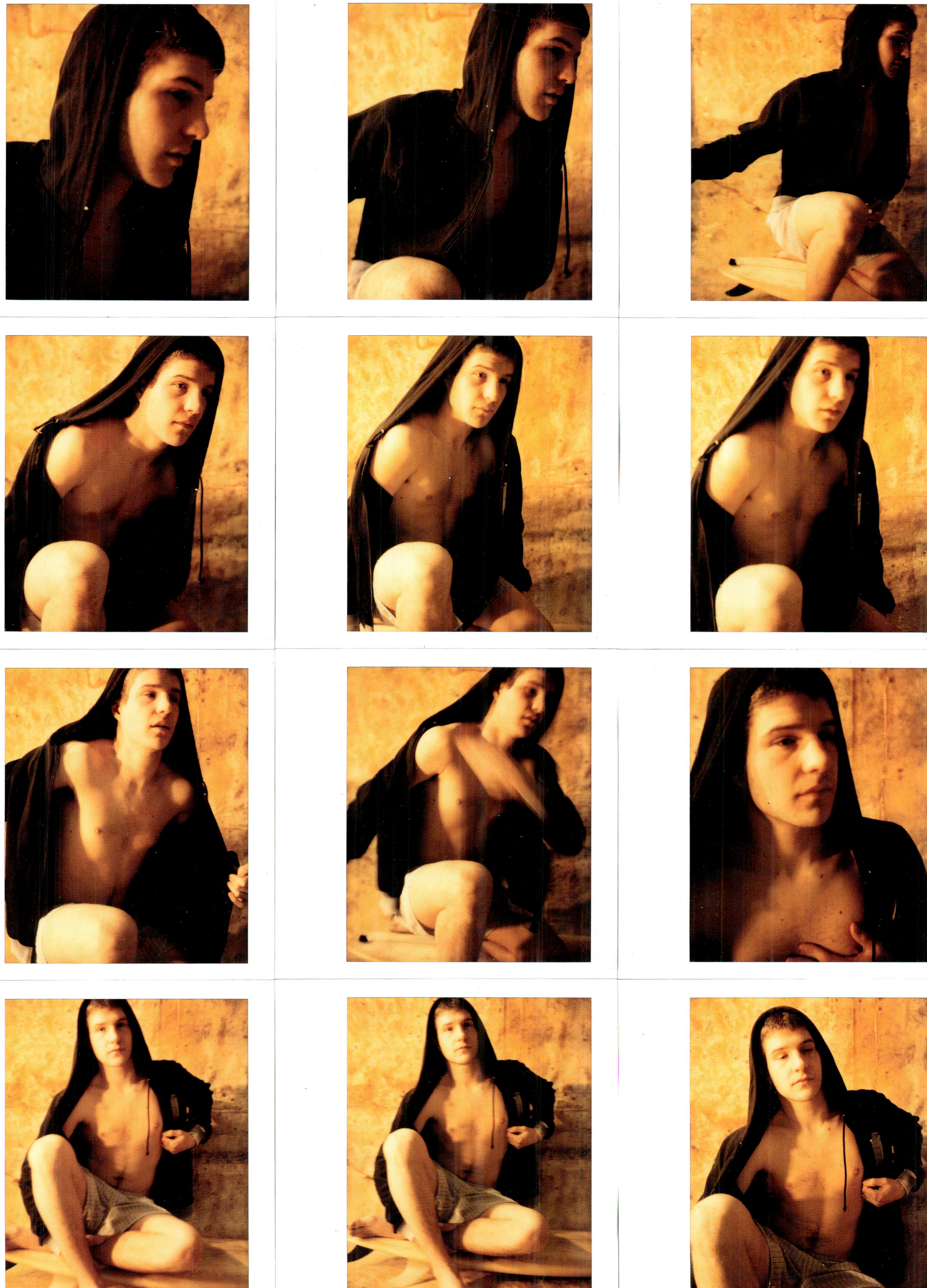

Study for *Saint Jerome*, da Vinci, Vancouver, 2005

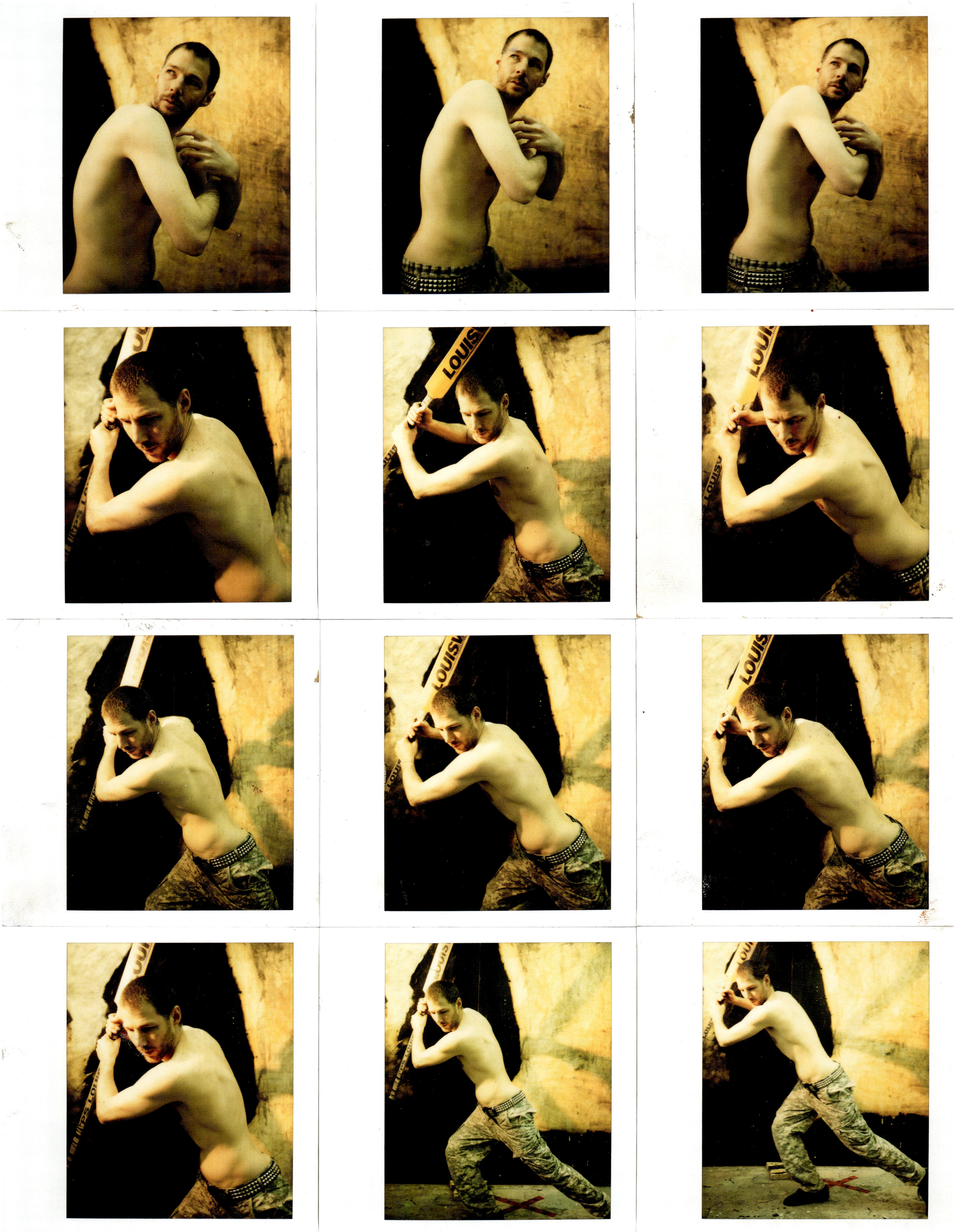

Kevin, study from *Scenes from the Life of Saint Benedict: XII – How God punished Florentius*, Luca Signorelli, Vancouver, 2008

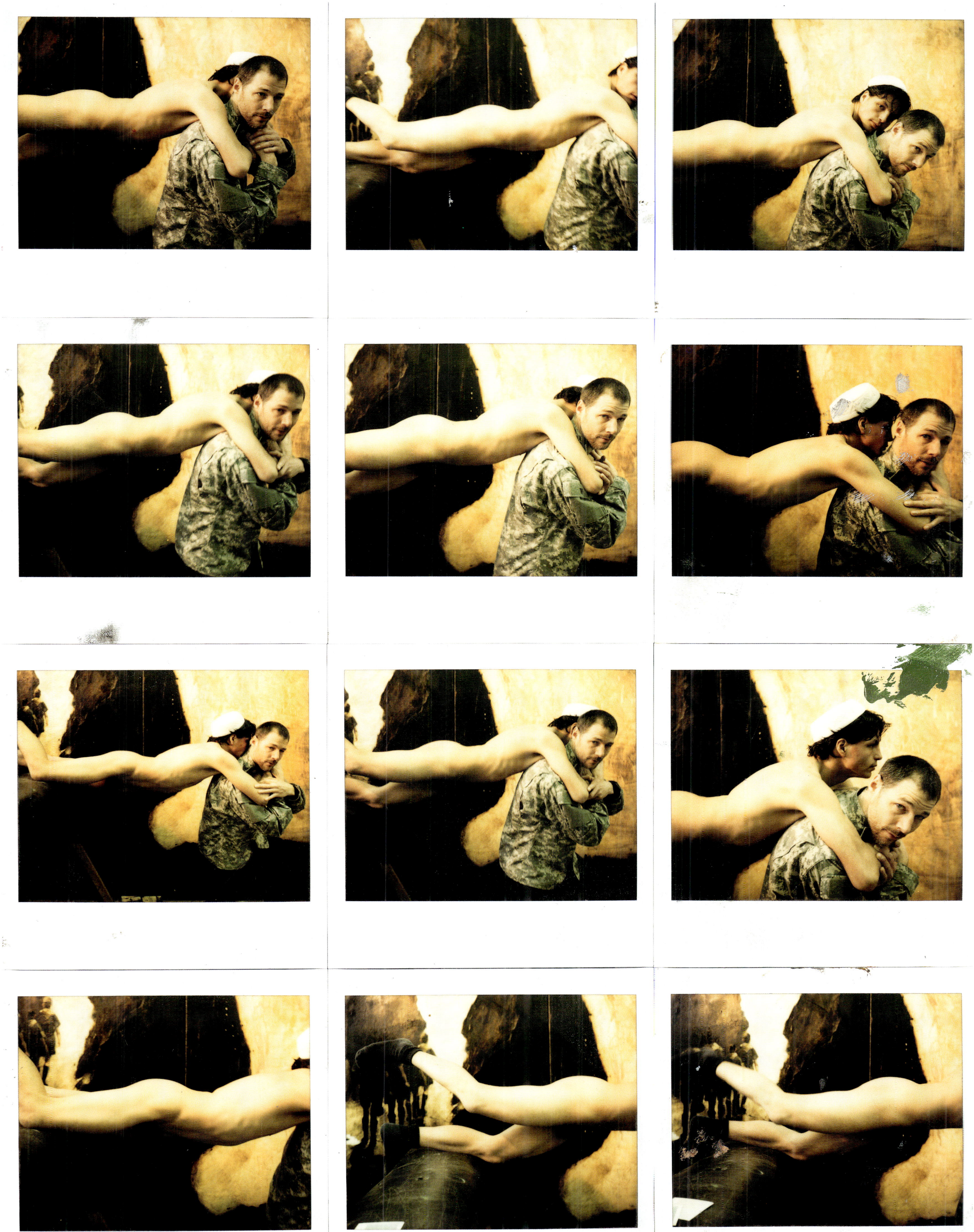

Kevin and Jason, study from *Scenes from the Life of Saint Benedict: XII – How God punished Florentius*, Luca Signorelli, Vancouver, 2008

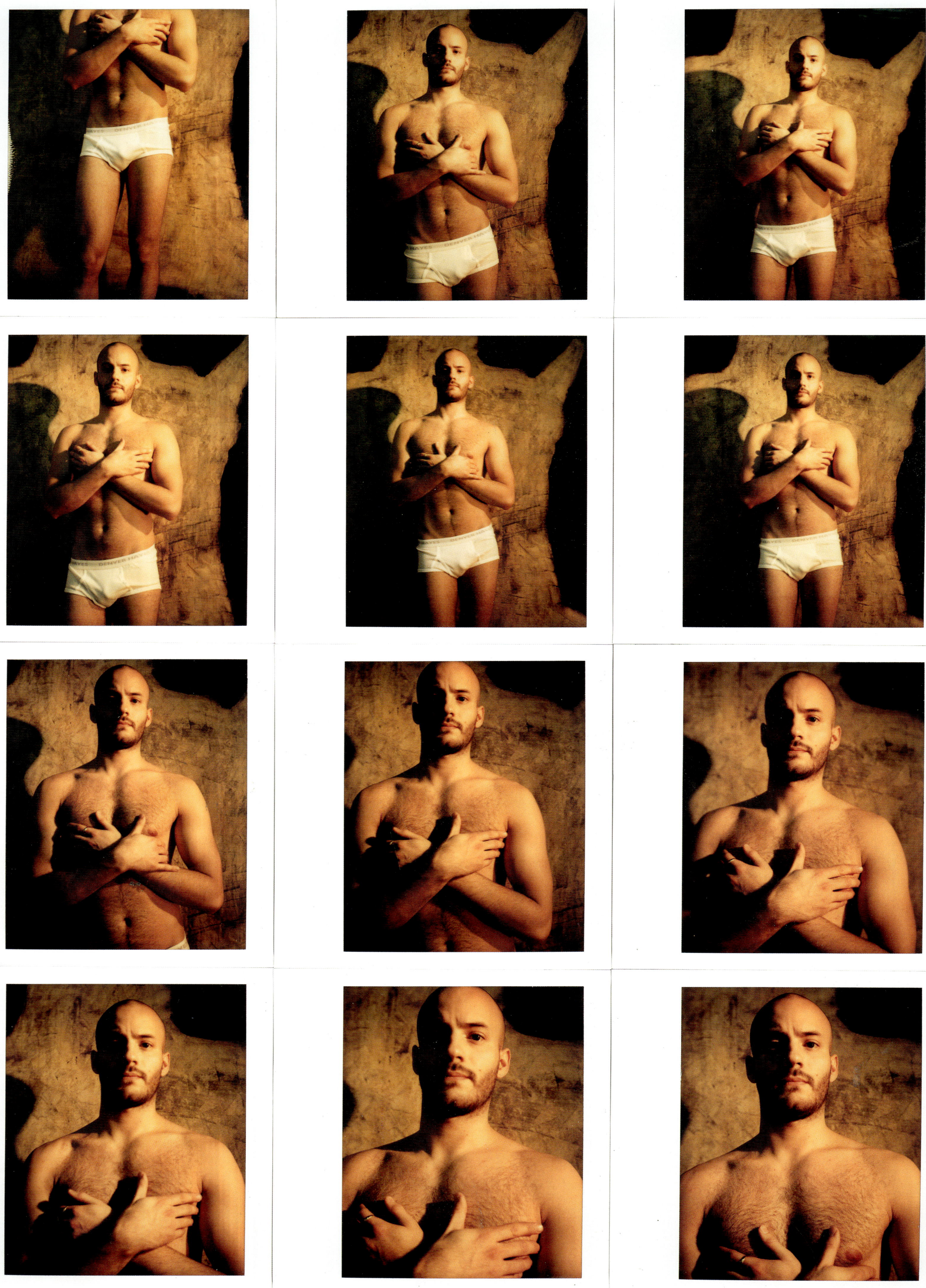

Lucien, Vancouver, 2007

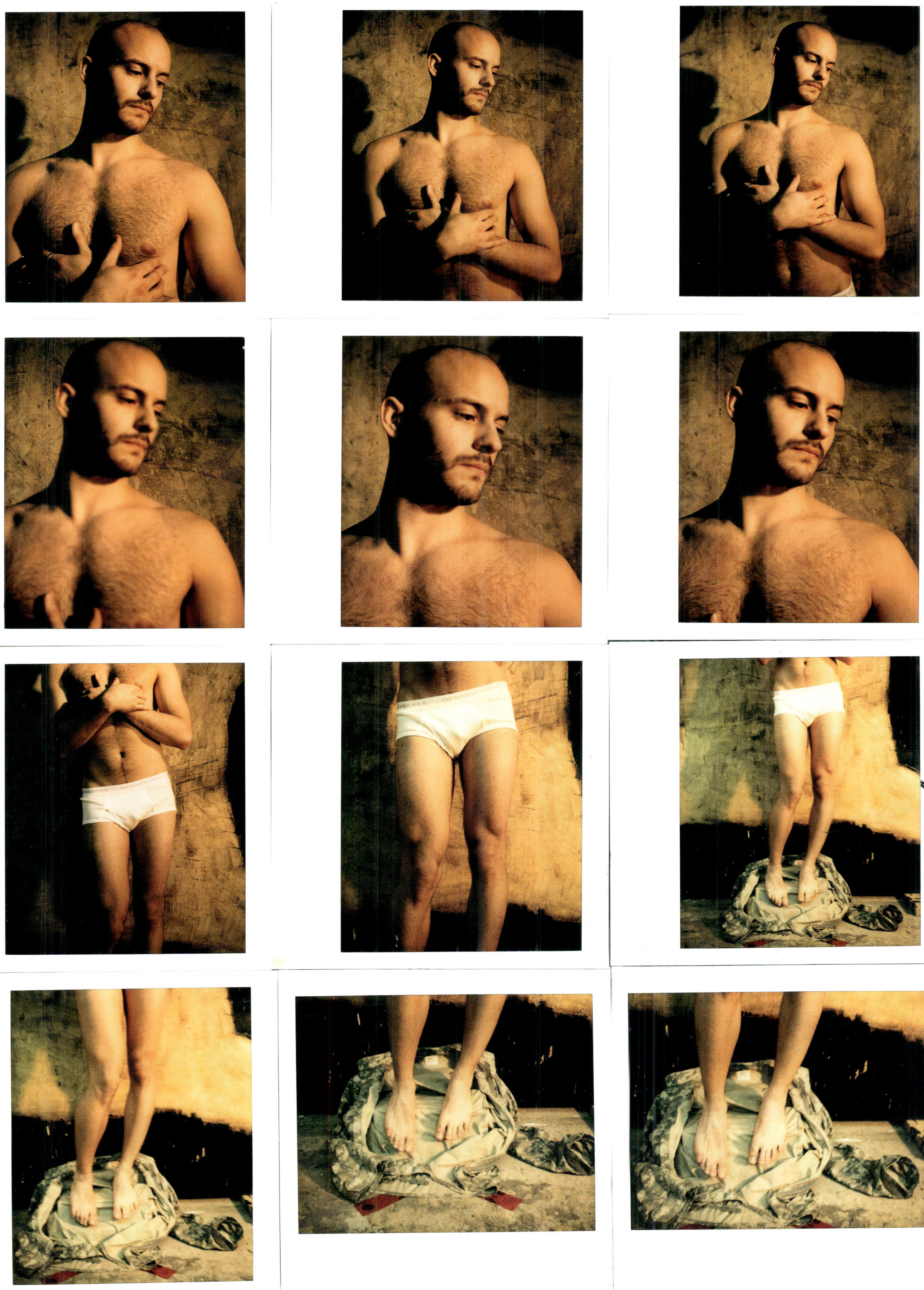

Lucien, Vancouver, 2007

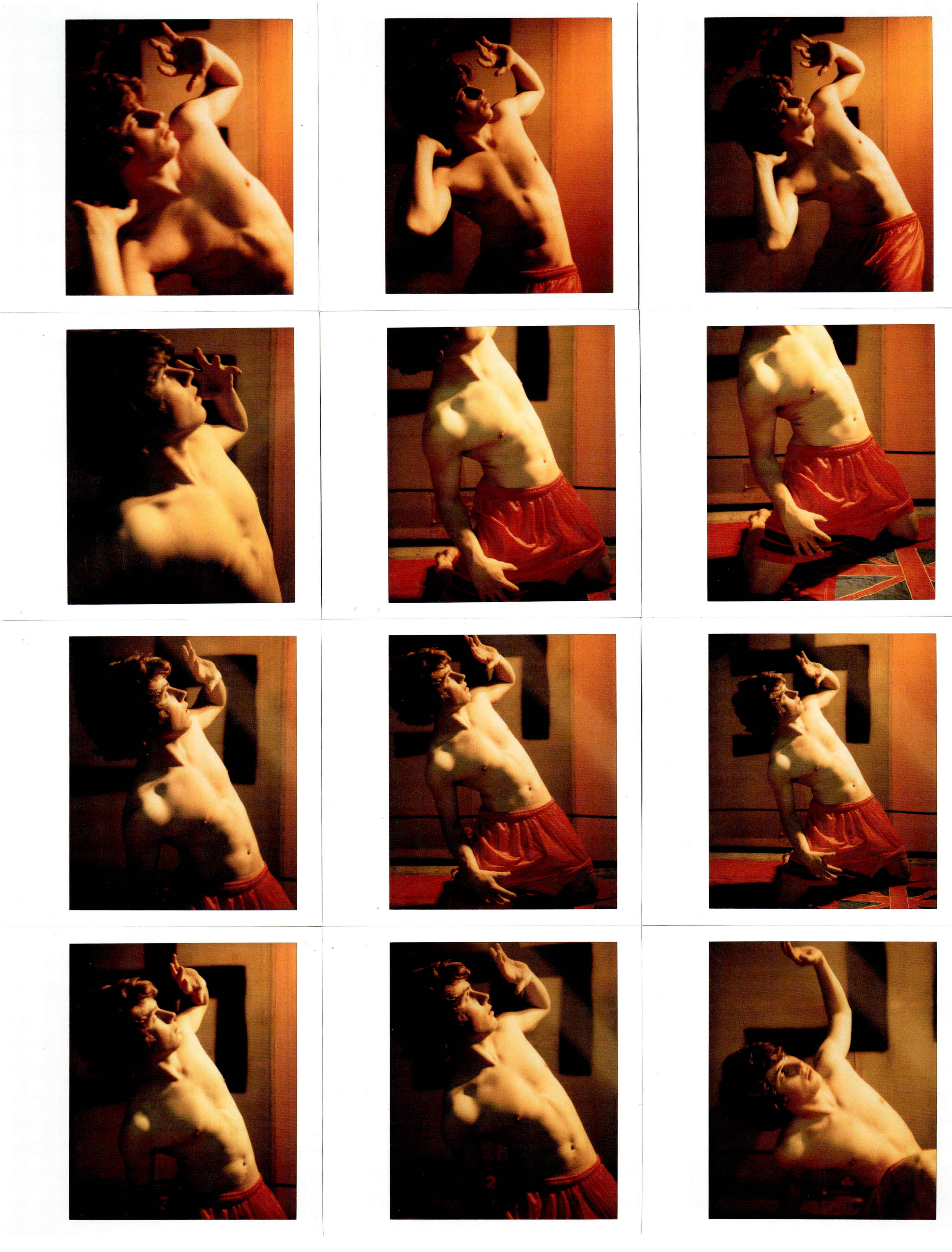

Jérémy, Vancouver, 2008

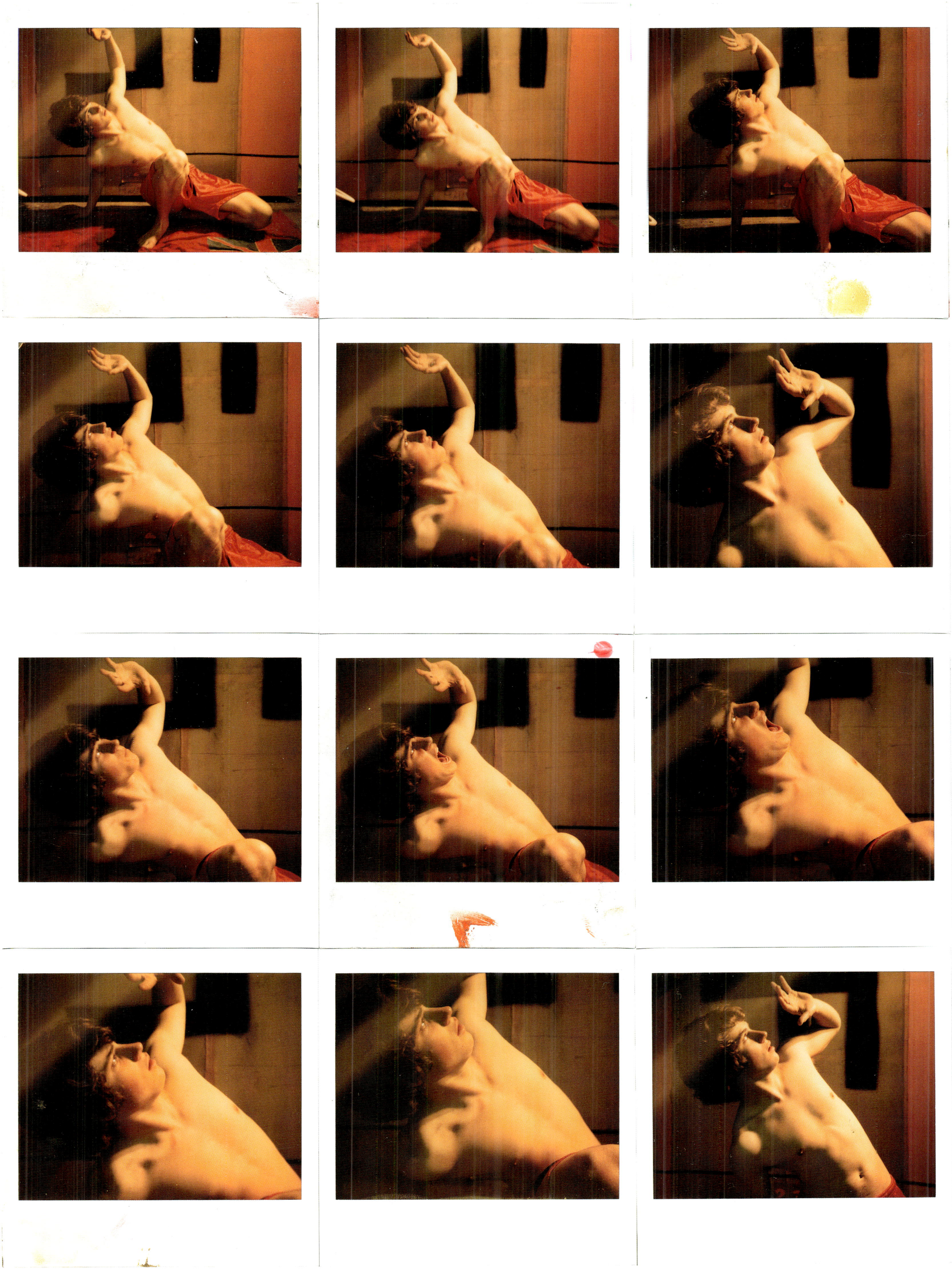

Jérémy, Vancouver, 2008

Attila Richard Lukacs

1962
Born in Alberta, Canada

1985
Graduated (Honours) Emily Carr College of Art and Design, Vancouver, British Columbia

Confirmed Upcoming Exhibitions

2009–2010
Polaroid Studies for Paintings, Illingworth Kerr Gallery, Calgary, Alberta, conceptualized and curated by Michael Morris
Polaroid Studies for Paintings, NGBK, Berlin, Germany, conceptualized and curated by Michael Morris
Reflected Glory, Givens/Shaw Public School, Toronto, Ontario
Vesica Piscis, Institute for Contemporary Culture, Royal Ontario Museum, Toronto, Ontario (solo)

Selected Exhibitions

2009
Polaroid Studies for Paintings, The Art Gallery of Alberta, Edmonton, Alberta, conceptualized and curated by Michael Morris

2008
Polaroid Studies for Paintings, Presentation House Gallery, North Vancouver, British Columbia, conceptualized and curated by Michael Morris
Inside Darkness, Musée d'art contemporain des Laurentides, Saint-Jérôme, Quebec, (solo)
Still Lifes, Walter Phillips Gallery, Banff Centre, Banff, Alberta (solo)

2006
Paint, Vancouver Art Gallery, Vancouver, British Columbia
Das achte Feld, Museum Ludwig, Köln, Germany
Antisocial Gallery, Vancouver, British Columbia (solo)
Le Corps Gay, Écomusée du fier monde, Montréal, Quebec
Vancouver School, Leo Marshall Corniculum Center, North Vancouver, British Columbia

2005
Beyond Redemption, Belkin Satellite, Vancouver, British Columbia

2004
Basement Show, Art Gallery of Calgary, Calgary, Alberta
Works from the permanent collection, National Gallery of Canada, Ottawa, Ontario (solo)

2003
Basement Show, Vancouver, British Columbia
New Works, Belkin Satellite, Vancouver, British Columbia (solo)

2002
Le Corps Gay, Centre d'exposition du Vieux-Palais, Saint-Jerome, Quebec
Jake, Xeno at Dadabase, Vancouver, British Columbia (solo)

2000
paperworx, Galerie Schedler, Zurich, Switzerland (solo)

1999
Arbor Vitae, Diane Farris Gallery, Vancouver, British Columbia (solo)
Fresh Flowers, Bellevue Art Museum, Bellevue, Washington
Heads, Galerie Schedler, Zurich, Switzerland (solo)
Myths about my Garden, Phyllis Kind Gallery, New York, New York (solo)

1998
Galerie OZ, Paris, France (solo)
Galerie Schedler, Zurich, Switzerland (solo)
Detention, Toronto, Ontario (solo)
Justina M. Barnicke Gallery, Hart House, University of Toronto, Toronto, Ontario (solo)
Telling Tales, Vancouver Art Gallery, Vancouver, British Columbia

1997
Phyllis Kind Gallery, New York, New York (solo)
E-werk, Beaverbrook Art Gallery, Fredericton, New Brunswick (solo)
Odd Bodies, The National Gallery of Canada, Ottawa, Ontario
Galerie Schedler, Zurich, Switzerland

1996
E-werk, Mendel Art Gallery, Saskatoon, Saskatchewan (solo)
E-werk, London Regional Art and Historical Museums, London, Ontario (solo)
E-werk, Morris and Helen Belkin Art Gallery, University of British Columbia, Vancouver, British Columbia (solo)
Naked Truths, University of Hawaii Art Gallery, Honolulu, Hawaii

1995
E-werk, The Edmonton Art Gallery, Edmonton, Alberta (solo)
E-werk, The Nickle Arts Museum, University of Calgary, Calgary, Alberta (solo)
Portraits, Diane Farris Gallery, Vancouver, British Columbia (solo)
Phyllis Kind Gallery, New York, New York (solo)
The Reconstructed Figure, Katonah Museum of Art, Katonah, New York
Ark, Illingworth Kerr Gallery, Alberta College of Art and Design, Edmonton, Alberta (Solo)

1994
E-werk, Musée d'art contemporain de Montréal, Montreal, Quebec (solo)
E-werk, Institute of Theoretical Painting Kunstwerke, Berlin, Germany (solo)
Kunsthaus Mürzzuschlag, Mürzzuschlag am Semmering, Jahresmuseum, Austria
E-werk, Chromapark, Berlin, Germany (solo)
Informing Visions, Walter Phillips Gallery, Banff Centre for the Arts, Banff, Alberta
'64–'94 Contemporary Decades, Emily Carr Institute of Arts & Design, Vancouver, British Columbia

1993
Different Strokes, Guggenheim Gallery, Chapman University, Orange, California
The Anxious Salon, MIT List Visual Art Center, Cambridge, Massachusetts
The New Renaissance, Bill Lowe Gallery, Atlanta, Georgia
AIDS Project, NGBK, Berlin, Germany

1992
Varieties of Love, Diane Farris Gallery, Vancouver, British Columbia (solo)
Die Schonen Sohne der Wuste, Moderne Kunst Dietmar Werle, Cologne, Germany (solo)
Boudoir, Berlin, Germany (solo)
Documenta IX, Kassel, Germany
Schwules Museum, Berlin, Germany

1991
Das Goldene Zeitalter, Württembergischer Kunsteverein, Stuttgart, Germany
Sixty Years Sixty Artists, Vancouver Art Gallery, Vancouver, British Columbia
Interferenzin-Kunst aus West Berlin 1960–90, Riga, Latvia and St. Petersberg, USSR
The National Museum of Contemporary Art, Seoul International Art Festival, Seoul, Korea
Myth and Magic in America: The Eighties, Museo de Contemporáneo de Monterrey, Monterrey, Mexico
Vollbild, Tableaux du Sida, Kulturzentrum Reithalle, Bern, Switzerland
Vollbild, Tableaux du Sida, La Fondation Deutsch, Belmont-sur-Lausanne, Switzerland
Outrageous Desire, Rutgers University, New Brunswick, New Jersey

1990
Bilder, Moderne Kunst Dietmar Werle, Cologne, Germany (solo)
Teck Gallery, Simon Fraser University, Vancouver, British Columbia (solo)
Illingworth Kerr Gallery, Alberta College of Art, Calgary, Alberta (solo)
London Regional Art and Historical Museums, London, Ontario (solo)
Diane Farris Gallery, Vancouver, British Columbia (solo)
Artropolis '90, The Roundhouse, Vancouver, British Columbia

1989
The Power Plant, Toronto, Ontario (toured to Walter Phillips Gallery, Banff, Alberta (solo)
49th Parallel, New York, New York (solo)

1988
Kunstlerhaus Bethanien, Berlin, Germany (solo)
Plug-In Institute of Contemporary Art, Winnipeg, Manitoba (solo)
Galerie Dietmar Werle, Cologne, Germany (solo)
Vollbild, NGBK, Berlin, Germany
Diane Farris Gallery, Vancouver, British Columbia (solo)

1987
Morality Tales: History Painting in the 1980s, Grey Art Gallery, New York University, New York (toured)
Toyama Now '87: New Art Around the Pacific, The Museum of Modern Art, Toyama, Japan
London Life Young Contemporaries, London Regional Art Gallery, London, Ontario
West Coast Painting: New Directions, Canada House, London, England

1986
Attila Richard Lukacs / Charles Rea, Mercer Union, Toronto, Ontario
4 Vancouver Young Romantic Painters, Centre Canadien Culturel, Paris, France
25 Young Canadian Artists, Convertible Showroom, Vancouver, British Columbia

1985
Young Romantics, Vancouver Art Gallery, Vancouver, British Columbia
Five Young Artists, Diane Farris Gallery, Vancouver, British Columbia
Contemporary Canadian Painting, Thomas Barry Fine Arts, Minneapolis, Minnesota
Futura Bold Installation, Convertible Showroom, Vancouver, British Columbia
Futura Bold, Pitt International Galleries, Vancouver, British Columbia

1984
Warehouse Show, Vancouver, British Columbia
Four Painters, Diane Farris Gallery, Vancouver, British Columbia

1983
Unit Pitt Gallery, Vancouver, British Columbia (solo)

Performance / Lectures

1997
Harvard Graduate School of Architecture, Lecture Series

2002
Alberta College of Art and Design, Calgary, Alberta (performance)

2000
Berlin, Ich hole meinen Koffer ab' Club Spyder Galaxy, Zurich, Switzerland (performance)
National Ballet of Canada, 'Glen Gould': 3 short works, costumes and design

Residencies

2004
School of the Museum of Fine Arts, Boston, Massachusetts

2002
Alberta College of Art and Design, visiting artists program & lecture series

1989
Banff Centre, Banff, Alberta

1986–88
Studio Residency Program, Künstlerhaus Bethanien, Berlin, Germany

Michael Morris

1942
Born in Saltdean, Sussex, England
Immigrated to Canada in 1946

1960–1961
University of Victoria, Victoria, British Columbia

1962–1964
Vancouver School of Art, graduated with honors

1965–1966
Post-Graduate Studies, Slade School of Fine Art, University College, London, Great Britain

1967
Acting Curator of the Vancouver Art Gallery, Vancouver, British Columbia

1967–1968
Curator, Centre for Communications and the Arts, Simon Fraser University, Burnaby, British Columbia

1973–1980
Co-founder and co-director of Western Front Society, a center for the production and presentation of new art activities in Vancouver, British Columbia

1992
Established the Morris/Trasov Archives at the Morris and Helen Belkin Gallery, Vancouver, British Columbia

2005
Honorary Doctorate of Humanities, Emily Carr Institute of Art + Design, Vancouver, British Columbia

Selected Exhibitions

2009
Zig Zags & Other Motifs, Belkin Annex, Vancouver, British Columbia
All That Is Solid Melts into Air MUHKA, Mechelen, Belgium
Polaroid Studies for Paintings Attila Richard Lukacs & Michael Morris, The Art Gallery of Alberta, Edmonton, Alberta

2008
Light on in Babyland, Justina M. Barnicke Gallery, Hart House, University of Toronto, Toronto, Ontario
Polaroids, Presentation House Gallery, North Vancouver, British Columbia

2007
Documentary Protocols, Leonard & Bina Ellen Gallery, Concordia University, Montreal, Quebec
Monochrome, Morris and Helen Belkin Gallery, Vancouver, British Columbia
LIVE Performance Art Biennale, Western Front, Vancouver, British Columbia

2006
Paint: BC Painting since the 1960s, Vancouver Art Gallery, Vancouver, British Columbia
One man show: Winchester Galleries, Victoria, British Columbia

2005–06
Intertidal: Vancouver Art & Artists, Museum van Hendendaagse Kunst Antwerpen, Antwerp, Belgium

2005
Art of the Sixties, The National Gallery of Canada, Ottawa, Ontario
Photography in Question, Canadian Museum of Contemporary Photography, Ottawa, Ontario
Classified Material: Archives, Accumulations, Artists, Vancouver Art Gallery, Vancouver, British Columbia

2004
Hidden Histories, The New Art Gallery, Walsall, Great Britain

2003
Robert Smithson & Vancouver, Vancouver Art Gallery, Vancouver, British Columbia

2002
The Sixties, Art Gallery of Greater Victoria, Victoria, British Columbia
Golden Streams, curated by Luis Jacob, The Blackwood Gallery, University of Toronto, Mississagua, Ontario

2001
Search for the Spirit of Miss General Idea from the Morris/Trasov Archive, Helen Pitt Gallery, Vancouver, British Columbia
Art City: Mr Peanut for Mayor from the Morris/Trasov Archives, Morris and Helen Belkin Gallery, Vancouver, British Columbia

2000
Making It New: The Big Sixties Show, Glenbow Museum, Calgary, Alberta and Art Gallery of Windsor, Windsor, Ontario
Gay Chic of the '70s from the Morris/Trasov Archive, Helen Pitt Gallery, Vancouver, British Columbia

1999
How Sad I Am Today: The Art of Ray Johnson and the New York Correspondence School, Morris/Trasov Archive and Morris and Helen Belkin Gallery, Vancouver

1998
One man show: Art Konsult, New Delhi, India

1997
Max Mueller Bhavan Artists Centre, New Delhi, India; Gallery Chemould, Mumbai, India
One man show: Winchester Galleries, Victoria, British Columbia

1996
Metropolitan Art Gallery, Kolkata, India
One man show, Art Konsult, New Delhi, India
Morris/Trasov Archive, Colour Research, Morris and Helen Belkin Art Gallery, Vancouver, British Columbia
One man show: Winchester Galleries, Victoria, British Columbia
Transient Moments: Vancouver and the Performance Photograph, Presentation House Gallery, North Vancouver, British Columbia

1995
Crawford Municipal Art Gallery, Cork, Ireland
One man show: Paul Petro Contemporary Art, Toronto, Ontario
Morris / Trasov Archive, Colour Research, Plug In Contemporary Art Gallery, Winnipeg, Manitoba
One man show: Winchester Galleries, Victoria, British Columbia
Vancouver 1965–1975: Context and Influences, Vancouver Art Gallery, Vancouver, British Columbia

1994
Morris / Trasov Archive, Colour Research, XXII Bienal Internacional São Paulo, Brazil
5 Jahre Danach, Haus Am Lützoplatz, Berlin, Germany

1993
Werkshau, Malerei und Skulptur, Neues Kunstquartier, Berlin, Germany

1992
Morris / Trasov Archive inaugural exhibition, Morris and Helen Belkin Gallery, Vancouver, British Columbia
Hormones Schwules Museum, Berlin, Germany

1991
Under the Influence of Fluxus, Rutgers University, New Jersey; Winnipeg, Manitoba; Toronto, Ontario; Montreal, Quebec

1987
DAAD Galerie, Video Installation and Exhibition, Berlin, Germany
Interferenzen: Kunst aus West Berlin 1960–1990, Riga; St. Petersburg; Moscow; Berlin
One man show: Eveyln Aimis Gallery, Toronto, Ontario
One man show: Galerie Dietmar Werle, Koln, Germany

1986
Making History: Recent Acquisitions, Vancouver Art Gallery, Vancouver, British Columbia
Das andere Land: Auslandische Kunstler in der Bundesrepublik, Grosse Orangerie, Schloss Charlottenburg, Berlin, Germany

1985
video, DAAD Galerie, Berlin, Germany
Berlin Notes, Walter Philips Gallery, Banff, Alberta
Articule, Montreal, Quebec

1984
performance, Kunsthalle, Berlin, Germany
performance, De Fabrik, Einhoven, Holland

1983
Museums by Artists, organized by Art Metropole, Toronto, Ontario
performance, J & J Donguy Gallery, Paris, France
Vancouver Art & Artists, Vancouver Art Gallery, Vancouver, British Columbia

1982
Video Narcissus, Ars Viva Gallery, Berlin, Germany
New Video Work, Akademie der Kunste, Berlin, Germany

1980
Pret-a-Porter, Nova Gallery, Vancouver, British Columbia

1979
Galerie Gaetan, Geneva
Colour research, Centre Culture Canadien, Brussels, Belgium

1978
Image Bank correspondence at the Centre Culturel Canaden, Paris France, and Arte Fiera, Bologna, Italy
Between the Frames, Nova Gallery, Vancouver, British Columbia

1976
Gallery Allen, Vancouver, British Columbia
Das Sofortbild Polaroid, Akionsgalerie, Bern, Switzerland

1975
Gallery Allen, Vancouver, British Columbia
Saidye Bronfman Centre for the Arts, Montreal, Quebec

1973
Section Envoie, Paris Biennial, Museum of Contemporary Art, Paris, France
Trajectories 73, Museum of Contemporary Art, Paris, France
Action and the Avant Garde, Akademie der Kunste, Berlin, Germany

1972
Image Bank Cultural Ecology, 1974 projects, Annual Report, and colour research

1971
Image Bank Postcard Show, University of British Columbia Fine Arts Gallery, Vancouver, British Columbia
Miss General Idea Pageant, Art Gallery of Ontario, Toronto, Ontario
Art City and other Image Bank L.I.P. projects

1970
Realism '70, Montreal Museum of Art, Montreal, Quebec and Art Gallery of Ontario, Toronto, Ontario
A Room with Props, with Vincent Trasov, Vancouver Art Gallery, Vancouver, British Columbia
Intermedia, Vancouver Art Gallery, Vancouver, British Columbia and Victoria Art Gallery, Victoria, British Columbia

1969
Galerie Godard, Montreal, Quebec
Art d'Aujourd'hui, Montreal Museum of Art, Montreal, Quebec and Paris Bienale, Paris, France
New Art of Vancouver, Newport Harbor Nautical Museum, Newport Beach, California

1968
Survey '68, Art Gallery of Ontario, Toronto, Ontario
Prisma with Gary Lee Nova, Vancouver Art Gallery, Vancouver, British Columbia
Letter Series, Douglas Gallery, Vancouver, British Columbia

1967
Perspective '67, Art Gallery of Ontario, Toronto, Ontario
Douglas Gallery, Vancouver, British Columbia

1966
Painting '66, Vancouver Art Gallery, Vancouver, British Columbia

1965
New Design Gallery, Vancouver, British Columbia
Art Gallery of Greater Victoria, Victoria, British Columbia

Residencies/Performance

1981–1998
Berliner Kunstler program, DAAD Galerie, Berlin, Germany

1990
Art Studio, Banff Centre, Banff, Alberta

2003
Open Studio, Toronto, Ontario

2004
Guest artist for Performance, University of Victoria, Victoria, British Columbia

2006
Art Studio, Banff Centre, Banff, Alberta

Curatorial Projects

1999
Ray Johnson: How Sad I Am Today, curated by Michael Morris & Sharla Sava, Morris & Helen Belkin Art Gallery, and Morris/Trasov Archive, Vancouver, British Columbia

2005
Maxwell Bates: A Canadian Expresionist, curated by Michael Morris & Nancy Townshend, Art Gallery of Alberta, Edmonton, Alberta. Exhibit traveled to The Nickle Museum, Calgary, Alberta; The Mendel Art Gallery, Saskatoon, Saskatchewan; and the Victoria Art Gallery, Victoria, British Columbia

2009
Attila Richard Lukacs: Polaroids, curated by Michael Morris; travel exhibition organized by the Art Gallery of Alberta, Edmonton, Alberta
Vision to Reality: West Coast Modernism, curated by Michael Morris & Mary-Jo Hughes, Art Gallery of Greater Victoria, Victoria, British Columbia

About the Contributors

Vince Aletti reviews photography exhibitions for the *New Yorker*'s "Goings on About Town" section and writes a regular column about photo books for *Photograph*. He is the winner of the 2005 Infinity Award in writing from the International Center of Photography, where he is currently an adjunct curator. Aletti co-curated "Weird Beauty: Fashion Photography Now" with Carol Squiers and is the curator of "This Is Not a Fashion Photograph," both at ICP; he and Squiers worked together on "Avedon Fashion 1944–2000," the museum's summer 2009 exhibition, as well as on its Abrams catalog. *Male*, a book of photographs and other artwork from Aletti's collection, was published by Andrew Roth's PPP Editions at the end of 2008. *The Disco Files 1973–1978*, a collection of Aletti's weekly columns on disco, was published in spring 2009 by DJhistory in the UK.

Stan Persky teaches philosophy at Capilano University in North Vancouver, BC, and is the author of *Buddy's: Meditations on Desire*, *The Short Version*, and *Topic Sentence*.

Michael Turner is an award-winning author of fiction, songs, and criticism. Books include *Hard Core Logo*, *The Pornographer's Poem*, *Fred Herzog: Vancouver Photographs* and *8 x 10*. He lives in Vancouver.

Scott Watson is a Professor in the Department of Art History, Visual Art and Theory and Director/ Curator of the Morris and Helen Belkin Art Gallery at the University of British Columbia where he is also Chair of the graduate Critical Curatorial Studies program. He has published an award-winning book on Canadian artist Jack Shadbolt, a monograph on Stan Douglas, as well as many articles and catalogue essays on post-war and contemporary art. Watson's research focus is contemporary art and issues, art theory and criticism, twentieth-century art history, and curatorial and exhibition studies. He is currently researching concrete poetry for an upcoming publication and exhibition, and editing a book on British Columbia's studio pottery movement.

List of Works

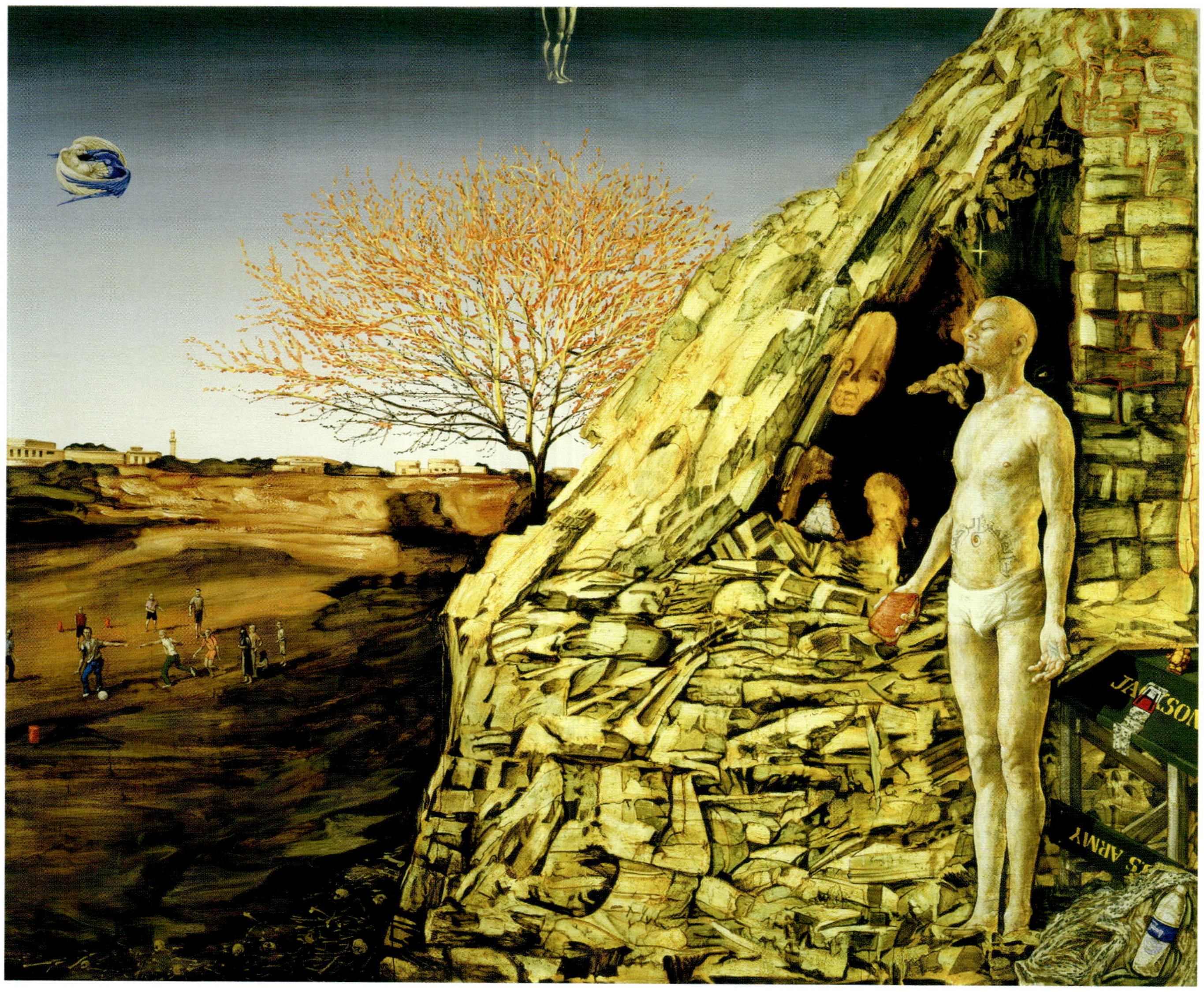

Attila Richard Lukacs, *Slave in the Graveyard*, 2007, oil on canvas, 307 x 366 cm.